The Possessive Investment in Whiteness

HOW WHITE PEOPLE PROFIT

TEMPLE UNIVERSITY PRESS
PHILADELPHIA

The Possessive

Investment

in Whiteness

FROM IDENTITY POLITICS

George Lipsitz

Temple University Press, Philadelphia 19122
Copyright © 1998 by Temple University
Published 1998
Printed in the United States of America

∞   The paper used in this publication meets the requirements of the American National
Standard for Information Sciences—Permanence of Paper for Printed Library Materials, ANSI
Z39.48–1984

Text design by Kate Nichols

Library of Congress Cataloging-in-Publication Data

Lipsitz, George
    The possessive investment in whiteness : how white people profit
from identity politics / George Lipsitz.
        p.   cm.
    Includes bibliographical references and index.
    ISBN 1-56639-634-4 (hbk. : alk. paper).—ISBN 1-56639-635-2
(pbk. : alk. paper)
    1. Racism—United States.   2. Prejudices—United States.
3. Whites—United States—Race identity.   4. United States—Race
relations.   5. United States—Social policy—1993–   I. Title.
E184.A1L56   1998
305.8′00973—dc21   97-53204

CONTENTS

Bill Moore's Body

I began to suspect that white people did not act as they did because they were white, but for some other reason, and I began to try to locate and understand the reason. —JAMES BALDWIN

This book argues that both public policy and private prejudice have created a "possessive investment in whiteness" that is responsible for the racialized hierarchies of our society. I use the term "possessive investment" both literally and figuratively. Whiteness has a cash value: it accounts for advantages that come to individuals through profits made from housing secured in discriminatory markets, through the unequal educations allocated to children of different races, through insider networks that channel employment opportunities to the relatives and friends of those who have profited most from present and past racial discrimination, and especially through intergenerational transfers of inherited wealth that pass on the spoils of discrimination to succeeding generations. I argue that white Americans are encouraged to invest in whiteness, to remain true to an identity that provides them with resources, power, and opportunity. This whiteness is, of course, a delusion, a scientific and cultural fiction that like all racial identities has no valid foundation in biology or anthropology. Whiteness is, however, a social fact, an identity created and continued with all-too-real consequences for the distribution of wealth, prestige, and opportunity.

The term "investment" denotes time spent on a given end, and this book also attempts to explore how social and cultural forces encourage white people to expend time and energy on the creation and re-creation of whiteness. Despite intense and frequent disavowal that whiteness means anything at all to those so designated, recent surveys have shown repeatedly that nearly every social choice that white people make about where they live, what schools their children attend, what careers they pursue, and what policies they endorse is shaped by considerations involving race.[1] I use the adjective "possessive" to stress the relationship between whiteness and asset accumulation in our society, to connect attitudes to interests, to demonstrate that white supremacy is usually less a matter of direct, referential, and snarling contempt than a system for protecting the privileges of whites by denying communities of color opportunities for asset accumulation and upward mobility. Whiteness is invested in, like property, but it is also a means of accumulating property and keeping it from others. While one can possess one's investments, one can also be possessed by them. I contend that the artificial construction of whiteness almost always comes to possess white people themselves unless they develop antiracist identities, unless they disinvest and divest themselves of their investment in white supremacy.

I hope it is clear that opposing whiteness is not the same as opposing white people. White supremacy is an equal opportunity employer; nonwhite people can become active agents of white supremacy as well as passive participants in its hierarchies and rewards. One way of becoming an insider is by participating in the exclusion of other outsiders. An individual might even secure a seat on the Supreme Court on this basis. On the other hand, if not every white supremacist is white, it follows that not all white people have to become complicit with white supremacy, that there is an element of choice in all of this. White people always have the option of becoming antiracist, although not enough have done so. We do not choose our color, but we do choose our commitments. We do not choose our parents, but we do choose our politics. Yet we do not make these decisions in a vacuum; they occur within a social structure that gives value to whiteness and offers rewards for racism.

I write this book in response to the crisis that confronts us in regard to race. But as with most books, its origins are complex and complicated. Perhaps the best way I can situate my engagement with the possessive investment in whiteness is to relate my connection to a crime that took place more than thirty-five years ago when I was a teenager. On April 23, 1963, Bill Moore was shot to death at close range alongside a highway in northern Alabama. The thirty-five-year-old father of three children received two .22 caliber slugs in his head and one in his neck.

When Moore was murdered, he was just beginning a one-man civil rights march from Chattanooga, Tennessee, to Jackson, Mississippi. A white man raised in the deep South but working as a postman in Baltimore, Moore had been horrified in 1962 by Mississippi governor Ross Barnett's role in fighting the desegregation of the University of Mississippi. When a federal court judge had to intervene to order the university to admit a fully qualified twenty-nine-year-old air force veteran as its first black student, Barnett pledged resistance, declaring the state's authority to be superior to that of the federal government. President Kennedy sent National Guard troops to Mississippi to force compliance with the court's order, but a rioting mob of whites resisted with a rampage that left two people dead and almost four hundred injured.[2]

Distressed by the violence in Mississippi, Moore asked himself what he could do to help. He had recently moved from Binghamton, New York, to Baltimore for the express purpose of becoming active in the front lines of the civil rights movement. Encouraged by the positive publicity surrounding a march on the Maryland state capital that had been organized by the Baltimore chapter of the Congress of Racial Equality earlier that year, Moore decided that he would stage his own one-man march. Playing on his identity as a postman, he decided to "deliver a letter" expressing support for integration to Governor Barnett. In his message, Moore advised the Mississippi governor "not to go down in infamy as one who fought the democracy for all which you have not the power to prevent."[3]

Born in upstate New York, Moore had moved to Mississippi as a child. As an adult, he continued to express great affection for the South and its people. He felt particularly embarrassed by Mississippi's image as a bastion of white supremacy. "I dislike the reputation this state has acquired as being the most backward and most bigoted in the land," he asserted in his letter to Barnett. "Those who truly love Mississippi must work to change this image." Before starting his journey, Moore left a letter for President Kennedy at the White House advising the president, "I am not making this walk to demonstrate either Federal rights or state rights, but individual rights. I am doing it to illustrate that peaceful protest is not altogether extinguished down there. I hope that I will not have to eat those words."[4]

Moore rode by bus from Washington, D.C., to Chattanooga, Tennessee, where he began his march on April 21, pulling a small two-wheeled postal cart containing his belongings. He wore two placards, sandwich-board style, on his chest and back. One read, "Equal Rights for All: Mississippi or Bust"; the other read, "Black and White: Eat at Joe's." On the first days of his trip one white woman smiled at him and another bought him a milkshake, but most of the whites he encountered (and at least one of the blacks) greeted him with jeers and arguments. In Georgia, one group of young white males shouted threats at Moore from a passing car, and another group pelted the postman with rocks and stones. A news broadcaster for WGAD reported that the Gadsden, Alabama, radio station had received an anonymous telephone call hours before the shooting reporting Moore's entrance into Etowah County, advising that "there might be a news story of consequence."[5] Moore walked through Gadsden on the afternoon of April 23; a passing motorist discovered his body that night on the pavement of U.S. Highway 11 near Attalia, about ten miles from Gadsden. The sandwich board signs, stained with blood, lay a few feet from his body. Investigators found fifty-one dollars in Moore's pocket and a diary among his possessions. An entry for April 23 noted that he had been confronted by two men who had learned about his walk from television news reports and warned him that he would not finish the march alive. In a final entry he wrote that "a couple of men who had talked to me before, drove up and questioned my religious and political beliefs and one was sure I'd be killed for them."[6]

Even Alabama's segregationist governor George Wallace publicly condemned the shooting as "a dastardly act," and he offered a $1,000 reward for information leading to the arrest and conviction of Moore's assailant.[7] Alabama authorities filed charges almost immediately against the operator of a store and filling station near Fort Payne, Alabama, Floyd L. Simpson, who had been seen speaking with Moore on the day of the murder. The indictment accused Simpson of killing William L. Moore "unlawfully and with malice aforethought."[8] An FBI ballistics test on the bullets found in Moore's body and on a .22 caliber rifle belonging to Simpson led to Simpson's arrest. The case was referred to a grand jury, and Simpson was released on $5,000 bond. Outside the glare of national publicity the grand jury deliberated slowly and in mid-September announced its refusal to indict Simpson—or anyone—for Moore's murder. The results of the ballistics tests were not made public. Grand jury foreman Robert Tinsley explained that several witnesses had been called, but he refused to explain why no indictment was issued.[9]

In the meantime, civil rights activists had responded immediately to Moore's murder. An integrated group of more than one hundred students in Nashville, Tennessee, marched from the chapel at Fisk University, a historically black institution, to the city's Federal Building carrying signs proclaiming "Moore Died for Love. Let's Live and Act in Love" and "William Moore. Who Will Be Next?"[10] Diane Nash Bevel led a delegation of eight black civil rights workers from Birmingham to Gadsden to take up the letter carrier's march at the spot where he was killed. Not sponsored by any organized civil rights group, the eight participants in the march told reporters that "they hoped to prove that a person preaching love of his fellow man, as Mr. Moore had, could walk safely though Alabama."[11] Members of the group intended to walk all the way to Jackson and were encouraged during the first hour of their march when they received positive comments from white spectators along their route. But Etowah County Sheriff's Office deputies soon arrested all eight marchers, charging them with "peace disturbance."

One week later, civil rights advocates announced another attempt to resume Bill Moore's march. Marvin Rich, community relations director of the Congress of Racial Equality, explained from the group's national headquarters in New York, "This is to give the people of Alabama and America another chance. William Moore traveled through this country to express his hopes for equality and justice and he died. This was a failure for the people of Alabama and the people of America."[12] When the group of six white and six black demonstrators started their walk from the Greyhound Bus Station in Chattanooga, bystanders taunted them and threatened them with violence. "Hope you stop a .22," one white man shouted to the group, in reference to the bullets that killed Bill Moore. On the second day of the marchers' journey, a convoy of cars filled with whites chased them across the Alabama-Tennessee border, throwing rocks and bottles and screaming, "Throw them niggers in the river" and "Kill them." Officers of the Alabama Highway Patrol met the march at the border and arrested the civil rights demonstrators for "breach of peace," manhandling them and attacking them repeatedly with electric-shock cattle prods as they lay on the pavement in nonviolent protest. From their cells in the Kilby State Prison in Montgomery, the arrested demonstrators announced that they would not accept bail, that they intended to remain incarcerated as a way of calling attention to the assault on their rights of free speech and free assembly. They remained in jail for nearly a month.[13]

In mid-May, civil rights groups tried once again to deliver Bill Moore's letter to Governor Barnett. When marchers held a memorial service on the spot where Moore had been killed, Alabama highway patrol officers and Etowah County sheriff's deputies arrested and jailed the entire delegation of five whites and six blacks for breach of the peace.[14] Later, about thirty African American men, women, and children from a local church joined civil rights workers from around the nation for a memorial service honoring Moore at a roadside park. James Peck, editor of the Congress of Racial Equality's national newsletter, praised Moore as "a genuine idealist—he worked for brotherhood all his life."

Reverend E. W. Jarrett of Galilee Baptist Church in Gadsden eulogized Moore as having "died but not in vain." A twenty-six-year-old white participant in the march, a native of Chattanooga then living in New York, explained, "I have come down here to make amends for the way this thing has been going on for the last 200 years. If Christ was on this earth today, I'm sure he would be killed just like William Moore."[15]

Bill Moore's murder made many people feel that they had to act, that it was no longer acceptable to be a spectator in the struggle over civil rights. To be sure, many others claimed that Moore had no one to blame but himself, that he had brought about his own death through provocative actions that he should have known would inflame the anger of white supremacists. A *New York Times* editorial on April 26 condemning the murder nonetheless described Moore's march as "a pitifully naive pilgrimage." An investigator for the Alabama State Police reported that he had spoken with Moore thirty minutes before his death and asked the postman to cancel his march or at least remove his signs. "I warned him about the racial situation in Alabama but he wouldn't listen," A. G. McDowell related. "He told me in a very nice way that he wanted to prove something and he couldn't if he turned back."[16] U.S. Attorney General Robert Kennedy withheld the support of the Department of Justice to those attempting to complete Moore's march, arguing that "perhaps their energies might be better used in a different direction than taking a walk."[17]

About six weeks after Moore's murder, Medgar Evers, field secretary for the Mississippi chapter of the National Association for the Advancement of Colored People (NAACP), addressed a mass meeting in Jackson, vowing to carry on the struggle against all forms of segregation in that city. When he returned to his home that night, Evers was killed, shot in the back by a sniper. Although his assassin, Byron de la Beckwith, would successfully avoid a conviction for more than thirty years, the brutal repression required to silence people like Moore, Evers, and their supporters exposed the venomous pathology of white supremacy to people across the nation.[18] In Los Angeles and San Francisco mass rallies protesting the murders of Moore and Evers attracted more than twenty thousand participants.[19] All across the nation during the summer of 1963, the deaths of Bill Moore and Medgar Evers made people ask themselves what they were prepared to do to about the pervasive presence of white supremacy in their society.

I was one of those people. The bullets that killed Bill Moore changed my life. I remember hearing news reports about his disappearance and death on the old gray radio in my bedroom on the second story of my family's home in Paterson, New Jersey. I was fifteen years old. The first broadcasts advised that Moore was missing; the next morning newscasters reported his death. I can still remember the impression that his murder made on me: Moore was a white man murdered by other white men because he opposed white supremacy. I had never encountered a story like that. It made me look into myself and provoked me to think about what I was willing to risk for my own beliefs.

The city that I grew up in was racially diverse, and I had seen enough even at the age of fifteen to realize that good and bad people came in all colors, that both virtue and vice characterized every community. But Bill Moore made me think harder about what it meant for me to be white in a world where the advantages of whiteness were carved out of other people's disadvantages. I knew that those of us in the almost exclusively white neighborhoods on the east side of Paterson lived in better houses and had more money than our classmates in minority or mixed neighborhoods. I did not know then the way residential segregation and home-loan discrimination skewed life chances along racial lines and inhibited opportunities for asset accumulation among members of aggrieved "minority" groups. Yet I did know that my own neighbors included slumlords who failed to provide decent, sanitary, or even safe living conditions for the tenants they gouged, that profits produced by charging high rates for broken-down tenements in slum neighborhoods in another part of town paid country club dues and college tuition fees for people in my part of town.

The murder of Bill Moore opened up new possibilities and personalized the civil rights struggle for me in dramatic ways. For Bill Moore, disapproving of white supremacy in principle wasn't enough; he felt he needed to put his life on the line trying to end it. Bill Moore fought against white racism because he personally found it intolerable, not just because he imagined it might be intolerable for someone else. Certainly I had been aware of many of the black martyrs before him in the civil rights movement, whose deaths were equally tragic and dramatic. Over the years many writers have justifiably criticized the dynamics whereby white people martyred in the civil rights movement have received a disproportionate share of attention compared to the overwhelmingly greater number of black people killed in that struggle. As Rita Schwerner noted when the murder of her husband, Michael, and his fellow civil rights workers James Chaney and Andrew Goodman led to a massive federal investigation and search in Mississippi's rivers and coastal waters for the three victims' missing bodies in 1964, "We all know this search with hundreds of sailors is because Andrew Goodman and my husband are white. If only Chaney was involved, nothing would have been done."[20] Hollywood films, made-for-television movies, and books have similarly honored white seminarian James Reeb but not Jimmy Lee Jackson, a black youth. They have chronicled the killing of white civil rights volunteer Viola Liuzzo, but not that of Herbert Lee, a black farmer and voting rights activist shot and killed by a member of the Mississippi state legislature who was never prosecuted for the killing.[21] History textbooks still routinely credit President Lincoln with freeing the slaves or Presidents Kennedy and Johnson with ending segregation without mentioning the grass roots pressures from people of color that forced those leaders to act as they did.

In addition, films about the murders of Medgar Evers (*Ghosts of Mississippi*) and Chaney, Schwerner, and Goodman (*Mississippi Burning*) rewrite the historical record by placing white FBI agents and white attorneys at the center of a struggle for social justice that actually depended almost entirely upon the determination and persistence of black people in the face of indifference and even outright hostility among most whites, including those in law enforcement agencies. I hope that my attention to Bill Moore does not contribute to the erasure of black people from the story of their own struggle for emancipation. I have to admit, however, that the murder of Bill Moore did affect me to an unusual degree, even more than the many reports of the deaths of dozens of blacks in the civil rights struggle. It is only fair to ask myself if my own conditioning as a white person did not make me somehow value a white life more than a black life. Yet I also now see that our society does not often produce or even imagine genuinely antiracist white people. To be sure, many whites are embarrassed by the benefits they receive from white supremacy, and other are inconvenienced or even threatened by the resentments it creates. Some view white supremacy as economically wasteful and socially destructive, while others wish they could live in a society without racial distinctions. Yet individuals like Bill Moore are rare, people willing to risk their lives in the fight against white supremacy, eager to join a movement with minority leadership, and cognizant of the fight as something for themselves rather than for others. Our history and our fiction contain all too many accounts of whites acting with unctuous paternalism to protect "helpless" people of color, but very few stories about white people opposing white supremacy on their own. Members of aggrieved racialized groups appear most often as threatening strangers or servile sidekicks in the stories we tell about our past and present, and only rarely as self-active agents operating in their own behalf. The difficulty of imagining an antiracist white subject is part of what made Bill Moore's story so compelling to me thirty-five years ago and what makes it resonate for me even today.

At the moment I learned of Bill Moore's death, I found myself thinking about commitment as well as color. What would it mean to believe in something so powerfully that you would give your life for it? I thought I understood how Moore felt, how tormented he must have been by the terrible injustices in our society and by his own inability to do anything meaningful about them. Later I would learn about the dangers of individual action, about the ways in which any one person's intentions—no matter how sincere—need to be coordinated with a collective social movement and connected to carefully thought out strategies and tactics produced by a democratic process that changes individuals and society at the same time. I learned later that Moore had been advised against his one-man march by officers of national civil rights organizations, that he had been a mental patient at the Binghamton State Hospital between 1953 and 1955, and that personal desperation as well as social commitment shaped his decision to march on Mississippi and deliver a letter to the governor.[22] Yet I think it would be a mistake to let Bill Moore's human problems and contradictions overshadow the basic idea that he got absolutely right. Like another man often described as mentally ill—John Brown—Bill Moore found white supremacy an abomination even though he was white. He did not imagine himself innocent of the privileges he had received as a result of being white, nor did guilt drive him to seek the approval of those he might have oppressed. He correctly identified white supremacy as the problem and took resolute action toward a solution.

Bill Moore's murder was a terrible crime, but culpability for it does not rest solely with the person who fired the shots that killed him. Bill Moore was murdered because too few people had his kind of courage and commitment, because too many white people kept silent about white supremacy even though they knew it was wrong. Today, I think his example remains more relevant than ever, not because dramatic moments of individual heroism will solve our problems, but because white Americans like myself have not yet come to grips with the structural and cultural forces that racialize human rights, opportunities, and life chances in our country. Too many of us continue to imagine that we would have supported the civil rights struggle of thirty years ago, when our actions and opinions today conform more closely to the record of that struggle's opponents. We have so demonized the white racists of 1960s Mississippi that we fail to see the ways in which many of their most heinous practices and policies have triumphed in our own day.

At the time of Bill Moore's murder, Mississippi began to emerge as a public symbol of the sickness at the center of race relations in the United States. In some ways the state deserved that reputation. The rioters in Oxford opposing the desegregation of their state's university knew that they could count on overt and covert support from Mississippi's elected officials and leading citizens. Antiblack vigilantes operated with impunity throughout the state, burning the homes and churches of civil rights leaders, bombing black-owned businesses, and shooting civil rights workers. A state agency, the Mississippi Sovereignty Commission, gave covert support to white supremacist groups, including those distributing license plate holders emblazoned with slogans like "Federally Occupied Mississippi, Kennedy's Hungary" and "Most Lied About State in The Union." The Sovereignty Commission helped Byron de la Beckwith escape a conviction for the murder of Medgar Evers by helping the defense screen jury members, and its agents conspired with Klansmen to set up the murders of James Chaney, Michael Schwerner, and Andrew Goodman.[23]

In 1964, the challenge by the Mississippi Freedom Democratic Party to the openly white supremacist state delegation to the Democratic National Convention, coupled with the murders of Chaney, Schwerner, and Goodman, attracted national and international attention. Magazine articles and best-selling books attempted to diagnose the conditions that gave rise to the state's racial antagonisms, while popular songs by the Chad Mitchell Trio, Phil Ochs, and Nina Simone criticized Mississippi's practices as outside the pale of civilized society. Nightclub and television audiences viewed Mississippi through the bitter and biting satire of black comedians Moms Mabley and Dick Gregory, whose topical humor singled out the state's white supremacist culture for special ridicule and critique.[24] Gregory joked that the state was so racist that "a white moderate in Mississippi is a cat who wants to lynch you from a *low* tree."[25]

At the same time, however, a different side of the state of Mississippi became visible through the actions and ideas of the state's African American residents as they mobilized for change along with a small number of white allies. I remember watching the televised testimony of Fannie Lou Hamer before the Credentials Committee at the 1964 Democratic National Convention as she described her attempts to register to vote as well as the harassment and retaliation she suffered for those efforts. As a warning, local authorities once charged her with failure to pay a one-month water bill of $9,000, even though her family's cabin had no running water.[26] Hamer told the committee that she had been fired from her job, evicted from her home, and beaten by sheriff's deputies, but she continued to battle for her rights. "Is this America, the land of the free and the home of the brave where we are threatened daily because we want to live as decent human beings?" she asked.[27]

In an election supervised by the Mississippi Freedom Democratic Party

(MFDP) and open to all voters regardless of race, Mississippi voters had chosen Hamer and her colleagues to represent their state at the convention. The national Democratic Party, however, seated the all-white segregationist delegation of party regulars, many of whom had already pledged to support Republican nominee Barry Goldwater, who campaigned as an opponent of the 1964 Civil Rights Act. As I learned later, President Johnson sent liberal senator Hubert Humphrey as his representative to a secret meeting at the convention with members of the MFDP in an attempt to persuade them to drop their demands to be seated as official delegates. Hamer had been eager to meet the senator, whom she had admired because of his reputation as a proponent of civil rights, but she was disappointed to find "a little round-eyed man with his eyes full of tears." When warned by the MFDP attorney, Joseph Raugh, that their effort to be seated at the convention would damage Humphrey's chances for nomination as Johnson's running mate, Hamer asked, "Well, Mr. Humphrey, do you mean to tell me that your position is more important to you than four hundred thousand black people's lives?"[28] Humphrey's inability to answer that question embodied a larger inability among white liberals to distance themselves sufficiently from the possessive investment in whiteness, an inability that plagues them to this day.

At college in St. Louis in 1964, I encountered some Mississippians who had worked with Fannie Lou Hamer and who displayed the same kinds of courage and commitment. Joyce and Dorie Ladner especially impressed me. They had worked almost alone in Natchez, Mississippi, as civil rights organizers in the early 1960s when nearly everyone else was afraid to challenge white supremacy in that section of the state. I heard the Ladner sisters speak at the campus YMCA at meetings organized by civil rights supporters, and their knowledge, tactical insights, and commitment left a lasting impression on me. As Charles Payne shows in his excellent study of the civil rights struggle in Mississippi, people like Fannie Lou Hamer and the Ladner sisters emerged from an entire community that made up for a lack of material resources and political power with an abundance of courage and vision. Their example provided hope and inspiration to many people living in circumstances far different from their own.[29]

With the passage of the 1964 and 1965 civil rights laws, Mississippi's brand of white supremacy was revealed as symptomatic of a much broader psychosis. Ending de jure (by law) segregation in the South did little or nothing to end de facto (by fact) segregation in the North. Mississippi, the home of William Faulkner, Chester Himes, and Eudora Welty, of Elvis Presley, Jimmie Rodgers, and Robert Johnson, was not an aberration isolated from the rest of the United

States. Although the form differed from state to state and from region to region, the possessive investment in whiteness that poisoned political and private lives in Mississippi was a quintessentially American problem. We discovered that laws guaranteeing the right to eat at a lunch counter did little to correct the elaborate web of discrimination in housing, hiring, and education that left minorities less able to pay for a lunch-counter meal, let alone raise the capital necessary to own a lunch counter. We found that school segregation and unequal education did not end when courts banned "separate but equal" Jim Crow schools, but left intact segregated neighborhoods and school districts. Even the right to vote meant less than we thought when gerrymandering and the high costs of political campaigns left aggrieved minority communities with no one to vote for who would be likely to represent their interests accurately. Those of us who might have been inclined to view white racism as a particularly Southern problem at the time of Bill Moore's murder soon saw the wisdom in Malcolm X's observation that as long as you're south of the Canadian border, you're in the South.

This book identifies the ways in which power, property, and the politics of race in our society continue to contain unacknowledged and unacceptable allegiances to white supremacy. I write it, in part, to pay the debts I owe to Joyce and Dorie Ladner, to Fannie Lou Hamer, and to many other Mississippians. I want to make it clear that Fannie Lou Hamer's appeals did not fall on deaf ears and that Bill Moore's letter can still be delivered after all these years.

Yet I would not be honoring the work of these Mississippians properly if I let it go at that. I now live and work in California, a state where demagogic political leaders and a frightened electorate have recently launched a series of decidedly racist attacks on communities of color. The mendacity and meanness of Governor Pete Wilson, the passage of the anti-immigrant Proposition 187 and the anti–affirmative action Proposition 209, initiatives against bilingual education, and the refusal by legally constituted authorities to enforce laws protecting the civil rights, wages, and working conditions of the people of the state have made California in the 1990s the human rights equivalent of Mississippi in the 1960s.

Thirty years ago, Californians could afford to view the events transpiring in Mississippi with pity and contempt. California then was a high-wage and high-employment state where taxpayer support provided quality schools and social service programs geared toward bringing chances for upward mobility to an impressively broad range of its population. The state's political leaders acted with foresight and vision, preparing for the future by speaking honestly and openly with the citizens of their state about the things they needed to do to insure the common good. Mississippi, on the other hand, used the power of the state to maintain a low-wage, low-employment economy characterized by vivid contrasts between the dire poverty and financial anxiety of most state residents and the monopoly power and luxury life-styles of a handful of wealthy plutocrats. It trailed most of the other states in educational expenditures per pupil. Its political leaders rarely leveled with citizens, resorting instead to demagogic scapegoating of powerless and nonvoting populations to divide and conquer. As John Dittmer points out in his fine book *Local People*, one of the intended consequences of racially segmenting the labor force in Mississippi in the 1950s and 1960s was to preserve wealth in a few hands by deterring workers from joining together to seek union representation or legislation regulating the conditions of labor.[30]

Today, California has caught up with the Mississippi of 1963. State agencies fail to enforce laws regulating wages, hours, and working conditions, much less bans on discrimination in housing, hiring, and education. The growth of unregulated low-wage labor has launched a race to the bottom that enables wealthy consumers to pay less for foodstuffs and food preparation, for construction and maintenance, for child care and domestic cleaning, while the majority of the population confronts the stagnation and even the decline of its real wages. California now stands near the bottom in state school spending per pupil—in no small measure because most public school students are now members of racial "minorities." We discover to our sorrow that our elected officials cannot lead us so they lie to us, fomenting hatred against the poor, immigrants, and racial minorities to hide the ways in which their own policies are destroying the economic and social infrastructure of our state. If this book represents an effort to deliver at last the letter that Bill Moore wished to bring to Ross Barnett in 1963, I hope that it will also help send a message to Sacramento as well.

I think I now know why Bill Moore's murder affected me so deeply in 1963. His actions forced my first confrontations with the possessive investment in whiteness—a poisonous system of privilege that pits people against each other and prevents the creation of common ground. Exposing, analyzing, and eradicating this pathology is an obligation that we all share, white people most of all. I hope that this book will be a step in that direction.

In the darkest days of the 1990s, as the governor of California and his political puppets on the board of regents were resorting to the crudest kinds of racist scapegoating to protect the possessive investment in whiteness, a group of young students at the University of California, San Diego, where I teach, created an interethnic antiracist coalition that expressed and enacted a compelling vision of social justice. Their dignity, discipline, and determination to fight every measure designed to increase the "wages of whiteness" (including Proposition 209, Proposition 187, and SP1 and SP2) have provided an inspiring alternative to the unjust and immoral policies advanced by the most powerful and wealthy individuals in their state. They have learned the lessons of history well, and their actions point the way toward a better and more just future. The members of the No Retreat! coalition have inherited the vision and the courage of Fannie Lou Hamer, Bill Moore, and many others. I dedicate this book to them, with deep respect and gratitude.

The Possessive Investment in Whiteness

The Possessive Investment
in Whiteness

Blacks are often confronted, in American life, with such devastating examples of the white descent from dignity; devastating not only because of the enormity of white pretensions, but because this swift and graceless descent would seem to indicate that white people have no principles whatever.

—JAMES BALDWIN

Shortly after World War II, a French reporter asked expatriate Richard Wright for his views about the "Negro problem" in America. The author replied, "There isn't any Negro problem; there is only a white problem."[1] By inverting the reporter's question, Wright called attention to its hidden assumptions—that racial polarization comes from the existence of blacks rather than from the behavior of whites, that black people are a "problem" for whites rather than fellow citizens entitled to justice, and that, unless otherwise specified, "Americans" means "whites."[2] But Wright's formulation also placed political mobilization by African Americans during the civil rights era in context, connecting black disadvantages to white advantages and finding the roots of black consciousness in the systemic practices of aversion, exploitation, denigration, and discrimination practiced by people who think of themselves as "white."

Whiteness is everywhere in U.S. culture, but it is very hard to see. As Richard Dyer suggests, "[W]hite power secures its dominance by seeming not to be anything in particular."[3] As the unmarked category against which difference is constructed, whiteness never has to speak its name, never has to acknowledge its role as an organizing principle in social and cultural relations.[4] To identify, analyze, and oppose the destructive consequences of whiteness, we

1

need what Walter Benjamin called "presence of mind." Benjamin wrote that people visit fortune-tellers less out of a desire to know the future than out of a fear of not noticing some important aspect of the present. "Presence of mind," he suggested, "is an abstract of the future, and precise awareness of the present moment more decisive than foreknowledge of the most distant events."[5] In U.S. society at this time, precise awareness of the present moment requires an understanding of the existence and the destructive consequences of the possessive investment in whiteness that surreptitiously shapes so much of our public and private lives."

Race is a cultural construct, but one with sinister structural causes and consequences. Conscious and deliberate actions have institutionalized group identity in the United States, not just through the dissemination of cultural stories, but also through systematic efforts from colonial times to the present to create economic advantages through a possessive investment in whiteness for European Americans. Studies of culture too far removed from studies of social structure leave us with inadequate explanations for understanding racism and inadequate remedies for combating it.

Desire for slave labor encouraged European settlers in North America to view, first, Native Americans and, later, African Americans as racially inferior people suited "by nature" for the humiliating subordination of involuntary servitude. The long history of the possessive investment in whiteness stems in no small measure from the fact that all subsequent immigrants to North America have come to an already racialized society. From the start, European settlers in North America established structures encouraging a possessive investment in whiteness. The colonial and early national legal systems authorized attacks on Native Americans and encouraged the appropriation of their lands. They legitimated racialized chattel slavery, limited naturalized citizenship to "white" immigrants, identified Asian immigrants as expressly unwelcome (through legislation aimed at immigrants from China in 1882, from India in 1917, from Japan in 1924, and from the Philippines in 1934), and provided pretexts for restricting the voting, exploiting the labor, and seizing the property of Asian Americans, Mexican Americans, Native Americans, and African Americans.[6]

The possessive investment in whiteness is not a simple matter of black and white; all racialized minority groups have suffered from it, albeit to different degrees and in different ways. The African slave trade began in earnest only after large-scale Native American slavery proved impractical in North America. The abolition of slavery led to the importation of low-wage labor from Asia. Legislation banning immigration from Asia set the stage for the recruitment of low-wage labor from Mexico. The new racial categories that emerged in each of these eras all revolved around applying racial labels to "nonwhite" groups in order to stigmatize and exploit them while at the same time preserving the value of whiteness.

Although reproduced in new form in every era, the possessive investment in whiteness has always been influenced by its origins in the racialized history of the United States—by its legacy of slavery and segregation, of "Indian" extermination and immigrant restriction, of conquest and colonialism. Although slavery has existed in many countries without any particular racial dimensions to it, the slave system that emerged in North America soon took on distinctly racial forms. Africans enslaved in North America faced a racialized system of power that reserved permanent, hereditary, chattel slavery for black people. White settlers institutionalized a possessive investment in whiteness by making blackness synonymous with slavery and whiteness synonymous with freedom, but also by pitting people of color against one another. Fearful of alliances between Native Americans and African Americans that might challenge the prerogatives of whiteness, white settlers prohibited slaves and free blacks from traveling in "Indian country." European Americans used diplomacy and force to compel Native Americans to return runaway slaves to their white masters. During the Stono Rebellion of 1739, colonial authorities offered Native Americans a bounty for every rebellious slave they captured or killed. At the same time, British settlers recruited black slaves to fight against Native Americans within colonial militias.[7] The power of whiteness depended not only on white hegemony over separate racialized groups, but also on manipulating racial outsiders to fight against one another, to compete with each other for white approval, and to seek the rewards and privileges of whiteness for themselves at the expense of other racialized populations.

Aggrieved communities of color have often curried favor with whites in order to make gains at each other's expense. For example, in the nineteenth century some Native Americans held black slaves (in part to prove to whites that they could adopt "civilized" European American ways), and some of the first chartered African American units in the U.S. army went to war against Comanches in Texas or served as security forces for wagon trains of white settlers on the trails to California. The defeat of the Comanches in the 1870s sparked a mass migration by Spanish-speaking residents of New Mexico into the areas of West Texas formerly occupied by the vanquished Native Americans.[8] Immigrants from Asia sought the rewards of whiteness for themselves by asking the courts to recognize them as "white" and therefore eligible for naturalized citizenship according to the Immigration and Naturalization Act of 1790; Mexican Americans also insisted on being classified as white. In the early twentieth century, black soldiers accustomed to fighting Native Americans in the Southwest participated in the U.S. occupation of the Philippines and the punitive expedition against Pancho Villa in Mexico.[9] Asian American managers cracked down on efforts by Mexican American farm workers to unionize, while the Pullman Company tried to break the African American Brotherhood of Sleeping Car Porters by importing Filipinos to work as porters. Mexican Americans and blacks took possession of some of the property confiscated from Japanese Americans during the internment of the 1940s, and Asian Americans, blacks, and Mexican Americans all secured advantages for themselves by cooperating with the exploitation of Native Americans.

Yet while all racialized minority groups have sometimes sought the rewards of whiteness, they have also been able to come together in interethnic antiracist alliances. Native American tribes often harbored runaway slaves and drew upon their expertise in combat against whites, as in 1711 when an African named Harry helped lead the Tuscaroras against the British.[10] Native Americans secured the cooperation of black slaves in their attacks on the French settlement near Natchez in colonial Louisiana in 1729, and black Seminoles in Florida routinely recruited slaves from Georgia plantations to their side in battles against European Americans.[11] African Americans resisting slavery and white supremacy in the United States during the nineteenth century sometimes looked to Mexico as a refuge (especially after that nation abolished slavery), and in the twentieth century the rise of Japan as a successful non-white world power often served as a source of inspiration and emulation among African American nationalists. Mexican American and Japanese American farm workers joined forces in Oxnard, California, in 1903 to wage a successful strike in the beet fields, and subsequently members of the two groups organized an interracial union, the Japanese Mexican Labor Association.[12] Yet whether characterized by conflict or cooperation, all relations among aggrieved racialized minorities stemmed from recognition of the rewards of whiteness and the concomitant penalties imposed upon "nonwhite" populations.

Yet today the possessive investment is not simply the residue of conquest and colonialism, of slavery and segregation, of immigrant exclusion and "Indian" extermination. Contemporary whiteness and its rewards have been created and recreated by policies adopted long after the emancipation of slaves in the 1860s and even after the outlawing of de jure segregation in the 1960s. There has always been racism in the United States, but it has not always been the same racism. Political and cultural struggles over power have shaped the contours and dimensions of racism differently in different eras. Antiracist mobilizations during the Civil War and civil rights eras meaningfully curtailed the reach and scope of white supremacy, but in each case reactionary forces engineered a renewal of racism, albeit in new forms, during succeeding decades. Racism has changed over time, taking on different forms and serving different social purposes in each time period.

Contemporary racism has been created anew in many ways over the past five decades, but most dramatically by the putatively race-neutral, liberal, social democratic reforms of the New Deal Era and by the more overtly race-conscious neoconservative reactions against liberalism since the Nixon years. It is a mistake to posit a gradual and inevitable trajectory of evolutionary progress in race relations; on the contrary, our history shows that battles won at one moment can later be lost. Despite hard-fought battles for change that secured important concessions during the 1960s in the form of civil rights legislation, the racialized nature of social policy in the United States since the Great Depression has actually increased the possessive investment in whiteness among European Americans over the past half century.

During the New Deal Era of the 1930s and 1940s, both the Wagner Act and the Social Security Act excluded farm workers and domestics from coverage, effectively denying those disproportionately minority sectors of the work force protections and benefits routinely afforded whites. The Federal Housing Act of 1934 brought home ownership within reach of millions of citizens by placing the credit of the federal government behind private lending to home buyers, but overtly racist categories in the Federal Housing Agency's (FHA) "confidential" city surveys and appraisers' manuals channeled almost all of the loan money toward whites and away from communities of color.[13] In the post–World War II era, trade unions negotiated contract provisions giving private medical insurance, pensions, and job security largely to the white workers who formed the overwhelming majority of the unionized work force in mass production industries, rather than fighting for full employment, medical care, and old-age pensions for all, or even for an end to discriminatory hiring and promotion practices by employers in those industries.[14]

Each of these policies widened the gap between the resources available to whites and those available to aggrieved racial communities. Federal housing policy offers an important illustration of the broader principles at work in the possessive investment in whiteness. By channeling loans away from older inner-city neighborhoods and toward white home buyers moving into segregated suburbs, the FHA and private lenders after World War II aided and abetted segregation in U.S. residential neighborhoods. FHA appraisers denied federally supported loans to prospective home buyers in the racially mixed Boyle Heights neighborhood of Los Angeles in 1939, for example, because the area struck them as a "'melting pot' area literally honeycombed with diverse and subversive racial elements."[15] Similarly, mostly white St. Louis County secured five times as many FHA mortgages as the more racially mixed city of St. Louis between 1943 and 1960. Home buyers in the county received six times as much loan money and enjoyed per capita mortgage spending 6.3 times greater than those in the city.[16]

The federal government has played a major role in augmenting the possessive investment in whiteness. For years, the General Services Administration routinely channeled the government's own rental and leasing business to realtors who engaged in racial discrimination, while federally subsidized urban renewal plans reduced the already limited supply of housing for communities of color through "slum clearance" programs. In concert with FHA support for segregation in the suburbs, federal and state tax monies routinely funded the construction of water supplies and sewage facilities for racially exclusive suburban communities in the 1940s and 1950s. By the 1960s, these areas often incorporated themselves as independent municipalities in order to gain greater access to federal funds allocated for "urban aid."[17]

At the same time that FHA loans and federal highway building projects subsidized the growth of segregated suburbs, urban renewal programs in cities throughout the country devastated minority neighborhoods. During the 1950s and 1960s, federally assisted urban renewal projects destroyed 20 percent of the central-city housing units occupied by blacks, as opposed to only 10 percent of those inhabited by whites.[18] More than 60 percent of those displaced by urban renewal were African Americans, Puerto Ricans, Mexican Americans, or members of other minority racial groups.[19] The Federal Housing Administration and the Veterans Administration financed more than $120 billion worth of new housing between 1934 and 1962, but less than 2 percent of this real estate was available to nonwhite families—and most of that small amount was located in segregated areas.[20]

Even in the 1970s, after most major urban renewal programs had been completed, black central-city residents continued to lose housing units at a rate equal to 80 percent of what had been lost in the 1960s. Yet white displacement declined to the relatively low levels of the 1950s.[21] In addition, the refusal first to pass, then to enforce, fair housing laws has enabled realtors, buyers, and sellers to profit from racist collusion against minorities largely without fear of legal retribution. During the decades following World War II, urban renewal helped construct a new "white" identity in the suburbs by helping to destroy ethnically specific European American urban inner-city neighborhoods. Wrecking balls and bulldozers eliminated some of these sites, while others were transformed by an influx of minority residents desperately competing for a declining supply of affordable housing units. As increasing numbers of racial minorities moved into cities, increasing numbers of European American ethnics moved out. Consequently, ethnic differences among whites became a less important dividing line in U.S. culture, while race became more important. The suburbs helped turn Euro-Americans into "whites" who could live near each other and intermarry with relatively little difficulty. But this "white" unity rested on residential segregation, on shared access to housing and life chances largely unavailable to communities of color.[22]

During the 1950s and 1960s, local "pro-growth" coalitions led by liberal mayors often justified urban renewal as a program designed to build more housing for poor people, but it actually destroyed more housing than it created. Ninety percent of the low-income units removed for urban renewal during the entire history of the program were never replaced. Commercial, industrial, and municipal projects occupied more than 80 percent of the land cleared for these projects, with less than 20 percent allocated for replacement housing. In addition, the loss of taxable properties and the tax abatements granted to new enterprises in urban renewal zones often meant serious tax increases for poor, working class, and middle-class home owners and renters.[23] Although the percentage of black suburban dwellers also increased during this period, no significant desegregation of the suburbs took place. From 1960 to 1977, 4 million whites moved out of central cities, while the number of whites living in suburbs increased by 22 million; during the same years, the inner-city black population grew by 6 million, but the number of blacks living in suburbs increased by only 500,000.[24] By 1993, 86 percent of suburban whites still lived in places with a black population below 1 percent. At the same time, cities with large numbers of minority residents found themselves cut off from loans by the FHA. For example, because of their growing black and Puerto Rican populations, neither Camden nor Paterson, New Jersey, in 1966 received one FHA-sponsored mortgage.[25]

In 1968, lobbyists for the banking industry helped draft the Housing and Urban Development Act, which allowed private lenders to shift the risks of financing low-income housing to the government, creating a lucrative and thor-

oughly unregulated market for themselves. One section of the 1968 bill authorized FHA mortgages for inner-city areas that did not meet the usual eligibility
criteria, and another section subsidized interest payments by low-income families. If administered wisely, these provisions might have promoted fair housing goals, but FHA administrators deployed them in ways that actually promoted segregation in order to provide banks, brokers, lenders, developers,
realtors, and speculators with windfall profits. As a U.S. Commission on Civil
Rights investigation later revealed, FHA officials collaborated with blockbusters
in financing the flight of low income whites out of inner city neighborhoods,
and then aided unscrupulous realtors and speculators by arranging purchases
of substandard housing by minorities desperate to own their own homes. The
resulting sales and mortgage foreclosures brought great profits to lenders (almost all of them white), but their actions led to price fixing and a subsequent
inflation of housing costs in the inner city by more than 200 percent between
1968 and 1972. Bankers then foreclosed on the mortgages of thousands of these
uninspected and substandard homes, ruining many inner-city neighborhoods.
In response, the Department of Housing and Urban Development essentially
red-lined inner cities, making them ineligible for future loans, a decision that
destroyed the value of inner-city housing for generations to come.[26]

Federally funded highways designed to connect suburban commuters with
downtown places of employment also destroyed already scarce housing in minority communities and often disrupted neighborhood life as well. Construction of the Harbor Freeway in Los Angeles, the Gulf Freeway in Houston, and
the Mark Twain Freeway in St. Louis displaced thousands of residents and bi-
sected neighborhoods, shopping districts, and political precincts. The processes
of urban renewal and highway construction set in motion a vicious cycle: population loss led to decreased political power, which made minority neighborhoods more vulnerable to further urban renewal and freeway construction, not
to mention more susceptible to the placement of prisons, incinerators, toxic
waste dumps, and other projects that further depopulated these areas.

In Houston, Texas—where blacks make up slightly more than one quarter
of the local population—more than 75 percent of municipal garbage incinerators and 100 percent of the city-owned garbage dumps are located in black
neighborhoods.[27] A 1992 study by staff writers for the *National Law Journal* examined the Environmental Protection Agency's response to 1,177 toxic waste
cases and found that polluters of sites near the greatest white population received penalties 500 percent higher than penalties imposed on polluters in minority areas—an average of $335,566 for white areas contrasted with $55,318

for minority areas. Income did not account for these differences—penalties for low-income areas on average actually exceeded those for areas with the highest median incomes by about 3 percent. The penalties for violating all federal environmental laws regulating air, water, and waste pollution were 46 percent lower in minority communities than in white communities. In addition, superfund remedies left minority communities waiting longer than white communities to be placed on the national priority list, cleanups that began from 12 to 42 percent later than at white sites, and with a 7 percent greater likelihood of "containment" (walling off a hazardous site) than cleanup, while white sites experienced treatment and cleanup 22 percent more often than containment.[28]

The federal Agency for Toxic Substances and Disease Registry's 1988 survey of children suffering from lead poisoning showed that among families with incomes under $6,000 per year, 36 percent of white children but 68 percent of black children suffered from excess lead in their bloodstreams. Among families with incomes above $15,000 per year, only 12 percent of white children but 38 percent of black children suffered from toxic levels of lead.[29] In the Los Angeles area, only 34 percent of whites inhabit areas with the most polluted air, but 71 percent of African Americans and 50 percent of Latinos live in neighborhoods with the highest levels of air pollution.[30] Nationwide, 60 percent of African Americans and Latinos live in communities with uncontrolled toxic waste sites.[31]

Scholarly studies reveal that even when adjusted for income, education, and occupational status, aggrieved racial minorities encounter higher levels of exposure to toxic substances than white people experience.[32] In 1987, the Commission for Racial Justice of the United Church of Christ found race to be the most significant variable in determining the location of commercial hazardous waste facilities.[33] In a review of sixty-four studies examining environmental disparities, the National Wildlife Federation found that racial disparities outnumbered disparities by income, and in cases where disparities in race and income were both present, race proved to be more important in twenty-two out of thirty tests.[34] As Robert D. Bullard demonstrates, "race has been found to be an independent factor, not reducible to class" in predicting exposure to a broad range of environmental hazards, including polluted air, contaminated fish, lead poisoning, municipal landfills, incinerators, and toxic waste dumps.[35] The combination of exposure to environmental hazards and employment discrimination establishes a sinister correlation between race and health. One recent government study revealed that the likelihood of dying from nutritional deficiencies was two and a half times greater among African Americans than among European Americans.[36] Another demonstrated that Asian and Pacific Islander recipients of aid for at-risk families exhibited alarming rates of stunted growth and underweight among children under the age of five.[37] Corporations systematically target Native American reservations when looking for locations for hazardous waste incinerators, solid waste landfills, and nuclear waste storage facilities; Navajo teenagers develop reproductive organ cancer at seventeen times the national average because of their exposure to radiation from uranium mines." [38] Latinos in East Los Angeles encounter some of the worst smog and the highest concentrations of air toxins in southern California because of prevailing wind patterns and the concentration of polluting industries, freeways, and toxic waste dumps.[39] Environmental racism makes the possessive investment in whiteness literally a matter of life and death; if African Americans had access to the nutrition, wealth, health care, and protection against environmental hazards offered routinely to whites, seventy-five thousand fewer of them would die each year.[40]

Minorities are less likely than whites to receive preventive medical care or costly operations from Medicare. Eligible members of minority communities are also less likely than European Americans to apply for food stamps.[41] The labor of migrant farm workers from aggrieved racialized groups plays a vital role in providing adequate nutrition for others, but the farm workers and their children suffer disproportionately from health disorders caused by malnutrition.[42] In her important research on health policy and ethnic diversity, Linda Wray concludes that "the lower life expectancies for many ethnic minority groups and subgroups stem largely from their disproportionately higher rates of poverty, malnutrition, and poor health care."[43]

Just as residential segregation and urban renewal make minority communities disproportionately susceptible to health hazards, their physical and social location gives these communities a different relationship to the criminal justice system. A 1990 study by the National Institute on Drug abuse revealed that while only 15 percent of the thirteen million habitual drug users in the United States were black and 77 percent were white, African Americans were four times more likely to be arrested on drug charges than whites in the nation as a whole, and seven to nine times more likely in Pennsylvania, Michigan, Illinois, Florida, Massachusetts, and New Jersey. A 1989 study by the Parents' Resource Institute for Drug Education discovered that African American high school students consistently showed lower levels of drug and alcohol use than their European American counterparts, even in high schools populated by residents of low-income housing projects. Yet, while comprising about 12 percent of the U.S population, blacks accounted for 10 percent of drug arrests in 1984, 40 percent in

1988, and 42 percent in 1990. In addition, white drug defendants receive considerably shorter average prison terms than African Americans convicted of comparable crimes. A U.S. Sentencing Commission study found in 1992 that half of the federal court districts that handled cases involving crack cocaine prosecuted minority defendants *exclusively*. A *Los Angeles Times* article in 1995 revealed that "black and Latino crack dealers are hammered with 10-year mandatory federal sentences while whites prosecuted in state court face a minimum of five years and often receive no more than a year in jail." Alexander Lichtenstein and Michael A. Kroll point out that sentences for African Americans in the federal prison system are 20 percent longer than those given to whites who commit the same crimes. They observe that if blacks received the same sentences as whites for these offenses, the federal prison system would require three thousand fewer prison cells, enough to close completely six of the new five-hundred bed institutions.[44]

Racial animus on the part of police officers, prosecutors, and judges accounts for only a small portion of the distinctive experience that racial minorities have with the criminal justice system. Economic devastation makes the drug trade appealing to some people in the inner city, while the dearth of capital in minority neighborhoods curtails opportunities for other kinds of employment. Deindustrialization, unemployment, and lack of intergenerational transfers of wealth undermine parental and adult authority in many neighborhoods. The complex factors that cause people to turn to drugs are no more prevalent in minority communities than elsewhere, but these communities and their inhabitants face more stress while having fewer opportunities to receive private counseling and treatment for their problems.

The structural weaknesses of minority neighborhoods caused by discrimination in housing, education, and hiring also play a crucial role in relations between inner-city residents and the criminal justice system. Cocaine dealing, which initially skyrocketed among white suburban residents, was driven into the inner city by escalating enforcement pressures in wealthy white communities. Ghettos and barrios became distribution centers for the sale of drugs to white suburbanites. Former New York and Houston police commissioner Lee Brown, head of the federal government's antidrug efforts during the early years of the Clinton presidency and later mayor of Houston, noted, "There are those who bring drugs into the country. That's not the black community. Then you have wholesalers, those who distribute them once they get here, and as a rule that's not the black community. Where you find the blacks is in the street dealing."[45]

You also find blacks and other minorities in prison. Police officers in large cities, pressured to show results in the drive against drugs, lack the resources to effectively enforce the law everywhere (in part because of the social costs of deindustrialization and the tax limitation initiatives designed to shrink the size of government). These officers know that it is easier to make arrests and to secure convictions by confronting drug users in areas that have conspicuous street corner sales, that have more people out on the street with no place to go, and that have residents more likely to plead guilty and less likely to secure the services of attorneys who can get the charges against them dropped, reduced, or wiped off the books with subsequent successful counseling and rehabilitation. In addition, politicians supported by the public relations efforts of neoconservative foundations often portray themselves to suburban voters as opponents of the "dangerous classes" in the inner cities.

Minority disadvantages craft advantages for others. Urban renewal failed to provide new housing for the poor, but it played an important role in transforming the U.S. urban economy from one that relied on factory production to one driven by producer services. Urban renewal projects subsidized the development of downtown office centers on previously residential land, and they frequently created buffer zones of empty blocks dividing poor neighborhoods from new shopping centers designed for affluent commuters. To help cities compete for corporate investment by making them appealing to high-level executives, federal urban aid favored construction of luxury housing units and cultural centers like symphony halls and art museums over affordable housing for workers. Tax abatements granted to these producer services centers further aggravated the fiscal crisis that cities faced, leading to tax increases on existing industries, businesses, and residences.

Workers from aggrieved racial minorities bore the brunt of this transformation. Because the 1964 Civil Rights Act came so late, minority workers who received jobs because of it found themselves more vulnerable to seniority-based layoffs when businesses automated or transferred operations overseas. Although the act initially made real progress in reducing employment discrimination, lessened the gaps between rich and poor and between black and white workers, and helped bring minority poverty to its lowest level in history in 1973, that year's recession initiated a reversal of minority progress and a reassertion of white privilege.[46] In 1977, the U.S. Civil Rights Commission reported on the disproportionate impact of layoffs on minority workers. In cases where minority workers made up only 10 to 12 percent of the work force in their area, they accounted for from 60 to 70 percent of those laid off in 1974. The principle of seniority, a trade union triumph designed to protect workers from age discrimination, in this case guaranteed that minority workers would suffer most from technological changes, because the legacy of past discrimination by their employers left them with less seniority than white workers.[47]

When housing prices increased dramatically during the 1970s, white home-owners who had been able to take advantage of discriminatory FHA financing policies in the past realized increased equity in their homes, while those excluded from the housing market by earlier policies found themselves facing even higher costs of entry into the market in addition to the traditional obstacles presented by the discriminatory practices of sellers, realtors, and lenders. The contrast between European Americans and African Americans is instructive in this regard. Because whites have access to broader housing choices than blacks, whites pay 15 percent less than blacks for similar housing in the same neighborhood. White neighborhoods typically experience housing costs 25 percent lower than would be the case if the residents were black.[48]

A recent Federal Reserve Bank of Boston study revealed that Boston bankers made 2.9 times as many mortgage loans per 1,000 housing units in neighborhoods inhabited by low-income whites than in neighborhoods populated by low-income blacks.[49] In addition, loan officers were far more likely to overlook flaws in the credit records of white applicants or to arrange creative financing for them than they were with black applicants.[50] A Los Angeles study found that loan officers more frequently used dividend income and underlying assets as criteria for judging black applicants than for whites.[51] In Houston, the NCNB Bank of Texas disqualified 13 percent of middle-income white loan applicants but 36 percent of middle-income black applicants.[52] Atlanta's home loan institutions gave five times as many home loans to whites as to blacks in the late 1980s. An analysis of sixteen Atlanta neighborhoods found that home buyers in white neighborhoods received conventional financing four times as often as those in black sections of the city.[53] Nationwide, financial institutions receive more money in deposits from black neighborhoods than they invest in them in the form of home mortgage loans, making home lending a vehicle for the transfer of capital away from black savers toward white investors.[54] In many locations, high-income blacks were denied loans more often than low-income whites.[55]

When confronted with evidence of systematic racial bias in home lending, defenders of the possessive investment in whiteness argue that the disproportionate share of loan denials to members of minority groups stems not from discrimination, but from the low net worth of minority applicants, even those who have high incomes. This might seem a reasonable position, but net worth is almost totally determined by past opportunities for asset accumulation, and therefore is the one figure most likely to reflect the history of discrimination. Minorities are told, in essence, "We can't give you a loan today because we've discriminated against members of your race so effectively in the past that you have not been able to accumulate any equity from housing and to pass it down through the generations."

Most white families have acquired their net worth from the appreciation of property that they secured under conditions of special privilege in a discriminatory housing market. In their prize-winning book *Black Wealth/White Wealth*, Melvin Oliver and Thomas Shapiro demonstrate how the history of housing discrimination makes white parents more able to borrow funds for their children's college education or to loan money to their children to enter the housing market. In addition, much discrimination in home lending is not based on considerations of net worth; it stems from decisions made by white banking officials based on their stereotypes about minority communities. The Federal Reserve Bank of Boston study showed that black and Latino mortgage applicants are 60 percent more likely to be turned down for loans than whites, even after controlling for employment, financial, and neighborhood characteristics.[56] Ellis Cose reports on a white bank official confronted with evidence at a board of directors' meeting that his bank denied loans to blacks who had credit histories and earnings equal to those of white applicants who received loans. The banker replied that the information indicated that the bank needed to do a better job of "affirmative action," but one of his colleagues pointed out that the problem had nothing to do with affirmative action—the bank was simply letting prejudice stand in the way of its own best interests by rejecting loans that should be approved.[57]

Yet bankers also make money from the ways in which discrimination creates artificial scarcities in the market. Minorities have to pay more for housing because much of the market is off limits to them. Blockbusters profit from exploiting white fears and provoking them into panic selling. Minority home owners denied loans in mainstream banks often turn to exploitative lenders who make "low end" loans at enormously high interest rates. If they fail to pay back these loans, regular banks can acquire the property cheaply and charge someone else exorbitant interest for a loan on the same property.

Federal home loan policies have put the power of the federal government at the service of private discrimination. Urban renewal and highway construction programs have enhanced the possessive investment in whiteness directly through government initiatives. In addition, decisions about where to locate federal jobs have also systematically subsidized whiteness. Federal civilian employment dropped by 41,419 in central cities between 1966 and 1973, but total federal employment in metropolitan areas grew by 26,558.[58] While one might naturally expect the location of government buildings that serve the public to follow population trends, the federal government's policy of locating offices and records centers in suburbs aggravated the flight of jobs to suburban locations less accessible to inner-city residents. Because racial discrimination in the private sector forces minority workers to seek government positions disproportionate to their numbers, these moves exact particular hardships on them. In addition, minorities who follow their jobs to the suburbs must generally allocate more for commuter costs, because housing discrimination makes it harder and more expensive for them than for whites to relocate.

The policies of neoconservatives in the Reagan and Bush administrations during the 1980s and 1990s greatly exacerbated the racialized aspects of more than fifty years of these social welfare policies. Regressive policies that cut federal aid to education and refused to challenge segregated education, housing, and hiring, as well as the cynical cultivation of an antiblack consensus through attacks on affirmative action and voting rights legislation clearly reinforced possessive investments in whiteness. In the U.S. economy, where 86 percent of available jobs do not appear in classified ads and where personal connections prove the most important factor in securing employment, attacks on affirmative action guarantee that whites will be rewarded for their historical advantage in the labor market rather than for their individual abilities or efforts.[59]

Attacking the civil rights tradition serves many functions for neoconservatives. By mobilizing existing racisms and generating new ones, neoconservatives seek to discredit the egalitarian and democratic social movements of the post-World War II era and to connect the attacks by those movements on wealth, special privilege, and elite control over education and opportunity to despised and unworthy racial "others."

Attacks on the gains made by civil rights activism also act as a wedge to divide potentially progressive coalitions along racial lines, a strategy that attained its peak moment with the defection of "blue collar" trade unionists from the Democratic Party in the 1980s to become "Reagan Democrats." In addition to protecting centralized power and wealth and dividing its opponents, the neoracism of contemporary conservatism also functions as an important unifying symbol for a disparate and sometimes antagonistic coalition that includes Hamiltonian big-government conservatives as well as antistate libertarians, and that incorporates born-again Christians into an alliance with "objectivist" free market thinkers who celebrate selfishness and view the love of gain as the engine of human progress. This coalition often has trouble agreeing on the things it favors, but it has no difficulty agreeing about the alleged bad behavior and inferior morality of minority individuals and communities. Most important, by generating an ever repeating cycle of "moral panics" about the family, crime, welfare, race, and terrorism, neoconservatives produce a perpetual state of anxiety that obscures the actual failures of conservatism as economic and social policy, while promoting demands for even more draconian measures of a similar nature for the future. The neoracism of contemporary conservatism plays a vital role in building a countersubversive consensus because it disguises the social disintegration brought about by neoconservatism itself as the fault of "inferior" social groups, and because it builds a sense of righteous indignation among its constituents that enables them to believe that the selfish and self-interested politics they pursue are actually part of a moral crusade.

Yet even seemingly race-neutral policies supported by both neoconservatives and liberals in the 1980s and 1990s have increased the absolute value of being white. In the 1980s, changes in federal tax laws decreased the value of wage income and increased the value of investment income—a move harmful to minorities, who suffer from a gap between their total wealth and that of whites even greater than the disparity between their income and white income. The failure to raise the minimum wage between 1981 and 1989 and the decline of more than one-third in the value of Aid to Families with Dependent Children (AFDC) payments injured all poor people, but they exacted special on costs on nonwhites, who faced even more constructed markets for employment, housing, and education than poor whites.[60]

Similarly, the "tax reforms" of the 1980s made the effective rate of taxation higher on investment in actual goods and services than on profits from speculative enterprises. This change encouraged the flight of capital from industrial production with its many employment opportunities toward investments that can be turned over quickly to allow the greatest possible tax write-offs. Government policies thus discouraged investments that might produce high-paying jobs and encouraged investors to strip companies of their assets to make rapid short-term profits. These policies hurt almost all workers, but they fell particularly heavily on minority workers, who because of employment discrimination in the retail and small business sectors were overrepresented in blue-collar industrial jobs.

On the other hand, while neoconservative tax policies created incentives for employers to move their enterprises elsewhere, they created disincentives for home owners to move. Measures like California's Proposition 13 (passed in 1978) granting tax relief to property owners badly misallocate housing resources, because they make it financially unwise for the elderly to move out of large houses, further reducing the supply of housing available to young families. While one can well understand the necessity for protecting senior citizens on fixed incomes from tax increases that would make them lose their homes, the rewards and punishments provided by Proposition 13 are so extreme that they prevent the kinds of generational succession that have routinely opened up housing to young families in the past. This reduction works particular hardships on those who also face discrimination by sellers, realtors, and lending institutions.

Subsidies to the private sector by government agencies also tend to enhance the rewards of past discrimination. Throughout the country, tax increment financing for redevelopment programs offers tax-free and low-interest loans to developers whose projects use public services, often without having to pay taxes to local school boards or county governments. In St. Louis, for example, tax abatements for wealthy corporations deprive the city's schools (and their majority African American population) of $17 million a year. Even if these redevelopment projects eventually succeed in increasing municipal revenues through sales and earnings taxes, their proceeds go to funds that pay for the increased services these developments demand (fire and police protection, roads, sewers, electricity, lighting, etc.) rather than to school funds, which are dependent upon property tax revenues.[61] Nationwide, industrial development bonds resulted in a $7.4 billion tax loss in 1983, which ordinary taxpayers had to make up through increased payroll taxes. Compared to white Americans, people of color, more likely to be poor or working class, suffer disproportionately from these changes as taxpayers, as workers, and as tenants. A study by the Citizens for Tax Justice found that wealthy Californians spend less than eleven cents in taxes for every dollar earned, while poor residents of the state pay fourteen cents out of every dollar in taxes. As groups overrepresented among the poor, minorities have been forced to subsidize the tax breaks given to the wealthy.[62] While holding property tax assessments for businesses and some home owners to about half of their market value, California's Proposition 13 deprived cities and counties of $13 billion a year in taxes. Businesses alone avoided $3.3 billion to $8.6 billion in taxes per year under this statute.[63]

Because they are ignorant of even the recent history of the possessive investment in whiteness—generated by slavery and segregation, immigrant exclusion and Native American policy, conquest and colonialism, but augmented by liberal and conservative social policies as well—Americans produce largely cultural explanations for structural social problems. The increased possessive investment in whiteness generated by disinvestment in U.S. cities, factories, and schools since the 1970s disguises as *racial* problems the general social problems posed by deindustrialization, economic restructuring, and neoconservative attacks on the welfare state. It fuels a discourse that demonizes people of color for being victimized by these changes, while hiding the privileges of whiteness by attributing the economic advantages enjoyed by whites to their family values, faith in fatherhood, and foresight—rather than to the favoritism they enjoy through their possessive investment in whiteness.

The demonization of black families in public discourse since the 1970s is particularly instructive in this regard. During the 1970s, the share of low-income households headed by blacks increased by one-third, while black family income fell from 60 percent of white family income in 1971 to 58 percent in 1980. Even adjusting for unemployment and for African American disadvantages in life-cycle employment (more injuries, more frequently interrupted work histories, confinement to jobs most susceptible to layoffs), the wages of full-time year-round black workers fell from 77 percent of white workers' income to 73 percent by 1986. In 1986, white workers with high school diplomas earned $3,000 per year more than African Americans with the same education.[64] Even when they had the same family structure as white workers, blacks found themselves more likely to be poor.

Recent economic gains by blacks brighten the picture somewhat, but the deindustrialization and economic restructuring of the 1970s and 1980s imposes yet another racial penalty on wage earners from minority communities, who suffered setbacks while members of other groups accumulated equity-producing assets. And even when some minority groups show improvement, others do not. In 1995, for example, every U.S. ethnic and racial group experienced an increase in income except the twenty-seven million Hispanics, who experienced a 5.1 percent drop in income during that year alone.[65]

Forty-six percent of black workers between the ages of twenty and twenty-four held blue-collar jobs in 1976, but only 20 percent by 1984. Earnings by young black families that had reached 60 percent of white families' income in 1973, fell to 46 percent by 1986. Younger African American families experienced a 50 percent drop in real earnings between 1973 and 1986, with the decline in black male wages particularly steep.[66] Many recent popular and scholarly studies have delineated the causes for black economic decline over the past two decades.[67] Deindustrialization has decimated the industrial infrastructure that formerly provided high wage jobs and chances for upward mobility to black workers. Neoconservative attacks on government spending for public housing, health, education, and transportation have deprived members of minority groups of needed services and opportunities for jobs in the public sector. A massive retreat at the highest levels of government from the responsibility to enforce antidiscrimination laws has sanctioned pervasive overt and covert racial discrimination by bankers, realtors, and employers.

Yet public opinion polls of white Americans reflect little recognition of these devastating changes. Seventy percent of whites in one poll said that African Americans "have the same opportunities to live a middle-class life as whites," and nearly three-fourths of white respondents to a 1989 poll believed that opportunities for blacks had improved under Reagan.[68] If such optimism about the opportunities available to African Americans does not demonstrate ignorance of the dire conditions facing black communities, it indicates that many whites believe that blacks suffer deservedly, because they do not take advantage of the opportunities offered them. In opinion polls, favorable assessments of black chances for success often accompanied extremely negative judgments about the abilities, work habits, and character of black people. A National Opinion Research Report in 1990 disclosed that more than 50 percent of U.S. whites viewed blacks as innately lazy and less intelligent and less patriotic than whites.[69] More than 60 percent said that they believed that blacks suffer from poor housing and employment opportunities because of their own lack of will power. Some 56.3 percent said that blacks preferred welfare to employment, while 44.6 percent contended that blacks tended toward laziness.[70] Even more important, research by Mary Edsall and Thomas Byrne Edsall indicates that many whites structure nearly all of their decisions about housing, education, and politics in response to their aversions to black people.[71]

The present political culture in this country gives broad sanction for viewing white supremacy and antiblack racism as forces from the past, as demons finally put to rest by the passage of the 1964 Civil Rights Act and the 1965 Voting Rights Act.[72] Jurists, journalists, and politicians have generally been more vocal in opposing what they call "quotas' and "reverse discrimination"—by which they usually mean race-specific measures, designed to remedy existing racial discrimination, that inconvenience or offend whites—than in challenging the thousands of well-documented cases every year of routine, systematic, and unyielding discrimination against minorities. It is my contention that the stark contrast between nonwhite experiences and white opinions during the past two decades cannot be attributed solely to individual ignorance or intolerance, but stems instead from liberal individualism's inability to describe adequately the collective dimensions of our experience.[73] As long as we define social life as the sum total of conscious and deliberative individual activities, we will be able to discern as racist only *individual* manifestations of personal prejudice and hostility. Systemic, collective, and coordinated group behavior consequently drops out of sight. Collective exercises of power that relentlessly channel rewards, resources, and opportunities from one group to another will not appear "racist" from this perspective, because they rarely announce their intention to discriminate against individuals. Yet they nonetheless give racial identities their sinister social meaning by giving people from different races vastly different life chances.

The gap between white perception and minority experience can have explosive consequences. Little more than a year after the 1992 Los Angeles rebellion, a sixteen-year-old high school junior shared her opinions with a reporter from the *Los Angeles Times*. "I don't think white people owe anything to black people," she explained. "We didn't sell them into slavery, it was our ancestors. What they did was wrong, but we've done our best to make up for it." A seventeen-year-old senior echoed those comments, telling the reporter, "I feel we spend more time in my history class talking about what whites owe blacks than just about anything else when the issue of slavery comes up. I often received dirty looks. This seems strange given that I wasn't even alive then. And the few members of my family from that time didn't have the luxury of owning much, let alone slaves. So why, I ask you, am I constantly made to feel guilty?"[74]

More ominously, after pleading guilty to bombing two homes and one car, vandalizing a synagogue, and attempting to start a race war by planning the murder of Rodney King and the bombing of Los Angeles's First African Methodist Episcopal Church, twenty-year-old Christopher David Fisher explained that "sometimes whites were picked on because of the color of their skin. . . . Maybe we're blamed for slavery."[75] Fisher's actions were certainly extreme, but his justification of them drew knowingly and precisely on a broadly shared narrative about the victimization of "innocent" whites by irrational and ungrateful minorities.

The comments and questions raised about the legacy of slavery by these young whites illuminate broader currents in our culture, with enormous implications for understanding the enduring significance of race in our country.

These young people associate black grievances solely with slavery, and they express irritation at what they perceive as efforts to make them feel guilty or unduly privileged because of things that happened in the distant past. The claim that one's own family did not own any slaves is frequently voiced in our culture. It is almost never followed with a statement to the effect that of course some people's families did own slaves and we will not rest until we track them down and make them pay reparations. This view never acknowledges how the existence of slavery and the exploitation of black labor after emancipation created opportunities from which immigrants and others benefited, even if they did not personally own slaves. Rather, it seems to hold that, because not all white people owned slaves, no white people can be held accountable or inconvenienced by the legacy of slavery. More important, having dispensed with slavery, they feel no need to address the histories of Jim Crow segregation, racialized social policies, urban renewal, or the revived racism of contemporary neoconservatism. On the contrary, Fisher felt that his discomfort with being "picked on" and "blamed" for slavery gave him good reason to bomb homes, deface synagogues, and plot to kill black people.

Unfortunately for our society, these young whites accurately reflect the logic of the language of liberal individualism and its ideological predispositions in discussions of race. In their apparent ignorance of the disciplined, systemic, and collective *group* activity that has structured white identities in U.S. history, they are in good company. In a 1979 law journal article, future Supreme Court justice Antonin Scalia argued that affirmative action "is based upon concepts of racial indebtedness and racial entitlement rather than individual worth and individual need" and is thus "racist."[76] Yet liberal individualism is not completely color-blind on this issue. As Cheryl I. Harris demonstrates, the legacy of liberal individualism has not prevented the Supreme Court from recognizing and protecting the group interests of *whites* in the Bakke, Croson, and Wygant cases.[77] In each case, the Court nullified affirmative action programs because they judged efforts to help blacks as harmful to whites: to white expectations of entitlement, expectations based on the possessive investment in whiteness they held as members of a group. In the Bakke case, for instance, where the plaintiff argued that medical school affirmative action programs disadvantaged white applicants like himself, neither Bakke nor the Court contested the legitimacy of medical school admissions standards that reserved five seats in each class for children of wealthy donors to the university or that penalized Bakke for being older than most of the other applicants. The group rights of not-wealthy people or of people older than their classmates did not compel the Court or Bakke to make any claim of harm. But they did challenge and reject a policy designed to offset the effects of past and present discrimination when they could construe the medical school admission policies as detrimental to the interests of whites as a group—and as a consequence they applied the "strict scrutiny" standard to protect whites while denying that protection to people of color. In this case, as in so many others, the language of liberal individualism serves as a cover for coordinated collective group interests.

Group interests are not monolithic, and aggregate figures can obscure serious differences within racial groups. All whites do not benefit from the possessive investment in whiteness in precisely the same ways; the experiences of members of minority groups are not interchangeable. But the possessive investment in whiteness always affects individual and group life chances and opportunities. Even in cases where minority groups secure political and economic power through collective mobilization, the terms and conditions of their collectivity and the logic of group solidarity are always influenced and intensified by the absolute value of whiteness in U.S. politics, economics, and culture.[78]

In the 1960s, members of the Black Panther Party used to say that "if you're not part of the solution, you're part of the problem." But those of us who are "white" can only become part of the solution if we recognize the degree to which we are already part of the problem—not because of our race, but because of our possessive investment in it. Neither conservative "free market" policies nor liberal social welfare policies can solve the "white problem" in the United States, because both reinforce the possessive investment in whiteness. But an explicitly antiracist interethnic movement that acknowledges the existence and power of whiteness might make some important changes. Antiracist coalitions also have a long history in the United States—in the political activism of John Brown, Sojourner Truth, and the Magon brothers among others, but also in our rich cultural tradition of interethnic antiracism connected to civil rights activism of the kind detailed so brilliantly in rhythm and blues musician Johnny Otis's book, *Upside Your Head! Rhythm and Blues on Central Avenue.* These all too infrequent but nonetheless important efforts by whites to fight racism, not out of sympathy for someone else but out of a sense of self-respect and simple justice, have never completely disappeared; they remain available as models for the present.[79]

Walter Benjamin's praise for "presence of mind" came from his understanding of how difficult it may be to see the present. But more important, he called for presence of mind as the means for implementing what he named "the only true telepathic miracle"—turning the forbidding future into the fulfilled present.[80] Failure to acknowledge our society's possessive investment in whiteness prevents us from facing the present openly and honestly. It hides from us the devastating costs of disinvestment in America's infrastructure over the past two decades and keeps us from facing our responsibility to reinvest in human resources by channeling resources toward education, health, and housing—and away from subsidies for speculation and luxury. After two decades of disinvestment, the only further disinvestment we need is from the ruinous pathology of whiteness, which has always undermined our own best instincts and interests. In a society suffering so badly from an absence of mutuality, an absence of responsibility and an absence of justice, presence of mind might be just what we need.

CHAPTER 2

Law and Order: Civil Rights
Laws and White Privilege

People who know so little about themselves can face very little in another; and one dare hope for nothing from friends like these.—JAMES BALDWIN

For more than fifty years, the consensus between U.S. liberals and conservatives in favor of the possessive investment in whiteness has been so complete that the issue has not even come under debate. Neither side has been required to make its arguments in explicit racial terms, but both have been able to carry out racialized agendas—the liberals under the name of respecting prevailing market practices, encouraging business investment in cities, and helping the "middle class," the conservatives under the guise of promoting states' rights, protecting private property, and shrinking the welfare state.

Because American society has not acknowledged the ways in which we have created a possessive investment in whiteness, the disadvantages of racial minorities may seem unrelated to the advantages given to whites. Minority disadvantages are said to stem from innate deficiencies, rather than from systematic disenfranchisement and discrimination. Especially since the passage of the 1964 and 1965 Civil Rights Acts, the dominant discourse in our society argues that the problems facing communities of color no longer stem primarily from discrimination but from the characteristics of those communities themselves, from unrestrained sexual behavior and childbirths out of wedlock, crime, welfare dependency, and a perverse sense of group identity and group entitlement that stands in the way of individual achievement and advancement.

In this regard, it is vital to look at the actual record of civil rights laws and their enforcement. Contrary to their stated intentions, civil rights laws have actually augmented the possessive investment in whiteness, not because civil rights legislation is by nature unwise or impractical, but because these particular laws were structured to be ineffective and largely unenforceable. The conservatives are not wrong when they attribute the problems facing aggrieved racial minorities to a crisis of values, rampant violations of law and order, and pernicious group politics. But by projecting these negative judgments onto minority individuals and groups, they evade the fact that the history of the past five decades demonstrates that the most fanatical group politics, the most flagrant violations of the law, and the vilest evasions of responsible and moral behavior have been enacted by whites. Massive white opposition to the implementation (rather than the mere articulation) of antidiscrimination statutes stands as a stunning indictment of the character of European Americans and shows how the racial problem in the United States remains at heart a white problem. At every stage over the past fifty years, whites have responded to civil rights laws with coordinated collective politics characterized by resistance, refusal, and renegotiation.

Fair Housing

In 1890, San Francisco's board of supervisors passed an ordinance mandating the removal of Chinese Americans from neighborhoods ripe for redevelopment close to downtown. The law ordered their resettlement in isolated industrial areas of the city filled with waste dumps and other environmental hazards. Although overturned by the courts, the San Francisco Segregation Ordinance of 1890 prefigured laws in other cities aimed mainly at preventing racial minorities (especially African Americans) from moving into houses on blocks where whites were the majority of the homeowners.[1] All across the nation in the years immediately before World War I, city governments put the force of law behind residential segregation through racial zoning. When the Supreme Court declared these ordinances unconstitutional in 1917, real estate brokers, political leaders, and bankers turned to restrictive covenants and other private deed restrictions to prevent integration and consequently enhance the material rewards of whiteness.

Between 1924 and 1950 realtors throughout the United States subscribed to a national code that bound them to the view that "a realtor should never be instrumental in introducing into a neighborhood a character of property or occupancy, members of any race or nationality, or any individual whose presence will clearly be detrimental to property values in the neighborhood." Local codes were even more explicit in excluding "detrimental" groups from white neighborhoods.[2]

Mob violence and vigilante action accompanied the legal sanctioning of segregation in many places. As evidenced in the important scholarship of Thomas Sugrue and Arnold Hirsch, northern whites especially succeeded in preserving racially exclusive neighborhoods during the 1940s and 1950s through mob actions that went largely unpunished by law enforcement authorities afraid to challenge crimes enacted on behalf of the possessive investment in whiteness.[3] Most of the time violence was not needed to preserve segregation because restrictive covenants achieved the same ends through peaceful although still coercive means. As private agreements written into deed restrictions on the resale of property, restrictive covenants satisfied the courts and effectively constricted the housing market for groups subject to discrimination, while providing an artificially inflated equity for those practicing it. African American community organizations, who took the lead in opposing restrictive covenants in the courts, attained partial success in 1948 when the Supreme Court ruled in *Shelley v. Kraemer* that state courts who enforced these deed restrictions against the will of buyers and sellers violated the Constitution. Yet even while acknowledging the unfairness of restrictive covenants, the Court's decision provided justification, legitimation, and guidance for resisting racial desegregation. Although it prevented states from enforcing restrictive covenants on their own, it did not make it illegal for property owners to adhere to them voluntarily, and it did not ban the registration of restrictive covenants with local authorities. This meant that people denied the opportunity to buy a home (and thus accumulate assets) because of a restrictive covenant had to initiate legal action and bear the complete cost and burden of securing justice themselves.[4]

When the courts ruled on behalf of minorities, white resistance grew into outright refusal. After the Supreme Court decision in *Shelley v. Kraemer,* the FHA persisted in its policy of recommending and even requiring restrictive covenants as a condition for receiving government-secured home loans.[5] White home owners, realtors, and bankers realized that restrictive covenants could remain in force despite *Shelley v. Kraemer* and, more important, that the ruling did nothing to challenge the other major mechanisms for real estate discrimination, including redlining (denying loans to areas inhabited by racial minorities), steering (directing minority buyers solely to homes in minority neighborhoods), and block busting (playing on the white fear of a change in neighborhood racial balance to promote panic sales, getting whites to sell their homes for small amounts and then selling those same homes to minority buyers at extremely high prices).[6]

In the wake of *Shelley v. Kraemer,* resistance and refusal to desegregate the private housing market helped preserve the possessive investment in whiteness for white home owners for the next twenty years. In the life of a nation, twenty years is not long, but in the lives of individuals, twenty years of rights denied can have devastating effects—inhibiting their accumulation of assets, depriving them of the increased equity that comes with home ownership, and devaluating the assets that they might have passed on to their children. Resistance and refusal preserved the possessive investment in whiteness and forced those excluded from its benefits to try to renegotiate the issue of residential segregation through other channels.

In the presidential election of 1960, African American voters in key northern cities provided the crucial margin that elected John F. Kennedy. Afraid to challenge the segregationists in his own party who held key positions in Congress, Kennedy attempted to respond to minority demands for fair housing by issuing his own executive orders, especially Order 11063 that required government agencies to oppose discrimination in federally supported housing. Once again, white resistance rather than compliance was the order of the day. Federal officials quickly realized that the president would not object if they simply did not communicate his order to local housing authorities. The FHA even refused to apply Executive Order 11063 to its own loans, even though that agency ran the largest federally supported housing program.

White resistance to Kennedy's executive order reflected and exacerbated popular support among whites for racial discrimination. In 1964, California voters overwhelmingly supported a referendum repealing that state's fair-housing law. California governor Edmund G. "Pat" Brown, who supported the open-housing law, later admitted he "was completely out of tune with the white citizens of the state who felt that the right to sell their property to whomever they wanted was a privileged right, a right of ownership, a constitutional right."[7] These acts of resistance and refusal forced a renegotiation of the legal status of open-housing laws. The 1964 Civil Rights Act specifically *exempted* federal mortgage insurance programs from antidiscrimination requirements—a stipulation that virtually guaranteed the continuation of discrimination in home lending.[8] When Lyndon Johnson asked Congress to pass a fair-housing bill in 1966, his request produced "some of the most vicious mail LBJ received on any subject," according to White House aide Joseph Califano (and Johnson certainly received more than his share of hate mail on a variety of subjects).[9] Republican minority leader Everett Dirksen attacked the proposed 1966 bill with particular relish, claiming that white opposition to fair housing stemmed not from whites' racial prejudice but from blacks' bad behavior when they moved into white areas. The House of Representatives passed a bill that accomplished the opposite of what Johnson had requested, acknowledging the "right" of individuals to discriminate in selling their homes and to require their realtors to discriminate as well. Martin Luther King, Jr., and other civil rights leaders argued that the bill was not worth passing, and only a filibuster by its opponents in the Senate prevented it from becoming law.[10]

The death of Dr. King in 1968—and the riots that erupted in its wake—forced another renegotiation of fair-housing issues twenty years after *Shelley v. Kraemer*. When Congress finally passed a comprehensive fair-housing law, it actually encouraged white resistance through provisions that rendered it virtually unenforceable. Title VIII of the Fair Housing Act authorized the Department of Housing and Urban Development to investigate complaints made directly to the HUD secretary but forbade that agency to initiate investigations on its own. The act gave the HUD secretary only thirty days to process complaints and to decide if action was warranted, but even if the agency pursued cases, it had no enforcement power and could only encourage the party guilty of discrimination to accept "conference, conciliation, and persuasion." In rare instances, HUD could refer cases to the attorney general for legal action, but Title VIII authorized action by the Justice Department only when cases "raised an issue of general public importance" or revealed "a pattern or practice" of discrimination. Denial of an individual's constitutional rights was not considered serious enough for action in this realm. People faced with discrimination in the housing market were required to file suit within 180 days of the alleged discriminatory act or within 30 days of the end of mediation. This meant that people suffering from violations of their rights had to bring action on their own behalf, hire their own attorneys, pay their own legal fees and court costs, and bear the burden of proof to establish that "serious" acts of discrimination had indeed taken place. After all that, the act restricted punitive damages in clear-cut cases of discrimination to a maximum of $1,000.[11]

Surely the contours of the 1968 Fair Housing Act make it unique in the annals of legal discourse. As Patricia Roberts Harris noted when she served as secretary of housing and urban development during the Carter administration, there are very few incidents of law breaking where authorities cannot punish the lawbreakers but instead may only ask if the law breaker wishes to talk about the matter with the victim.[12] Despite its palpable weaknesses, however, the 1968 law provoked thousands of complaints about housing discrimination each year, which foundered on the opportunities for resistance and refusal built into the act itself. During the 1970s fewer than 30 percent of the complaints filed with HUD led to mediation, and close to 50 percent of those remained in noncompliance. A study conducted in 1980 demonstrated that only slightly more than one-third of the complaints to HUD led to voluntary consent agreements, and half of those were settled in favor of the party accused of discrimination. As of 1980, only five victims of discrimination has received damages in excess of $3,500. By 1986, the antidiscrimination mechanisms established in the 1968 law had led to decisions on only about four hundred fair-housing cases. Subsequent changes have strengthened aspects of the enforcement and punitive mechanisms of the law, but even today most experts estimate more than two million cases of housing discrimination occur every year without legal action being taken against them.

The process of resistance, refusal, and renegotiation that plagued fair-housing efforts from *Shelley v. Kraemer* through the 1968 Fair Housing Act was not an aberration; it has characterized every judicial, legislative, and executive effort on behalf of open housing for the past fifty years. For example, when plaintiffs filed suit in federal court charging racial discrimination by Chicago's public-housing authority in the 1960s, a federal judge initially skeptical of their claims eventually found the housing authority guilty in 1969. He ordered the city to construct seven hundred new units of public housing in white neighborhoods and to locate 75 percent of new public housing outside the inner-city ghetto. The Chicago Housing Authority resisted this order initially and, when finally faced with the necessity of compliance, responded by ceasing construction of *all* new public housing as a means of evading integration.[13]

Similarly, the St. Louis suburb of Black Jack reincorporated and changed its zoning laws in 1970 in order to block construction of a low- and middle-income integrated housing development. Secretary of Housing and Urban Development George Romney filed a lawsuit against the municipality in federal court, as he was required to do by law, but Attorney General John Mitchell intervened in order to protect Black Jack's resistance to desegregation by ordering Romney to drop the suit. The executive branch put even more clout behind this resistance when President Nixon announced he would suspend enforcement of all civil rights laws for a year while his staff studied the situation. Over that year, hundreds of grants were approved by the government without seeing if they complied with federal civil rights laws. Nixon conceded that denying housing to people because of their race was wrong, but he added that he found it equally wrong for cities opposed to federally assisted (and therefore integrated) housing to "have it imposed from Washington by bureaucratic fiat."[14] Nixon's tactic of affirming support for integration in the abstract while acting to undermine the mechanisms that made it possible in practice became a standard response among white politicians to desegregation demands during the civil rights and post–civil rights eras. These politicians soon discovered that their obstructionism made them tremendously popular among white voters.

White resistance manifested as refusal to abide by fair-housing laws continued to guide federal policy in the 1970s and 1980s. A survey conducted by HUD in the 1970s disclosed that black "testers" sent out to inquire about housing for rent or sale received less information than white testers on housing for sale 15 percent of the time, and they received less information than white testers about the availability of rental housing 27 percent of the time.[15] As late as 1970, officials of the Federal Home Loan Bank Board redlined postal zip code areas where the black population was increasing.[16] Training manuals designed for use by private appraisers in 1977 continued to describe desirable neighborhoods as "100 percent Caucasian" along with the phrase "without adverse effects from minorities."[17] Yet federal and state officials remained virtually inactive in the enforcement of fair-housing laws.

Because white resistance and refusal has always led to renegotiation of the terms of open housing, every triumph by fair-housing advocates has turned out to be an empty victory. For example, opponents of the racially unequal consequences of urban renewal won a long-sought victory in 1970 with the passage of the Uniform Relocation Assistance and Real Property Acquisition Act, which mandated for the first time that local housing authorities replace the low-income units they destroy (most often occupied by racial minorities). Congress responded by eliminating the urban renewal program altogether, replacing it with community development block grants that emphasized luxury housing for upper- and middle-class home owners. In St. Louis, the city evicted five hundred families (almost all of them African American) from the Pershing Waterman Redevelopment area, gave $5.8 million in tax abatements to developers, demolished nine buildings at city expense, secured $1.4 million in federal block grant funds, and sold 106 parcels of land to the developers for $122 per parcel. Yet because the Pershing Redevelopment Company was a private enterprise, and because the funding came from block grants rather than urban renewal funds, none of the dislocated families received a single dollar in relocation assistance.[18]

Similarly, Congress passed the Equal Credit Opportunity Act in 1974, which expressly prohibited discrimination in real estate lending, requiring banks to record the racial identities of applicants rejected and accepted for loans. When bankers refused to collect the required data, ten civil rights groups filed suit in 1976, asking the courts to order the comptroller of the currency, the Federal Deposit Insurance Corporation (FDIC), and the Home Loan Bank Board to obey the 1974 law. These agencies did sign a court order agreeing to collect the required materials, but the comptroller of the currency and the FDIC ceased keeping records based on race in 1981 when the court order expired. Home Loan Bank Board records revealed that blacks continued to face rejection rates several times higher than those encountered by white applicants. Having resisted the law initially, the federal agencies complied with the law for a short time when compelled to do so by a court order, then reverted to absolute refusal.

Advocates of fair housing attempted to renegotiate the issue with the passage of the 1975 Home Mortgage Disclosure Act and the 1977 Community Investment Act. These bills required lenders to identify which neighborhoods received their home-improvement and mortgage loans, and to demonstrate their willingness to supply capital to worthy borrowers in low-income areas.[19] If enforced, these acts might have made a substantial difference, but the Reagan administration rendered them moot by ignoring the law. Reagan's appointee as director of the Justice Department's Civil Rights Division, William Bradford Reynolds, filed only two housing discrimination suits in his first twenty months in office, a distinct drop from the average of thirty-two cases a year filed during the Nixon and Ford presidencies or even the nineteen per year during the final two years of the Carter administration.[20]

When the number of housing discrimination complaints filed with HUD doubled, the Reagan Justice Department neglected nearly every serious complaint and initiated frivolous suits against plans that maintained integrated housing and prevented block busting by regulating the racial balance in housing developments. For example, the administration took action aimed at invalidating deed restrictions in one of the few genuinely integrated areas of Houston, the Houston Oaks subdivision, because the original deeds contained restrictive covenants (which were neither enforced nor honored by the residents). The administration also used the Paperwork Reduction Act as an excuse to stop HUD from gathering data on the racial identities of participants in its housing programs.[21] By refusing to gather data on true discrimination, the Reagan administration strengthened resistance to fair-housing laws to the point of encouraging outright refusal to obey them.

Precisely because of white resistance to desegregation, the subsidized housing program had the highest percentage of black recipients of any federal benefits program—38.5 percent in 1979. In 1980, language in an amendment to the Housing and Community Development Act would have allowed local housing authorities to address directly the urgent housing situation of racial minorities by designating housing for those in greatest need, but the Reagan administration came to power shortly afterwards and made the victory a hollow one by virtually eliminating all federal funding for subsidized housing—from $26.1 billion in 1981 to $2.1 billion in 1985.[22] While cutting allocations for these programs aimed at providing simple subsistence and income maintenance for a primarily black clientele, the Reagan administration retained the home owner mortgage deduction, a federal housing policy more costly to the government but one that helps a primarily white clientele accumulate assets.

The 1988 Fair Housing Amendments Act, which addressed many important shortcomings in previous fair-housing legislation, came at a time when high housing prices kept many people of color out of the market. In addition, housing in the United States has become so hypersegregated, loan procedures so discriminatory, and enforcement of fair-housing laws so infrequent that federal law acknowledging the rights of all people to secure housing on a fair basis may have no effect on their ability to actually do so. Whites who became home owners under blatantly discriminatory circumstances condoned and protected by the judicial, legislative, and executive branches of government have also become more formidable competitors for housing, as value of their homes has increased as a result of appreciation and inflation. Median prices on new homes and on sales of existing homes increased by almost 230 percent between 1970 and 1985, while the consumer price index rose by 177 percent.[23]

The possessive investment in whiteness generated by failure to enforce fair-housing legislation has concrete costs for people of color. Melvin Oliver and Tom Shapiro estimate that discrimination in the home loan industry alone costs black homeowners $10.5 billion in extra payments, and that every black home owner is deprived of nearly $4,000 as a result of the 54 percent higher rate they pay on home mortgages. The costs for those who cannot enter the housing market, and who consequently neither build equity nor qualify for the home owners' tax deduction, is, of course, much higher.[24] The appreciated value of owner-occupied homes constitutes the single greatest source of wealth for white Americans. It is the factor most responsible for the disparity between blacks and whites in respect to wealth—a disparity between the two groups much greater than their differences in income. It is the basis for intergenerational transfers of wealth that enable white parents to give their children financial advantages over the children of other groups. Housing plays a crucial role in determining educational opportunities as well, because school funding based on property tax assessments in most localities gives better opportunities to white children than to children from minority communities. Opportunities for employment are also affected by housing choices, especially given the location of new places of employment in suburbs and reduced funding for public transportation. In addition, housing affects health conditions, with environmental and health hazards disproportionately located in minority communities.

Whiteness has a value in our society. Its value originates not in the wisdom of white home buyers or the improvements they have made on their property, but from the ways in which patterns of bad faith and nonenforcement of antidiscrimination laws have enabled the beneficiaries of past and present discrimination to protect their gains and pass them on to succeeding generations. These benefits stem directly from the pattern of resistance, refusal, and renegotiation that white individuals and their elected representatives have fashioned in response to antidiscrimination legislation. If these dynamics applied only to housing, they would be damaging enough, but the same process of resistance, refusal, and renegotiation has characterized the history of antidiscrimination legislation and court rulings in education and employment as well.

School Desegregation

Unequal opportunities for education play a crucial role in racializing life chances in the United States. Just as the 1948 *Shelley v. Kraemer* decision and the 1968 Fair Housing Act are often credited incorrectly with ending discrimination in housing, the Supreme Court's 1954 ruling in *Brown v. Board of Education* is widely acknowledged as the turning point in ending school segregation. Yet once again, mere articulation of antidiscrimination principles did not lead to their implementation. Like laws against discrimination in housing, official policies designed to end segregated education have been consistently undermined and defeated by white resistance and refusal.

The 1954 *Brown* case culminated sixteen years of school desegregation lawsuits filed by the NAACP and other civil rights and community groups. In that decision, the Court conceded that government bodies had played a crucial role in promoting and preserving racial differences by limiting black students to separate and therefore inherently unequal educations. Yet while ruling against de jure segregation in the abstract, the decision provided no means for dismantling the structures that crafted advantages for white students out of the

disadvantages of students of color. The plaintiffs in *Brown* sought more for their
children than physical proximity to whites; they pursued desegregation as a
means of securing for black students the same educational resources and opportunities routinely provided to whites. The *Brown* decision helped frustrate
their aims, however, because it outlawed only one technique of inequality—de
jure segregation—without addressing the ways in which discrimination in
housing, employment, and access to public services enabled whites to resegre-
gate the schools by moving to suburban districts. In addition, as Cheryl I. Harris argues, by ordering implementation of its decision "with all deliberate
speed," the Supreme Court in *Brown I* and *Brown II* allowed for more deliber-
ation than speed. The Court allowed the white perpetrators of discrimination
"to control, manage, postpone, and if necessary, thwart change."[25]

Just as the absence of enforcement mechanisms made violations of fair-
housing laws an unusual class of criminal offenses—crimes that carried virtually no penalties—*Brown I* and *Brown II* invented new kinds of constitutional
rights. In most previous decisions, the Supreme Court considered constitu-
tionally protected rights as "personal and present," meaning that their violation
required immediate redress. But the rights of black children in *Brown I* and
Brown II received no such protection. The level of white resistance to desegregation dictated the remedy, an approach that Harris correctly concludes invited
"defiance and delay" and, I would add, outright refusal as well.[26] Efforts to desegregate schools provoked massive resistance in the North as well as the South,
but even with clear evidence of massive refusal on the part of whites to respond
to *Brown,* the courts did not begin to evaluate proposed remedies for segregation critically until the 1968 *Green v. County School Board of New Kent County,
Virginia.*[27] Federal courts did not direct school districts to adopt specific remedies like busing until 1971 with *Swann v. Charlotte-Mecklenburg Board of Education,* and the Supreme Court did not announce that the time for "all deliberate speed" had run out until the 1975 and 1977 *Bradley v. Milliken* cases.

By inviting more than two decades of delay, the Supreme Court condoned
the systematic denial of black children's constitutional rights, responding to
white parents and their representatives who argued that remediation inconvenienced them and interfered with their expected privileges as whites.[28] Perhaps
most important, two decades of delay and denial of the rights of minority children encouraged whites to view the inconvenience of busing as worse than the
systematic practices of discrimination that provoked it. As in later discussions
about affirmative action, resistance to busing as judicial activism and unwar-
ranted federal intervention in community affairs proceeded as if white resis-

tance and refusal had not caused it to be necessary, as if whites were innocent victims of remedies for a disease that did not even exist.

The power of white resistance and refusal to desegregate education was demonstrated most powerfully in the 1973 *San Antonio Independent School District v. Rodriguez* case. Here the Supreme Court acknowledged that the education provided to Mexican American children in San Antonio was inferior to that offered to Anglo children but contended that education was not so fundamental a right that it enjoyed constitutional protection, and consequently the courts could not order equalization of resources.[29] In a parallel display of the power of the possessive investment in whiteness, in *Bradley v. Milliken I* and *II* the Court ruled against cross-district city-suburb busing as a remedy for segregation. In this case, the justices received ample evidence that various governments and government agencies had participated in the construction, maintenance, and perpetuation of discriminatory policies in the Detroit school system. They received the findings of a lower federal court that private sector actions in real estate and home lending led to residential segregation that made school integration by district impossible. Yet by a five-to-four decision the justices ruled against cross-district busing, apparently persuaded by Justice Potter Stewart's stupefyingly innocent assertion that racial segregation in Detroit's schools was caused by "unknown and unknowable factors."[30]

White political leadership played an important role in solidifying the resistance to and refusal of school desegregation. Close to 70 percent of northern whites told pollsters that they supported the Johnson administration's efforts to desegregate the South in 1964, but when urban riots, fair-housing campaigns, and efforts to end de facto school segregation reached their localities, a conservative countersubversive mobilization (made manifest in the Goldwater and Wallace campaigns for the presidency and in the efforts by Californians to repeal fair-housing laws) changed public opinion. By 1966, 52 percent of northern whites told pollsters that they felt that the government was pushing integration "too fast."[31] Richard Nixon secured the key support of Strom Thurmond in the 1968 presidential campaign in return for a promise to lessen federal pressure for school desegregation. White southern voters consequently provided him with a crucial vote margin in a closely contested election.[32] Nixon supervised the abandonment of the school desegregation guidelines issued in the 1964 Civil Rights Act, nominated opponents of busing to the Supreme Court, and in his 1972 reelection campaign urged Congress to pass legislation overturning court-ordered busing.[33]

Opposition to school desegregation has enabled whites to preserve de facto advantages they held as a result of an earlier era's overt de jure segregation. As Gary Orfield suggests, the superiority of suburban schools is taken for granted as a right attendant to home ownership, while desegregation is viewed as a threat to a system that passes racial advantages from one generation to the next. In Orfield's words, "Whites tell pollsters that they believe that blacks are offered equal opportunities, but fiercely resist any efforts to make them send their children to the schools they insist are good enough for blacks." At the same time, "the people who oppose busing minority students to the suburbs also tend to oppose sending suburban dollars to city schools."[34]

Efforts to desegregate higher education have also provoked white resistance. In the 1978 *Regents of the University of California v. Bakke* case, an unsuccessful white applicant to the UC-Davis medical school charged that he had been denied admission to the school because of his race. Bakke claimed that he had compiled a higher undergraduate grade point average (GPA) than the average GPA of minority students admitted through a special admissions program. He did not challenge the legitimacy of the thirty-six white students with GPAs lower than his who also secured acceptance to the UC-Davis medical school the year he applied, nor did he challenge the enrollment of five students admitted because their parents had attended or given money to the school. He did not challenge his exclusion from the other medical schools to which he applied that did not have minority special admissions programs but favored younger applicants over the thirty-six-year-old Bakke. Nor did he mention that he had been the beneficiary of special privileges as an elementary school student in the illegally segregated Dade County, Florida, school district.[35] But Bakke did claim that the sixteen minority special admits to UC-Davis took spots that he deserved, even though the graduation rate for special admission students in the past had ranged from 91 to 95 percent, and at least one of the minority special admits the year Bakke applied had an undergraduate GPA of 3.76, much higher than Bakke's.[36]

In her generative and important article "Whiteness as Property," Cheryl Harris notes that Bakke's case rested on the expectation "that he would never be disfavored when competing with minority candidates, although he might be disfavored with respect to other more privileged whites."[37] While conceding the legality of the UC-Davis minority special admissions program, the Supreme Court nonetheless ordered Bakke's admission to medical school. Justice Powell ruled that while universities could not consider race as a factor in admission procedures merely to correct past injustices, they could consider race as a factor in admissions in order to enhance the educational environment for other (that is, white) students. In this case, the California Supreme Court applied the standard of strict scrutiny traditionally used only on behalf of "discrete and insular minorities" likely to suffer "invidious discrimination." In his deciding opinion supporting the state court's level of scrutiny, Justice Lewis Powell did not argue that whites were part of a discrete and insular minority likely to suffer invidious discrimination, but he did say that white individuals might be so upset by what they viewed as preferential treatment for Chicanos and blacks that they might *perceive* a denial of equal rights amounting to invidious discrimination.[38] In this case as in many others, guesses about the perceptions and expectations of whites supersede the constitutional rights and empirical realities of blacks and other minorities. It certainly stands in sharp contrast to the 1973 *Rodriguez* decision, which minimized the importance of education as a federally guaranteed right when the case involved Mexican American children. In *Bakke,* white expectations and perceptions of being hindered in their pursuit of the educational opportunities they desired were considered worthy of federal protection.

The value attached to white perceptions by Justice Powell was not an aberration; it is the logical consequence of the success of white resistance and refusal in forcing renegotiation of antidiscrimination law. Its centrality to educational issues is best illustrated by a comparison of the litigation over Bakke with the universally recognized legality of special admissions plans that routinely benefit whites, such as "legacy" admits at elite institutions, including Harvard, Yale, Dartmouth, the University of Pennsylvania, and Stanford. These programs give special preference to children of alumni and children of large donors to the schools. At the University of California and the University of Virginia, alumni children from out of state secure the advantage of being treated as if they were in state students. Since the 1950s, 20 percent of the undergraduate students entering Harvard have secured admission because their parents were Harvard alumni.[39] The judiciary that intervened on behalf of Allan Bakke has never found this system, which routinely channels rewards to the beneficiaries of past discrimination and their children, to disadvantage minority students, nor has the system met with disfavor from the conservative foundations, politicians, and university regents who attacked and dismantled the University of California's commitment to race-and gender-based affirmative action policies in 1995 on the grounds that they opposed special preferences and privileges rather than merit-based procedures.

White resistance and refusal in housing and education works to deprive minority children of both intergenerational transfers of wealth and the tools to better their own conditions. Inadequate funding for inner-city schools means that minority youths frequently encounter larger classes, fewer counselors, more inexperienced teachers, and more poorly equipped laboratories and libraries than their white counterparts.[40] According to a National School Boards Association study in 1993, 70 percent of black and Latino students attend schools with a predominately minority enrollment; in the northeastern states nearly half of black and Latino students attend schools where minority enrollment exceeds 90 percent.[41] Yet, in education as well as in housing, the highest levels of judicial, legislative, and executive power have worked together to preserve white privileges and raise barriers to education and to asset accumulation for members of minority groups. As Cheryl Harris astutely concludes, "When the law recognizes, either implicitly or explicitly, the settled expectations of whites built on the privileges and benefits produced by white supremacy, it acknowledges and reinforces a property interest in whiteness that reproduces black subordination."[42] It also recognizes that white resistance and refusal justifies the renegotiation of opportunities for equality not just in education, but in housing and hiring.

Fair Hiring

Federal labor policies have systematically advantaged whites over minorities, creating and preserving a possessive investment in whiteness with respect to jobs. The Social Security Act of 1935 exempted from coverage the job categories most likely to be filled by African Americans, Asian Americans, and Mexican Americans—farm workers and domestics—while the National Labor Relations Act put the force of federal law behind racially restrictive union rules and regulations. When the NAACP proposed that the Wagner Act contain a prohibition against racial discrimination by trade unions, the American Federation of Labor announced that it would not support the legislation if it contained such a provision. Thus, organized labor was willing to forego federally sanctioned collective bargaining in order to preserve its more important privilege of racial monopolies for white workers. Eventually, the New Deal sided with the unions, granting them federal protection for collective bargaining recognition *and* racial exclusivity.[43]

President Roosevelt's Executive Order 8802 mandated fair hiring in defense industries, but it took concerted direct-action strikes and mass demonstrations by minority workers and their supporters to secure even a modicum of what Roosevelt's executive order promised.[44] When postwar layoffs and discriminatory hiring practices by private employers reversed wartime gains, minority workers launched twenty years of struggle on a variety of fronts, trying to win access to fair employment opportunities. By 1964 thirty-four states had passed fair-hiring legislation, but these laws had few provisions for enforcement and were largely ineffective. They followed the pattern we have seen earlier of affirming a commitment to nondiscriminatory practices in the abstract while doing nothing to challenge the reality.[45] Consequently, racially based hiring and racialized segmentation of the labor market remained the norm rather than the exception in the U.S. economy. Employer preferences and trade union discrimination consistently relegated minority workers to the worst jobs with the lowest rewards. By the 1950s, black workers aged twenty-four to forty-four faced unemployment levels three times those confronting their white counterparts. Only half of black workers labored full-time, while nearly 67 percent of white workers had year-round employment. Compared to whites, black workers endured lower median incomes, a greater likelihood of layoffs, less access to medical and pension plans, and more injuries at work.[46] Because of shorter life spans, lower life earnings, and the regressive nature of Social Security taxes, African American workers paid more into Social Security than they took out, actually subsidizing the Social Security benefits received by more privileged groups. Small wonder then, that at the grass-roots level the civil rights struggles so often represented as exclusively concerned with voting rights or desegregating public accommodations often revolved around fair and full employment.

Starting in the early 1960s, black workers and their allies in Philadelphia, Newark, and New York City staged nonviolent direct-action protests against construction projects financed by taxpayer dollars that hired few, if any, black workers.[47] In St. Louis, demonstrators led by Percy Green temporarily halted construction on the federally funded Gateway Arch. Green climbed up one leg of the structure and chained himself to it in order to dramatize his complaints against the project's all-white construction crew.[48] Such demonstrations sought to desegregate the workplace, but in some cities they also had broader social goals. In New York and Philadelphia community groups linked their demands for construction jobs for minorities to protests against the construction of new schools in all-black neighborhoods, which they viewed as an effort to insure segregated and therefore inferior educations for their children.[49]

In Cambridge, Maryland, the militant Cambridge Nonviolent Action Committee conducted a survey of the black community and disclosed that 42 percent considered unemployment their most pressing problem; 26 percent pinpointed housing, and 6 percent considered access to public accommodations their top priority.[50] In 1960, a study by the U.S. Commission on Civil Rights condemned "persistent and undeniable" racial discrimination in employment, expressly rebuking the leadership of the trade union movement for its inaction. The massive March on Washington in August 1963, most often remembered as the occasion for Martin Luther King, Jr.'s "I Have a Dream" speech, was officially a march for jobs and justice, with signs prominently displayed calling for stronger fair-employment practices legislation. An investigation by Attorney General Ramsey Clark into the causes of the 1965 Watts riots found employment issues paramount in the minds of community residents.[51]

Confronted with incessant direct-action protests and indirect political pressure, the AFL-CIO reluctantly threw its support behind Title VII of the 1964 Civil Rights Act, a section of the bill ostensibly designed to promote fair hiring. Yet resistance and refusal remained part of the union strategy. According to one highly placed source, the AFL-CIO leadership supported this bill because they believed that a commitment to integration in principle might ward off measures that could bring it about in practice. A leading lobbyist working on behalf of the Civil Rights Act later recalled that the unions "had just been so beaten for their racism that they wanted a bill and then they could blame it on the bill if it wasn't enforced."[52] To that end, they helped write a law that resembled many of the existing ineffective state fair-hiring laws, especially in their assumptions that discriminatory hiring was an individual act and an individual problem rather than a systemic feature of the economy.

Just as the 1968 Fair Housing Act and the 1954 *Brown* decision established principles about discrimination never designed to be translated into practice, Title VII of the 1964 Civil Rights Act contained provisions that undermined its stated goals. The Equal Employment Opportunity Commission (EEOC) established by the act lacked its own enforcement mechanisms, such as cease-and-desist orders, and could offer only "conciliation" as a remedy to aggrieved individuals.[53] In addition to its weak enforcement provisions, this section of the bill provided explicit special protection for the beneficiaries of past discrimination. As a condition of its support, the AFL-CIO insisted that the bill protect current seniority rights—even those obtained through overtly discriminatory practices. The federation insisted that the mandate for fair hiring applied only to future appointments. Section 703(h) of the bill secured all of these guarantees. In the judgment of Herbert Hill, former national labor director of the NAACP, these provisions offered protection to "the racial status quo of seniority systems for at least a generation."[54]

As had been the case in efforts to fight discrimination in housing and education, white resistance prevented equality in hiring for at least a generation, forcing a renegotiation of the terms, conditions, and procedures of antidiscrimination measures. Yet like the modest changes in the laws governing school segregation and real estate discrimination created by *Brown* and the 1968 Fair Housing Act, the fair-hiring sections of the 1964 Civil Rights Act met with massive resistance by whites, in this case white employers, white workers, and their political representatives. Some of the St. Louis unions targeted by Percy Green's direct-action protests at the Gateway Arch responded to Title VII by adding a grandfather clause to their apprenticeship regulations, giving extra points on an exam to applicants whose fathers were journeyman construction workers. Construction unions in Philadelphia initiated confidential oral interviews as prerequisites for admission to apprenticeship programs in plumbing, pipefitting, sheet metal work, roofing, and electrical work. All of the black applicants failed this section of the "exam." Forty percent of the apprentices accepted by the Philadelphia Plumbers Union were the sons of union plumbers.

One construction worker in that city bristled when told that blacks considered these practices discriminatory, explaining, "Some men leave their sons money, some large investments, some business connections and some a profession. I have none of these to bequeath to my sons. I have only one worthwhile thing to give: my trade . . . For this simple father's wish it is said that I discriminate against Negroes. Don't all of us discriminate? Which of us when it comes to choice will not choose a son over all others?"[55] This worker understood very well the value of his whiteness and what it would be worth to his son to pass it across generations. Like white parents able to leave suburban homes to their children or provide them with exclusive educations, he understood that whiteness is property, to borrow a concept from legal scholars Derrick Bell and Cheryl Harris. Perhaps he also knew that government officials, union leaders, and employers would help him protect that property.

The weaknesses of the EEOC undermined efforts at fair employment. The commission received more than 1,300 complaints about discrimination in its first hundred days of operation. By 1967 it received more than 8,000 complaints—a total accounting for an average of 23 per day. By 1972, little more than half of the 80,000 cases referred to the agency had even been investigated. Frustration with the backlog of complaints at the EEOC forced private individuals to file suits on their own. Between 1965 and 1971, private lawsuits against job discrimination outnumbered actions taken by the Department of Justice by twenty-five to one.[56]

Title VII of the 1964 Civil Rights Act gave the Department of Labor's Bureau of Apprenticeship Training responsibility for ending discrimination in the building trades unions. The bureau failed to take this responsibility seriously. Staffed by individuals with long histories in the trade union movement, it disregarded most of the complaints it received and failed to take any action when several of its very few investigations revealed clear evidence of discrimination. Three years after the bill became law the agency was still in the process of compiling a list of apprenticeship programs that had been "warned" about discrimination, but even unions notified of violations of the law needed only to issue a statement announcing their intention to comply with the law in the future to get back into the good graces of the government. While the bureau dawdled, unions developed a vast number of tests, oral interviews, and new "education" requirements as a means of continuing to discriminate under the guise of raising standards. In 1968, an exasperated secretary of labor ruled that, in the future, government contractors would not receive any contracts unless they took "affirmative action.[57]

Auto worker Alphonso Lumpkins informed St. Louis Mayor James F. Conway about the weaknesses in fair hiring law enforcement in a 1980 letter. Describing his ten-year involvement in a campaign to challenge discrimination in the auto industry, Lumpkins complained, "We have found it very difficult to get local attorneys to stand up to the judges in getting required documents, time to present witnesses, and documents on behalf of our cases."[58] When General Motors closed its Chevrolet Shell plant, the mostly female and minority work force learned that they lost all seniority rights and had to seek employment at other GM plants as new workers. Yet when the same company merged its Fisher Body plant with its Chevrolet Truck facility, the workforce at these facilities— 89 percent white males at Fisher and 74 percent white males at Chevrolet Truck—kept their seniority rights. That same year, the Equal Employment Opportunity Commission revealed the pattern in St. Louis federal courts that prevented workers like Lumpkins from receiving justice. The EEOC found that federal judges undermined the letter and intent of civil rights laws by denying fees to attorneys for successful plaintiffs in the amounts they would usually receive as reimbursement for their expenses. Thus, the commission's findings confirmed a 1978 brief by the American Civil Liberties Union that charged "an unusual degree of hostility" by federal judges in St. Louis toward people filing civil rights cases. In a successful 1973 suit against discrimination in Iron Workers Local 396 by black worker Walee Abdul Hameed, one attorney worked 368 hours, and another put in 438, but when they tried to get the losing defendants to play their usual $60 and $80 per hour fees, Judge James H. Meredith denied their request with no comment. In another case Judge John H. Nangle gave no award to attorneys for black fire fighters, and in yet another Judge Kenneth Wangelin awarded an attorney only $300 for a successful suit.[59]

Broader economic changes turned justice delayed into justice denied. When deindustrialization, downsizing, and economic restructuring produced large numbers of layoffs during the 1970s, the seniority rights of white workers insulated them from the worst consequences of these dramatic changes. The provisions in Title VII designed to protect the seniority rights of those workers rewarded them in perpetuity for having benefited from racial discrimination before 1964. As argued in chapter 1, a study conducted for the U.S. Commission on Civil Rights found that seniority-based layoffs worked particular hardships on black workers during the 1973–1974 recession. In areas where blacks made up only 10 to 12 percent of the work force, they accounted for 60 to 70 percent of the workers laid off.[60] Unprotected by seniority in the present because they had been discriminated against in the past, blacks paid disproportionate costs for the economic restructuring of the 1970s and 1980s. In addition, because discrimination in hiring did not magically cease with the passage of the 1964 bill, employees who had benefited from discrimination since 1964 also got to retain the seniority rights they had accrued, while others had to struggle against overt and covert discrimination in order to get jobs with lesser seniority. Along with plant closings, layoffs have devastated minority communities. One study found that between 1979 and 1984, 50 percent of black males in durable goods manufacturing in five Great Lakes cities lost their jobs.[61]

The impact of these seniority-based layoffs might have been less had the laws banning discriminatory practices in hiring been enforced effectively, but here again, white resistance and refusal preserved the possessive investment in whiteness. The Supreme Court has repeatedly thwarted efforts to find fair solutions to the ways in which seniority-based layoffs unfairly and disproportionately affect minority workers. In the 1986 *Wygant v. Jackson Board of Education* case, the Court overturned a voluntary collective bargaining agreement that called for laying off some senior white teachers before junior black teachers, in order to remedy previous discrimination and to prevent budget crises from causing the district to lose all of its minority teachers. In deciding that this agreement violated the constitutional rights of white workers, Justice Powell posed the decision as a "color-blind" defense of the principle of seniority, arguing that "the rights and expectations surrounding seniority make up what is probably the most valuable capital asset that the worker 'owns,' worth even more than the current equity in his home."[62]

Based on arguments similar to those employed by the Philadelphia construction worker defending nepotism in his union, Powell's comparison to home equity is an appropriate one, but perhaps not for the reasons he intended.

Like the equity in homes secured in discriminatory housing markets, white seniority rights secured in discriminatory labor markets routinely receive protection from the courts as if they were constitutional rights. In addition, race rather than seniority stood at the center of this case. Justice Thurgood Marshall observed in his dissent in *Wygant* that all layoffs burden someone, but they are rarely treated as violations of constitutional rights. Marshall noted that the plan the Court rejected did more to protect seniority rights than random layoffs would have, but by the Court's reasoning, random layoffs would have been constitutional. Thus the only kinds of layoffs the majority opinion ruled out were those designed to implement the letter and the spirit of antidiscrimination laws. The violation here was not of seniority, but of white expectations that their past advantages will be secured by the courts. As Cheryl Harris explains, "Although the existing state of inequitable distribution is the product of institutionalized white supremacy and economic exploitation, it is seen by whites as part of the natural order of things that cannot legitimately be disturbed."[63]

The Supreme Court carried its protection of white expectations to a ridiculous degree in the 1989 *City of Richmond v. J.A. Croson* decision. In overturning the Richmond, Virginia, City Council's legislation setting aside 30 percent of construction contracts for minority-owned businesses, the Court ruled that the requirement violated the constitutional rights of white contractors who previously had secured 99.33 percent of city contracting business. In this case, the Court applied to white male business owners the "strict scrutiny" standard originally developed in the 1938 *United States v. Carolene Products Co.* case and later applied to protect "discrete and insular" minorities subject to pervasive discrimination. Justice Sandra Day O'Connor's majority opinion ignored evidence about systematic discrimination in the construction industry, including the fact that between 1973 and 1978 minority businesses received only .67 percent of construction contracts in a city whose population was evenly divided between white and black. Like Justice Stewart in *Bradley v. Milliken I* and *II*, Justice O'Connor could not fathom why blacks had not received construction contracts from the City of Richmond prior to the set-aside program. "Blacks may be disproportionately attracted to industries other than construction," she mused, dismissing national statistics on discrimination in the industry because she claimed that they proved nothing about discrimination in the industry in Richmond.[64] Yet while finding no pattern of discrimination against blacks that might compel remedial action, the majority of the Court did find the claim by a white contractor that he might be relegated to competing for 70 percent of Richmond's construction work instead of 99.33 percent sufficiently serious to warrant strict scrutiny and to overturn the policy of Richmond's democratically elected but predominately black city council. Unlike the city council of the all-white municipality of Black Jack, Missouri, whose desires to be free of outside "bureaucrats" caused Richard Nixon to suspend enforcement of civil rights laws in 1970, the Richmond City Council's actions were overturned as a violation of constitutional rights.

This special sensitivity to potential civil rights violations against whites has proven part of a broader pattern. The Court ruled in *Martin v. Wilks* that white male fire fighters in Birmingham who felt they experienced "reverse discrimination" should be allowed to reopen a collective bargaining agreement containing a court-approved affirmative action promotion plan many years after the original case had been settled. Yet in the parallel case of *Lorance v. ATT Technologies, Inc.* in the same year, the Court told female employees that they could not file claims against discriminatory policies in their place of employment because they had waited too long to complain. In fact, the women filed suit as soon as they were aware of the policy's adverse affect on them, but the Court ruled they should have questioned the procedures at the precise moment when they were adopted, even though they could not have possibly known then what results the policies would bring.[65] Thus, the same Supreme Court that granted "suspect-class" status to Birmingham's white male firefighters and Richmond's white contractors denied that status in other cases to women, to minorities, and to persons with below-average incomes.[66]

Resistance, Refusal, Renegotiation, and Racial Progress

Derrick Bell aptly sums up the state of civil rights law in the 1990s in a two-part formulation: "(1) Because most policies challenged by blacks as discriminatory make no mention of race, blacks can no longer evoke the strict-scrutiny shield in absence of proof of intentional discrimination—at which point, strict scrutiny is hardly needed. (2) Whites challenging racial remedies that usually contain racial classifications are now deemed entitled to strict scrutiny without any distinction between policies of invidious intent and those with remedial purposes. Thus, for equal protection purposes, whites have become the protected 'discrete and insular minority.' "[67] White resistance and refusal has led to renegotiation of antidiscrimination law to such a degree that efforts to combat discrimination are now considered discriminatory.

The problems confronting communities of color in the 1990s are not just the residual consequences of slavery and segregation; they are, as well, the product of liberal and conservative policies that have encouraged resistance, refusal, and renegotiation of antidiscrimination measures. The "disadvantages" facing minority communities have everything to do with having been taken advantage of in the past and present. Without fundamental change, we can only expect the impact of race on opportunities to increase in the years ahead.

Failure to enforce civil rights laws banning discrimination in housing, education, and hiring, along with efforts to undermine affirmative action and other remedies designed to advance the cause of social justice, renders racism structural and institutional rather than private and personal. Whites may or may not be openly racist in their personal decisions or private interactions with others, but they nonetheless benefit systematically from the structural impediments to minority access to quality housing, schools, and jobs. Michael Omi makes a useful distinction between "referential" racism (the snarling, sneering, cross-burning displays of antipathy toward minorities) and "inferential" racism (a system of structured inequality that allows white people to remain self-satisfied and smug about their own innocence). Inferential racism allows whites to disown Louisiana politician David Duke or Los Angeles Police Department detective Mark Fuhrman as individual "racists" (although Duke has twice received the majority of white votes in statewide elections and Fuhrman appeared frequently on talk shows and placed a book on the bestseller list after escaping jail time for his acts of perjury in the O.J. Simpson case), while assuming that the houses they own, the schools they attend, and the jobs they hold come to them exclusively on the basis of individual merit.

For more than fifty years our nation's public commitments to equal opportunity have been fatally undermined by our practices of resistance, refusal, and renegotiation. Rather than ushering in a golden age where people are judged by the content of their character rather than by the color of their skin, we have augmented and intensified the possessive investment in whiteness. Our policies in the realm of antidiscrimination law conform to the analogy offered more than thirty years ago by Malcolm X. Challenging a reporter who suggested that the passage of civil rights legislation proved that things were improving in the United States, Malcolm X argued that it did not show improvement to stick a knife nine inches into someone, pull it out six inches, and then call that progress. Pulling the knife all the way out would not be progress either. Only healing the wound that the knife had caused would show improvement. "But some people," Malcolm X observed, "don't even want to admit the knife is there."[68]

CHAPTER 3

Immigrant Labor and Identity Politics

That victim who is able to articulate the situation of the victim has ceased to be a victim; he, or she, has become a threat.—JAMES BALDWIN

On election day in 1994, nearly 60 percent of the California electorate voted in favor of Proposition 187, a measure designed to deny medical treatment and education and to deliver excruciating pain and punishment to undocumented workers and their families. The initiative required the expulsion from school of close to 500,000 students, mandated denial of prenatal care to pregnant women, deprived deaf children of sign language instruction, and demanded that doctors refuse to provide their patients with immunization shots and refuse tests and treatment for victims of AIDS, tuberculosis, alcoholism, and all other diseases. Phrased in especially punitive language and fueled by a demagogic and hate-filled public relations campaign blaming "illegal" immigrants from Mexico for the many problems confronting California's economy, the statute created chilling new categories of public obligation and citizenship. It required private citizens to become government informants, ordering doctors, nurses, teachers, social workers, and other state employees to report to immigration authorities all persons "suspected" of living in the United States without proper documentation.

Although surveys showed that many Canadian, Italian, Israeli, and Irish citizens lived and worked in California without proper credentials from the Immigration and Naturalization Service (INS), the popular campaign on behalf of

Proposition 187 expressly targeted immigrants from Mexico and Central America (and to a lesser extent those from Asia) as the focal point of concern about the alleged "costs" of providing medical care and education to undocumented immigrants. Reinforcing longstanding white supremacist practices of viewing all Latinos and Asians as eternally "foreign" while celebrating assimilation as the unique achievement of European immigrants and their descendants, Proposition 187 effectively criminalized Latino and Asian American identity, creating a previously unheard of legal category—the "suspected" illegal immigrant—and then subjecting these "suspects" to vigilante surveillance, supervision, and invasion of privacy.

Federal jurists delayed the implementation of Proposition 187 as they were required to do by constitutional law. Its provisions improperly granted the power of regulating immigration to the State of California rather than to the federal government. Some of the provisions of the initiative eventually became law through the welfare reform act of 1996 passed by Congress and signed by President Clinton, although a few of its more dramatic and draconian provisions were thrown out by the federal courts. Yet the passage of Proposition 187 marked an important event in the contemporary reinscription of the possessive investment in whiteness. It not only unleashed an inflammatory and hate-filled wave of nativist antiforeign scapegoating, but it also served as a key component in a campaign to insulate white voters and property owners from the ill effects of neoconservative economic policies. Blaming the state's fiscal woes on immigrants rather than taking responsibility for the ruinous effects of a decade and a half of irresponsible tax cuts for the wealthy coupled with disinvestment in education and infrastructure enabled the state's political leaders and wealthy citizens to divert attention away from their own failures. They knew full well that Proposition 187 and the many schemes that surfaced in its wake to deny social services, health care, and education to undocumented and even documented immigrants would have no effect on the numbers of migrants coming to the United States, most of whom migrate in order to escape even greater austerity in their home countries. They knew that the state would lose more money in federal aid (to education based on school enrollment, for example) than it would save by cutting off benefits to undocumented workers and their families, that denying medical treatment to people in need of care would cause more financial and social damage to the state through unchecked epidemics and untreated diseases than such measures would save in tax revenues.

The wealthy white voters who provided the bulwark of support for Proposition 187 had no intention of giving up the benefits they derived from the unregulated, low-wage work performed by immigrants as agricultural laborers, short order cooks, porters, bellhops, janitors, pool cleaners, domestic servants, gardeners, and construction workers. But these voters knew that creating a climate of terror among racialized immigrants and fostering a lynch-mob atmosphere among whites would constrain minority low-wage workers from organizing unions or demanding state enforcement of existing laws on minimum wages, safe and humane working conditions, and employer social security contributions. The process of demonizing undocumented workers as "illegal aliens" emanated not from a respect for legality, but rather from efforts by executives from large corporations, small business owners, and individual employers to escape their own legal obligations and moral responsibilities to obey statutes mandating safe working conditions, a living wage, and dignified relations between employers and employees.

Taking advantage of an already vulnerable population, the proponents of Proposition 187 used their ballot initiative as a device to terrorize the low-wage work force into accepting even worse working conditions for even lower wages. Perhaps more important, they relied on the campaign for Proposition 187 to solidify a countersubversive coalition held together by images that inverted actual power relations, presenting whites, the wealthy, and males as "victims" of the unfair advantages purportedly secured by racial minorities, the poor, and women. Part of a politics by moral panic that characterized the Reagan years and culminated in the capture of Congress by the Republican Party in the 1994 election, this manifestation of privilege masquerading as powerlessness does not really need to convince the electorate at large in order to succeed; its true aim is to build a sense of besieged solidarity within its own group. When it secures actual victories as in the case of Proposition 187, it simply supplies an added fringe benefit for its adherents.

The proponents of Proposition 187 officially disavowed any racist intent behind their initiative, but their own words and actions indicated otherwise. Linda Hayes, the campaign's media director for southern California, exhibited her group's obsession with race in a letter to the *New York Times* published a few weeks before the election. She explained that illegal immigration stemmed from a secret plan by "Mexicans" to establish Spanish as California's official language, to drive English speakers from the state, and to then hold a plebiscite annexing California to Mexico.[1] Though preposterous as a basis for public policy, Hayes's letter exemplified an important element in the debate over Proposition 187—its role in inviting whites to express openly and in public the racial resentments, prejudices, and paranoid fantasies that they previously entertained in private. In the aftermath of the election, a series of ugly incidents illustrated the success of this dimension of the campaign. A fifth grade teacher ordered her Latino pupils to write a paper detailing their citizenship status and that of their parents. A counter attendant at a fast-food restaurant refused to serve hamburgers and soft drinks to three English speaking Mexican American teenagers (all U.S. citizens, it turned out). A restaurant customer entered the establishment's kitchen and demanded proof of citizenship from the cooks. A school security guard told two Latinas, "We don't have to let Mexicans in here any more." A receptionist at a public health clinic told all Spanish speaking women that they were no longer eligible for medical treatment. The registrar at a California State University campus submitted a proposal to notify all students with Spanish surnames that they needed proof of citizenship to remain enrolled.[2] At the same time, however, many courageous educators and health care professionals announced their firm intention to defy the new law by refusing to comply with its provisions requiring them to become informants for the INS.

Political opportunism accounted for much of the campaign on behalf of Proposition 187. During his first term in office, California governor Pete Wilson saw his approval ratings in public opinion polls drop below 20 percent as the state suffered from a devastating economic recession. Less than 20 percent approval represents a nadir for any incumbent, much less for Pete Wilson, a career politician lavishly subsidized throughout his career by contributions from wealthy attorneys, developers, and bankers in his successful previous races for mayor of San Diego, U.S. senator, and governor.[3] To improve his chances for election, Wilson attempted to deflect anger away from himself and toward some of the most powerless and defenseless people in California. In a state where government allotments to single mothers raising two children already fell $2,645 below the official poverty line, Wilson successfully advocated reducing payments so that these women and their children would be even poorer. He showed himself to be motivated more by spite and contempt than by fiscal restraint when he explained that the new payments should not produce hardships for welfare mothers and their children because the cuts simply meant "one less six pack per week."[4]

Unable to run on his own record, the only resource Wilson owned to advance his ambitions was his whiteness, which he used ruthlessly and effectively. In his 1994 reelection campaign, he deflected criticism away from his dismal performance as the state's chief executive by scapegoating immigrants for California's problems. His commercials repeatedly broadcast a film showing a dozen Mexican nationals running past U.S. border guards as a voice-over narrative seething with racist contempt intoned, "*They* just keep coming." Wilson's speeches and statements in support of his own campaign and on behalf of Proposition 187 made special and nearly obsessive mention of the relatively small number of Mexican immigrant women who give birth to children in California hospitals, taking advantage of stereotypes of Mexicans as sexually unrestrained—as if forming families is an illicit activity, as if childbirth is an unnatural and perverse practice of the poor, and as if anyone would be better off if expectant mothers and their children were denied prenatal care or childbirth under safe conditions.

Undocumented workers pay far more in taxes than they receive in services. In addition, they benefit the U.S. economy as productive low-wage laborers, ineligible for direct welfare assistance, and vulnerable as "illegal" immigrants to employers who can mistreat them—and in some cases run out on paying them any wages at all—secure in the knowledge that the workers' undocumented status makes it all but impossible for them to file complaints with the legally constituted authorities. To be sure, not all of the federal taxes paid by undocumented workers return to California, and it is true that city, county, and state agencies bear primary responsibility for some of the medical and educational expenses of immigrants. Yet Californians also enjoy the overwhelming majority of the economic benefits in the form of lower prices for goods and services created by the hard work and legal vulnerability of largely unregulated low-wage immigrant labor.[5]

Particular sectors of the California work force may well be hurt by the influx of undocumented workers, especially members of other minority groups competing for unskilled low-wage employment. One can see clearly that jobs cleaning and maintaining office buildings, hotels, and restaurants that used to go routinely to African Americans now seem increasingly to be the domain of Central Americans. Immigrants are sometimes favored by employers over blacks because those doing the hiring suffer from racist preconceptions about African American workers. Employers also generally prefer to hire workers who do not speak English, who are unfamiliar with U.S. labor laws, and whose noncitizen status makes them reluctant to become trade union activists, to file grievances on the job, or to complain to state and federal agencies about violations of labor laws or health and safety regulations. This change is part of a conscious strategy by employers nationwide to create a "union proof" work force, a strategy in evidence from the rise of prison labor in the United States to the emergence of low-wage data-processing jobs in India, from the entry of Central Americans into jobs as janitors in Los Angeles office buildings to the recruitment of longshore workers in the Persian Gulf as replacements for unionized dock workers in Australia, from increases in part-time employment in the poultry industry in the Midwest and South to the development of computer-generated automation as a means of turning high-paying, high-skill jobs into low-skill, low-wage employment.[6]

After a long educational campaign by civil rights groups, African American voters opposed Proposition 187 by a slight majority, but the utility of dividing African American from Latino or Asian workers provided an unanticipated fringe benefit for the Republican Party, which put hundreds and thousands of dollars behind the campaign to pass Proposition 187—and which would later spend millions on a demagogic campaign against affirmative action. The party directed its efforts mainly at white voters, who comprise an overwhelming majority of the electorate in an off-year election. The strategy aimed at mobilizing anti-immigrant sentiment and using it to slip Pete Wilson past the voters once again despite his poor performance as governor. The Republicans received a major assist from Wilson's opponent, Kathleen Brown, the state treasurer and Democratic Party nominee for governor. Brown nominally opposed Proposition 187 but failed to challenge its basic premises. Unable to oppose the interests of the transnational corporations backing her expensive campaign efforts by calling for improvements in the wages and working conditions of all workers, Brown wound up agreeing with Wilson that illegal immigrants posed serious problems for California while claiming that Proposition 187 was an extreme and ineffective way to address the issue.

The leaders of the Democratic Party, of the trade unions, and of the state's civil rights organizations shied away from the fight over Proposition 187. They failed to expose the enormous economic benefits that come to Californians from the exploitation of immigrant workers. They failed to expose the active role played by big corporations and wealthy individuals in promoting immigration and encouraging the rise of undocumented labor in the United States. They failed to offer proposals to seize the assets of businesses and individuals employing undocumented workers, or to campaign for laws making retailers responsible for selling products secured from illegal sweatshop labor. Offered a choice between the arguments proposed by Pete Wilson that things are bad and that illegal immigrants were to blame, and the arguments offered by Kathleen Brown that things are bad but that nothing in particular could be done, close to 60 percent of the voters predictably enough chose Wilson's position.

Proposition 187 and the plethora of anti-immigrant measures that have emerged in its wake draw on a long history of laws designed to insure the unimpeded importation of low-wage labor in order to drive down wages for all workers while blaming the resulting social and economic catastrophes on the immigrants themselves. In this endeavor, the posture of protecting the property interests of "whiteness" plays an indispensable role. The proponents of Proposition 187 articulated their concerns in unambiguous language when the leader of the campaign to pass the measure described his group as the "posse" and Proposition 187 as "the rope." Key architects of Proposition 187 received funds from the well-known white supremacist Pioneer Fund, an organization dedicated to research in eugenics purporting to prove the superiority of the white race and the threat posed to it by interaction with people of color. In television and newspaper advertisements, in public pronouncements and privately circulated propaganda, supporters of Proposition 187 relied on racist and sexist stereotypes, on the "menace" posed by Mexican women coming to California to have babies at taxpayers' expense. This argument has little basis in fact; the amount of public funds spent on prenatal care and childbirth for undocumented immigrants is both minimal and cost effective. Yet by feminizing and infantilizing the enemy, by connecting the social transgression of nonwhite immigrants coming to California with the fear of unrestrained "Latin" sexuality and procreation, the advocates of Proposition 187 "played the race card, evoking powerful stereotypes that are especially well suited for concealing the real social relations between undocumented immigrants and California's white voters.

Asian American studies scholar and activist Lisa Lowe presented a brilliant and useful analysis of the stereotyping central to the Proposition 187 campaign in an address to the Modern Language Association national meetings in San Diego a little more than a month after the 1994 election. Lowe argued that successful racist stereotypes are not just picturesque untruths, but carefully constructed images designed to make lies more attractive than truth.[7] The truth in California in 1994 was that the standard of living enjoyed by the state's middle and upper classes increasingly depended upon the desperation of immigrants, especially low-wage women workers from Mexico, El Salvador, Guatemala, China, the Philippines, and other sites in Latin America and Asia. These women's labor lowers the price of garments made in primitive sweatshops as well the price of computer chips vital to the profits of high-tech industries. The low-wage women workers demonized as parasites by Pete Wilson actually do much of the hard work on which middle-class prosperity relies. They clean offices, hotel rooms, and homes. They plant, harvest, prepare, and serve food. They sew clothes they cannot afford to buy. For all their hard and underrewarded work, they find themselves hated and defamed as lazy dependents living off the largesse of the very people whose lives they make easier and more remunerative. The hypocrisy of Proposition 187's supporters did not need to be well hidden. During the election campaign reporters discovered that million-aire senatorial candidate and Proposition 187 supporter Michael Huffington had long benefited from the work done for him and his family by an undocu-mented immigrant housekeeper, and little more than a year after the election the *Washington Post* reported that Pete Wilson himself employed as his house-keeper an "illegal alien" from Tijuana.[8]

Lowe's analysis uncovers the importance of white identity politics within the immigration issue. The possessive investment in whiteness seeks support for transnational capital by promising to confine its worst effects to communi-ties of color while preserving and extending the benefits of present and past dis-crimination enjoyed by European Americans. At the same time, it works as a wedge against the welfare state in general, using the denial of benefits to "un-worthy" recipients like illegal and later legal immigrants as the prelude to fu-ture campaigns to "privatize" education and health services for everyone, ef-fectively reserving them only for the rich. The portrayal of massive immigration to the United States from Mexico as a consequence of the desire of individual immigrants for welfare benefits completely disregards the neoliberal "reforms" imposed on Mexico by U.S. and transnational capital that have made flight from that country a necessity for many formerly self-sufficient workers and farmers. The U.S. government insists on free trade and unlimited mobility for U.S. capital; works to lower wages, cut social spending, and disrupt traditional economies in poor nations; encourages the growth of low-wage jobs in North America; and then expresses shock and dismay when these decisions all lead to increased immigration to the United States.

Border Crossers and Double Crossers: Immigrant Labor and Transnational Capital

The rhetoric that demonizes low-wage workers for crossing international boundaries elides the existence of the most important border crossers in the Southwest, the U.S. firms that use special tax breaks and the provisions of in-ternational trade agreements to set up *maquiladora* plants on the U.S.-Mexico border. Instigated and sustained by tax breaks that offer subsidies to U.S. firms who abandon workers in the United States by fleeing to locations of low-wage labor like Mexico, maquiladora zones provide opportunities for large profits for California businesses and investors. By moving across the border, such U.S. firms as Xerox, RCA, Chrysler, ITT, IBM, and Eastman Kodak have employed nearly a half million workers in their Mexican plants at a savings of between $16,000 to $25,000 per worker per year. Low wages, low taxes, weak unions, high unemployment, and nonenforcement of environmental protection laws make maquiladora plants the locus of terrible exploitation and disruption in Mexico.[9]

Corporations gain state-subsidized advantages over workers in both the United States and Mexico by crossing the border. For example, in 1992, the Smith-Corona Company closed a typewriter plant in Cortland, New York, dismissing eight hundred workers from their jobs. The company then relocated its operations to Tijuana, Mexico. Management abuses motivated the Mexican workers to go on strike in October 1994. When the employees announced their work stoppage, the Smith-Corona Company in Mexico "disappeared from the social security records as if it had been shut down," according to Mary Tong of the San Diego Support Committee for Maquiladora Workers. The workers still made the same products at the same plants, but they could not find out the identity of their employer in order to bargain with management. At least sixteen companies "disappeared" in Tijuana in this way in 1994, sometimes simply sneaking out of town, abandoning plants built with subsidies from the Mexican government, and avoiding all payroll and tax obligations including the severance pay required in such situations by Mexican law.[10]

Unconstrained by Mexican environmental laws that are not enforced, companies in one Tijuana industrial park release unlawful and dangerous concentrations of lead, copper, cadmium, chromium, zinc, and arsenic into drainage ditches, polluting sources of drinking water for some two thousand people who live in the *colonia* nestled beneath the industrial park. One study showed that more than 40 percent of the people in this neighborhood suffered from pollution-related illnesses and learning disabilities. Between 1993 and 1995 alone, nine women in this colonia gave birth to anencephalic babies (babies born without brains). Corporate and government officials denied that pollution caused these birth defects, attributing the poor health of mothers and children to deficient amounts of folic acid in the diets of the workers and their families. Yet these workers subsist largely on corn and beans, two food with high levels of folic acid.[11]

The passage of the North American Free Trade Agreement in 1993 compounded already depressed conditions in Mexico's agricultural sector, promoting massive migration to cities like Tijuana. For their maquiladora plants, transnational companies seek out young women workers, whom they believe will be more obedient and less militant than men or older women, and whom they intend to work hard for a brief period and then replace with other willing recruits fleeing the devastated economic conditions in the agricultural regions of central and southern Mexico. Because Mexican law leaves to companies the responsibility for prenatal care and childbirth expenses for women workers, the firms try to force pregnant women to quit their jobs. In one plant owned by a Japanese firm, management put a pregnant worker in a fume-filled soldering room with no ventilation in hopes of making her quit her job. She remained at work because she needed the money. Her baby was born anencephalic.[12]

Maquiladora plants offer great advantages to investors, owners, and their families in the United States, especially California. They make products that can be sold for less because of their lower labor costs, while the practice or even the possibility of runaway shops constrains the demands of U.S. workers. Chaos in Mexico insures a steady flow of desperate immigrant workers across the border; the undocumented status of some of them insures greater exploitation, forcing wages and working conditions for all workers even lower.

Immigration, Ideology, and Ethnic Studies

A desire for short-term political advantage propelled Pete Wilson and his allies into politics designed to secure the benefits of past and present discrimination in perpetuity for affluent white voters, at the same time deflecting the anger of downwardly mobile whites toward the exploited immigrant workers upon whom the life-styles of the rich depend. Right-wing attacks on affirmative action and on ethnic studies programs in schools support this strategy: they aim at suppressing any institutional site capable of generating a critique of racism's role in winning political consent for an emerging economic order that harms the interests of the majority. These attacks, however, also underscore the importance of ethnic studies: when connected to activist efforts to establish cross-border solidarity and to organize low-wage workers into militant collectives, ethnic studies can help shape a popular rejection of politics based on the possessive investment in whiteness.

Most of the best work in ethnic studies—work often derided as identity politics—in fact addresses the ways in which new social relations have given rise to new coalitions and conflicts that change the meaning of ethnic and racial identity. Rather than seeking to separate society into discrete warring camps, ethnic studies scholars assume that we can be unified eventually only if we examine honestly and critically the things that divide us in the present. They presume that very few social problems can be solved by knowing *less* about them. They argue that the same processes that exacerbate old divisions while generating new ones may open the way to unexpected affiliations and alliances based on the pursuit of social justice and on resistance to unjust hierarchies and exploitative practices.

Lowe's original and generative book, *Immigrant Acts,* explains how the Asian American experience with racialization, economic exploitation, immigrant exclusion, and barriers to citizenship is not the property of Asian Americans alone but the legacy of all Americans. These practices have shaped the meaning of what it means to be a citizen, a low-wage worker, a gendered subject, or an aggrieved racialized "minority." Similarly, in a singularly impressive study, Yen Le Espiritu underscores the importance of normative gender categories in branding all subordinate groups as alternatively "deviant, inferior, or overachieving," while leaving each group with a fundamentally distinct race-gender-sex economy.[13] All racialized populations suffer from the possessive investment in whiteness in some ways, but the historical and social circumstances confronting each group differ. Consequently, alliances *and* antagonisms, conflicts *and* coalitions, characterize the complex dynamics of white supremacy within and across group lines.

Lowe identifies hybridity, heterogeneity, and multiplicity as component parts of ethnic identity. In her formulation, people develop ethnic identities through hybridity, a growing together of more than one element—for example, through relations across ethnic lines or through the ways in which one's gender, sexual identification, or class intersects with one's race or ethnicity. Lowe defines ethnic groups as always heterogeneous, as coalitions made up of people with different interests, aims, ages, genders, sexual preferences, religions, languages, and so on. Identities are also multiple in Lowe's formulation; no one lives their life entirely as an ethnic subject. At a given moment in one's life, ethnicity might be more important than, say, gender, but under other circumstances gender might become more important. People play different roles under different conditions; their identities emerge though complex interactions with others as well as through constant internal dialogue and negotiation.[14]

The generative insights in Lowe's work emerge in the context of a rich dialogue among scholars in ethnic studies about the dynamism of all social identities, including but not limited to ethnic identities. Juan Flores defines an important component of Puerto Rican identity in New York as "branching out"—"the selective connection to and interaction with the surrounding North American society." Flores notes that the social location of Puerto Rican migrants encourages them to first branch out to black Americans and other migrants from Latin America and the Caribbean, and later to groups with a history of social disadvantage, including Chinese, Arabs, and, "more cautiously," Irish, Italians, and Jews. Consequently, Puerto Rican "assimilation" is not into the dominant culture and does not entail the disappearance of distinct national backgrounds, but rather involves a fusion of diverse working-class cultures shaped by marginalization and exclusion in order to create "a healthy interfertilization of cultures." Similarly, Jack D. Forbes explores the long history of coalition and conflict that makes Native American and African American identities mutually constitutive as well as mutually exclusive, while Gary Y. Okihiro examines the complex connections and points of convergence between Asian Americans and African Americans. Peter Narvaez's research on the influence of Hispanic music cultures on African American blues musicians reminds us that the proximity of Mexico as a destination for escaped slaves undermined the growth of the slave system in Texas while activists of Mexican origin on both sides of the border provided moral and material assistance to slaves seeking freedom. Kevin Gaines notes that African Americans chafing at the white practice of addressing them by their first names rather than as Mister or Miss or Mrs. subverted the practice by naming their children after anti-imperialist black heroes from Latin America like Antonio Maceo, a general in the Cuban struggle for independence. James Howard delineates how the Shawnee tribe came to align itself with the antislavery Union forces during the Civil War and how, thirty years later, a band of antiacculturationist Shawnees emigrated to Mexico in hopes of constructing a pan-Indian nation.[15]

Creative scholars from all backgrounds have carried out important work in ethnic studies, but the situated experiences of scholars from aggrieved minority groups has often proven a source of special insights and analyses. A. Philip Randolph told the 1963 March on Washington that it has often fallen to "the Negro" to remind other Americans about the importance of giving human rights priority over property rights, because "our ancestors were transformed from human persons into property." In similar fashion, gays and lesbians have often been the most perceptive critics and analysts of heterosexuality as a social force because their situated experiences compel them to recognize, analyze, and understand existing sexual hierarchies and to theorize alternatives to them.[16] It should not be surprising then, that outstanding research on social identities emanates from scholars of color and from the institutional sites of ethnic studies designed to ask and answer questions that are both particular and universal, that see ethnicity and race both from close up and from far away.

Scholarship in Chicano studies has been especially rich in exploring the the-
oretical and practical causes and consequences of racism in recent years, in part
because of the crises confronting Chicano communities as a result of the white
identity politics put in play by people like Pete Wilson, but also because the
complex realities of Chicano existence have always called into question the
simplistic binary oppositions that produce the possessive investment in whiteness. Chicano communities are connected to the national histories of the
United States, Mexico, and Spain, to indigenous nations and tribal groups, to
cultures that include diverse languages, religions, and social practices. Issues of
national culture, ethnic identity, and language emerge as parts of complex contradictions in Chicano history, and consequently scholars studying Chicanos
need to develop fully theorized definitions of social roles that go beyond the
parochial experiences of any one group. The best scholarship in Chicano studies does not simply tack some new information about Chicanos onto what we
already know from the study of other groups, but like all good work in ethnic
studies uses the situated knowledge and experiences of Chicanos to ask and answer important new questions about the general dynamics of social identities.

For example, Ramón Gutiérrez has fashioned a brilliant narrative about the
Spanish and Anglo conquest of indigenous people in New Mexico between
1600 and 1850 in his book, *When Jesus Came, the Corn Mothers Went Away*. Using Inquisition records and anthropological sources to construct a record of
how successive conquests changed the character of both everyday activities and
political allegiances, Gutiérrez stresses the syncretic and relational nature of
ethnic identities, refuting the romantic and essentialist assumptions of previous scholars about Anglos, Indians, and Chicanos. Gutiérrez's ability to represent competing and conflicting points of view offers an important alternative
to the kind of monologic history that presents only one story told from one
point of view. In the process, he demonstrates definitively how ethnic and racial
identities always intersect, how they emerge in concert with identities of gender, sexual preference, class, religion, and nationality.[17] Gutiérrez demonstrates
the interconnections between macrosocial structures of power and the experiences of everyday life by showing how all three societies in his study structure
inequality through categories of marriage and kinship, but do so in distinctly
different ways.

George Sánchez brings a similar dynamism to his history of the East Side of
Los Angeles between 1900 and 1945 in *Becoming Mexican American*. He shows
how a specific confluence of residential segregation, class and generational ho-
mogeneity, political alliances, and cultural practices coalesced to produce a dis-

tinctive Mexican American identity in that city. Like Gutiérrez, Sánchez tells a significant story about one community, but in the process he illuminates general principles about the ways in which ethnic and racial identities are constructed dynamically through practical activity. Sánchez shows, for instance, how Mexican migration helped fill the shortage of low-wage labor created by laws mandating the exclusion of Asians, how restrictive covenants and racial zoning by whites helped create a Mexican American community with fixed spatial boundaries, and how discrimination against other minority groups occasionally encouraged interethnic alliances based on physical proximity and shared experiences.[18]

One important feature of the scholarship of Gutiérrez and Sánchez is their view of ethnicity as relational rather than atomized and discrete. Group identities form through interaction with other groups. As a result, Spaniards, Mexicans, Pueblo Indians, and Anglos in New Mexico changed each other as well as themselves through complicated experiences of conflict and cooperation. Mexican American identity in Los Angeles in Sánchez's account emerged out of complex interactions with Asian Americans, blacks, and Native Americans to be sure, but also with Molokans, Jews, and Anglo Protestants. Vicki Ruíz argued along similar lines in *Cannery Women, Cannery Lives,* her excellent study about Chicana working women in Los Angeles during the 1930s and 1940s. Ruíz's research revealed the ways in which physical proximity in neighborhoods enabled Chicana workers to unite with women of other backgrounds to fight for trade union representation to address their common grievances on the job, including problems they faced specifically as women, such as sexual harassment. Similar research on Chicanos in Texas by David Montejano exposes the importance of Anglo-Mexican relations, while Neil Foley's study of cotton economy in that state demonstrates the mutually constitutive as well as competitive nature of relations among Anglos, Mexicans, and blacks. In a brilliant and generative study of *testimonios* by nineteenth-century Californios, Rosaura Sánchez draws upon a stunning repertoire of theories from literary criticism, cultural geography, sociology, and social history to delineate the ways in which the displaced Californio elite both resisted and paradoxically reinforced the racist hierarchies of their Anglo conquerors, establishing themselves as an aggrieved and racialized U.S. ethnic group while simultaneously participating in and endorsing the exclusion and subordination of Native Americans.[19]

As a dynamic, fluid, and relational category, ethnic identity emerges as contested within Chicano studies scholarship. In *Walls and Mirrors,* a vitally important study of Mexican immigration to the United States, David Gutiérrez shows how the value of "whiteness" and its concomitant imperatives of racialized exclusion have divided Mexican American communities between those who favor citizenship and cultural incorporation in the United States and those oriented more toward maximizing group resources by maintaining solidarity with all people of Mexican origin on both sides of the border. Gutiérrez shows how settled descendants of previous immigrants develop interests and political positions different from those of new immigrants. In an important twist, however, he also identifies the significance of a core contradiction among Anglos who demand low-wage Mexican labor to benefit the U.S. economy while maintaining a racialized view of Mexicans as unwelcome and unfit for cultural or political inclusion.[20] For Gutiérrez, the power of the possessive investment in whiteness means that ethnic identity among Chicanos changes its boundaries over time: internal politics and the external opportunity structure help shape Chicanos as assimilationist or separatist, united in defense of immigrants or divided into inclusive and exclusive factions, eager to identify themselves as "white" or determined to ally with other aggrieved communities of color.

This excellent body of historical work helps explain the subtlety and supple nature of contemporary Chicano cultural criticism. José Saldívar's brilliant *Border Matters* ranges over diverse forms of cultural expression to explore the ways in which the existence of the U.S.-Mexico border shapes Chicano imagination and expression. In an innovative and persuasive study, Carl Gutiérrez-Jones shows how police surveillance, brutality, and incarceration shape the subtexts of a broad range of Chicano fiction and film representations. Ramón Saldívar explains how oral and written traditions among Chicanos contain a consistent aesthetic and challenge prevailing power relations by "opting for open over closed forms, for conflict over resolution and synthesis."[21]

One of the main generative achievements of Chicano studies scholarship has been to illuminate the ways in which complex cultural meanings become encoded in unlikely sites, unassuming artifacts, and ordinary practices of everyday life. Rosa Linda Fregoso's *The Bronze Screen*, for example, presents a scintillating study of the ways in which collective memory, popular culture products, religious rituals, and decidedly gendered images and ideas serve as impetus for a feminist politics of "differential consciousness." Similarly, Gloria Anzaldúa reads the Virgin of Guadalupe as a complex "religious, political, and cultural image" symbolizing "the mestizo true to his or her Indian values" as well as "rebellion against the rich, upper and middle class; against their subjugation of the poor and the *indio*." José Limón blends cultural critique, ethnography, social history, and folklore in his richly textured and insightful studies of social interactions among Tejanos at barbecues, dance halls, and the myriad other sites where everyday life activities shape and reflect social identities.[22]

Yvonne Yarbro-Bejarano shows how the poisonous legacy of sexism in popular Chicano narratives, songs, and theatrical traditions suppresses the experiences and criticisms of women while constituting the community along masculinist lines. Norma Alarcón analyzes the layers of sexism sedimented in the Malintzin legends, as well as the problems they pose for Chicana writers and critics. While Chicano critics have been insightful about the ways in which a shared group identity can hide serious divisions within the group, they have also been brilliant in detailing the ways in which widely divergent interests and practices might emerge from common roots. Steven Loza offers an example of the latter in his pathbreaking and carefully researched examination of the plurality and diversity of Chicano music from Los Angeles, *Barrio Rhythm*. James Diego Vigil shows how the aesthetics of the *ranflas* (low riders) driven by Chicano car customizers mimic the methodical, slow, and smooth kinesics manifested in the stylized dress and body language of Chicano street gangs, while Brenda Bright explores the ways in which low-riding practices in three cities in Texas, New Mexico, and California reveal both unity and division within and across Chicano communities.[23]

These extraordinary works illustrate the importance of ethnic studies scholarship in providing perspective, understanding, and analysis of the problems we face in the present as a result of the cultural transformations transnational capital engenders. Yet Chicano studies draws its determinate shape not just from the imperatives of the present, but from the practices of the past. Anxieties about identity that may appear new and daunting to relatively privileged people raised in monolingual environments in metropolitan countries have a long history among aggrieved groups for whom cultural complexity and creative code switching constitute the baseline realities of life. Consequently, some of the most sophisticated vocabularies and grammars of cultural criticism and cultural practice come from groups with comparatively little political and economic power. In the case of Chicano studies, the brilliant innovations of the present draw upon collective resources shaped and honed through the struggles of the past, as exemplified in the enduring relevance of a Chicano Studies work from the 1950s—Américo Paredes's *With His Pistol in His Hand*.

Paredes's book explores the ballad of Gregorio Cortez, a popular *corrido* from South Texas based (as corridos are) on an actual incident that took place in 1901. According to Paredes, the popularity of many versions of the song celebrating the struggles of Gregorio Cortez stemmed from its utility as an allegory about all Tejano people. Relating the story of a peaceful and hardworking man minding his own business who was unjustly attacked and forced to flee in order to avoid being charged for a crime that he did not commit, the ballad's verses systematically unmasked the falsity of prevailing Anglo slurs against Mexicans.

The incident starts when the Anglo, monolingual sheriff of a Texas county learns that a stolen horse might be in his vicinity. Discovering that Gregorio Cortez recently traded for a mare, the sheriff travels to the Tejano's ranch, accompanied by an Anglo deputy known for his bilingual skills. The deputy does not know Spanish as well as he thinks he does, however. He informs Reynaldo Cortez that the sheriff wishes to speak with Gregorio, and when Reynaldo tells his brother in Spanish "someone wants you" (as in someone wants to speak with you), the deputy translates the words back to the sheriff as "you are a wanted man." Furthermore, when the deputy asks Cortez if he recently traded for a horse, he uses the word equivalent to the generic English term for a horse (*caballo*) rather than the more precise gender-specific Spanish term for a mare (*yegua*). When Cortez replies that he has not traded for a caballo, the deputy tells the sheriff that the rancher is lying. The sheriff pulls out his gun and shoots at but misses Cortez's brother. Cortez returns the fire in self-defense and kills the sheriff.[24] Cortez's skill as a rider enables him to escape the posses chasing him. He becomes a folk hero among Tejanos and even earns the respect of Anglos who recognize that he has been falsely accused of murder for acts committed in self-defense. Cortez is never captured, but in order to save his family and his community from reprisals, he turns himself in to the law, walking in proudly "with his pistol in his hand."

The key elements in the Gregorio Cortez narrative inverted prevailing Anglo stereotypes about Mexicans. In a society where racist slurs depicting Mexicans as dishonest, stupid, and cowardly served to legitimate Anglo conquest and fraudulent expropriation of land legally held by Tejanos, the ballad of Gregorio Cortez offered an eloquent alternative. Paredes notes that just as white slave owners raped black women and then portrayed black males as sex fiends, Anglo Texans stole land from Mexicans and then defamed their victims as people prone to steal. To initiate and legitimate the expropriation of Chicano land and labor, they developed stories about Mexicans as unintelligent, lazy, and cowardly. In the ballad of Gregorio Cortez, the charge of thievery turns out to be inaccurate, simply a product of Anglo ignorance and linguistic incompetence. Gregorio Cortez is hardworking, highly skilled, intelligent, and courageous. One particularly important verse inverts one of the most sacred legends of the

Anglo Texans. For years, admirers of the state law enforcement agency, the Texas Rangers, celebrated the courage of their heroes through a story about a riot in a border town. When local authorities ask the Texas Rangers for help in subduing hundreds and maybe thousands of Mexican insurgents, the state agency sends only one ranger, arguing that there is only one riot. The "humor" of this anecdote relies upon knowledge of a common racist slur that holds the courage of whites is so great that it takes only one white man to subdue an entire group of Mexicans. In the ballad of Gregorio Cortez, however, these odds are reversed, as just one elusive Mexican frustrates the combined efforts of the Texas Rangers, local sheriffs, and posses. A powerful couplet in the song demonstrates this inversion: "Decia Gregorio Cortez, con su pistola en la mano,/ Ah, cuanto rinche montado para un solo mexicano!" (Then said Gregorio Cortez, with his pistol in his hand,/ Ah, so many mounted Rangers, against one lone Mexican!)[25]

The ballad of Gregorio Cortez and the practices of topical songwriting and singing from which it emerged testify to the presence among Chicanos of what art historian Robert Farris Thompson calls "alternative academies."[26] These sites provide opportunities for personal and collective artistic expression. They offer education in the guise of entertainment, and they serve as conduits for the moral economy that oppressed people need in order to deal with the ideological, political, economic, and police power of their enemies. Paredes's book shows how it fell to one popular song to keep alive historical memory of an incident of injustice, to invert dominant stereotypes, celebrate individual heroism, identify group loyalty as the ultimate moral obligation, and call a community into being through performance.

Of course, changes in historical conditions can give new meaning to old cultural expressions. The rise of Chicana feminism in the 1970s and 1980s created a consciousness sensitive to the masculinist biases built into the ballad of Gregorio Cortez, what Renato Rosaldo calls its "primordial patriarchy." A song that served emancipatory purposes at one moment may become reactionary in another era, just as a group identity forged in struggle under one set of circumstances may become an obstacle to emancipation at a later moment. Chicana feminists as well as gay and lesbian Chicano and Chicana writers have been particularly active in rereading and reevaluating the traditions of their own communities in order to fuse the traditional antiracism of Chicanos with the necessity for projecting "a heterogeneous, changing heritage into the future."[27]

Yet for all of its grounding in a previous era, Paredes's study of the ballad of Gregorio Cortez remains relevant to understanding, analyzing, and acting upon the oppressive power of racial hierarchies in our lives. While adding important and historically specific knowledge to what we already know about Chicanos, *With His Pistol in His Hand* speaks to the experiences of other groups as well. It demonstrates how popular culture and indigenous voices offer evidence about social history, and it challenges us to explore the relationship between all cultural texts and their social and historical contexts. It shows how people act in the arenas that are open to them with the tools they have available.

Most important, Paredes's book reminds us that in any moment of danger, people from aggrieved communities can be a source of enormous insight and empowering analysis. Ethnic studies scholarship is no substitute for systematic and coordinated political action, but action without understanding is always doomed to fail. Scholars from aggrieved communities can play a particularly important role in solving our present problems, not primarily because of who they are, but rather because of what they and their communities have been forced to learn from the hands dealt them by history. Especially when many of the wealthiest and best-educated people in positions of leadership are attempting to escape responsibility for the consequences of their own policies by scapegoating immigrants, non-English speakers, and low-wage workers, ethnic studies and Chicano studies scholars have a key role to play in determining what kind of future we will have, or more ominously, whether we will have any future at all.

Unity and Division

We live in an age of painful contradictions. Mass communication and mass migration bring the people of the world closer together in unprecedented ways, uniting diverse populations through common participation in global markets, investments, and mass media. Yet the practices and processes that affect everyone do not affect everyone equally. At the very moment that we find the people of the world becoming more united, we also find that economic inequality, cultural insecurity, and ethnic, religious, and racial rivalries renew old antagonisms and engender new conflicts, leaving us paradoxically more divided than ever before.

Ethnic divisions and racial conflicts have a particularly poisonous presence at the present moment. From Bosnia to Belfast, from Rwanda to Russia, from East Timor to Tel Aviv, we see the destructive consequences of ethnic antagonisms everywhere. It is understandable that under these circumstances people might be wary of any kind of "identity politics" in which racial, religious, and ethnic identities become the basis for political solidarity and cultural practice. Writers arguing from a variety of political perspectives have critiqued identity politics as encouraging allegiance to group interests rather than a sense of civic responsibility extending across racial and ethnic lines, as an assault on the traditions and values most responsible for human progress, and as a diversion from real social problems that have nothing to do with social identities. Alarmist articles in majors news magazines bemoan the erosion of a "common" culture in the United States, while neoconservatives sneer about the emergence of "victim studies" in academia. Critics attack minority artists and intellectuals as guilt-mongering whiners demanding special privileges and seeking to elevate inferior works in order to elevate their own self-esteem, while on a broader front, politicians demagogically dismantle the antidiscrimination mechanisms established as a result of the civil rights movement, mislabeling antiracist remedies as instruments of "reverse racism." All around us, we see evidence of a fundamentally new era for the possessive investment in whiteness, fueled by ferment over identity politics.

Yet once we remember that whiteness is also an identity, one with a long political history, contemporary attacks on "identity" politics come into clear relief as a defense of the traditional privileges and priorities of whiteness in the face of critical and political projects that successfully disclose who actually holds power in this society and what has been done with it. Contrary to the claims of neoconservatives that they stand for universal interests, the politics of whiteness as exemplified by attacks on immigrants and on affirmative action amount to little more than a self-interested strategy for preserving the possessive investment in whiteness, a politics based solely on identity. Conversely, the best ethnic studies scholarship, cultural production, and community organizing aims at opening up an understanding of ethnicity as hybrid, heterogeneous, and multiple (in the eloquent formulation of Lisa Lowe)—as a political project aimed at creating identities based on politics rather than politics based on identities. These projects rely on egalitarian politics and struggles for social justice to counter the identity politics of whiteness that generates identities based on the defense and perpetuation of inequality.[28] Different ethnic groups have different histories and experiences; as long as that is the case, organizing along ethnic lines will always make sense. Yet ethnic groups still must decide which things bring them together and which things divide them, which groups offer them useful alliances and which do not. Mobilizing around a common group identity does not preclude forming strategic and philosophical alliances with other groups.

Under current conditions, defending immigrants requires solidarity among Asian, Latino, and Caribbean communities. Attacks on linguistic diversity create opportunities for coalitions between Latinos and Asians, while incidents of racially motivated police brutality bring together immigrants and citizens with common concerns. Efforts to organize trade unions among low-wage workers require coalitions that include African Americans, Latinos, Asian Americans, Native Americans, and European Americans. For example, the Committee against Anti-Asian Violence in New York defends Asian victims of vigilante violence and police brutality, but it also unites with the National Congress for Puerto Rican Rights to stage a Racial Justice Day rally and march and publicizes the activities of Project REACH, a multicultural organization established to provide drop-in centers that offer safe havens to gay and lesbian youths, support HIV-positive youth, help women defend themselves against sexual assaults, and train youth leaders.[29] Asian Immigrant Women Advocates in Oakland, California, brings together second- and third-generation Asian American women united in their commitment to help empower Asian immigrant women working in the electronics, hotel, and garment industries. AIWA's members come from different national backgrounds, speak different languages, and belong to different classes, yet their shared concern about the lives of low-wage women workers from Asia leads them to political actions that address the class problems that women face as workers, the gender problems they confront as women, the legal problems they experience as immigrants, and the racial problems they encounter as members of racialized groups.[30] Organizing efforts among Latino workers at the New Otani Hotel in Los Angeles have drawn upon ethnic solidarity in Mexican and Salvadoran communities, but they have also fused a strategic alliance with Chinese veterans of Japanese slave labor camps with longstanding grievances against the hotel's Japanese owner, the Kajima Corporation, for its role in Japanese imperialism during World War II.[31]

The Bus Riders Union in Los Angeles originated in problems with public transportation in the city that affect all ethnic groups. Yet the group's analysis showed that the transportation routes favored by inner-city residents generated funds for the transit system that subsidized the commuter trains favored by suburban residents. Arguing that neighborhood race effects accounted for the disproportionate resources made available to commuters from mostly white suburbs, the union brought suit against the transit authority on civil rights grounds. In this case, the 10 to 20 percent of white bus riders in the inner city experienced violations of their civil rights because they relied on services utilized disproportionately by minorities. The Bus Riders Union reached an impressive settlement with the transit authority. Their strategy demonstrated the centrality of race in determining access to public services, yet they mobilized a struggle that did not revolve around racial identities, but rather one that united members of all races in a common struggle for social justice.[32]

Action within and across ethnic groups in these struggles is made possible by what the participants know, not who they are. Their situated knowledges, historical experiences, and current struggles with power give their ethnic identities their determinant meanings. Like scholars in Chicano studies and other ethnic studies fields, their knowledge comes from their experiences, their strategic insights from the ways in which having less power than your enemies makes it important to know the truth and dangerous to deny reality. Political struggle, social analysis, and social theory are mutually constitutive; each is better when linked to the other. As James Baldwin pointed out years ago, "People who cling to their delusions find it difficult, if not impossible, to learn anything worth learning: a people under the necessity of creating themselves must examine everything, and soak up learning the way the roots of a tree soak up water. A people still held in bondage must believe that *Ye shall know the truth, and the truth shall make ye free.*"[33]

CHAPTER 4

Whiteness and War

*The question of identity is a question involving the
most profound panic—a terror as primary as the
nightmare of the mortal fall. An identity is questioned
only when it is menaced, or when the mighty begin to
fall, or when the wretched begin to rise, or when the
stranger enters the gates, never thereafter, to be a
stranger; the stranger's presence making you the
stranger, less to the stranger than to yourself.*

—JAMES BALDWIN

In 1982, two unemployed white male auto workers in Detroit attacked Chinese American draftsperson Vincent Chin with a baseball bat, smashed his skull, and beat him to death. Although they denied any racist intent, one of the auto workers remarked during the incident, "It's because of you we're out of work"—apparently thinking that Chin was Japanese and therefore responsible for layoffs in the auto industry caused by competition from cars made in Japan. Neither perpetrator ever served a day in prison for the murder.[1] In 1984, a white male high school teacher pushed Ly Yung Cheung, a pregnant nineteen-year-old Chinese American woman, off a New York City subway platform into the path of a moving train that decapitated her. In his successful plea of not guilty by reason of insanity, the teacher claimed that he suffered from "a phobia of Asian people" that led him to murder Cheung.[2] In 1989, a white man wearing combat fatigues fired more than one hundred rounds of ammunition from an AK-47 assault rifle into a crowd of mostly Asian American children at the Cleveland Elementary School in Stockton, California, killing five children and wounding close to thirty others. Four of the children killed were Cambodian refugees—Ram Chun, Sokhim An, Rathanar Or, and Oeun Lim. The fifth was a Vietnamese American, Tran Thanh Thuy. An investigation by state officials found it "highly probable" that the assailant picked that particular school because of his animosity toward "Southeast Asians," whom the gunman described as people who get "benefits" without having to work.[3] In 1992, a group of white males attending a party in Coral Gables, Florida, beat nineteen-year-old Luyen Phan Nguyen to death when he objected to racial slurs directed at him. At least seven of the men ran after Nguyen as he attempted to flee, shouting "Viet Cong" and hunting him down "like a wounded deer" while bystanders refused to intervene and stop the beating.[4]

Although these incidents sprang from different motivations and circumstances, they share a common core—the identification of Asians in America as foreign enemies, unwelcome and unwanted by white Americans. Hate crimes enact the rage of individual sociopaths, but they also look for justification to patterns of behavior and belief that permeate the rest of society in less extreme form. The logic that legitimated the attacks on Vincent Chin, Ly Yung Cheung, the school children in Stockton, and Luyen Phan Nguyen stemmed from long-standing patterns and practices in the United States. As Lisa Lowe, Yen Le Espiritu, and Gary Okihiro among others have demonstrated repeatedly in their sophisticated research, for more than a century and a half Asian immigrants have met the need for cheap labor by U.S. businesses without receiving recognition as vital contributors to the national economy. Diplomats and corporate officers have obtained access to vital markets and raw materials by integrating Asia into the North American economy, yet through law, labor segmentation, and "scientific" racism, Asians in America have been seen as forever foreign and outside the rewards of white identity.[5]

U.S. wars in Asia over the past five decades have also contributed significantly to this view of Asian Americans and Asians as foreign enemies incapable of being assimilated into a U.S. national identity. Military action against Japan in World War II led to the internment of more than 100,000 Japanese Americans and to the forced sale and seizure of their property. No other group of immigrants and their descendants have been identified with their country of origin in this way, not even German Americans during World War I. The national groups from countries allied with the United States at different moments in these wars—Chinese, Koreans, Filipinos, Japanese, Vietnamese, and Cambodians—have often found themselves identified as undifferentiated "Asians" in the United States and vilified for the actions of governments and nations that they have also opposed. Armed conflicts against Asian enemies in the Philippines, Korea, China, Vietnam, Laos, and Cambodia functioned geopolitically to decide control over markets and raw materials after the demise of European imperialism, to contain China and the Soviet Union, and to determine access to the rim economies of Southeast and Northeast Asia. Yet they functioned culturally to solidify and reinforce a unified U.S. national identity based in part on antagonism toward Asia and Asians.

During the 1980s, Asians accounted for nearly half of all legal immigrants to the United States. More than a million Southeast Asians entered the country as refugees after the war in Vietnam, and between 1970 and 1990 more than 855,000 Filipinos, 600,000 Koreans, and 575,000 Chinese immigrated to the United States. During the same era, the rise of Japanese businesses as competitors with U.S. firms, the painful legacy of the U.S. war in Vietnam, the stagnation of real wages, and increasing class polarization combined to engender intense hostility toward Asia and Asian Americans. As Yen Le Espiritu explains, hostility toward Asian competitors overseas and Asian American immigrants at home functions as components in an interlocking system. "In a time of rising economic powers in Asia, declining economic opportunities in the United States, and growing diversity among America's people," Espiritu observes, "this new Yellow Perilism— the depiction of Asia and Asian Americans as economic and cultural threats to mainstream United States—supplies white Americans with a united identity and provides ideological justification for U.S. isolationist policy toward Asia, increasing restrictions against Asian (and Latino) immigration, and the invisible institutional racism and visible violence against Asians in the United States."[6]

Anti-Asian sentiment in the United States depends upon its necessary correlative—the assumption that true cultural franchise and full citizenship requires a white identity. This violence against Asian Americans stems from the kinds of whiteness created within U.S. culture and mobilized in the nation's political, economic, and social life. The "white" identity conditioned to fear the Asian "menace" owes its origins to the history of anti-Indian, antiblack, and anti-Mexican racism at home as well as to anti-Arab and anti-Latino racisms shaped by military struggles overseas and by condescending cultural stereotypes at home. White racism is a pathology looking for a place to land, sadism in search of a story.

Reginald Horsman's study of nineteenth-century racism and Manifest Destiny explains how presumptions about racial purity and fears of contamination encouraged white Americans who envisioned themselves as Anglo-Saxons to fabricate proof of the inferiority of other groups. Horsman shows how racialized hierarchies on the home front served as impetus for imperial expansion abroad, with the rationalizations originally developed to justify conquest of Native Americans eventually applied to Mexicans and Filipinos. Yet the categories created for racist purposes displayed great instability—at one time or another, depending on immediate interests and goals, Native Americans, blacks, Mexicans, and Asians might be either elevated above the others or labeled the most deficient group of all. Similarly, David Roediger's research shows how the derogatory term "gook" originated among U.S. forces to deride the Nicaraguans fighting with Cesar Augusto Sandino during the U.S. occupation of that nation in the 1920s before it was applied as a racial slur against Koreans, Vietnamese, and even Iraqis in subsequent conflicts.[7]

Yet whiteness never works in isolation; it functions as part of a broader dynamic grid created through intersections of race, gender, class, and sexuality. The way these identities work in concert gives them their true social meaning. The renewal of patriotic rhetoric and display in the United States during and after the Reagan presidency serves as the quintessential example of this intersecting operation. Reagan succeeded in fusing the possessive investment in whiteness with other psychic and material investments—especially in masculinity, patriarchy, and heterosexuality. The intersecting identity he offered gave new meanings to white male patriarchal and heterosexual identities by establishing patriotism as the site where class antagonisms between men could be reconciled in national and patriotic antagonisms against foreign foes and internal enemies. By encoding the possessive investment in whiteness within national narratives of male heroism and patriarchal protection, Reagan and his allies mobilized a crossclass coalition around the premise that the declines in life chances and opportunities in the United States, the stagnation of real wages, the decline of basic services and infrastructure resources, and the increasing social disintegration stemmed not from the policies of big corporations and their neoliberal and neoconservative allies in government, but from the harm done to the nation by the civil rights, antiwar, feminist, and gay liberation movements of the 1960s and 1970s. By representing the national crisis as a crisis of the declining value of white male and heterosexual identity, Reagan and his allies and successors built a countersubversive coalition mobilized around protecting the privileges and prerogatives of the possessive investments in whiteness, in masculinity, in patriarchy, and in heterosexuality.

The murders of Vincent Chin, Ly Yung Cheung, the Southeast Asian school children in Stockton, and Luyen Phan Nguyen become understandable as more than the private and personal crimes of individual criminals when placed in these two contexts: widely shared social beliefs, practices, and images that render Asians as foreign enemies, and the decline of life chances and opportunities in the United States viewed as the result of the defeat in Vietnam and the democratic movements for social change that helped end that war.

The key to the conservative revival that has guided leaders of business and government since the 1970s has been the creation of a countersubversive consensus mobilized around the alleged wounds suffered by straight white men. At the heart of this effort lies an unsolvable contradiction between the economic goals of neoconservatives and neoliberals and the cultural stories they have to tell to win mass support. The advocates of surrendering national sovereignty and self-determination to transnational corporations rely on cultural stories of wounded national pride, of unfair competition from abroad, of subversion from within by feminists and aggrieved racial minorities, of social disintegration attributed not to systematic disinvestment in the United States but to the behavior of immigrants and welfare recipients. Thus we find ourselves saturated with stories extolling American national glory told by internationalists who seek to export jobs and capital overseas while dismantling the institutions offering opportunity and upward mobility to ordinary citizens in the United States.

The seeming paradox of reconfirmed nationalism during the 1991 Gulf War and the globalization of world politics, economics, and culture that emerged in its wake represents two sides of the same coin. For more than twenty years, reassertions of nationalism in the United States have taken place in the context of an ever increasing internationalization of commerce, communication, and culture. Furthermore, some of the most ardent advocates of public patriotism and militant nationalism have been active agents in the internationalization of the economy. Wedded to policies that have weakened the nation's economic and social infrastructures in order to assist multinational corporations with their global ambitions, political and economic leaders have fashioned cultural narratives of nationalism and patriotic excess to obscure and legitimize the drastic changes in national identity engendered by their economic and political decisions. In times of crisis, the illusion that all contradictions and differences would be solved if we would only agree to one kind of culture, one kind of education, one kind of patriotism, one kind of sexuality, and one kind of family can be comforting.

Exploring the dynamics of nationalistic rhetoric and patriotic display during an era of economic and political internationalization can help us understand the role of whiteness as a defining symbolic identity that mobilizes gender and sexual elements in the service of obscuring class polarization. Close study of the patriotic revival of the post-Vietnam era, especially, reveals organic links between discussions of white male identity and the U.S. defeat in the Vietnam War, deindustrialization, changes in gender roles, and the rising emphasis on acquisition, consumption, and display that has characterized the increasingly inegalitarian economy of the postindustrial era. Perhaps most important, analysis of the connections among these events and practices will enable us to see how the whiteness called forth by dominant narratives of "American patriotism" has functioned paradoxically to extend the power of transnational corporations beyond the control of any one nation's politics.

The New Patriotism

In his brilliant analysis of the 1915 D. W. Griffith film *The Birth of a Nation*, Michael Rogin demonstrates the persuasive power of scenarios depicting "the family in jeopardy" for the construction of nationalistic myths. By representing slave emancipation and the radical reforms of the Reconstruction era as threats to the integrity and purity of the white family, Griffith's film fashioned a new narrative of national unity and obligation based on connections between patriotism and patriarchy—between white patriarchal protection of the purity of the white family and the necessity for whites to forget the things that divide them in order to unite against their nonwhite enemies.[8]

   The kind of patriotism articulated by neoconservative politics in the United States since the 1970s has successfully updated the formula advanced by Griffith in 1915. It is perhaps best exemplified during ceremonies in 1984 commemorating the fortieth anniversary of the World War II Normandy invasion, when President Ronald Reagan read a letter written to him by the daughter of a veteran who had participated in the 1944 battle. The imagery created by Reagan and his media strategists for this ceremony encapsulates the conflation of whiteness, masculinity, patriarchy, and heterosexuality immanent in the patriotic renewal that revolved around the Reagan presidency. A serious illness had made it impossible for the veteran to attend the anniversary ceremonies himself, but his daughter had promised that she would travel to Normandy in his place and attend the commemoration, visit monuments, and place flowers on the graves of his friends who had been killed in combat. "I'll never forget," she promised him. "Dad, I'll always be proud."

   Her father died shortly before the anniversary, but she kept her word and sat in the audience at Omaha Beach as Reagan read her letter to a crowd of veterans and their families. In an image broadcast on network newscasts (and featured repeatedly in an advertisement for the president's reelection campaign that year), tears filled her eyes as the president read her words, his voice quivering with emotion. Media analyst Kathleen Hall Jamieson identifies the imagery encapsulated in that scene as emblematic of the key themes of the Reagan presidency. In one short, sentimental, and cinematic moment, the president depicted military service as a matter of personal pride and private obligation.[9] The drama of a father's military service and a daughter's admiring gratitude reconciled genders and generations (even beyond the grave) through a narrative of patriarchal protection and filial obligation. It offered a kind of immortality to the family by connecting it to the ceremonies of the nation state, and it served the state by locating and legitimating its demands for service and sacrifice within the private realm of family affections. Reagan's rhetoric eclipses the political purposes ostensibly served by the Normandy invasion—defeating fascism, defending democracy, and furthering freedom of speech, freedom of worship, freedom from fear, and freedom from hunger—in his enthusiasm for a story celebrating personal feelings and family ties.

World War II served as a suitable vehicle for patriotic revival in the post-Vietnam era because of the contrasts between the two wars. The United States and its allies secured a clear victory over the Axis powers in the Second World War, the postwar era brought unprecedented prosperity, and the unity forged in the face of wartime emergencies did much to define the nationalism and patriotism of the Cold War era. Yet the deployment of memories about World War II as a "good war" also rested on nostalgia for a preintegration America, when segregation in the military meant that most war heroes were white and de jure and de facto segregation on the home front channeled the fruits and benefits of victory disproportionately to white citizens.

Reagan's rhetoric had enormous appeal in the eighties—at least in part because it connected nostalgia for the whiteness of the pre–civil rights era with the affective power of nationalist narratives rooted in private family obligations and the responsibilities of paternal protection. From the popularity during the Korean War of Lefty Frizell's song "Mom and Dad's Waltz" with its improbable rhyme, "I'd do the chores and fight in wars for my momma and papa," to the government distribution of pin-up photos of blonde and snow-white Betty Grable as a symbol of white womanhood and companionate marriage to soldiers during World War II, to Senator Albert Beveridge's description of U.S. annexation of the Philippines in the 1890s as an "opportunity for all the glorious young manhood of the republic—the most virile, ambitious, impatient, militant manhood the world has ever seen," patriotism has often been constructed in the United States as a matter of a gendered and racialized obligation to paternal protection of the white family.[10]

As Robert Westbrook points out, appeals to private interests as motivations for public obligations in the United States stem from a fundamental contradiction within democratic liberalism as it has emerged in Western capitalist societies. Drawing upon the scholarship of liberal political theorist Michael Walzer, Westbrook explains that liberal states must present themselves as the defenders of private lives, liberty, and happiness. But precisely because they are set up to safeguard the individual, these states have no legitimate way to ask citizens to sacrifice themselves for the government. Lacking the ability to simply command allegiance as absolutist states do, and unable to draw on the desire to defend an active public sphere that might emerge within a broad-based participatory democracy, in Westbrook's view liberal capitalist states must cultivate and appropriate private loyalties and attachments if they are to mobilize their citizens for war.[11]

Westbrook's analysis helps us understand some of the deep-seated emotional appeal of Ronald Reagan's remarks at the Normandy commemoration as well as the political capital they built. Like so much recent scholarly work, it helps us see the connection between the nation and what has come to be called the "imagi-nation."[12] Westbrook captures one aspect of the relationship between citizens and the liberal state quite cogently and convincingly by showing how the state borrows legitimacy and commands obligation by insinuating itself into family and gender roles. But the state also creates those very family and gender roles in a myriad of ways: the state licenses marriages and legislates permissible sexual practices, regulates labor, commerce, and communication, and allocates welfare benefits, housing subsidies, and tax deductions to favor some forms of family life over others. Just as the state uses gender roles and family obligations to compel behavior that serves its interests, powerful private interests also use the state to create, define, and defend gender roles and family forms consistent with their own goals.

In his speech at Omaha Beach, Ronald Reagan not only used the family to serve a certain definition of the state, but he also put the power of the state behind specific definitions of acceptable gender and family roles, with enormous ramifications for the distribution of power, wealth, and life chances among citizens. While clearly colonizing private hopes and fears in the service of the state, Reagan's framing of the Normandy observance also mobilized the affective power of the state to address anxieties in the 1980s about private life, gender roles, jobs, community, and consumption patterns during the president's first term in office.

Reagan's celebration of a daughter's fulfillment of her father's last wish relied on clearly defined gender roles, situating women as dutiful, grateful, and proud. By taking her father's place at the ceremony, the letter writer wins the approval of the president, whose tears and quivering voice add a layer of paternal approval for her actions. The ceremony affirmed the continuity of white male heroism, female spectatorship, and national glory as the answer to anxieties about change, death, and decay. In the context of national politics in 1984, the Normandy observance celebrated gender roles and family forms consistent with Reagan's policies as president. It addressed anxieties about combat raised by Reagan's acceleration of the Cold War and by the deaths of U.S. service personnel in Lebanon and Grenada. It projected a sense of national purpose and continuity in an age of community disintegration engendered by deindustrialization, economic restructuring, and the evisceration of the welfare state. It offered spectacle without sacrifice, a chance for audiences to recommit themselves to the nation without moving beyond personal emotions and private concerns. By fashioning a public spectacle out of private grief, it combined the excitement of action with the security of spectatorship. In a country increasingly committed to consumption and sensual gratification, it presented the nation state as a source of spectacle, producing the most elaborate shows of all. As J. A. Hobson noted a century ago, "Jingoism is merely the lust of the spectator."[13]

Ronald Reagan's success in establishing himself as both president of the United States and as what some critics have jokingly called "the most popular television character of all time" depended in no small measure upon this ability to project reverent patriotism and confident nationalism. In 1980, the last year of the Carter presidency, two media events framed the nation's problems in distinctly racialized forms. Extensive media coverage made the Iranian hostage crisis a symbol of the military and diplomatic weaknesses of the United States (perhaps along with backdoor deals between the Reagan campaign staff and Iranian officials eager to procure the weapons that Reagan eventually did send secretly to that nation). The Iranians released all of their nonwhite captives, a move possibly aimed at building support in nonwhite communities but one that guaranteed the national crisis would be viewed as a crisis for whites. In the same year, the victory of the U.S. hockey team over the Soviet Union in the Olympics received unprecedented publicity as a Cold War triumph, especially since it came in a sport long dominated by the U.S.S.R. and Canada, and because it took place after the Soviet invasion of Afghanistan. Furthermore, although many previous U.S. athletic teams had defeated teams from the Soviet Union, the victory in hockey was achieved by a team composed entirely of white males.

Elected to the presidency in the wake of the Iranian hostage crisis and the U.S. hockey team's victory, Reagan cultivated support for his policies and programs by making himself synonymous with beloved national symbols. Making especially skilled use of mass spectacles like the ceremonies marking the Normandy invasion, the opening of the 1984 Olympics, and the centennial of the Statue of Liberty in 1986, the president guided his constituency into a passionate appreciation for displays of national power and pride. Yet for all of Reagan's skills as a performer and politician, he was more the interpreter than the author of the "new patriotism." Revived nationalistic fervor and public displays of patriotic symbols predated and followed his presidency. Popular support for the Gulf War and for the invasion of Panama, the tumultuous parades for soldiers returning home from Operation Desert Storm (and retroactively veterans of Vietnam and Korea), and the outpouring of films, television programs, and popular songs with nationalistic, militaristic, and heroic themes signal a broad base of support for nationalistic public patriotic celebration and display.

During the 1988 presidential election, for example, George Bush successfully depicted Michael Dukakis as an enemy of the Pledge of Allegiance because the Massachusetts governor supported a court decision exempting Jehovah's Witnesses and other religious objectors from school ceremonies saluting the flag. Dukakis responded, not by delineating the civil libertarian basis for his stance, but by circulating film footage of himself riding in an army tank. In 1992, Bush deflected attention away from his own performance in office with a stream of accusations and insinuations about William Clinton's absence from military service during the Vietnam conflict. For his part, Clinton identified himself with the Cold War rhetoric and actions of President Kennedy, and he selected Vietnam veteran Al Gore as his running mate, perhaps to contrast with Bush's vice-president, Dan Quayle, whose service in the Indiana National Guard had enabled him to avoid service in Vietnam. At the same time, third-party candidate Ross Perot called attention to his own education at the U.S. Naval Academy and to his efforts on behalf of U.S. prisoners of war held in Vietnam through his selection of a navy officer and former prisoner of war, Admiral James Stockdale, as his running mate.

Yet for all of its apparent intensity and fervor, the "new patriotism" often seemed strangely defensive, embattled, and insecure. Even after the collapse of the Soviet Union and the end of the Cold War, a desperate quality permeated the discourse and display of loyalty to the nation's symbols. Only in the rarest of cases did the new patriotism address aspects of national identity that might truly command the love, loyalty, and lives of citizens—the expressive freedoms of speech, press, assembly, and worship guaranteed by the Bill of Rights; the rule of law and the system of checks and balances; and the history of rectifying past injustices as exemplified in the abolitionist and civil rights movements. To the contrary, the covert activities carried on by Oliver North in the Reagan White House, press self-censorship about U.S. military actions in Grenada, Panama, and the Persian Gulf, and popular support for a constitutional amendment to prohibit flag burning, all indicate that (to borrow a phrase from singer and activist Michelle Shocked) many Americans are more upset by people like flag burners who would "wrap themselves in the Constitution to trash the flag" than by those like Oliver North who would "wrap themselves in the flag in order to trash the Constitution." Samuel Johnson called patriotism the "last refuge of a scoundrel," but scoundrels evidently had more patience in his day; in recent years refuge in patriotism has been the first resort of scoundrels of all sorts.

In place of a love for the historical rights and responsibilities of the nation, instead of creating community through inclusive and democratic measures, the new patriotism has emphasized public spectacles of power and private celebrations of success. It does not treat war as a regrettable last resort, but as an important, frequent, and seemingly casual instrument of policy that offers opportunities to display national purpose and resolve. In several instances, spectacle has seemed to serve as an end in itself, out of all proportion to the events it purports to commemorate. For example, after the thirty-six-hour war in Grenada in 1983, six thousand elite U.S. troops were awarded 8,700 combat medals for defeating the local police and a Cuban army construction crew. President Reagan announced that "our days of weakness are over. Our military forces are back on their feet and standing tall."[14]

When a group of antiwar Vietnam veterans picketed an appearance by actor Sylvester Stallone in Boston in 1985 because they thought his film *Rambo, First Blood: Part II* simplified issues and exploited the war for profit, a group of teenagers waiting to get Stallone's autograph jeered the veterans and pelted them with stones, screaming that Stallone was the "real veteran."[15] Stallone actually spent the Vietnam War as a security guard in a girl's school in Switzerland, but, like Pat Buchanan, Newt Gingrich, Dick Cheney, Phil Gramm, Clarence Thomas, and Rush Limbaugh—all of whom conveniently avoided military service in Vietnam themselves—Stallone established credentials as a "patriot" in the 1980s by retroactively embracing the Vietnam War and ridiculing those who had opposed it.

In contrast to previous periods of patriotic enthusiasm like World War II, when Americans justified military action by stressing citizen action in defense of common interests through their participation in armed forces firmly under civilian control, the patriotism of the last twenty-five years has often focused on the actions of small groups of elite warriors. In popular paramilitary magazines like *Soldier of Fortune,* in motion pictures ranging from *Red Dawn* to *Rambo* to *Missing in Action,* and in covert operations directed from the White House by Oliver North and John Poindexter during the Reagan administration, elite warriors defying legal and political constraints to wage their own personal and political battles have presented themselves as the true patriots.[16]

These men also offer hope for healing the nation's racial wounds. In Hollywood films, precombat racial rivalries disappear when the ordeal by fire builds communion among soldiers from different backgrounds. Rambo's character combines German and Native American ancestry in an identity that allows audiences to root for cowboys and Indians at the same time. Outside of motion pictures, life follows art as Republicans and conservative Democrats revere a man they know little about, General Colin Powell, because his combination of African American identity and military distinction promises a form of cultural unity at no real cost to whites.

Proponents of the new patriotism often cite their efforts as attempts to address the unresolved legacy of the Vietnam War. In their view, antiwar protest during that conflict undermined the welfare of U.S. troops in the field, contributed to the U.S. defeat, and ushered in an era of military and political weakness in the 1970s. Moreover, they claim that Vietnam-era opposition to the war, the military, and the government in general triggered a series of cultural changes with devastating consequences for U.S. society. As William Adams notes, "[I]n the iconography of Reaganism, Vietnam was the protean symbol of all that had gone wrong in American life. Much more than an isolated event or disaster of foreign policy, the war was, and still remains, the great metaphor in the neoconservative lexicon for the 1960s, and thus for the rebellion, disorder, anti-Americanism, and flabbiness that era loosed among us."[17]

Thus, the new patriotism not only seeks to address the issues of war and peace, unity and division, loyalty and dissent left over from Vietnam, but also contains a broader cultural project. While purporting to put Vietnam behind us, it actually tries to go back to Vietnam, to fight the war all over again, this time not only to win the war, but to undo the cultural changes it is thought to have generated. The new patriotism must redemonize the Vietnamese enemy, as in *The Deer Hunter,* and invert the power realities of the war by depicting Americans like Rambo as underequipped, feisty guerrilla fighters battling superior numbers and equipment. Just as former National Endowment for the

Humanities director Lynne Cheney called for the replacement of social science textbooks stressing "vacuous concepts" like "the interdependence among people" with textbooks filled with "the magic of myths, fables, and tales of heroes," the rosy new patriotic spectacles ignore the complex causes and consequences of U.S. involvement in Vietnam and celebrate the redeeming virtues of violent acts and heroic stories.[18]

These attempts to put Vietnam behind us began as early as 1976, less than a year after the communist victory in Southeast Asia, when President Ford sent an armed force to rescue thirty-eight U.S. merchant sailors aboard the cargo ship *Mayaguez.* The ship and crew had been seized by the Cambodian navy in the confusion of the Khmer Rouge's ascendance to power in that country. Forty-one U.S. Marines died (and forty-nine were wounded) in an effort to free thirty-eight Americans who had already been let go—the Cambodian government had released the *Mayaguez* crew before the U.S. attack began. Yet Senator Barry Goldwater, among many others, hailed the raid as a boost to America's self-image. "It was wonderful," according to the senator. "It shows we've still got balls in this country."[19]

Ronald Reagan boasted that the invasion of Grenada in 1983 and the bombing of Libya in 1985 proved that the United States "was back and standing tall," while George Bush contended that the U.S. invasion of Panama demonstrated the same point. In the mid to late 1980s, many cities including Chicago and New York held massive parades honoring Vietnam veterans—a decade after the conclusion of that war. On the eve of the Gulf War, Bush contrasted the forthcoming campaign with the Vietnam War where, he claimed, U.S. forces fought with "one hand tied behind their backs"; at the war's conclusion he proudly announced that "we've licked the Vietnam syndrome."[20]

When massive public parades welcomed home the veterans of Operation Desert Storm from the Persian Gulf, new patriots lost no opportunity to draw parallels to previous wars. In an opinion piece in the *Los Angeles Times,* a Vietnam-era veteran confessed his jealousy of the Desert Storm vets and their rousing homecoming receptions. Korean War veterans from New York staged a parade on their own behalf two months after the end of the Persian Gulf War, contrasting the immediate gratitude shown to Desert Storm veterans with their own perceived neglect. "My personal feeling was, God, they got it fast," said the executive director of the New York Korean Veterans Memorial Commission, adding, "Some guy came over to me and said is that the memorial for Desert Storm? I said, 'Do me a favor, walk the other way. We've waited 40 years. Desert Storm can wait a couple of months.'"[21]

Yet, no matter how many times they have been declared dead, the memories of Vietnam—and their impact on U.S. society—have not gone away, and that is as it should be. The deaths of more than fifty thousand Americans and more than two million Vietnamese, Laotians, and Cambodians demand our attention, grief, and sorrow. In a guerrilla war with no fixed fronts, savage punishing warfare took the lives of soldiers and civilians alike. U.S. forces detonated more explosives over Southeast Asia during those years than had been exploded by all nations in the entire previous history of aerial warfare. The devastation wrought by bombs, toxic poisons, napalm, fragmentation grenades, and bullets continues in succeeding generations in all nations affected by the conflict. Small wonder then that an overwhelming majority of respondents to public opinion polls for more than twenty years have continued to affirm that they view U.S. participation in the war to have been not just a tactical error but fundamentally wrong.[22]

The realities of mass destruction and death in Vietnam are not the realities addressed by the new patriotism. There has been no serious confrontation with the real reasons for the U.S. defeat in Vietnam—the unpopularity and corruption of the South Vietnamese government; the claim on Vietnamese nationalism staked by the communists through their years of resistance against the French, the Japanese, and the United States; the pervasive support for the other side among the Vietnamese people that turned the conflict into an antipersonnel war; and our own government's systematic misrepresentation of the true nature of the conflict to the American people.[23] All the subsequent celebrations of militarism, nationalism, and obedience to the state, have not salved the still-open wounds of Vietnam.

Perhaps this is not a failure; perhaps evocations of Vietnam have been designed less to address that conflict and its legacy than to encourage Americans to view *all* subsequent problems in U.S. society exclusively through the lens of the Vietnam War. This strategy not only prevents us from learning the lessons of Vietnam, but even more seriously, it prevents us from coming to grips with quite real current crises—the consequences of deindustrialization and economic restructuring, the demise of whole communities and their institutions, and the social and moral bankruptcy of a market economy that promotes materialism, greed, and selfishness, that makes every effort to assure the freedom and mobility of capital while relegating human beings to ever more limited life chances and opportunities.

Evocations of powerlessness, humiliation, and social disintegration that the new patriotism ascribes to the Vietnam War perfectly describe what has been

happening to U.S. society ever since. They transmit anxieties about social decay through metaphors about threats to the bodies of heterosexual white males,
who appear as put-upon victims, and present an economic and social crisis as
an unnatural disruption of racial and gender expectations. Since 1973, a combination of deindustrialization, economic restructuring, neoconservative politics, austerity economics, and the transformation of a market *economy* into a
privatized market *society* (in which every personal relation is permeated by
commodity relations) has revolutionized U.S. society. Stagnation of real wages,
automation-generated unemployment, the evisceration of the welfare state,
threats to intergenerational upward mobility, privatization of public resources,
and polarization by class, race, and gender have altered the nature of individual and collective life in this country. At the same time, the aggrandizement of
property rights over human rights has promoted greed, materialism, and narcissism focused on consumer goods, personal pleasure, and immediate gratification.

These changes have created a society in which people cannot participate in
the decisions that most affect their lives. Our society no longer offers enough
jobs at respectable wages; it discourages work while encouraging speculation,
gambling, and profiteering. Entertainment spectacles nurture voyeurism,
sadism, and sensationalism while stoking envy, avarice, and resentment. Advertising messages invade and exploit—in a word, colonize—the most intimate
areas of desire and imagination for profit, while the power of concentrated
wealth pits communities against each other in a competition for declining resources and services. As capital becomes more and more mobile—rapidly cir-
cling the globe in search of profitable returns on investments—people become
less and less mobile and less and less able to control the ordinary dimensions of
their own lives.

In such a society, patriotic spectacles serve an important function: the
imagined power and majesty of the nation state compensate for the loss of individual and collective power. As we control our own lives less and less, we look
increasingly to images outside ourselves for signs of the power and worth that
we have lost. Patriotism and patriarchy both ease the anxieties of powerlessness,
humiliation, and social disintegration, offering us identification with the power
of the state and larger-than-life heroes, or at least authority figures.

The new patriotism projects back onto the Vietnam War the alienations
and indignities generated in the present by our postindustrial market society.
We can best understand the social and cultural work performed by the new patriotism only when we understand how the death of industrial America and its

replacement by an expanded privatized market society has destabilized individual and collective identity, engendering feelings of displacement and powerlessness that leave people hungry for symbolic representations of the power and purpose they have lost in their everyday lives.

Systematic disinvestment in U.S. cities and manufacturing establishments has forced millions of people to suffer declines in earning and purchasing power, to lose control over the nature, purpose, and pace of their work, wreaking havoc in their lives as citizens and family members. Plant shutdowns have disrupted once stable communities, truncated intergenerational upward mobility, and made speculation, gambling, and fraud more valuable than work. Investments in plant and equipment by U.S. corporations declined from an average of 4 percent of the gross national product between 1966 and 1970 to 3.1 percent from 1971 to 1975, and 2.9 percent from 1976 to 1980. Unemployment averaged over 7 percent in the United States between 1975 and 1979, a rise from 5.4 percent between 1970 and 1974, and only 3.8 percent from 1965 to 1969. Real median family income, which doubled between 1947 and 1973, fell 6 percent between 1973 and 1980.[24] Despite massive spending on armaments and radical reductions in the tax obligations of corporations and wealthy individuals, capital continues its exodus to more profitable sites of exploitation in other parts of the globe. Thirty-eight million people in the United States lost their jobs in the 1970s as a result of computer-generated automation, plant shutdowns, and cutbacks in municipal and state spending.[25]

At the same time, the emerging postindustrial economy generated sales and service jobs with much lower wages, benefits, and opportunities for advancement than the jobs they replaced. Between 1979 and 1984 more than one-fifth of the newly created full-time jobs paid less than $7,000 per year (in 1984 dollars). For the entire decade, the lowest paying industries accounted for nearly 85 percent of new jobs. By 1987, 40 percent of the work force had no pension plans, and 20 percent had no health insurance. Between 1979 and 1986 the real income of the wealthiest 1 percent of the population increased by 20 percent, while the real income of the poorest 40 percent of the population fell by more than 10 percent. Real discretionary income for the average worker by the early 1980s had fallen 18 percent since 1973. At the same time, housing costs doubled, and the costs of basic necessities increased by 100 percent.[26] Changes in tax codes in the 1980s further penalized working people by making them pay more in the form of payroll taxes, while making investment and property income more valuable than wage income.[27]

By presenting national division during the Vietnam War as the root cause of the diminished sense of self and community experienced by many Americans during the past twenty years, the new patriotism deflects attention and anger away from capital, away from the disastrous consequences of neoconservative economics and politics. But it also makes a decidedly class-based appeal to resentments rooted in the ways that the working class unfairly shouldered the burdens of the war in Vietnam and has unfairly shouldered the burdens of deindustrialization and economic restructuring since. It also makes a decidedly race-based appeal by presenting the white U.S. combatant as the only true victim of the conflict, representing antiwar protesters as women or effete men who chose the well-being of Asian "others" over the survival needs of white American men.

The ground war in Vietnam was a working-class war, but not a white war. Out of a potential pool of 27 million people eligible to serve in the military, only 2.5 million went to Vietnam, according to a recent study by Christian Appy. Eighty percent of those who served came from poor or working-class backgrounds. As one veteran complained, "Where were the sons of all the big shots who supported the war? Not in my platoon. Our guys' people were workers. . . . If the war was so important, why didn't our leaders put everyone's son in there, why only us?"[28] The sons of the important people backing the war, like the sons of most of the important and unimportant people actively opposing it, did not serve in combat because of their class privileges. When protest demonstrations at home and insubordination, desertions, and low morale at the front made it politically dangerous to continue the war, President Nixon and other leaders chose to buy time for a decent interval, allowing them to withdraw gracefully by trying to turn resentment against the war into resentment against antiwar demonstrators. Richard Nixon realized that the public could be persuaded to hate antiwar demonstrators, especially college students, even more than they hated the war. Military leaders picked up on Nixon's cue, telling soldiers that antiwar demonstrators hated them, blamed them for the war, and actively aided and abetted the enemy. Of course, much of the antiwar movement made it easy for their enemies by all too often displaying elitist and anti-working-class attitudes and by failing to make meaningful alliances with the working-class public, which opposed the war (according to public opinion polls) in even greater numbers than did college students.[29]

The new patriots are certainly correct when they charge that the American people have neglected the needs of returning Vietnam veterans, but they reveal more about their own agendas than about neglect of veterans when they cite the absence of homecoming parades as proof of this maltreatment. The miserable state of Veterans Administrations hospitals, the scarcity of education and job-training opportunities for veterans, and corporate/government refusals to acknowledge or address the consequences to veterans of defoliants like Agent Orange have all demonstrated far more neglect of Vietnam-era veterans than has the absence of parades. Ironically the dishonorable treatment afforded Vietnam veterans has come in no small measure as a direct consequence of the neoconservative attack on the welfare state, which provided extensive social services for previous generations of veterans. Thus, by directing veteran resentment toward antiwar protesters, neoconservatives hide from the consequences of their own policies, from what they have done to social welfare programs, to the social wage in the United States, and to the ability of government to respond to the needs of its citizens.

In addition, the neoconservative new patriots have been extremely selective about which veterans should be given attention. When antiwar veterans attempted to tell their story at the 1971 Winter Soldier hearings, or when they flung their medals onto the steps outside the halls of Congress to protest the continuation of the war that same year, almost none of the individuals and groups angry about the lack of parades did anything about the veterans' concerns. The dangers faced and overcome in Vietnam by Chicano, black, Native American, and Asian American soldiers have not persuaded Anglo Americans to root out racism from the body politic and recognize the ways in which "American" unity is threatened by the differential distribution of power, wealth, and life chances across racial lines. Most important, by ignoring the ways in which social class determined who went to Vietnam, the new patriots evade the degree to which the veterans' station in life has been diminished because they were workers and members of minority groups.

The mostly working-class veterans of the Vietnam War returned to a country in the throes of deindustrialization. They participated in the wave of wild-cat strikes resisting speed-up and automation in U.S. factories during the 1960s and 1970s. They played prominent roles in the United Mine Workers strikes and demonstrations protesting black lung and in the Amalgamated Clothing Workers campaigns against brown lung and other industrially caused health hazards. They have been visible among the ranks of the unemployed and the homeless. But their status as workers victimized by neoconservative politics and economics in the 1970s and 1980s is far less useful to the interests of the new patriots than their role as marchers in parades and as symbols of unrewarded male heroism.

The official story disseminated by new patriots and the news media about

Vietnam veterans has obscured the connection between deindustrialization and the national welfare since the seventies, but many representations of Vietnam veterans in popular culture have brought it to the surface. Billy Joel's 1982 popular song "Allentown" and Bruce Springsteen's 1984 hit "Born in the USA" both connect the factory shutdowns of the post-1973 period to the unresolved anger of Vietnam veterans at broken promises and frustrated hopes. Joel's "Goodnight Saigon" has become the basis for the climactic moment at his live concert performances; audience members wave lighted matches and cigarette lighters as they sing the song's anthemlike verse, "We said we would all go down together." Similarly, Bobbie Ann Mason's novel *In Country* presents a Kentucky town filled with fast-food restaurants and advertising images, but no meaningful jobs for its disillusioned Vietnam veterans.[30] Unfortunately, even these progressive representations focus solely on U.S. veterans, obscuring the people of Southeast Asia and the war's dire consequences for them. They seem to presume that the psychic damage done to some Americans by the experience of defeat in Southeast Asia outweighs the nightmare visited on Vietnam, Cambodia, and Laos by the war itself. Yet, despite their callousness toward Asian victims of the Vietnam War, these representations call attention to an important unspoken dimension of the war—its class character.

Hollywood films about the Vietnam War have repeatedly drawn on its class character for dramatic tension and narrative coherence. In contrast to films about previous wars, where the experience of combat often leveled social distinctions and built powerful alliances among dissimilar soldiers, Vietnam War films seethe with what one critic called "a steady drone of class resentment." Perhaps expressions of class resentment only "drone" for those who feel they are being resented. For working-class audiences in the 1970s and 1980s, no less than for working-class soldiers in the 1960s and 1970s, expressions of class anger might be long overdue. In these films, draftees and enlisted men hate their officers, soldiers hate college students, and corruption almost always percolates down from the top.[31] For example, the Ukrainian American workers portrayed in *The Deer Hunter* fail in their efforts to protect themselves from surprises either in the dying social world of their hometown in the industrial steel-making city of Clairton, Pennsylvania, or in the equally unpredictable and rapidly disintegrating social world they enter in Vietnam.[32] The combat soldiers in *Hamburger Hill* constantly compare themselves to college students who have escaped military service, while Rambo reserves his greatest rage for the automated technology in his own supervisor's operations headquarters. Lone-wolf commandos in the *Rambo* films, *Missing in Action*, and other action/adventure stories assume underdog status by reversing reality: this time the Americans fight as guerrillas with primitive weapons against foes with vastly superior arms and technology.[33]

Nearly every Hollywood film about the Vietnam war tells its story from the perspective of white males. Yet the disproportionate numbers of African Americans and Latinos on the front lines in the actual war's combat situations complicate the racial politics of Vietnam War films, preventing a simple binary opposition between whites and Asians. Most often, these films depict initial hostilities between distrustful groups of whites and blacks, who then bond through the shared experiences of combat. Asian American soldiers are almost always absent, Latino soldiers appear rarely, but combat in Vietnam becomes a site where masculine bonds between black and white men magically resolve and dissolve racial antagonisms.[34] At the same time, the oppositions that provide dramatic tension in many of these films build upon long established narrative practices of racialized good and evil—especially the motifs of westward expansion with their hostile and "savage" Native Americans whose stealth and ferocity threaten white American troops, and the captivity story that once featured whites captured by Native Americans, reworked for Vietnam War films as a ghostly presence in accounts of U.S. soldiers missing in action or held as prisoners of war by the Vietnamese.

War as the Best Show of All

In spectacles on-screen and off, the new patriotism attempts to channel working-class solidarity into identification with the nation state and the military. To oppose the government and its policies is seen as opposing working-class soldiers in the field. But the class solidarity proclaimed in political and entertainment narratives rarely includes both genders. If there is a crisis for the working class in the Vietnam of the new patriotism, it is a distinctly gendered and racialized crisis for working-class white men only. They often become surrogates for all people in representations of Vietnam, in both politics and entertainment, that use the war to demonstrate and analyze a crisis of masculinity, centered on an alleged erosion of male prestige and power. The exploitation of low-wage women workers in the postwar economy or the burdens imposed on women raising children by the decline or disappearance of the "family wage" in heavy industry rarely appear in films about the Vietnam War and its aftermath.

In a compelling and quite brilliant analysis, Lynda Boose notes the narcissistic and homoerotic qualities of contemporary warrior films. Rather than citizen soldiers, the characters played by Sylvester Stallone and Chuck Norris more closely resemble World Wrestling Federation performers playing out a little boy's fantasy of bodily power and domination over other men. *Iron Eagle, Top Gun,* and *An Officer and a Gentleman* all revolve around anxious sons and absent fathers. For Boose, these representations reflect arrested development, "a generation stuck in its own boyhood" attempting to recover the father. She notes that in *The Deer Hunter* there are no fathers, only brothers. In that film and many others like it, the idealized nuclear family dies in Vietnam, providing audiences an opportunity to mourn the loss of patriarchal power and privilege produced not only by defeat in Vietnam, but by deindustrialization at home with its decline in real wages for white male breadwinners and the attendant irreversible entry of women into the wage-earning work force. But rather than presenting either the war or deindustrialization as political issues, these films and the national political narrative they support present public issues as personal. In Boose's apt summary: "The political is overwhelmed by the personal and adulthood by regressive desire."[35] But in our society, regressive desire and a preoccupation with the personal are intensely political phenomena—they nurture the combination of desire and fear necessary to our subordination as citizens and consumers. The binary oppositions between males and females reinforced by the Vietnam War narrative of the new patriotism serve broader ends in an integrated system of repression and control.

As Boose, Susan Jeffords, Philip Slater, and others have argued, the glorification of the military in our society has served as a key strategy for forces interested in airing anxieties about feminist and gay/lesbian challenges to traditional gender roles.[36] During the 1980s the core of Ronald Reagan's supporters from the extreme Right viewed patriotism as intimately connected to the restoration of heterosexual male authority. Religious writer Edward Louis Cole complained that in America, "John Wayne has given way to Alan Alda, strength to softness. America once had men," but now it has "pussyfooting pipsqueaks." Similarly, Reverend Tim LaHaye argued that "it has never been so difficult to be a man," because so many women are working outside the home for pay. In Reverend LaHaye's opinion, such women gain "a feeling of independence and self-sufficiency which God did not intend a married woman to have."[37] Yet the solutions offered by the New Christian Right, like the solutions offered by paramilitary culture or consumer society, do not prescribe adult interactions between men and women to determine mutually acceptable gender definitions. Rather, they offer men juvenile fantasies of omnipotence through the unleashing of childish aggression and desire for control over others.

They also encourage the most blatant forms of homophobia and misogyny. By attaching agency and heroism to the identities of heterosexual men and by requiring physical and emotional bonding based on a presumed common identity, the new patriotism seeks to equate social boundaries with natural limits, to present social transgression as biological transgression, and to fuse group loyalty through fear of foreigners. One might think that the desire on the part of previously excluded groups to share the burdens of combat and citizenship would augment rather than diminish one's own service, but the virulent reaction against gays and lesbians in the military or against women in combat reveal that primary attachments to identity politics transcend claims about citizenship and patriotic responsibility among large segments of the new patriots. It should come as no surprise that efforts to include women in combat or to acknowledge the obvious presence of gays and lesbians in the military were perceived as threatening by the new patriots rather than as confirming their values. Radio talk-show host Armstrong Williams, a black neoconservative, summed up much of the Right's anxiety in an October 1996 broadcast, when he explained, "If the feminists and the politically correct people had their way, they would turn our little boys into fairies and queers."[38]

War films and other narratives of military life prove ideal for representing and validating aggressive and regressive male behavior. Psychoanalyst Chaim Shatan observes that basic training can strip recruits of their identities, discouraging their participation in broader communities on or off base. All power is vested in the drill instructors and training leaders. In Shatan's view, "the dissolution of identity is not community, though it can relieve loneliness. Its success is due to the recruit's ability to regress to an earlier stage of development, in which he is again an unseparated appendage of the domain ruled over by the Giant and Giantess, the DIs of the nursery."[39] Rather than teaching independence and responsibility, the social relations and subjectivities glorified by the new patriotism fuse the narcissism of consumer desire with the nascent authoritarianism of the warfare state.

The glorification of masculine authority and conflation of patriotism with patriarchy in the military might make us think of combat films as exemplars of what our culture often calls an oedipal journey into adulthood—a rite of passage through sacrifices that make individuals distinct from others and responsible for their actions. If this were true, the films would help teach discipline, restraint, and responsibility. But the identities encouraged in the military by identification with the group, denials of difference, unquestioning obedience to authorities, and bonding through hatred, anger, and violence conform more closely to what our culture calls preoedipal traits—dissolution of the self into a more powerful entity, unleashing normally repressed behaviors and emotions, and fueling hatred for the subjectivities and desires of other people. Rather than teaching responsibility, the new patriotism stages sadomasochistic spectacles that use revenge motifs to justify unleashing the most primitive and unrestrained brutality, imitating the enemies we claim to fear. To manage the anxieties generated by this regression, the new patriots have to affirm all the more intensely their abstract fidelity to leaders, causes, and entities outside themselves.

The dynamics of militaristic spectacles have a self-perpetuating character. Oedipal and preoedipal identities play upon one another: regression to primitive desires generates an anxious longing for identification with powerful patriarchal authority; systematic submission to superior authority gives rise to anxious feelings of loneliness and isolation, which in turn fuels the desire for even more connection to powerful authorities. In *The Origins of Totalitarianism*, Hannah Arendt suggests that people in putatively democratic societies become ready for totalitarianism when loneliness becomes a routine feature of everyday existence. The combined effects of deindustrialization, economic restructuring, and the oppressive materialism of a market society where things have more value than people feed a sense of isolation and loneliness. Privatization prevents people from active engagement in civic society, from participating in processes that might lead to a healthy sense of self. Militarism becomes one of the few spaces in such a society where a shared sense of purpose, connection to others, and unselfish motivation have a legitimate place.

The denial of the political in combat films and fiction no less than in public patriotic rhetoric connects the new patriotism to the narcissism of consumer desire as the unifying national narrative. The ascendancy of greed and materialism in U.S. society during the 1980s has been widely acknowledged, but the distinctive form this greed assumed in an age of deindustrialization has attracted less attention and analysis. Changes in investment policies and tax codes during the Reagan years accelerated trends favoring consumption over production, leveraged buyouts over productive investments, short-term profits over long-term investment, and love of gain over collective obligations and responsibilities. People at the highest income levels embraced behaviors previously associated with the poor—seeking short-term sensations and pleasures rather than pursuing disciplined long-range investments, programs, or policies. At the macrosocial level, these policies have produced paralyzing levels of public and private debt, squandered the social resources and industrial infrastructure of the nation, and generated long-term costs to individuals and their environments while imposing burdens on future generations. On the microsocial level, they have encouraged the very attitudes displayed most often in adolescent warrior fantasies—regressive desire, narcissistic grandiosity, and anxieties about identity that lead to craving for sensations, distraction, and displays of power.

As president of the United States, no less than In his role as a performer in commercials for General Electric in the 1950s, Ronald Reagan communicated the language of consumer desire with extraordinary skill. He offered more for less, promising that tax cuts would not reduce government revenues because they would stimulate massive economic growth. He claimed that ending government regulation would free the private sector to find market-based solutions to social problems. He told Americans that they could have it all, as in his 1986 State of the Union speech when he announced, "In this land of dreams fulfilled where greater dreams may be imagined, nothing is impossible, no victory is beyond our reach, no glory will ever be too great. So now, it's up to us, all of us, to prepare America for that day when our work will pale before the greatness of America's champions in the 21st century."[40] When this philosophy led the government to accumulate a larger national debt during Reagan's terms in office than had been incurred by all previous presidents combined, when it produced massive unemployment, homelessness, and health hazards, and when it created the preconditions for massive fraud in the savings and loan industry leading to enormous debts that executives from deregulated industries then passed on to consumers, Reagan continued to insist that his policies were working. In their own way they were, not to solve problems and make the nation stronger, but to transform the political system into a branch of the entertainment industry, into an entity seeking scapegoats for social problems rather than solutions to them.

Of course, the severe economic decline experienced by most people in the United States during the 1980s should not be attributed solely to Reagan; it predated and postdated his terms in office. The stagnation of real wages owed much to long-term imbalances in the U.S. economy between the needs of capital and the needs of the majority of the population. But the political culture that Reagan nurtured in the wake of this devastation perfectly complemented the escape from responsibility promoted by a consumer commodity society fixated on instant gratification. Reagan basked in the glow of the glory he attained by invading Grenada, bombing Libya, and identifying himself with the overwhelming U.S. victory at the 1984 Olympics (gained largely because the Soviet Union and other Warsaw Pact nations did not participate). By timing the Libya bombing for maximum exposure on network prime time, he set the stage for the voyeurism of the Gulf War, where news reports often resembled video games or commercials by weapons manufacturers. In return for all of the broken promises and devastated lives of his era, Reagan left the nation with a better-developed taste for spectatorship of the kind described long ago by J. A. Hobson—gloating "over the perils, pains, and slaughter of fellow-men whom he does not know, but whose destruction he desires in a blind and artificially stimulated passion of hatred and revenge."[41]

The new patriotism arises from deeply felt contradictions in U.S. society. It arbitrates anxieties about changes in gender roles, jobs, communities, and collective identity brought on by deindustrialization and economic restructuring. Narratives of national honor take on increased importance as the practices of transnational corporations make the nation state increasingly powerless to advance the interests of its citizens. Private anxieties about isolation, loneliness, and mortality fuel public spectacles of patriotic identification that promise purposeful and unselfish connection to collective and enduring institutions. The new patriotism serves vital purposes for neoconservative economics and politics, providing psychic reparation for the damage done to individuals and groups by the operation of market principles, while at the same time promoting narcissistic desires for pleasure and power that set the stage for ever more majestic public spectacles and demonstrations of military might.

Yet while providing logical responses to the diminution of collective and individual power in an age of deindustrialization, the new patriotism encourages us to evade collective problems and responsibilities rather than to solve them. It interferes with serious public discussion of the world we have lost and the one we are building through deindustrialization and economic restructuring. It promotes male violence and female subordination, builds identification with outside authorities at the expense of personal integrity and responsibility, and inflames desires that can only be quenched by domination over others.

Perhaps most ominously, the new patriotism builds possessive identification with warfare and violence as solutions to personal and political problems. Although aggression is often portrayed as natural in our culture, the elaborate pomp of patriotic ceremonies and rituals may indicate precisely the opposite— that aggression needs to be nurtured and cultivated. It is not easy for humans to kill other humans; one study of the World War II Normandy invasion showed that even among specially trained combat troops, many failed to fire their weapons once the battle started. Nightmares, guilt, and other signs of postcombat stress have plagued veterans of all wars, not just Vietnam. The attention devoted to ceremonial commemoration of past wars may be not so much evidence of how easy it is for people to go to war, but rather how much persuasion, rationalization, and diversion are required to make warfare acceptable.

Unfortunately, elaborate public appeals to honor the memory of slain soldiers only create the preconditions for new generations of corpses. Shatan explains that "ceremonial vengeance" serves to perpetuate rather than resolve the legacy of past wars because it requires repression of the genuine agonies caused by combat. In his eloquent formulation, "unshed tears shed blood." Grief and mourning are transformed into scapegoating and fantasies of revenge. Unresolved grief and guilt lead us to inflict our wounds on others; reincarnating yesterday's dead as today's warriors "promises collective rebirth to all who have died for the Corps," but at the price of creating more martyrs whose deaths must be avenged in the future.[42]

Ceremonial celebrations of militarism perpetuate dangerous illusions about warfare. They hide the ambiguous outcome of every conflict, the limited utility of force in resolving conflicts of interest and ideology, and the ways in which the resolution of every war contains the seeds of the next one. But even beyond any practical shortcomings of war as a way of resolving conflicts lies its atrocious immorality. Our nation is not the first (and it will not be the last) to believe that participating in the systematic destruction of other humans will not fundamentally compromise our morality and our humanity, but the weight of the historical record is inescapable. Author and Vietnam War veteran Tim O'Brien counsels that moral lessons cannot be learned from warfare. He tells us that a war story "does not instruct, nor encourage virtue, nor suggest models of proper human behavior." O'Brien asks us to cease believing in the morality of war, advising us that any time we feel uplifted or righteous after reading a war story, we have been made the victim of "a very old and terrible lie."[43]

Of course, this is not to say that nothing of value is ever salvaged from war. Certainly many of the people who have seen combat become ferociously antiwar precisely because they have witnessed the waste and destructiveness of warfare firsthand. In addition, as George Mariscal points out in his important book *Aztlan and Vietnam,* for communities of color in the United States, the Vietnam War (like previous conflicts) sharpened contradictions and accelerated demands for civil rights from soldiers who saw themselves asked to fight and possibly die overseas for freedoms that they did not enjoy at home.[44] At the level of soldiers in the field, lessons about mutuality and interdependence often break down prejudice and parochialism. For these individuals and those they influence, warfare holds meanings that counteract the stories of heroism and glory that dominate combat narratives.

On the level of spectacle, however, war can be the best show of all. During World War I, Randolph Bourne argued that war was "the health of the state"—that nothing furthers the totalitarian projects of centralized power as effectively as warfare. During the Gulf War, Todd Gitlin amended Bourne's formulation, claiming that war is also the health of the networks—and we might add the health of the advertisers, toy makers, film producers, and other merchants of diversion, distraction, and vicarious thrill seeking. Even if only as symbolic compensation, war enables, or at least seems to enable, individuals to negotiate otherwise intolerable contradictions.

The Wages of War

If war remains "the health of the state," it nonetheless does great harm to individuals and groups. Psychoanalyst and cultural critic Joel Kovel reminds us that a false subject needs a false object—people who do not know who they are need demonized enemies in order to define themselves. Hatred of the external enemy does not end when the shooting stops; on the contrary, the spectacles of war and the rituals of ceremonial vengeance promote appetites that need to be sated. It is hardly an accident that with the end of the Cold War the neoconservative lobbyists and public relations specialists in the John M. Olin Foundation, the Heritage Foundation, and the Bradley Foundation among others who did so much to promote the new patriotism, now collaborate with overtly white supremacist organizations like the Pioneer Fund to publicize the most vulgar and discredited forms of white supremacist thought. In Charles Murray and Richard Herrnstein's *The Bell Curve,* but also in Dinesh D'Souza's *The End of Racism* and in Samuel P. Huntington's "The Clash of Cultures," neoconservatives present people of color at home and abroad as the new enemy to be scapegoated for the lost wages of whiteness. They offer the possessive investment in whiteness as reparation and consolation for the destructive consequences of the economic and political policies demanded by the transnational corporations that pay their salaries and fund their research. Their efforts to portray the victims of racism as the beneficiaries of unearned privileges given to them because of their race hide the history of the possessive investment in whiteness and invert the history of racial politics in the United States. Yet while deficient as history and shamefully indecent as intellectual argument, these public relations campaigns have enjoyed broad success, from attacks on affirmative action to the promotion of hate crimes against people of color.

In a brilliant analysis of the role of anti-immigrant attitudes in contemporary conservatism, Kitty Calavita observes that "balanced budget conservatism" promises wealth, stability, and security to taxpayers and home owners, but creates an economy characterized by uncertain relations between work and reward, the plunder of public resources for private gain, economic uncertainty, and social disintegration. Moral panics, military mobilizations, and nativist attacks on immigrants provide a useful safety valve for the fear, anger, and frustration fostered by the false promises of the "balanced budget" conservatives. Because of the possessive investment in whiteness and its history, people of color easily become the main targets of this meanness masquerading as morality.[45]

U.S. wars in Asia have pitted U.S. combat troops against soldiers and civilians of nearly every eastern Asian nation. The experiences of warfare in Asia and the propaganda attendant to it have had racist consequences for citizens of those nations as well as for Asian immigrants to the United States. Of course, racism against Asians has a long history in the United States that includes disgraceful acts of mob violence, bigoted legislation denying immigrants from that continent opportunities to become citizens or own property, persistent economic exploitation, and the forced internment of more than 100,000 Japanese Americans, most of them citizens. Yet while not new, anti-Asian racism has taken on an especially vicious character in the context of the U.S. defeat in Vietnam and the rise of Asian economies as competitors with the United States. The hate crimes against Asian Americans enumerated at the beginning of this chapter are only a tiny sample of a much broader pattern of criminal behavior directed against people of Asian origin in the United States.[46] At the same time, the conflation of patriotism with whiteness has also had disastrous consequences for racialized immigrant groups from Mexico, Central and South America, the Caribbean, and the West Indies.

Deliberately inflammatory metaphors by politicians and journalists describing undocumented workers as an invading army prepare the public to see immigrants as the enemy. At the same time, antidrug policies that focus on border interdiction rather than on the suppression of demand and supply incentives create a context for actual low-intensity warfare along the border. Government policy and vigilante actions complement one another in bringing the hurts and hatreds of warfare within our own borders. In San Diego, a group of young whites active in their high school's Junior Reserve Officers Training program participated in unofficial and unauthorized nighttime excursions on the border during which they fired air rifles at defenseless immigrants. In 1992 a U.S. Border Patrol agent fired rounds from an M-16 rifle into a group of undocumented immigrants traveling on foot near Nogales, Arizona, because he thought they were drug couriers. Although one of the immigrants was wounded by the agent's fire, the incident did not become public until three months later when the same agent shot an unarmed Mexican man running away from him in the back two times with an AR-15 rifle . The agent attempted to cover up his crime by dragging his victim some fifty yards out of sight, leaving him to die, then returning later to bury the body. Another agent encountered him in the act and agreed (reportedly at gunpoint) to keep quiet about the shooting, but fifteen hours later he reported the incident to authorities, who charged the first agent with first-degree murder. At his trial six months later, a jury found the agent not guilty on all charges, accepting defense arguments portraying him as a "law officer on the front line of our nation's war on drugs" whose actions were justified because he was operating in a "war zone."[47]

Immigrants detained for border violations in a private jail contracting with the INS in Elizabeth, New Jersey, succeeded in having the facility closed in 1995 because of inhumane conditions and brutality by guards. Some two dozen of the inmates from that facility found then themselves transferred to the Union County Jail in Elizabeth, where guards punched and kicked them, pushed their heads into toilets, and compelled a line of men to take off their clothes, kneel before the guards, and chant "America is Number One."[48] In May 1996, a group of marines assigned to a secret unit combating drug smuggling along the border shot and killed a teenaged U.S. citizen herding goats near his home. A county grand jury recommended that no charges be filed.[49]

Identities are complex, relational, and intersecting. By disguising the social crises of our time as assaults on white male heterosexual power and privilege, the new patriotism has fanned the flames of white supremacy, homophobia, and anti-immigrant hatred. It has encouraged workers to feel their losses as whites, as men, as heterosexuals, but not as workers or community members. It has channeled resentments against foreigners, immigrants, members of aggrieved racial groups, women, gays and lesbians, college students, and intellectuals—but not against transnational capital and the economic austerity and social disintegration it creates and sustains.

The great scholar W.E.B. Du Bois argued long ago that the United States lost its best chance to be an egalitarian and nonracist society in the years after the Civil War because elites successfully manipulated the class resentments of white workers, directing them away from themselves and toward African Americans, Asian Americans, and Mexicans. White workers endured hardships in exchange for the security of knowing that there would always be a group below them, that there was a floor below which they could not fall. Du Bois called this assurance of privilege "the wages of whiteness," what white workers received instead of the higher economic wages they would have earned had they joined with all other workers in an interracial, classwide alliance. Du Bois quotes a populist white Georgia newspaper editor who identified the fatal flaw in going along with the elites' strategy: "Since at least 1865, we have been holding back the Negro to keep him from getting beyond the white man. Our idea has been that the Negro should be kept poor. But by keeping him poor, we have thrown him into competition with ourselves and have kept ourselves poor."[50]

A century later, the egalitarian promise of the social movements of the 1960s has similarly been betrayed by a version of nationalism and identity politics that hides the attack on wages, hours, working conditions, education, transportation, health care, and housing by encouraging a possessive investment in the contemporary version of the wages of whiteness. By investing their identities in these narratives of the nation that depend on the demonization of others, white Americans only serve the interests of the transnational corporations whose policies are directly responsible for the disintegration of the nation's social and economic infrastructure. Accepting the possessive investment in whiteness as consolation and compensation is a bad deal. It guarantees that whiteness is the only thing whites will ever really own.

CHAPTER 5

White Fear: O.J. Simpson and the Greatest Story Ever Sold

Even the most thoughtless, even the most deluded black person knows more about his life than the image he is offered as the justification of it.—JAMES BALDWIN

"**W**hiteness" emerged as a relevant category in U.S. life and culture largely as a result of slavery and segregation, Native American policy and immigration restrictions, conquest and colonialism. Economics and politics relegated various racial groups to unequal access to property and citizenship, while cultural practices institutionalized racism in everyday life by uniting diverse European American subjects into an imagined community called into being through appeals to white supremacy. Wild West shows, minstrel shows, Hollywood films, and commercial advertising have not merely reflected the racism that exists in social relations but have helped produce a unified white racial identity through the shared experience of spectatorship.

Cultural practices and products have often played crucial roles in prefiguring, presenting, and preserving political coalitions grounded in an identification with the fictions of whiteness. Andrew Jackson's coalition of the common man enacted in politics the alliances and identities announced on stage in minstrel shows. Woodrow Wilson's New Freedom gave political form to the white unity represented in the cinema of D. W. Griffith. Franklin D. Roosevelt's New Deal depended upon the alliance between northern white ethnics and southern white supremacists that permeated blackface musicals like Al Jolson's *The Jazz Singer*.[1] In conjunction with racialized structures of opportunity in economics and politics, these cultural practices and products help us understand how people who left Europe as Calabrians or Bohemians or Lithuanians became "whites" when they arrived in America, and how that designation made all the difference in the world.

The sinister social consequences of cultural expressions continue today. Cultural categories frame our understanding of social issues; they arbitrate the things we can imagine and perceive. Perhaps nothing better illustrates the conflation of cultural images with social relations than the O.J. Simpson murder trial and the cultural discourse that emerged in its wake.

Prosecutors in Los Angeles announce the filing of first-degree murder charges against a handsome and athletic African American man. They claim that he used deadly force in assaulting a white woman and her male companion on a quiet street in an affluent section on the west side of Los Angeles. The defendant is represented by prominent defense attorney Johnnie Cochran, who claims that serious and deliberate misconduct on the part of law enforcement officers has tainted the evidence against his client. After a much publicized trial, the jury reaches a verdict.

The jury finds the defendant guilty and sends him to prison. The man is not O.J. Simpson. He is Elmer "Geronimo" Pratt, a former deputy defense minister of the Black Panther Party who was incarcerated for more than twenty-five years for his alleged involvement in the killing of Caroline Olsen and the wounding of her husband, Kenneth Olsen, near a Santa Monica tennis court in 1968. Before coming to Los Angeles to enter UCLA on the GI Bill, Pratt served two tours of duty in Vietnam, where he was a decorated paratrooper. Upon receiving an honorable discharge from the service, he entered college and became active in radical political organizations, including the Los Angeles chapter of the Black Panther Party. After assassins (egged on by the Federal Bureau of Investigation's COINTELPRO project) shot and killed local Panther leaders Alprentice "Bunchy" Carter and Jon Huggins, Pratt became a key leader of the group.

At Pratt's trial in 1972, prosecutors claimed that a car resembling his was seen near the site of the crime, that the murder weapon had been found in Jon Huggins's house, and that Kenneth Olsen, who survived the attack, had positively identified Pratt as the culprit. In addition, an expelled member of the Black Panther Party, Julio Carl Butler, gave testimony damaging to the defendant. For his part, Pratt denied any knowledge of the attack on the Olsens, claiming that he had been hundreds of miles away in Oakland, California, when the crime was committed. Prosecutors and police officials did not tell the jury that Kenneth Olsen had identified at least three other suspects before responding to police prodding to name Pratt as the man who killed Caroline Olsen. They did not disclose that the barrel was missing from the alleged murder weapon, making it impossible to conduct tests that could connect it definitively to the crime. They did not produce wiretap evidence that might have corroborated Pratt's story that he was in Oakland at the time of the attack.

In their 1988 book *Agents of Repression,* Ward Churchill and Jim Vander Wall revealed that agents from the Los Angeles office of the FBI targeted Pratt for special surveillance and prosecution as early as 1969 because of his political activities. Internal reports from that office described Pratt as "a key black extremist" and informed supervisors in Washington, D.C., that "constant consideration is given to the possibility of utilization of counter intelligence measures with efforts being directed toward neutralizing Pratt as an effective BPP [Black Panther Party] functionary." Los Angeles Police Department (LAPD) officers arrested Pratt several times on an assortment of charges, all of which were dropped or resulted in acquittals, before they attempted to connect him to the killing of Caroline Olsen. Pratt was in jail awaiting trial in 1971 when he learned that his wife, Sandra Lane Pratt, had been murdered. She was eight months pregnant when she was shot five times at close range and killed. Although her body was found stuffed in a sleeping bag alongside an L.A. freeway, the police department conducted no serious investigation into her death. Law enforcement officials also denied Geronimo Pratt permission to view his wife's body or to attend her funeral.[2]

Churchill and Vander Wall point out that key prosecution witness Carl Julius "Julio" Butler had been a deputy sheriff before joining the Black Panther Party, that he has been identified as an FBI infiltrator of the Black Panthers by Louis Tackwood, who himself worked as an undercover agent in black nationalist groups, and that even though Butler pleaded guilty to four major felonies, he received only a probationary sentence and has subsequently been allowed to complete law school and enter California's bar association.[3] Former FBI agent M. Wesley Swearingen claimed in a 1995 book that Carl Butler was an informant for the LAPD and for the FBI. Swearingen noted that the bureau closed its file on Butler before the trial so that they could say he was "not an FBI informant," and he alleged that the government indeed possessed wiretap logs proving that Pratt was in the San Francisco Bay Area before and after the shooting of Caroline Olsen. When Swearingen tried to check the bureau's wiretap records, he was told that the logs from November 15 to December 20, 1968, were "missing."[4]

In a 1996 hearing, files from the district attorney's office had Butler's name on a list of "confidential informants," and when Pratt's attorney asked him if he had acted as an informant to the FBI based on his own definition of the term "informant," Butler replied "You could say that." In addition, retired LAPD captain Edward Henry testified that Butler was "technically" an informant, and that he remembered that Butler had often used obscene language when members of the Black Panther Party confronted police officers. Asked if he considered Butler an agent provocateur—an agent sent into a radical group with the intention of provoking violent confrontations—Henry replied, "In effect, yes. My thoughts at the time were that I didn't think Julius Butler cared what happened to the Panthers."[5] Three members of the jury that convicted Pratt in 1972 now say they believe they would never have reached a verdict of guilty had they known about the wiretap evidence or about the allegations that Butler had been an informant.[6]

In 1997, a conservative Republican judge appointed by Ronald Reagan overturned Pratt's conviction, ruling that the Los Angeles district attorney's office acted illegally in suppressing evidence favorable to Pratt during the 1972 trial. After twenty-seven years in jail, eight of them in solitary confinement, Geronimo Pratt was released from prison on bail. The district attorney made no effort to indict those responsible for prosecutorial misconduct or to charge Julio Butler with perjury, but announced an effort to appeal the superior court judge's decision. The prosecution of Pratt continues, despite its obvious unfairness.[7]

Geronimo Pratt's story is at least as dramatic and interesting as O.J. Simpson's. It is a story of murder and misconduct, of lost liberty and a ruined reputation. Yet it is not a story that will sell. Pratt may well be an innocent man imprisoned for a crime that he did not commit, a man framed for his political activities. But he does not qualify as a famous black criminal defendant the way Johnnie Cochran's later client does. Pratt's story does not involve interracial sex, drug use, or spousal abuse. Although he managed to secure the services of Johnnie Cochran at an early stage of the attorney's career, Pratt had no "dream team" of lawyers working for $650 per hour, no ability to pay forensic consultants the $50,000 per week that they would receive from Simpson.[8] Most important, Geronimo Pratt's story will not sell because it goes against the grain of the story-telling apparatuses of commercial culture, which place entertainment and consumer purchases at the center of the social world. Pratt's story is about politics, racism, and history; consequently, he remains unknown to most of the public. Simpson's story is about sex and celebrities, about professional sports, Hollywood films, and television commercials; consequently, his story is universally known. Simpson may be guilty, but he is a free man today. Pratt may be innocent, but he remained incarcerated for twenty-five years and still faces prosecution for a crime that he most likely did not commit.

In publicizing the O.J. Simpson case, media conglomerates at the same time publicized themselves and the world in which they work. The "saleability" of this story stemmed from its smooth fit with the long history of sales that preceded it—sales of individual celebrity images, cross-marketing campaigns aimed at connecting fame to commercial endorsements, and the general dramatization of wealth and material goods that forms the subtext of so many television commercials, Hollywood films, and even news broadcasts. The O.J. Simpson case was about an entertainment figure, but it also was entertainment. The reach and scope of media interest in the trial bears a close relation to the financial benefits that media outlets derive from selling the kind of stories that fit their preexisting categories. The Simpson story made huge amounts of money for cable and broadcast television networks, for tabloid newspapers and magazines, and for the merchandisers whose video tapes and books have only just begun to reach the market. But beyond its utility as a money maker, the Simpson trial also enables us to ask and answer questions about the power of publicity, the meaning of money, and the interpenetration of public and private concerns in our culture. Why did this story take on the proportions that it did? What were its uses and effects? What can we say about a society that spends so much of its time and resources on a story like this one?

Cultural theorist Arthur Kroker claims that nothing happens in our society unless it happens on television. Of course we know that this is not quite correct, that one of the problems with television programs is that they do so little to reflect the realities that people confront every day. Kroker's overstatement is perhaps deliberately provocative, emphasizing the central role played by commercial culture in framing public events and private concerns. But even if Kroker's formulation is flawed, its obverse is true: if something happens over and over again on television, it "happens" to all of us. Television played the key role in the Simpson case in many ways. The trial was telecast live, and its details were aired endlessly on news and entertainment programs. The case opened up whole new television markets with gavel-to-gavel coverage on cable and broadcast outlets. It helped spur the development of new programs and the creation of new celebrities through specialized discussions on cable channels. It provided a constant frame of reference for late-night comedians, talk shows, and news features, and even served as the source of a new line of Halloween masks featuring its central characters.

Simpson's status as an already famous celebrity gave his case particular significance for television programming, not just because he has appeared often in the medium as an athlete, broadcaster, film star, and spokesperson famous for his commercial endorsements, but because his prominence in diverse areas of entertainment gave him the kind of visibility that television loves to recycle and repackage. His segue from athletics to entertainment to news simply augmented that capacity or, to be more precise, brought the news where news directors, advertisers, and public relations firms deeply desire it to be—squarely within the realm of entertainment.

Commercial television in the United States has long rested on intertextual engagement with other media—television presents motion pictures, sporting events, and concerts; it mixes celebrities from different realms of endeavor on talk and game shows; it engages in relentless cross-programming, plugging purchases of other kinds of entertainment by placing television at the nexus of publishing, broadcasting, filmmaking, music recording, and shopping. Television stars make films that enable them to appear on talk shows to prepare audiences for their best-selling books, which give them name recognition valuable for product endorsements. As Daniel Czitrom noted years ago, nearly everything on television is an advertisement for some form of entertainment or product available in another medium; the infomercial, or program-length commercial, that dominates late-night programming on cable is simply a refinement of what the medium does more crudely elsewhere.

The Simpson trial became a story that was easy to sell, in part, because it seemed to replicate so perfectly the world of commercial television and its generic conventions. The athlete/actor/celebrity defendant charged with murder could have come out of *Murder, She Wrote* or *Columbo,* while the details about his residence and vehicles might fit easily into segments of *Dallas, Dynasty,* or *Life Styles of the Rich and Famous.* For experienced television viewers, courtroom confrontations may have enacted half-remembered episodes of *L.A. Law, Perry Mason,* and *Quincy,* while the history of unheeded claims of spousal abuse evoked the concerns and conflicts often aired in the movie of the week. The search for justice by grieving relatives and the short, glamorous lives of the victims sparked associations with daily soap operas or weekly serial dramas. Indeed, one source of public dissatisfaction with the trial's participants and its outcome seems to stem from the failure of the trial to fit the frame that television established for it, to come to a "happy ending" in the form of an unambiguous verdict of guilty, which certainly would have been the case had this been a television melodrama. But instead of following the clearly defined character roles and unambiguous narrative closures offered by television programs,

the trial and its participants reflected the ambiguities, uncertainties, and contradictions of everyday life and its complex social relations, giving the entire enterprise an out-of-control look in comparison to the other stories that television tells and sells.

From start to finish, the O.J. Simpson story demonstrated an eerie engagement with, and an unusual affinity for, the money-making mechanisms of
commercial culture. If it was something less than the trial of the century in
terms of legal significance, it was certainly the sale of the century in terms of its
ability to unite the various apparatuses of advertising, publicity, spectator
sports, motion pictures, television, and marketing into a totality generating
money-making opportunities at every turn. As one communications industry
executive explained to a reporter from a trade publication, "When you have this
kind of public awareness and preconditioning, the long-term cash-in has got to
be enormous."[9]

A major Los Angeles radio station gave defense witness Brian "Kato" Kaelin
his own talk show because of the trial. Attorney Gerry Spence, an outside expert frequently employed by television networks during the trial, parlayed his
guest commentaries on the Simpson case into his own televised talk show on
CNBC. The William Morris Agency won a hotly contested battle to serve as theatrical and public relations representative for lead prosecutor Marcia Clark.[10]
Edward Billet Productions purportedly offered Judge Lance Ito a million dollars to star in a new version of the television program *The People's Court*.[11] Industry experts confided to *Advertising Age* reporters that "Simpson-related
marketing could produce as much as $1 billion in media and merchandising
sales." During the trial, Simpson had his lawyers take out patent protection for
his full name as well as for his nicknames, "O.J." and "The Juice," and he had
them file more than fifty lawsuits against merchandisers marketing items bearing his name. In addition, Simpson negotiated deals for a video, a book, pay-
per-view interviews, and other projects that might eventually net as much as
$18 million.[12]

During the trial, jurors were dismissed for allegedly keeping notes designed
to aid them in writing books about their experiences. One dismissed juror published a book that came out before the trial ended. After the verdict, some jurors asked television producers and magazine editors for as much as $100,000
for interviews; one agreed to pose nude for *Playboy*.[13] Prosecutor Christopher
Darden and defense lawyers Robert Shapiro and Johnnie Cochran produced
highly publicized and broadly marketed books that appeared some six months
after the trial. Within a year, prosecutor Marcia Clark and perjured police offi-

cer Mark Fuhrman followed with books of their own. In his memoir, Darden accused a member of Simpson's defense team of drafting a book on a laptop computer even while the trial was taking place. Journalist Brent Staples speculated in the *New York Times* that Shapiro hired Alan Dershowitz as part of the defense team not for his potential contributions to the case but mainly to prevent Dershowitz from serving as a television analyst and making comments that might embarrass Shapiro.[14] Proof of Mark Fuhrman's perjury emerged not through vigorous cross-examination but from remarks he made to an aspiring screenwriter in the hope that he could have his real and imagined deeds as a member of the LAPD immortalized and publicized in a Hollywood film.[15]

The story of O.J. Simpson on trial sold well. CNN (the Cable News Network) presented 631 hours of direct televised coverage of the Simpson case, attracting an average of 2.2 million viewers at any given time. This content increased the channel's ratings and revenues by close to 50 percent.[16] On the day of the verdict, an unusually large number of daytime viewers—representing 42 percent of the nation's television homes and more than 90 percent of the sets in use—were tuned to channels covering the case. For the entire week leading up to the verdict, Simpson programming gave CNN fourteen of the fifteen most watched basic cable programs. Court TV, available in only about 24 million homes, nonetheless accounted for three of the most watched shows on cable during the fall 1995 ratings period.[17] Industry officials attributed much of cable television's collective 25 percent jump in ratings between 1994 and 1995 to the Simpson case.[18] Tabloid television shows featuring the Simpson story registered dramatic gains as well. During the week the verdict was announced, *Entertainment Tonight* secured an audience 39 percent larger than the previous week's. *Inside Edition* increased its viewership by 24 percent over the same period the previous year, while *American Journal* attracted double its average audience for that season.[19]

Mass circulation magazines devoted fifty-four cover stories to the Simpson case during the last half of 1994, and ninety during 1995—almost three times the attention they gave to their second-favorite cover story personality, television talk-show host Oprah Winfrey.[20] More than one million internet users visited CNN's O.J. Simpson Web site in the first six hours after the trial verdict, an average of 3,800 per minute.[21] A live interview with O.J. Simpson in January 1996 enabled Black Entertainment Television (BET) to reach three million households and secure the highest ratings in the channel's sixteen-year history, easily surpassing the previous high of 1.2 million households, much less its average viewership of 300,000 homes in prime time. The network did not pay

Simpson for this interview as he initially requested, but it did allow him to purchase time before and after the program to advertise his mail-order video available at $29.95.[22]

Stories about the O.J. Simpson trial enjoyed such a powerful presence in the market in part because they could draw on the main themes that organize television discourse in the United States: products as the center of social life, the stimulation and management of appetites, and alarm about the family in jeopardy. A story linking any two of these categories will always make the news (a news event that resembles a popular motion picture—"a real-life *Home Alone* right here in your town"; a new product that can affect your appetite for another product—"Will a new exercise machine help you quit smoking?" "Are you eating fat-free foods and still gaining weight? Find out why at eleven."). A story that links all three is even better ("Could your children be receiving sexually explicit images on the internet?"). One reason the O.J. Simpson trial became so prominent in the media is that it contained all the elements necessary for televisual representation: it was a story about products, appetites, and the family in jeopardy.

O.J. Simpson's identity raises immediate associations with products. Over the years, he has done commercials as a spokesperson for Hertz, Chevrolet, Wilson Sporting Goods, and Royal Crown Cola. He has been visible as a commodity himself, as a football player, as an announcer for ABC television's Monday night football games, as an actor in motion pictures (including the *Naked Gun* series), as a motivational speaker at corporate events, and as a personality on exercise videos. He has become wealthy from these endeavors and lives a visibly affluent life. Each part of his career has served as a form of advertising for the other parts; his fame as a football player gave him an edge as an actor, his visibility as both an actor and athlete made him more desirable for commercial endorsements. His sources of fame are mutually reinforcing, and this history makes him quite desirable as the object of news or feature stories on television. Audiences will recognize him; their attention will translate into future commodity purchases. O.J. replicates the kinds of cross-marketing fundamental to television's relationship to other media.

These days, fame itself can sell a product. For example, in the early 1990s, low-wage women workers in Indonesia who sew Air Jordan athletic shoes for Nike received wages of about $1.35 per hour. The shoes they make cost Nike about $5 a pair in materials and labor but sell for anywhere from $45 to $80 in the United States. At the same time, basketball star Michael Jordan, for whom the line is named, received $20 million per year to endorse these shoes, more than the wages of all of Nike's workers in all six of their workplaces combined. Thus, Jordan's fame was worth more to Nike than the workers' labor; his reputation and visibility are themselves commodities more valuable than his own work as a basketball player, for which he received about one-fifth the amount he got for endorsements.[23] Connecting fame with a product enhances the value of both, and both are more likely to appear on television.

Media coverage of the Simpson trial drew upon and reinforced the connection between Simpson and commodities. Coincidentally, the key pieces of material evidence in the trial were almost all commodities—the white Bronco and the Rolls Royce, the mysterious knife and the expensive Italian shoes, the unusual pair of designer leather gloves, some missing luggage, a golf bag, and even O.J.'s socks. Like testimony about the swimming pool, guest house, or video equipment on Simpson's property, the prominence of these items allowed journalists to report the news and talk about shopping at the same time. News reports of the trial paid close attention to Robert Shapiro's ties and Marcia Clark's hairstyles. Perhaps that preoccupation with appearances helps explain Christopher Darden's compulsion in his book on the trial to comment on other attorneys' "expensive suits," Simpson's "thousand-dollar suit," and Johnnie Cochran's "off-white linen suit"— what reviewer Adam Hochschild describes as Darden's "suitomania."[24]

The priority given to products in televisual discourse raises the issue of appetites. By showing us how satisfied and fulfilled we will feel when we accumulate material goods, commercials promote desire, but they also create anxiety about desires run wild. Some commercials profess to monitor consumption by describing the dangers of reckless or foolish indulgence, for which they sell remedies ranging from indigestion medicine to diet pills to rehabilitation from drug, alcohol, or gambling addictions. In a similar way, television programs often simultaneously inflame our desires and make us fear excess. In the Simpson case, the same things that made O.J. a symbol of fulfilled desires also made him a focal point for rumination about unrestrained appetites, about cocaine use, indiscriminate sex, and violence. John Fiske points out the ways tabloid newspaper accounts emphasized these connections with stories like "Sex Secrets that Drove O.J. Crazy," and "Shocking Truth about Nicole's 911 Call, O.J. Caught Her Making Love while Kids Slept in the Next Room."[25] The talents that brought O.J. wealth may have led him to use drugs. The good looks that made him a movie star may have enabled him to engage in obsessive extramarital sex. The physical strength that made him a successful athlete may have enabled him to murder two people brutally.

Finally, the family in jeopardy is a major theme of television drama, comedy, and news as well as the central preoccupation of commercials. As literary scholars Nancy Armstrong and Roddy Reid remind us, the theme dates back to the mid–nineteenth century when domestic fiction first became a profitable market item. They suggest that the theme emerged less because families experienced new threats from the world at large than because the best way to organize the middle-class family around the acquisition of household products was to create fearful images of the outside world and then "sell" the family as a defense against them.[26] To this day, the media describe the family largely in terms of affection, intimacy, and its role as a haven in a heartless world, with little open acknowledgment of its central role as a site for spending, as an economic unit that transfers wealth and property across generations, and as an entity coveted by marketers.

Like previous forms of commercial culture aimed at families, television describes the family as always in jeopardy, not least as a result of television itself making commercial culture the arbiter of proper family behavior. The authority of the products and the people on television always appears more impressive than the authority of one's own family. Television organizes the family into separate market segments watching different programs at different times of the day (Monday night football, late-afternoon talk shows, Saturday morning cartoons). In order to fulfill its project completely, in an ideal world the television industry would detach everyone from their connections to roles other than shopping, thus enabling television to sell them things around the clock. But to market products effectively, television must represent them as noncommodities, as vehicles for creating and preserving affection, intimacy, and interpersonal relations. This contradiction creates in viewers an unstable, volatile, and ultimately unresolvable anxiety that is always susceptible to media manipulation.

The Simpson trial revolved around narratives of family closure and rupture. One tabloid ran a picture of O.J., Nicole, and their first child with the caption, "How this dream family portrait turned into a murderous nightmare."[27] Was Nicole Brown's marriage to a wealthy and handsome celebrity the fulfillment of the dreams of an Orange County suburban girl, or a cruel deception that trapped her in an tempestuous relationship with a jealous, violent, and philandering husband? Did O.J. love Nicole and their children, as evidenced by his presence at the piano recital the day that Nicole was murdered, or was his attention merely a device to control others while allowing himself unbridled liberty? Both sides used family solidarity as an emblem of what was at stake for their clients; the Goldman family's public weeping and timely press conferences served the prosecution in the same way that the tight family circle of sisters and O.J.'s mother presented proof of Simpson's virtue in the eyes of the defense. Hints of a sexual relationship between Nicole Brown Simpson and Ron Goldman or between Nicole and Kato Kaelin had to be quashed by the prosecution, while O.J.'s romantic and sexual entanglements with other women had to be proven by the defense to be irrelevant to his devotion to Nicole. From an entertainment perspective, the issue was not so much character or motivation for murder but rather exposure of the close relationship between foundational narratives of family fidelity and the lived experiences that revealed them as fictions. As in the daytime soap opera or nighttime serial drama, family ties are invoked more passionately in the abstract as they disintegrate in practice.[28] While affirmation of the family as the center of the social world is required, it can exist comfortably alongside practices that contradict it.

The primacy in television discourse of property, appetites, and the family in jeopardy made the Simpson trial unusually susceptible to media exposure. In any art form, it is easy to go with the conventions and core grammar of the form and difficult to go against them. The Simpson trial was a story that could be told easily on television because television had long been involved in preparing the audience for stories like it. Just as the western films of John Ford seemed immediately credible to audiences accustomed to representations of the region in the paintings of Remington and Russell, on the covers of western novels, and in Wild West shows, the O.J. Simpson trial could be comprehended instantly as "true" by viewers accustomed to television and its conventions.[29] In this context, there is no danger of overexposure; even disgust at the media attention devoted to the Simpson trial can be easily incorporated into the narrative, providing another aspect of the Simpson case to be marketed for discussion on talk shows or as the subject of magazine articles.

It is difficult not to feel contempt for the processes that employ powerful and sophisticated communications media for the voyeurism, idle speculation, and trivialities that dominated coverage of the Simpson trial. Its pervasive presence raises serious questions about the society in which we live. Yet the stories that the media sells would not work if they did not serve some purpose, if they did not engage the attention and interest of audiences. We might do well to defer our judgment about whether we like or dislike the world that the Simpson trial reveals to us until we understand how and why the story works, what wounds it salves, and what desires it expresses.

In an essay about the popular culture of the 1930s, C.L.R. James offered some ideas that may help. James suggested that people who perceive themselves as restricted and constrained by their life circumstances turn to popular culture for compensatory stories about "free individuals who go out into the world and settle their problems by free activity and individualistic methods." Movie stars and celebrities seem to "live grandly and boldly," enjoying the freedom that others desire for themselves. Fictional and real law breakers offer special opportunities for this investment and engagement because their stories titillate millions of people with the fantasy of active living. According to James, stories filled with bloodshed, violence, and the freedom from restraint that they symbolize allow audiences to release "the bitterness, hate, fear, and sadism which simmer just below the surface." For James, the source of popular anger lay in the Great Depression, in the lost hopes, blasted aspirations, cultural disillusionments, and economic hard times engendered by economic collapse in the 1930s.[30] It is certainly possible that economic restructuring and cultural change tied to deindustrialization, globalization, and the stagnation of real wages have had a similar effect on our own time.

James felt that fascination with popular heroes in the 1930s provided "an outlet for cheated, defrauded personality in vicarious living through a few striking personalities." With no freedom to make meaningful choices about work or politics, people turn to popular culture, where at least some choices seem possible. At the same time, people resent the freedoms they project onto their heroes, mixing adoration of famous individuals with "murderous rejection" of them. The intolerable impotence and rage of everyday life ultimately leads us to desire the downfall of the idols we have created. This is a perversion, James contends, but one inherent "in a society in which the actual deepest desires of the masses cannot find expression."[31] It creates as well an ambivalence toward one's own fascination. As the president of the Radio-Television News Directors Association intriguingly observed, "The public hates itself for its fascination with O.J. Simpson."[32]

Yet for James, what mattered about the stories that sell was less their immediate uses and effects on audiences than their ideological role in preventing other stories from emerging—stories about history, power, and social relations. In the Simpson case, the very affinities for products, appetites, and the family in jeopardy that drove the Simpson saga as a media event also made it nearly impossible for public discourse to go beyond the frames and boundaries imposed by television's rhetorical and ideological conventions, especially in respect to race.

Even *Time* magazine agreed with arts curator Thelma Golden that "if

Nicole had been black, this case would have been on a cover of *Jet* magazine and not much more."[33] In a society dominated by property, appetites, and family-in-jeopardy stories, race should disappear, but in a racialized society, concepts like property, appetites, and the family in jeopardy have racial implications. As Herman Gray points out so persuasively in his exemplary book, *Watching Race*, throughout much of the 1980s and 1990s, television has linked accumulation and protection of property, descriptions of uncontrolled appetites, and threats to the family to racialized and racist imagery.[34] In mass media imagery, the alleged uncontrolled behavior, unrestrained appetites, and family disintegration among African Americans emerges as the main threat to the unimpeded acquisition of wealth and its transfer across generations by the "American" family—a family unmarked by race but assumed to be white.

Media images and political discourse over the past two decades have hinged upon stories that connect crime, drugs, and family disintegration to nonwhite communities, while presenting whites as besieged.[35] As Ralph Ellison observed in 1949, "Because these things are bound up with their notion of chaos, it is almost impossible for many whites to consider questions of sex, women, economic opportunity, the national identity, historic change, social justice—even the 'criminality' implicit in the broadening of freedom itself—without summoning malignant images of black men into consciousness."[36]

On television, black people who do not belong on *The Cosby Show* belong on *Cops*. Once these images have been circulated and recirculated, they are extremely difficult to displace. As historian Nathan Irvin Huggins remarked years ago about the enduring and poisonous power of the minstrel show "darkie," black people have found it difficult to "step out character" either on or off stage because white people are often so attached to the images that they have created about blacks.[37] Sanctimonious and supercilious condemnations of alleged moral transgressions by people of color serve an important function for white people. They transfer the blame for the moral and spiritual emptiness of our materialistic and competitive market society on to its worst victims, fashioning a temporary unity among whites otherwise divided by interests, attitudes, and ambitions. Channeling concerns about morality exclusively into concerns about the morals of the poor and the afflicted leaves the morality of the wealthy and the would-be wealthy unexamined—no small accomplishment in an age of savings-and-loan frauds, political influence peddling, and many other forms of white-collar crime.

At the very moment when whites are reaping unprecedented benefits from past and present racism, an insatiable demand exists for stories about minority misbehavior. Any amount of money seems too much to spend on education, health care, job training, or housing for minorities, but no amount seems too much for incarcerating and punishing minorities. As James Baldwin observed decades ago, these impulses spring from deeply systemic causes, from the sadism and vengeance generated by intense social inequality. Writing in 1972 with a prophetic relevance, Baldwin observed:

> Now, not even the people who are the most spectacular recipients of the benefits of prosperity are able to endure these benefits: they can neither understand them nor do without them, nor can they go beyond them. Above all, they cannot, or dare not, assess or imagine the price paid by their victims, or subjects, for this way of life, and so they cannot afford to know why the victims are revolting. They are forced, then, to the conclusion that the victims—the barbarians—are revolting against all established civilized values—which is both true and not true—and, in order to preserve these values, however stifling and joyless these values have caused their lives to be, the bulk of the people desperately seek out representatives who are prepared to make up in cruelty what both they and the people lack in conviction.[38]

Elements in the O.J. Simpson trial that conformed to the story already in place about racial identity could be comprehended easily by the audience. Elements that contradicted it made the story harder to sell. A guilty O.J. easily fit this scenario, especially after national newsmagazines printed Simpson's mug shot and artificially darkened his picture on their covers in order to accentuate the threat that he embodied (and, as John Fiske points out, to promote "impulse" buys by whites for those very magazines).[39] An innocent O.J., or at least an O.J. technically not guilty because the largely black jury believed that the prosecution's case did not meet the legal standards of proof beyond a reasonable doubt, went against the grain of the narrative already in place.

Yet racial categories accounted for much of the emotional charge carried by the Simpson trial and verdict. How could it have been otherwise in a case involving a black defendant and two murdered white victims? Race provided the trial with its most significant subtext, and the racial identities of the judge, attorneys, witnesses, and, most of all, jurors, went far toward determining what stories could be told and sold. Commodifying racial identity proved easy. *Tonight Show* host Jay Leno and New York senator Alphonse D'Amato attracted different degrees of criticism when Leno presented a recurrent skit featuring the

"Dancing Itos" (bearded Japanese men in judge's robes performing a cancan) and D'Amato impersonated Ito speaking in a Japanese accent (which Ito does not have) during an appearance on the Don Imus radio show. Even though they transgressed the boundaries of taste and tolerance, D'Amato and Leno correctly assumed that racial identity could play in the media as a joke, as an anxious expression of the intrusion of otherness in a media discourse that assumes audiences are white. But more complicated stories about race, and racism, could not so easily fit the commodified form of television discourse.

Police officer Mark Fuhrman's testimony—and perjury—provides a case in point. Before Fuhrman took the stand, print journalists reported that he had applied for disability benefits on the grounds that his service in the LAPD had left him with a violent hatred toward blacks and other "minority" groups. Prosecutors denied these stories and provided the press with a completely different spin—that Fuhrman was a distinguished and disciplined professional. When F. Lee Bailey's initial cross-examination failed to crack Fuhrman's cover story, press reports gushed about how effective a witness Fuhrman had been, how handsome he was, and how credible his testimony seemed. They overlooked Fuhrman's preposterous assertion that the police did not consider Simpson a suspect and consequently did not need a search warrant when Fuhrman climbed over a fence to inspect the grounds of Simpson's estate. These same accounts ridiculed Bailey for asserting that Fuhrman might harbor racist antipathies toward blacks. Fuhrman's "composure" and media-friendly appearance (handsome, white, and male) led the press to imbue his story with credibility. When definitive evidence emerged that Fuhrman had committed perjury, that he not only had used the word "nigger" in conversation but also was a racist ideologue who boasted privately about using his position as a police officer to brutalize suspects and enact his own racist beliefs, the response was strange. Rather than expressing anger that a police officer had compromised an important murder case by lying in court and by boasting about breaking the law, media outlets and callers to talk shows largely adopted the prosecution's line of argument, treating Fuhrman as if he were an unsuccessful character whose part had to be written out of the show. They admitted that Fuhrman was "a racist" but contended that his racism was personal and had nothing to do with the widespread racist practices of the LAPD (witness Chief Gates) or the prosecutor's office.

No one was expected to take responsibility for Fuhrman's racism; even the detective himself, who was allowed to plea bargain his crime of perjury, for which he served no time in jail, paid no fine, and received probation, whose only condition is that he commit no more crimes. This sudden burst of leniency from California's right-wing attorney general Dan Lungren, who likes to present himself as a hard liner in his treatment of criminals, sent the clear and unmistakable message that Fuhrman's race and occupation won him special privileges and immunity.

By treating racism as individual rather than institutional, the media made sure that Fuhrman's racism would in no way taint the police department that hired and promoted him, and that continued to place him in positions where he could abuse his authority. It could not be permitted to reflect badly on the prosecutors who relied on his testimony despite what they knew about him, who ridiculed claims that Fuhrman was a racist; but who absolved themselves of any blame when these claims proved true. However, when Johnnie Cochran used Fuhrman's racism to undermine the credibility of his testimony, the Goldman family, prosecutors, and an overwhelming number of media commentators reacted with indignation and outrage. People who could find no racism in Mark Fuhrman felt comfortable in condemning Cochran for playing the race card. If Fuhrman's racism was a personal attribute that could not be used to undermine the credibility of any other white person or any social institution run by whites, Cochran, the jury, and all of black America could be indicted as "reverse racists" for the Simpson verdict. As Lewis Gordon points out, "What the aftermath of the OJ Simpson case has shown about contemporary racial ideology in the US is that it is considered bad taste, a violation of protocol, for blacks to identify racism where racism exists."[40]

Los Angeles district attorney Gil Garcetti set the stage for most of the reaction to the verdict when he accused the majority black jury of being "emotive" rather than intellectual in its deliberations.[41] Facing a potentially difficult re-election campaign because his office had also failed to secure convictions in the highly publicized Menendez case the previous year, Garcetti had ample political incentive to shift the blame for this acquittal away from the prosecutors and police and on to the jury. But his decision to blame the intellectual failings of the jury was no accident; it built upon longstanding slurs of black people, to be sure, but also on the 1994 public relations campaign of right-wing groups like the John M. Olin Foundation on behalf of Charles Murray and Richard Herrnstein's *The Bell Curve*. This book drew upon the most regressive and white supremacist traditions of eugenics to spin a story about the innate mental inferiority of black people. Although the book was thoroughly discredited as science by every reputable critic, neoconservatives continued to circulate and praise it, because it enabled them to blame the disasters that their policies have brought to communities of color on the alleged biological inferiority of minorities themselves. Garcetti's comments also played into the public relations campaign waged by congressional Republicans during and after the 1994 elections through the "Contract with America," which tried to reframe civil rights issues by presenting white people as the victims of reverse discrimination rather than as the perpetrators of discrimination against people of color.

Popular reaction to the Simpson case followed the line of least resistance in the realm of media logic. Consequently, *The Bell Curve* and the "Contract with America" provided a framework for denouncing the verdict, the jury, and Johnnie Cochran while absolving Fuhrman, the prosecutors, and the LAPD. Just as Dan Quayle attributed the 1992 Los Angeles turmoil to the "poverty of values" in the inner city (which he blamed on the television program *Murphy Brown*'s letting its lead character have a baby out of wedlock), political leaders and media commentators blamed the Simpson verdict on the propensity of black people to blame their problems on racism. Peniel Joseph attributes this dynamic to what he calls the "equal opportunity racism" of the present day, which "seeks to exculpate white America's unrepentant racism by claiming that blacks are just as 'racist'; and in some cases (such as the Simpson case) can be worse than whites."[42]

One reason this line of argument sometimes works rests on the logic of media, on the fact that *The Bell Curve*, the "Contract with America," and Quayle's attacks on *Murphy Brown* so easily recapitulate commercial media's concerns about property, appetites, and the family in jeopardy. White racist acts like Fuhrman's, or those of Charles Stuart (who killed his pregnant wife in Boston in 1989 to get insurance money and blamed the attack on a black man) or Susan Smith (who drowned her two young sons in South Carolina in 1994 and blamed the crime on a black man), never register as parts of a broader pattern of white racist blame fixing but get dismissed as the acts of individuals who themselves get dismissed as aberrations. On the other hand, broad systematic practices such as discrimination in housing, employment, and education are too remote and impersonal for media treatment—until a white individual claims to be a victim of reverse discrimination. The real racism that millions of people face every day is thus either too localized or too generalized to secure media attention, but stories like the Simpson trial that use race as a way of dramatizing already known stories about products, appetites, and the family in jeopardy receive unlimited coverage.

The core preoccupations of the commercial media determine the stories that sell, and these, in turn, become the stories we tell. This framework guarantees that some important stories cannot be told. During the O.J. Simpson case, particular angles escaped media scrutiny entirely because they could not fit the format that places products, appetites, and the family in jeopardy at the center of the social world. For example, in the midst of all the attention given to O.J. Simpson's possessions, escapades, and defense costs, where was the detailed scrutiny of how the prosecution was constrained by California's Proposition 13, the tax-limitation ballot initiative of 1978 that has funneled millions of dollars to multinational corporations, small businesses, and homeowners at the expense of general tax revenues? How can local prosecutors ever win a case against individuals with unlimited resources for their defense when budget constraints so badly limit the resources and personnel available to the representatives of the public? In addition, what was the role of Simpson's celebrity status in the police decision to do so little about the nine cases of spousal abuse at the Simpson home to which they had been summoned? Former LAPD officer Mike Rothmiller has charged that the Organized Crime Intelligence Division of the department uses informants, wiretaps, cameras, and personal surveillance to monitor "all kinds of celebrities." Rothmiller claims that the department gathers embarrassing evidence about the personal lives of celebrities so that it will have leverage with important people and can secure their cooperation for initiatives that the department desires. Is it possible that the police had to fabricate the story that Simpson was not a suspect when they climbed the wall of his estate not only to protect the evidence they seized on that occasion, but because admitting that he was a suspect would make them reveal sources of information that might call public attention to the secretive duties of the OCID?

The media could not relate Proposition 13 and the activities of the OCID to the Simpson story because they break the frame that limits social life to a series of personal problems and acts of consumption. They require attention to broad structural processes and acknowledgment of deeply unequal conditions and opportunities in our society. They cannot coast on their similarity to previous media messages; they do not reference the primacy of products, anxiety about appetites, or fears about the family as they have come to us in mediated texts over the years.

But if the stories that sell monopolize the stories we tell, we will have no way to understand, analyze, or alter the serious structural problems our society faces. The problem is not with stories themselves. Stories can expand our horizons and augment our understanding, but they can also imprison us, just as surely and just as securely as we can be imprisoned by stone walls and iron bars. Just ask Geronimo Pratt.

CHAPTER 6

White Desire: Remembering Robert Johnson

He who has been treated as the devil recognizes the devil when they meet.—JAMES BALDWIN

If white racism manifested itself exclusively through hostility and exclusion it would be easier to understand and to combat. Yet the long history of interracial relations has created a possessive investment in whiteness that includes an investment in certain conceptions about people of color. The recurrence of racial stereotypes in art and in life, the frequent invocation of people of color as sources of inspiration or forgiveness for whites, and the white fascination with certain notions of primitive authenticity among communities of color, all testify to the white investment in images that whites themselves have created about people of color. In his excellent study of blackface minstrelsy, Eric Lott identifies both "love and theft" as components of the white racist imagination, and a similar dynamic serves as the central force in this chapter's exploration of white desire as manifested in the reception of the blues music of Robert Johnson.

"Every crossroads has a story" proclaims the large bold lettering in an advertisement on the back cover of the November/December 1996 issue of *Living Blues* magazine, promoting the state of Mississippi to tourists. As told in the first person by an aspiring musician who has "tried to pick out those soulful notes on my guitar, but could never duplicate that feeling you get when Howlin' Wolf lets you know he is 300 pounds of joy," the story in the ad concerns going to Mississippi to get in touch with the spirit of Robert Johnson. "Supposedly he went down to a crossroads and sold his soul to the Devil to play like that," the narrator explains. "So I drove down Highway 61 to Highway 49 where most folks say the deal was struck. I didn't want to sell my soul, or anything. I just wanted to kind of pay my respects. I don't know if the Devil got the soul of Robert Johnson that night. But this intersection has still heard its share of music. B. B. King, Muddy Waters, and Charlie Patton all had something to say and crossed these roads many times."[1]

It should not be surprising that the state of Mississippi uses the story of Robert Johnson at the crossroads to sell tourism. The story has proven its extraordinary appeal and exceptional commercial value over and over again. In recent years a series of successful books, documentary films, and television programs has celebrated "the search for Robert Johnson." The compact disc reissue of Johnson's recordings in 1990 sold more than 400,000 units within six months of its release and more than 900,000 units within six years. When a producer and recording engineer working for Sony discovered original masters of Robert Johnson recordings at that company's archives in New York, a reporter for a music industry trade publication compared their find to the discovery of the tomb of King Tut. Rock guitarist Eric Clapton has long validated his own standing as an artist by claiming a psychic and spiritual connection to Johnson through renditions of Johnson's songs, including "Crossroads."[2] The crossroads metaphor, both with and without reference to Robert Johnson, has served as the focal point for a number of celebrated art exhibits, films, and popular novels.[3]

It might seem paradoxical that large numbers of European Americans who have such a possessive investment in whiteness have an affective investment in the art of Robert Johnson, a black man. The two investments, however, are not mutually exclusive. Indeed, one depends on the other. The very existence of racism adds to the mystery, distance, and inversions of prestige enacted in the reception of blues music by romantics like Eric Clapton and many of his fans. William Faulkner once argued that white Americans needed the Negro selves they encountered through culture because they were the only selves they've every really known. In other words, with African Americans relegated to primitive, natural, and mystical domains, the consumption of black culture salves the alienations and identity problems of European Americans.

The current commercial value of the crossroads story depends in no small measure on the ways it erases its cultural origins and suppresses its original social intentions. Derived from diasporic African legends and trickster tales intended to teach the importance of human agency, the crossroads story here functions instead as a register of Western culture's enduring attachment to romanticism, to separating life and art, to elevating individual emotions over collective conditions, and to making an aesthetic of social pain. The romanticism implicit in the circulation and reception of the story of Robert Johnson at the crossroads hides the hard facts of life and labor in the segregated South in Johnson's day. It obscures the ways in which unquestioned assumptions about artistic expression in our own time keep us wedded to the very practices that our art ostensibly deplores. This romanticism contributes to the possessive investment in whiteness by maintaining the illusion that individual whites can appropriate aspects of African American experience for their own benefit without having to acknowledge the factors that give African Americans and European Americans widely divergent opportunities and life chances.

In Yoruba and other West African cosmologies, crossroads can be sites of danger and of opportunity. Where paths come together, collision and confusion may occur, but also decisions need to be made and choices matter. Robert Farris Thompson suggests that Yoruba art itself exists largely as training for life, as an activity that cultivates the ability to recognize significant communications so that the right decisions will be made. Material places and objects become important in this process because artistic activity tries to capture the metaphorical power of the natural world and to imbue objects with "intuitions of the power to make right things come to pass."[4] The crossroads mediates power across physical and metaphysical worlds, but it also cultivates an appreciation of activity and imagination as tools for transforming immediate circumstances and conditions. The trickster figure at the crossroads—often interpreted in the romantic tradition as the devil—is really Eshu-Elegbara (Legba, Elegba, Esu), not the incarnation of evil, but an unpredictable deity with the power to make things happen, a god described by Thompson as "the ultimate master of potentiality."[5]

The story of the crossroads that emerges with such frequency and power in commercial culture, however, proceeds from very different assumptions about art and life. Walter Hill's 1986 film *Crossroads* featured Ralph Macchio, the star of *The Karate Kid,* playing a white youth who taps into the power of black blues by tracking down an elderly African American blues musician in a Harlem hospital and helping him return to Mississippi in return for "some long lost songs." We learn that the bluesman gained his talent by selling his soul to the devil. The climactic moment of the film comes from a guitar duel between Macchio playing the blues and the devil (played by guitar virtuoso Steve Vai) playing heavy metal music. In this case, heavy metal represents the contaminated culture of the music industry, while the blues appears as a precommercial form with magical powers owing to its purportedly pure and uncontaminated history.[6]

Walter Mosley's 1995 novel, *RL's Dream*, recalls Johnson's music nostalgically as an art form that involved its listeners in depths of feeling unknown to today's audiences. Mosley's central character can "play anything on my guitar," but even when the beauty of his playing brings tears to the eyes of his listeners he knows that "the music they was hearin' was just a weak shadow, just like some echo of somethin', that happened a long time ago. They was feelin' somethin', but not what Robert Johnson made us feel in Arcola. They can't get that naked. And they wouldn't want to even if they could, 'cause you know Robert Johnson's blues would rip the skin right off yo' back. Robert Johnson's blues get down to a nerve most people don't even have no more."[7] Once again, the blues are deployed as an antidote to the shallowness of contemporary commercial culture, as an art form precious because it is unapproachable and unknowable, locked in the past but superior to anything we can imagine in the present.

The blues music that emerges in the film *Crossroads,* in Walter Mosley's *RL's Dream,* and in Eric Clapton's construction of Robert Johnson as a spiritual ancestor has less to do with the blues itself than with the traditions of romanticism in Western culture that date back to the late eighteenth century. Romanticism imagines an art immune to commercial considerations, an art capable of reconciling antagonistic social realities, of bringing people from very different circumstances together through aesthetic and emotional affinities. As Nancy Rosenblum explains, "The romantic sensibility is marked by a sense of its own boundless potential for creativity and expression, by revulsion at constriction and closure and at the very thought of being authoritatively defined."[8]

Eric Clapton's career and his purported connection to Robert Johnson exemplify this romanticism. Clapton has hardly had an easy life; he was born out of wedlock and raised by his grandparents, and has suffered from drug addiction and the death of his child, among other personal problems. Yet the romance of Robert Johnson functions in his personal and professional narratives as an appropriation that hides the differences between the two men and their life circumstances. While both artists had their share of problems, on his best day Robert Johnson caught more hell than Eric Clapton has ever imagined, and the musical forms that Clapton has explored as a form of personal self-discovery came to Johnson as part of a shared social language honed under historically specific circumstances for eminently practical purposes.

Clapton biographer Harry Shapiro identifies "the search for the spirit of Robert Johnson" as a core component in Clapton's career, noting that both artists "have lived 'the rock life' with periods of self-imposed exile, sudden bouts of wanderlust, drinking and gambling."[9] It would no doubt come as a surprise to Johnson to learn that he lived something called "the rock life," but the validation of the blues that comes from connecting it to the success of rock 'n' roll—and the moral qualities that adhere to rock 'n' roll when connected to its blues heritage—testify to both the power of contemporary commercial culture and its painful contradictions. Audiences and critics want to "own" the pleasures and powers of popular music without embracing the commercial and industrial matrices in which they are embedded; they want to imagine that art that they have discovered through commercial culture is somehow better than commercial culture itself, that their investment in the music grants them an immunity from the embarrassing manipulation, pandering, and trivialization of culture intrinsic to a market society.

In another biography of Clapton, titled *Crossroads,* Michael Schumacher identifies "wanderlust, drinking, and womanizing" as activities that link Clapton to Johnson. Schumacher offers quotes from Clapton that illustrate the artist's own investment in being linked with Johnson and the authenticity and depth of feeling associated with him. "It was almost like I'd been prepared each step to receive him," Clapton told Schumacher, comparing his involvement with Johnson's music to "a religious experience that started out by hearing Chuck Berry, and then at each stage I was going further and further back, and deeper and deeper into the source of the music, until I was ready for Robert Johnson." It is hard to see in what sense Johnson could be considered "the source" of blues guitar playing or singing in any musical sense, but Clapton's comments stem less from an assessment of Johnson as a musician than from the British guitarist's sense of a shared emotional bond. "It was almost as if he felt things so acutely he found it almost unbearable," Clapton explained. "It called to me in my confusion, it seemed to echo something that I had always felt."[10]

While claiming a mystical connection with Robert Johnson as an individual, Clapton ignores the economic and social structures that enable him rather than an African American to make a fortune playing African American music. In addition, Clapton's connection to the pain in Robert Johnson's life has not led him to any degree of sympathy for those in similar straits today. At a moment of intense antiblack, anti-Asian, and anti-Arab sentiment in the United Kingdom during the summer of 1976, Clapton launched a drunken rant against "foreigners" at a concert in racially volatile Birmingham, telling the audience, "I think we should vote for Enoch Powell," a white supremacist member of the British Parliament. Clapton made things worse in succeeding weeks when he attempted to justify his comments on the basis of his resentment of "Arab money-spending and their total lack of respect for other people's property." For those unmoved by his economic argument, Clapton added a dose of paternal protection, explaining that "one foreigner had pinched my missus' bum."[11]

Despite Clapton's easy incorporation of antiforeign racism in his romanticism about an African American artist, the motivations behind romanticism are not necessarily racist. The enduring appeal of romanticism in art and music in Western culture testifies to the alienation and isolation of bourgeois life, as well as to the relentless materialism of capitalist societies. The wounds that romanticism attempts to salve are real, but the categories that undergird romantic thinking perpetuate rather than mitigate the alienations and injustices that it seeks to address and redress. The life and legend of Robert Johnson can be made to conform perfectly to the contours of romanticism; it is not difficult to see what ends Johnson's story serves for Eric Clapton and his many fans, as well as for the Mississippi Tourism Commission and for a host of writers, filmmakers, visual artists, musicians, and television producers. Yet incorporating Robert Johnson into a romantic narrative hides both the social circumstances and the cultural strategies that informed his life and art.

When Robert Johnson started to play music in public, it was not at all evident that he would one day become the king of the Delta blues singers. In the ice houses, juke joints, and general stores around Robinsonville, Mississippi, in 1930, most people felt that the nineteen-year-old Johnson could play the harmonica tolerably well and that he could sing acceptably enough, but they judged him one of the worst guitar players they had ever heard. Son House remembers that when he and his fellow musicians would put down their instruments during breaks to go outside into the cool night air, Johnson often picked up one of their guitars and start playing so poorly that the patrons would beg the band members to come back and play so he would leave the stage. House remembers scolding the teenager, "Don't do that, Robert. You drive the people nuts. You can't play nothing."[12]

Johnson left Robinsonville in 1931 and moved to Hazlehurst—about forty miles south of Jackson. When he returned to Robinsonville two years later, House saw that the young musician now owned his own guitar. "What can you do with that thing?" House teased. "You can't do nothing with it." Johnson smiled and said, "Let me have your seat a minute," and when he started to play, House could hardly believe what he was hearing. "He was so good! Our mouths were standing open," House recalled.[13] Years later, blues scholar Mack McCormick interviewed many of Johnson's relatives, who claimed that Robert had gone out to a deserted crossroads just before midnight and met a large black man. The stranger took the guitar from Johnson's hands, tuned it to his liking, played a piece, and then handed it back. From that point on, the story goes, Robert Johnson played like an expert.[14]

Despite the seemingly universal appeal of this story, anyone who has ever attempted to play music may prefer to think that *practice* had something to do with Robert Johnson's improved skills as a guitar player. Yet the crossroads metaphor should not be dismissed as irrelevant or foolish. Robert Johnson's family members and fans interpreted his history through the lens of their experiences and beliefs as African people in America. They drew upon a large repertoire of folkways originating in Africa to solve the problems they faced as exploited workers, second-class citizens, and members of a despised racial group. They put mirrors outside their homes to catch the "flash of the spirit," and they left the Bible open at night or tacked newspapers onto their walls to secure the protections offered by "spirit writing." They scattered the possessions of the dead—especially broken glass, dishes, and cups—on burial sites to acknowledge the ruptures between the living and the dead, but also to observe the memories and rituals that can connect people across generations and continents. They looked to African practices for guidance in everyday life activities like cooking, healing, and farming, but also for explanation and transformation, for ways of rendering the hegemony of white supremacy in America relative, provisional, and contingent rather than natural, necessary, and inevitable. By remembering and retaining aspects of Africa in their lives, they could turn themselves from an oppressed national minority into part of the global majority of nonwhite people.

Robert Johnson may not have actually met a man at the crossroads at midnight, but he did infuse a material object—the guitar—with sufficient spiritual power to earn himself escape from the twin pillars of power in the Depression-era South, the plantation and the prison. The guitar enabled him to earn a living on the road, to move from town to town playing the blues for farm workers and factory hands all across the country. "He didn't care anything about working in the fields," Son House once remarked to a reporter who asked him why Johnson cared so much about music.[15] Robert Johnson's responses to his life choices resembled those of his Mississippi contemporary Charley Patton, who according to Robert Palmer also used the blues to create a life for himself where "he rarely worked for whites except to furnish a night's entertainment, and he was never tied to a menial job or plot of land for very long." Muddy Waters described his own interest in the blues in similar fashion, telling Robert Palmer that he longed to be a preacher, ballplayer or musician because "I al-

ways felt like I could beat plowin' mules, choppin' cotton, and drawin' water. I did all that, and I never did like none of it. Sometimes they'd want us to work Saturday, but they'd look for me, and I'd be *gone*, playin' in some little town or some juke joint."[16]

We can well imagine the labor that awaited Robert Johnson in the cotton fields and timber camps of the Mississippi Delta in the 1930s had he not been able to make a living as a musician. He was humiliated because of both his class and his race in a context where brutal police officers, lynch mobs, and labor exploitation combined to shape the contours of his existence. He may not have met the devil at a crossroads at midnight, but he certainly met the devil every morning at six A.M. when he had to say "Good morning, boss." Leaving home for him was not a romantic venture into the lonely life of the artist, but a way out of the constraints of a racialized class system.

Nothing underscores the desperation of Johnson's life circumstances more than his struggle simply to find a name. The person we gave come to call Robert Johnson was known as Robert Dodds, Little Robert Dusty, Robert Spencer, and R.L. Spencer during different parts of his life, but almost no one knew him as Robert Johnson until he took that name when he started his career as a musician. His many names reflect the precariousness and uncertainty of the life he led.

Johnson's mother, Julia Major Dodds, lived in Hazlehurst with her husband, Charles Dodds, and their ten children in 1909, two years before Robert was born. Charles Dodds provided for his wife and children by laboring on the farm that he owned and by making wicker furniture for sale. In 1909, however, he got into a disagreement with two wealthy white landowners and had to sneak out of town disguised in women's clothing just ahead of a lynch mob eager to punish him for standing up to white people. Dodds escaped to Memphis, where—just in case vigilantes from Hazlehurst came looking for Robert Dodds— he changed his name to Charles Spencer. Julia Dodds sent eight of her children one by one to live with their father in Memphis to protect them from retaliation by local whites, who eventually got her evicted from her land—ostensibly because of delinquent tax payments, but in reality as retribution for Robert Dodds's successful escape. Left with two children, no husband, no land, and no money, Julia Dodds hired out as a farm worker and lived in local labor camps. She met Noah Johnson on a cotton plantation, and their son Robert was born on May 8, 1911.[17]

Julia Dodds persisted in her efforts to reunite with her children and their father in Memphis. Yet even though her husband had himself fathered two children with his mistress from Hazlehurst, he never accepted his wife back because of her liaison with Noah Johnson. He did give in to her wishes in one respect, however, when he allowed Robert to live with him and his other children in Memphis for a few years, starting in 1914. Robert returned to the Delta in 1920 to live with his mother and her new husband, Willie "Dusty" Willis, in Robinsonville. As Robert Palmer notes, "With three different fathers before he was seven, a series of sudden uprootings and a succession of name changes, Robert had a confused and confusing childhood."[18]

Robert Johnson took the name by which he is known to us today only when he started his career as a musician. Even then, commercial considerations rather than bloodlines or voluntary identification most likely determined his decision. Audiences already knew blues singers Lonnie Johnson and Tommy Johnson, and Robert found that it helped him secure jobs when people confused him with the other Johnsons or when he could help their confusion along by encouraging them to think that he was related to Lonnie or Tommy. He introduced himself as "one of the Johnson boys" and claimed that the initials R. L. stood for Robert Lonnie.[19] In the 1920s, Tommy Johnson was telling people that he secured his talents by making a deal with the devil at a crossroads, and it is possible that Robert Johnson saw the commercial advantage in telling the same story about himself.[20]

Commercial considerations shaped Johnson's persona at every stage of his career. He is celebrated as a pure Mississippi blues player, but he actually listened extensively to phonograph records by musicians who played very different styles, including Leroy Carr and Lonnie Johnson. His songs "Malted Milk" and "Drunken Hearted Man" reveal Lonnie Johnson's influence, and "Love in Vain" owes much to Carr. Robert Johnson's "Walkin Blues" came from Son House and James McCoy. The influence of Kokomo Arnold and Peetie Wheatstraw is evident in "Sweet Home Chicago" and "Me and the Devil Blues." Robert Johnson was "perpetually inquisitive about all kinds of music and would probably have perfected an electric, jazz-influenced brand of modern blues had he lived into the 1940s."[21] His artistry was truly exceptional, but he deployed no formal or stylistic devices that were not also common to his fellow Delta blues musicians Charley Patton, Son House, and Skip James.[22]

Romanticist critics might prefer to imagine blues musicians as folk artists outside the culture industry, but in order to survive, much less record, they had to master the codes of commercial culture, even at the local level. The experience of Honeyboy Edwards is instructive and typical. He remembers that "sometimes the man who owned a country store would give us something like a couple of dollars on Saturday afternoon. We'd sit in the back of the store on some oat sacks or corn sacks and play while they sold groceries and whiskey and beer up front, and the people would come in and listen to us and pitch in. In the afternoon or maybe in the evenin' we'd go to a movie theater and play between the movies."[23]

To place in perspective the harm done by romantic myths, we have to explore the origins of African American music and the system of racialized labor out of which it emerged. In *Black Culture, Black Consciousness* Lawrence Levine observes that slaves employed music to send messages to other slaves, sometimes about resistance and running away, but also to shame their fellow workers into working harder and to criticize them for not pulling their weight.[24] Booker T. Washington claimed that slave owners cultivated the singing talents of their chattel because they believed that exceptionally good singers on their plantations could increase productivity.[25] Cosmopolitan contemporary audiences might find Robert Johnson's music refreshingly free of the conventions of commercial culture, but the materials that he used and the spaces open to him for artistic expression never escaped the reach of commerce or the logic of labor exploitation.

Robert Johnson came into this world shortly after a lynch mob drove Charles Dodds out of Hazlehurst, depriving him of his land and his livelihood. The blues singer never knew his biological father, Noah Johnson, and he fought so bitterly with his stepfather, Dusty Willis, that he eventually had to run away from home to play music. His rootlessness and restlessness were legendary. Fellow blues musician Johnny Shines remembers that "you could wake him up anytime and he was ready to go."[26] He wandered all over the United States playing the three-line twelve-bar blues, a hybrid of African and European forms developed in America on the guitar, an instrument that came to the United States from Mexico but had previously migrated from Spain to Mexico and from North Africa to Spain. He turned homelessness into an art and consequently is ripe for appropriation by romanticists who prize people who lose their identities through art, who pursue pleasure and evoke intense emotions, who develop highly individualized and original means of expression, and who live lives that seem to fall outside the bounds of bourgeois society and the world of commercial culture.

Yet all the qualities that seem to qualify the legendary artist Robert Johnson as a romantic hero do not apply to the historical Robert Johnson, whose identity changes had nothing to do with walking away from the security of bourgeois society, whose pursuit of pleasure and emotional intensity compensated for his systematic disenfranchisement as a worker, citizen, and racial subject, whose art had less to do with his own originality than with his mastery of shared social codes and forms of expression, and whose life and art were shaped at every stage by economic and commercial considerations.

Even his celebrated womanizing takes on another cast when we locate it within Johnson's actual life experiences. At the age of eighteen Johnson met and married sixteen-year-old Virginia Travis and lived with her on the Klein plantation near Robinsonville, sharing a cabin with his half-sister and her husband. Their marriage was not destroyed by Robert's lust or wanderlust but by the death of Virginia and her child during childbirth a year into the marriage. During his sojourn near Hazlehurst in 1931, where he supposedly made his deal with the devil, Johnson married an older woman who worked to support him while the young guitarist took lessons from an Alabama-born musician named Ike Zinneman (who claimed to have learned music himself during midnight visits to graveyards). Later, Johnson enjoyed an intimate and ongoing relationship with the mother of his fellow blues musician and pupil, Robert Lockwood, Jr. [27] His death at the hands of a man jealous of his sexual and romantic conquests has long made Johnson a symbol of reckless passion, but his disconnection from stable relationships has to be viewed in the context of the high female mortality, inadequate male wages, and pressures that poverty and racism imposed upon family formation in his era.

It is only at the level of reception and critical commentary that Robert Johnson's life takes on the contours of romanticism. Much of what we encounter about Robert Johnson comes from the ways in which his story can be made to fit another story already in place. This does harm to our understanding of both cultural practices and social relations. As Chris Waterman observes in his important discussion of commercial culture, folk traditions, and critical categories, Charley Patton and Robert Johnson come to represent the quintessential blues players more than someone like Bo Chatmon—"a light-skinned, somewhat finicky teetotaler who dressed in suits, owned a model-T Ford, and developed professional skills such as carpentry and gramophone repairing." Chatmon is simply too complex a personality and an artist to fit the frame through which Johnson is interpreted, but that frame does a disservice to Johnson's identity and history as well. As B. B. King notes about blues critics, "The scholars love to praise the 'pure' blues artists or the ones, like Robert Johnson, who died young and represented tragedy. It angers me how scholars associate the blues strictly with tragedy."[28]

None of this is to deny the astounding artistry of Robert Johnson, nor would it make sense to downplay the importance of the crossroads story when it is properly and carefully understood. But it is to warn against a kind of romanticism that looks so hard for individuality, emotion, and an aesthetic rendering of social pain that it overlooks the collective, material, and political dimensions of our lives. All art entails understanding the world as it appears to others; identification with others and their experiences is what enables art to exist. As Mikhail Bakhtin observes, culture is always dialogic and the "word" always half belongs to someone else. But if we are going to be honest about the words we share—and the worlds we share—we have to face the harsh facts that divide us as well as the fond hopes that might one day unite us. Romanticism gives us a wishbone, but combating racism requires us to display some backbone.

Visual artist Renee Stout offers an alternative way of receiving the art and life of Robert Johnson that uses what we can learn from our own experiences and from those of others without colonizing their pain for our own pleasure. Her installation "Dear Robert, I'll Meet You at the Crossroads" engages with Johnson's life and legend playfully, recreating a Depression-era juke joint, the furnishings in Johnson's living room, and a "man trap" featuring a pair of red shoes and see-through fabric that Stout hopes will entice Johnson and capture his love. Yet she plays with the romantic legends about the blues singer as well, placing teethlike spikes around the frame of the bed. Stout uses Johnson as a foil for her own strong identity, confiding, "God put me on the planet to challenge a man like that! So, it is like trying to tame that man and by doing this work on him, I am trying to understand all the power he had over women. . . . In a sense I'm relating him to my father, who tried to mold me into a woman who would listen to a man. He used to tell me, all your boyfriends are going to be henpecked, and I said, so what?"[29] Stout challenges Johnson and promises to heal him at the same time, offering a letter from Madame Ching, a fictional healer, with a suggested cure for the ailment described in Johnson's song "Dead Shrimp Blues"—male impotence caused by worry about an unfaithful spouse.

It is fitting and appropriate that Robert Johnson's encounter at the crossroads inspires Renee Stout, an artist whose extensive engagement with African artistic traditions informs all of her creations and infuses them with a strong sense of moral critique, intellectual complexity, and historical connection. Her figures, constructions, and assemblages deploy Kongo cosmograms, *minkisi* bags, fetishes, *minkondi* figures, and ceremonial mirrors in imaginative and innovative ways, mixing traditional African signs and symbols with contemporary North American cultural concerns and forms of expression. Unlike other artists who have turned to Africa for images and inspiration (Picasso, Brancusi, and the early Aaron Douglas, for example), Stout does more than appropriate designs and decoration. She explores the complex totality of art as a social practice in Africa—as religion, medicine, and philosophy, as well as ornamentation. Yet Stout does not pretend to be a traditional Kongo artist making fetishes for spiritual and practical purposes, but appropriately presents herself as someone who adapts African practices to African American realities.[30]

Her work displays both connection and separation from Africa; it exudes a rooted independence, using African beliefs and practices as a baseline reality for playful and provocative interventions designed to show how place and space, objects and images, all interact to mediate relations among people in the modern world. She returns to the past in order to engage the present; she displays images that might seem exotic and far away at first, only to reveal through them regimes of power, exploitation, and silencing that are very close to home. As Michael D. Harris observes, "[W]hen an artist like Renee Stout examines a particular African object and its context, he or she may find meanings and functions that already are familiar because its form, logic, or function are echoed or resembled in African-American cultural expression."[31]

In her strategic redeployment of the African past as an enduring part of the African American present, Renee Stout expresses what Paul Gilroy has described as "diasporic intimacy"—the ability of displaced Africans and their descendants to perpetuate African beliefs, values, and ideas in often hostile environments.[32] Diasporic intimacy enabled enslaved Africans in the American South to keep alive memories of the continent they came from through a wide range of covert and overt practices. They gathered for secret night meetings in remote corners of plantations to chant songs around overturned pots in the African manner. They buried their dead facing east, toward their homelands. They danced the "ring shout," moving slowly counterclockwise in circles that contained cosmic moral significance for them. They peppered their speech with African words and made music based on the West African pentatonic scale rather than on the European diatonic scale.[33] In the face of the most brutal forms of repression and the most sinister measures of surveillance, they kept part of Africa alive in America. African retentions helped them understand their captivity as a crime; it encouraged them to resist the European American ideology that defamed them as less than human, that attributed their subordination to their own nature rather than to the historical actions of their oppressors.

Denied their native languages, forbidden literacy, and prevented by law from defending themselves from beatings and whippings, American slaves turned to elements of African culture as a crucible of covert resistance, as a way of undermining the domination of white supremacy in America. But the retention and reinvention of African forms in America necessitated perpetual struggle. Ex-slave Ben Sullivan identified part of a much larger process when he told an interviewer from the Works Progress Administration's Federal Writers Project on the American Slave in the 1930s his memories of an incident during slavery times: "Old man Okra said he wanted a place like he had in Africa, so he built himself a hut, but Master made him pull it down. He said he didn't want an African hut on his place."[34] After emancipation ex-slaves and their descendants continued that struggle. They built shotgun houses that resembled dwellings in West Africa and protected their dwellings through a variety of traditional practices from their home continent—placing mirrors on outside walls, setting ceramic jars on both sides of front doors, ringing yards with whitewashed stones, and decorating inside walls with dynamic script called "spirit writing."[35] But their links to Africa were not limited to the physical presence of African objects. As Charles Joyner argues, even when slaves and free blacks found themselves dependent upon European or American tools and artifacts, they put them to use in distinctly African fashion.[36] Although rarely acknowledged or accepted by the dominant culture, Africanisms in American society have shaped the mind and spirit of black Americans, and, in turn, their cultural expressions have informed the basic vocabulary of most American music, dance, speech, style, and visual imagery.[37]

The struggle continues today. Many Americans still don't want an African hut in their country. They understand that the unity forged through the possessive investment in whiteness depends upon the erasure—or at least the eclipse—of the African, Asian, Latin American, and Native American pasts. Critics of Afrocentrism and multiculturalism deny, deride, and denigrate claims of enduring African contributions to American culture. Their vehemence makes Renee Stout's acknowledgment and celebration of the African presence in America that much more important, not just for what she has to say about Africa, but for demonstrating that the aspects of our identity tied to ethnic affiliations do not have to produce prejudice and parochialism but can offer us independence rooted in knowledge, enabling us to see things both from close up and from far away.

In his 1991 best-selling book, *The Disuniting of America: Reflections on a Multicultural Society,* Pulitzer Prize–winning historian Arthur Schlesinger, Jr., condemned efforts by educators to explore the connections between African Americans and the culture of the African continent. Denouncing "Afrocentric" education as part of a "cult of ethnicity" designed to "protect, promote, and perpetuate separate ethnic and racial communities," Schlesinger claimed that "it is hard to see what living connection exists between American blacks today and their heterogeneous West African ancestors three centuries ago." He concedes that "[f]rom time to time, black leaders, notably Martin Delany in the mid-nineteenth century and Marcus Garvey in the 1920s, excited passing interest in Africa," but he nonetheless maintains that "until very recent times, few black Americans have regarded the African connection as a major theme in their lives." Moreover, he charges that "American Afrocentrism" is a recent and "invented" tradition whose advocates operate from chauvinist and even racist motivations based on "the theory that race determines mentality."[38]

It is hard to imagine a historian being any less historical about the role of Africa in America; Schlesinger's argument displays ignorance of the historical record in nearly every respect.[39] Extensive research over the last three decades has consistently confirmed the judgment that Carter G. Woodson offered back in the 1920s, that "what the Negro accomplished in Africa was not lost. His art tended to revive in the slave on the American plantation. It appeared in the tasks, proverbs, and riddles of the plantation Negroes. The tribal chants of the African paved the way for the spirituals, the religious expression of the slave."[40] Following Woodson's analysis, we know that not just the spirituals, but the blues as well derived from Africa—from the AAB three-line form of West African poetry, from the antiphony, pitch changes, and "impure" tones of African musical systems, and from the ways the dynamic tensions between European diatonic and African pentatonic scales produce flatted fifths, thirds, and sevenths in blues music.[41]

Although comments from two distinguished and apparently equally uninformed historians appear on the back cover of Schlesinger's book (C. Vann Woodward called the work "brilliant" and John Morton Blum found it "learned, persuasive, and sound"), most knowledgeable reviewers have deemed Schlesinger's argument seriously deficient. Lawrence Levine, an expert on African American culture, singled it out for an especially devastating critique in his presidential address to the Organization of American Historians.[42] But although Schlesinger's book failed as a historical argument, it proved a public relations success, largely because of the support it received from individuals and institutions with a stake in its ideology. *The Disuniting of America* was originally commissioned and published by the Whittle Corporation, a purportedly education-oriented business that started Channel One: the corporation that donates television equipment to schools in return for the exclusive right to program into classrooms light feature stories bracketed by noisy commercials for candy and soda. The Time-Warner conglomerate held a financial interest in Channel One, and that company's *Time* magazine gave extensive publicity to Schlesinger's book, including a cover story in the July 8, 1991, issue that featured an excerpt from it.[43]

When one of the nation's most powerful multimedia conglomerates joins forces with an influential and politically connected educational entrepreneur and a Pulitzer Prize–winning historian to ridicule claims about the influence of Africa in America, the evidence supporting those claims in Renee Stout's work takes on enormous significance. Even more important than the physical and ethical proof that pervades her art, Stout's self-reflexive disclosures about her own processes of creation reveal the power and depth of organic popular traditions, community art institutions, and private family memories in nurturing and sustaining African imagery, icons, and ideas in America. Moreover, the compelling moral vision that arises from her work bears no resemblance to the parochial prejudice and "racism" that Schlesinger sees at the root of African American interest in Africa. Instead, Stout encourages an open-minded engagement with all cultures.

Her interest in the sense of separation and loss within the African diaspora leads Stout to an empathetic identification with the experiences of immigrants to America from Europe, Asia, Central America, and Haiti. Her honest explorations into her own family's history lead her on a quest to reconnect with the African past, but they also enable her to claim Native American and Irish ancestry. "They are all part of my heritage and influence my work," she affirms.[44] The pluralism and panethnic antiracism of Renee Stout's art and worldview are hardly inhibited by her interest in Africa and the Caribbean. On the contrary, her grounding in African forms and philosophies connects her to powerful traditions of social justice and moral critique capable of generating interest, concern, and attachment from many different kinds of people.

Growing up in the working-class East Liberty section of Pittsburgh, Pennsylvania, Stout encountered diverse forms of art and artisanship through that city's established cultural institutions as well as through informal cultural activities in her home and neighborhood . Saturday morning art classes at the Carnegie Museum exposed her to the institution's natural history and art collections. A display of shrunken heads from South America and a Central African *nkisi nkondi* figure made especially strong impressions on Stout, inspiring some of her later work.[45] Even today when she returns to Pittsburgh to visit with family and friends, she often returns to the *nkisi nkondi* in the Carnegie Museum "because I feel like I'm coming back with a little more knowledge each time."[46] She learned about a wide variety of artistic practices and traditions from her everyday life experiences as well. Stout's father worked as a mechanic, and her grandfather labored in a steel mill. They displayed pride in their skills as artisans and offered her important lessons in economy and ingenuity by never throwing anything out and by using all available resources in their work. Her grandfather also played music, providing her with important lessons about intercultural communication when he frequently entertained an interracial crowd of friends and neighbors at his home on summer evenings.[47] These early experiences shaped Stout's disposition toward music as another artistic, religious, and even medical practice—a way of understanding, experiencing, and perhaps even healing the world.

Stout also received artistic instruction and inspiration at home from her mother's brother, whose passion for painting was not diminished by a dearth of resources—he painted on any available spare surface, even the lids of shoe boxes when necessary.[48] Just as her classes at the Carnegie Museum started Stout on the road toward representations based on African imagery and icons, her family's ways of working as artisans and artists set the stage for her subsequent success with sculpture and assemblages made up of everyday items and found objects, including an ironing board, sardine cans, slippers, and a mousetrap.[49]

African practices influenced Stout in indirect ways when she was growing up, although she did not recognize or understand their full significance until later in life. For example, she remembers being fascinated by an old house on Renfrew Street in East Liberty because the woman who lived there filled the yard with dolls, stuffed animals, and a scarecrow—all mounted on poles. Only later did she learn of the close correspondence between this African American yard art and traditional West African practices. As art historian Robert Farris Thompson reminds us, yard art provides "an alternative classical tradition" for black artists, serving as "an invisible academy, reminding them who they are and where they come from."[50] She returned to Pittsburgh in 1980 to photograph the dressed figures in front of the house on Renfrew Street as part of her ongoing effort to incorporate physical artifacts from her life into her assemblages.[51] Once Stout became conscious of the African presence in her life, she began to recognize how pervasive it had been. While working on a 1992 installation at Woodlawn Cemetery in New York, Stout learned from her grandmother of a relative who died at a time when the family had no money for a headstone. "My mother took this jar and put things all over it," her grandmother remembered. Like many other African Americans, Stout's family had commemorated their dead in an African way, placing broken objects, household containers, and personal objects on the grave to mark and heal the rupture created by death. Later, during a trip home to Pittsburgh, Stout stopped at a pharmacy that she had been to many times before in Homewood, a mostly African American neighborhood. She noticed a collection of products designed for natural healing according to African and African American folk practices. "I didn't know that when you go to the back in the corner you have roots and oils, and it was there all along," she recalls. "And I didn't know until I knew what to look for."[52] Yet once she knew what to look for, African items and icons appeared all around her.

On a visit to California in 1986, she noticed newspapers covering the interior walls of a black woman's home and recognized their connection to African "protective print" and "spirit writing."[53] The Mande people in Africa, among others, placed religious writing inside leather charms. They brought the African-Islamic belief in the protective power of the written word with them to America. Throughout the southern United States, black people often placed newsprint on walls and in shoes, or left the Bible open at night as a continuation of African ways in America.[54]

Awareness of these influences on her life has enabled Renee Stout to incorporate African objects and artifacts into her visual images in imaginative and original ways. Protective writing decorates the mixed-media piece "Instructions and Provisions/Wake Me Up on Judgment Day."[55] Her celebrated "Fetish #2" comprises a cast of her own body in plaster layered with black paint and decorated with cowrie shells, parts of her deceased grandfather's watch, braided hair extensions, a pelt of monkey hair, medicine bags, dried flowers, a photograph of a baby, and a postal stamp from Africa. In this work, Stout presents herself as a Zairean *nkisi* figure decorated with objects of magic and power, including a mirrored back panel to suggest the necessity of "seeing beyond the visible."[56] The mixed-media assemblage "She Kept Her Conjuring Table Very Neat" combines ceremonial candles, roots, bones, beaded slippers, and a photograph of Colonel Frank, a semifictional character who often appears in her work along with his love interest, Dorothy.[57]

In "Ancestral Power Object" Stout presents a standing figure resembling an African nail fetish decorated with pins, jewelry, and her own fingerprints, among other items. Embellished with the names of Haitian and Yoruba deities, mysterious protective writing, the year of her own birth and that of her maternal grandmother, and a stamp from the Belgian Congo, this mixed-media work expresses Stout's figurative and literal "correspondence" (the postal stamp) with African ideas and arts. Stout mixes dirt and pebbles from West Africa with African American grave dirt as a means of "symbolically putting the whole back together again." She displays an incomplete circle on the front panel of her "Ancestral Power Object" to express "the incomplete destiny and development of the African American people."[58] Here she deploys an old metaphor in a new way. The circle has long been a powerful generative concept in African American life and culture, as Sterling Stuckey's singularly important research on the "ring shout" demonstrates. The counter-clockwise circle of the ring shout imported from "the Congo" (Angola) became the crucible of moral uplift and political instruction for generations of black people in slavery and in freedom. While generated in African American communities and serving critical functions for them, the semiotics of the circle articulated values and beliefs important to all people. As Stuckey shows, when black intellectuals (including W.E.B. Du Bois, Henry Highland Garnet, and Paul Robeson) applied the lessons taught them by the ring shout about solidarity across generations, national borders, and colors, they articulated a humane and egalitarian vision that educated and inspired people from all backgrounds.[59]

In similar fashion, the art of Renee Stout draws powerfully upon African American traditions and her own history. It uses personal and community knowledge to address the problems of a wider world. For example, her penchant for working with ordinary objects has meaning for Stout not simply because they reflect the traditions of her family and her ethnic group, but because they offer instruction for dealing with inequality and injustice. "When I look at society," she explains, "I see the emphasis on money and material things. Everyone is bogged down in competition. The reason I use found objects in my art is to say to everyone, 'Use what you have and be positive, whatever it is that you have, try to make something good from it.' My relatives were always able to make any situation elegant or wonderful. They made 'home' a very secure and nourishing place physically and spiritually." Within her own art, the use of found objects offers her a chance to exercise some control over her own environment. "I realized that I was taking objects from a painfully cruel environment and trying to turn them into something positive by creating with them," she says.[60]

Because she knows her own culture and its struggles so well, Stout finds herself especially appreciative of the spiritual, cultural, and political struggles of others. Discussing her use of images from Native American, Mexican, and Haitian folk traditions, she confesses, "I'm attracted to spiritual societies. . . . It [spirituality] seems like a means of survival in a world that you can't always understand." Her work on the African diaspora has honed her sensitivity to the experiences of immigrants to America from other parts of the world. She expresses particular concern about "how some people who have come to this country have had to change their whole way of thinking and identity in order to be accepted, even though they'll never be fully accepted. It is a hard thing to think about. Even though you tried and adapted to the ways of the existing culture, you are never going to be accepted. So, maybe it is not a good idea to throw away your old beliefs and ideas, maybe you should still hold onto them. I want people to think about those [people of other] cultures who come to the United States and have to totally change who they are. It is so unfair."[61]

Contrary to Arthur Schlesinger's assumption that contemporary interest in Africa evidences "the virus of tribalism" and "a cult of ethnicity" mandating ethnic and racial separation, Stout's engagement with African art expresses understanding of the important inflection that the African presence has always given to American society and culture. Rather than leading to racism or ethnic separatism, her art uses the situated knowledge emerging from the African American experience to illuminate broader truths and to imagine ways of branching out so that all people can draw on useful traditions from all cultures, a purpose Stout has articulated:

> I can't understand why people are trying to melt everything down, when what actually makes America interesting is the fact that no one originated here except the Native Americans. You have all these wonderful different flavors going into making this one great whole. I don't understand why people are fighting against that. Why is it that people cannot tolerate differences? I think that if people in America could open themselves up to all the different nationalities and customs that we have right here in this country, it would make every individual more worldly without even having to travel. We have so much right here that people are not taking advantage of.[62]

Her comments may be motivated as much by tactical as by philosophical concerns; with reactionary nationalists around the world seeking foundational certainty in mythologies of pure, discrete, and unified cultural origins for their ethnic or national group, Stout argues for creative responses to contradictions, ruptures, and fissures. Her art displays a clear concern for how difficult it will be to appreciate these "wonderful different flavors" when our histories leave us with unequal access to resources, wealth, and life chances—much less to the mechanisms of cultural expression and their distribution.

Renee Stout's engagement with African aesthetics and ideologies continues a long tradition among African American artisans and artists. The Mississippi-born rhythm-and-blues musician Ellas McDaniel touched on these links when he adopted the stage name Bo Diddley, naming himself for the diddley bow, a one-string instrument of African origin.[63] Like Stout, he turned to African culture and its uses among African Americans to create an identity and an artistic practice capable of changing the ways people experience their lives. Stout's interest in Robert Johnson's music and life complements perfectly her concentration on objects associated with healing, on devices designed to make life better.

Stout draws directly on a broad range of popular African practices surviving in the United States through diverse forms of vernacular artistic expression; but she also builds on a legacy of struggle by important individuals and community institutions that have insisted on a conscious connection between Africa and America. Her work is reminiscent of that of Henry O. Tanner, who began to select African Americans as the subjects of his genre paintings shortly after he appeared before the week-long Congress of Africa symposium at the 1894 Chicago World's Fair.[64] Stout follows in the tradition established by the Hampton Institute when it acquired one of the first collections of African art in North America at the turn of the century, largely through the efforts of that school's alumnus William H. Sheppard, who collected art in what later became the nation of Zaire between 1890 and 1910. Throughout the twentieth century, art historians and artists such as James A. Porter, R. O'Hara Lanier, and John Biggers, working at historically black institutions, have been in the vanguard of knowledge about and respect for the relationship between African and African American art.[65] Similarly, during the Harlem Renaissance Alain Locke asked his fellow intellectuals to explore and emphasize the African origins of their art.

The American interest in African art is neither recent nor symbolic; it is a product of the ways in which the history of the United States is organically linked to the history of the rest of the world. In the art of Renee Stout, it reaches new levels of complexity, depth, and imagination. Stout offers us an art as complicated and challenging as our history, an art with great affective power that nonetheless brings us face to face with the social relations that divide and unite us. Anyone open to acknowledging and appreciating the African presence can derive great wisdom and enjoyment from her images. Alarmists like Arthur Schlesinger may continue to resist the many things that the African presence in America can teach all of us, but as Ellas McDaniel might say, they don't know diddley. Whether in Renee Stout's art or in Robert Johnson's music, the African influences in America contain intellectual, aesthetic, and spiritual meanings important to all people.

CHAPTER 7

Lean on Me: Beyond Identity Politics

Once the victim's testimony is delivered, however, there is thereafter, forever, a witness somewhere: which is an irreducible inconvenience for the makers and shakers and accomplices of this world. These run together, in packs, and corroborate each other. They cannot bear the judgment in the eyes of the people whom they intend to hold in bondage forever, and who know more about them than their lovers.

—JAMES BALDWIN

In making the motion picture *Lean on Me* in 1989, director John Avildsen interrupted his *Karate Kid* series to turn his attention temporarily toward education. Defying skeptics who charged that he would probably keep making *Karate Kid* films until someone drove a stake through his heart, the director of *Rocky* presented a depiction of the adventures of an inner-city high school principal in a film that offered viewers a cross between *To Sir with Love* and *The Terminator.* Television and newspaper advertisements for *Lean on Me* boasted that the film told the story of a "real life" hero—Joe Clark, the African American principal of Eastside High School in Paterson, New Jersey. But Joe Clark is no hero. He exemplifies a new kind of cowardice, not a new kind of heroism. By celebrating his actions, this film expresses nothing that is new, just a very old and very destructive form of racism.

I have a personal connection to this film and to the situations it depicts. I grew up in Paterson and attended Eastside High School, graduating in 1964. Even then, Paterson was a dying industrial city plagued by high rates of poverty and unemployment. Half my high school class dropped out before graduation; five of the minority and white working-class students who graduated were killed in the Vietnam War. During the summer after our graduation, frustrated and angry black youths staged a civil insurrection in Paterson, setting fire to ghetto buildings and assaulting police officers and civilians with rocks, bottles, and sniper fire. A feature story in the *New York Times* commenting on the disturbance described Paterson as "a burned out inferno of crippled factories and wasted lives."

Growing up in Paterson during those years offered a young person an education inside and outside of the classroom. In a school whose population was divided among whites, blacks, and Puerto Ricans, racial tensions permeated every interaction. We knew that no matter what group we belonged to, somebody hated us. People could get jumped, robbed, and maybe even killed simply for being in the wrong place at the wrong time. Yet we also learned to deal with differences, to make friends with people from all backgrounds, to recognize the things we had in common and the things that divided us.

Ten percent of my class went on to college, mostly those who came from comfortable middle-class homes like my own. We had known all our lives that we would get college educations. Regardless of how hard we worked or how well or poorly we performed as students, our parents' aspirations, intentions, and material support would see to it that we went to college somewhere. At the same time, most of our classmates knew that for them higher education was out of the question, that no matter how hard they worked or how well they performed in school, their futures almost certainly lay in low-wage jobs in Paterson's declining industrial sector. Soon, even those jobs disappeared. My classmates and I went to school in the same building and seemed to receive the same education, but there was a big difference between those whose class and race made it seem natural and necessary to take college prep courses and those channeled into business and vocational tracks who faced, at best, a future of low-paid labor.

During the years that I attended Eastside, my father served as the principal of Central High, a school with an even larger minority population and dropout rate than Eastside's at that time. My father was a gentle and generous man who cared deeply about the students in his school. He could be a strict disciplinarian when he had to be, but he knew that a positive self-image and a sense of social connection could motivate students more effectively and more permanently than punishment. He befriended the students in his school who had behavior problems, learning their names and inquiring about their interests. He helped them with personal and family problems and worked tirelessly to help them secure employment so they could experience the responsibilities, respect, and sense of purpose that a job can bring to a young person. He turned the schools he ran into community centers, involved parents in the educational process, and fashioned after-school and evening programs that spoke to the broader needs of the neighborhood and the city.

My father and my mother had both attended Paterson's public schools in their childhood years. As children of immigrant parents they felt that they owed a great debt to the United States for many reasons, but most of all because of the education they received and the ways in which it encouraged, nurtured, and sustained their growth as critical, contemplative, and creative people and citizens. They knew that had their families remained in Europe, they would certainly have been sent to Hitler's concentration camps. That realization left them with a strong sense of social justice and an empathy for all oppressed people, not just their fellow Jews. My mother and father became teachers to repay they debt they felt they owed to this country, to give to others the great gifts that they had received. After my father died from a heart attack at the age of forty-nine during my senior year in high school in 1964, my family remained involved in public education in Paterson. My sister and my mother both taught at Eastside at different times during the 1960s and 1970s and established reputations as the kind of demanding and dedicated instructor that students remember long after their school years have been completed. Over the years, I have learned a great deal about what it means to try to offer a quality education in an inner-city school from them. My father, my mother, my sister, and many of their colleagues and friends have devoted much of their lives to that effort. I know how hard a job they have, how much patience and love it takes to try to neutralize the effects of poverty and racism even temporarily. I know as well that no amount of good intentions, no mastery of teaching techniques, and no degree of effort by individual educators can alter meaningfully the fundamentally unequal distribution of resources and opportunities in this society.

Neither the true history of Paterson's economic decline nor the actual conditions facing its educators appear in *Lean on Me*. Instead, the director of *Rocky* and *The Karate Kid* presents us with another kind of fairy tale, a story about how serious social problems can be solved simply by reciting rules, how challenges to public order by women and members of aggrieved racial minorities can be quelled by male heroes strong enough and determined enough to bully and intimidate their opponents. This glorification of a small-time demagogue and grandstander ignores the structural problems facing cities like Paterson, the realities of unequal funding for schools, or the health and nutrition problems of more and more children growing up in poverty.

Joe Clark rose to public prominence during the mid-1980s as part of a co-ordinated campaign by neoconservatives to hide from the consequences of their own actions in cutting social programs and educational opportunities during the Reagan years. A favorite of right-wing foundations and their educational spokesperson William Bennett, Clark blamed liberals and the civil rights movement for the sorry state of inner-city schools. He offered his own record as an administrator who ruled with an iron hand as a model for improving the schools without spending any more money on education. He called Reverend Jesse Jackson "a constipated maggot" and claimed that young black men were "barbarians who are out of control."[1] He became famous among conservatives because he patrolled Eastside High School carrying a baseball bat and a bull-horn, behavior that titillated neoconservative politicians and public relations flacks with the dream of enlisting blacks (whom they had already demonized as brutal) in a campaign of counterinsurgency against unruly inner-city minority youths. Although Clark has never developed any following in or connection with African American communities, his ability to enact white fantasies have made him a favorite among what James Baldwin called "the makers and shakers and accomplices of this world."

Lean on Me opens with a montage that portrays the predominately black students and staff of Eastside High School as lazy, licentious, boisterous, and brutal. With stereotypical caricatures that hearken back to nineteenth-century minstrel shows and D. W. Griffith's 1915 white supremacist film, *The Birth of a Nation,* Avildsen raises the specter of out-of-control black bodies to set the stage for his authoritarian black hero. *Lean on Me* glamorizes the way Clark resorts to physical intimidation and verbal abuse to make teachers, parents, and students knuckle under to law and order as he defines them. The film attributes the demise of discipline in Eastside High School to the control over school policy won by black female parents and teachers as a result of the civil rights movement of the 1960s. Like *The Birth of a Nation,* it summons up authoritarian patriarchal power as the necessary antidote to a broad range of misbehavior by blacks, ranging from lascivious attacks on white women to the laziness of public employees, from the uninhibited speech and body movements of black teenagers to brutal assaults on white authority figures and on "innocent" fellow blacks. Fusing elements of previous high school disruption films with the theme of the lone vigilante, Avildsen's motion picture displays no awareness of the aspirations, experiences, or feelings of students, parents, and teachers, much less any acknowledgment of the actual social conditions they confront.

As principal of Eastside High School, Clark illegally expelled large numbers of students from school on the grounds that he viewed them as troublemakers. He fueled fights between teacher and parent factions and—most important for his cinematic image—roamed the halls of his school carrying a baseball bat in order to threaten unruly students. These actions won praise from neoconservative pundits, but they did nothing to solve the educational problems facing the school and its students. Clark failed to lower the dropout rate, to improve academic performance, or to raise scores on standardized tests. Instead, his incessant self-promotion exacted serious costs on the school, which eventually became clear even to his patrons in conservative foundations.

Clark took a "sick leave" from his $65,000 a year principal's job so that he could continue to collect his salary while he toured the country giving lectures to conservative groups at $7,000 per appearance. He was in Los Angeles preparing to appear on the Arsenio Hall show when a musical act hired for an Eastside High School assembly featured several G-string clad male dancers. Clark declared himself innocent of any failure to supervise his school, blaming the whole affair on "the essence of some kind of surreptitious act" and in the process offering his students a negative lesson in taking responsibility for one's actions.[2] He sought appointment to an unexpired term on the Board of Freeholders in Essex County (about ten miles from Paterson), explaining that he needed experience in an administrative office as preparation for running for national office; "I'm not going to be a Jesse Jackson," he declared, referring to questions about the civil rights leader's lack of administrative experience during his 1984 and 1988 campaigns for the presidency. Clark turned his leave of absence into an extended audition for more support from conservative foundations, avoiding the actual work of running a school so that he could pontificate about education and pursue more lucrative and less taxing employment as a full-time speaker.

When his year on leave expired, Clark retired from his post. He filed a workman's compensation claim against the Board of Education, charging that his endocarditis (deterioration of the aortic valve) had been caused by the board's lack of appreciation of his efforts. Clark vowed that the school district "will pay for the damage they inflicted upon my mortal soul."[3] Conservative foundations are not usually supportive of government workers who defy their superiors, expect taxpayers to support them during sick leaves while they rake in thousands of dollars lecturing about their favorite political causes, and then file highly dubious workman's compensation claims; nevertheless, these foundations continued to embrace Clark because of his utility to their efforts to increase the possessive investment in whiteness.

The Joe Clark portrayed in *Lean on Me* gave white audiences one more chance to blame the victim, one more opportunity to believe that the anguish in African American ghettos stems from the underdeveloped character of the poor rather than from routine and systematic inequality in resources and opportunities. Since 1973, when President Nixon abandoned public housing and diverted War on Poverty funds into revenue-sharing schemes designed to lower local taxes on real estate, this country has been systematically exacerbating the crises facing the urban underclass. The value of grants given through the Aid to Dependent Children program fell by one-third from 1969 to 1985 when inflation is taken into account. The 1981 Deficit Reduction Act took away from the poor one dollar of benefits for every dollar earned. Critics charged that these policies would have disastrous effects on poor families and their children, and consequently on the nation's future. Time has shown these critics to be correct.

At the same time, federal policies have fueled a spending spree by and for the rich. Defense boondoggles, insider trading, speculation, hostile takeovers, and profiteering from bad loans have wreaked havoc in the U.S. economy over the past decades, but the taxpayer has always been there to pick up the tab, protecting the savings-and-loan bandits and other corporate looters from the consequences of their own actions. How does a country that has spent most of the past twenty years exploiting its poor children in order to feed the greed of the rich justify itself to itself? How do politicians and public relations flacks who promise to return us to family values explain their participation in the construction of a casino economy that brings an apocalypse on the installment plan to inner-city families? The answer to both questions is to blame the victims, to channel middle-class fears into a sadistic and vindictive crusade that racializes the poor and then blames them for their powerlessness.

The neoconservatism of our time has not only widened the gap between rich and poor, between whites and communities of color, but it has also encouraged the growth of a vigilante mentality, as violent and sadistic as the crime it purports to oppose. From Bernhard Goetz's shooting of four youths on a New York subway car to the Philadelphia Police Department's bombing of MOVE headquarters to the Los Angeles police roundups of fourteen-year-olds in the name of stopping gang violence, we seem to have convinced ourselves that once we have identified our enemies we no longer need to observe the due process of law. Most often invoked in the name of fighting criminality, this attitude instead elevates a criminal mentality to the front lines of social policy. It is an attitude rooted in resentment and fear, exploited by law-and-order politicians and the makers of vigilante films alike.

The problem with this attitude is that it only works as a way to treat someone else—none of us would allow ourselves to be treated in that fashion. Thus,
Joe Clark's belittling and humiliating of his students won audience approval because audiences believed that such treatment would be legitimate and might
work against the faceless "others" in the ghetto that have been created for us by
the media. If they were to think of those students as their own children, they
would never allow anyone to treat them in that fashion. Indeed, the conservative pundits who fawned over Clark did not line up to send their own children
to Eastside High School. Yet, as we have seen over and over again, once the erosion of civil liberties and the diminution of human dignity gets started, it does
not stop with its original victims. As Jesse Jackson warns, there is no way we can
hold the other person down in the dirt without climbing into the dirt ourselves.

In this context, it is not hard to see why there is a major motion picture
about Joe Clark—an honor denied to Septima Clark, Reverend Buck Jones,
Paul Robeson, Fannie Lou Hamer, Ella Baker, and other courageous fighters for
the African American community. Hollywood does not believe that white
American audiences want to see black heroes who love their own communities
and struggle to win resources for them. In Hollywood, there is no room for
adult blacks operating in their own interests, only for black sidekicks or terri-
fied blacks in need of white protection. The prototypical example was Alan
Parker's *Mississippi Burning,* which presented the 1964 civil rights struggle in
Mississippi as if black people played only the role of passive victim. From *The
Birth of a Nation* to *Gone with the Wind,* from *Lean on Me* to *Driving Miss Daisy,*
Hollywood has always preferred its faithful black servants. Joe Clark is only the
latest in a long line of smiling sycophants on- and offscreen, reassuring white
America that it will never have to wake up to its racial record and face its re-
sponsibilities.

Yet *Lean on Me* adds a new and frightening aspect to this traditional scenario. Clark's purported heroism stems from no positive accomplishment. He
does not help his own students nor does he serve as a role model for other educators. His sole function is to fuel the spite, resentment, and rage of the privileged. His mass-mediated image maintains the myth that counterinsurgency
will prevail when justice does not, that schools can succeed by becoming prisons—or more precisely that prisons are more important to society than
schools. In keeping with the neoconservative contempt for public education,
Clark brings the model of the military and the penitentiary to urban education.
It does not matter to his admirers that such behavior cannot develop the intellectual and personal resources necessary for a lifetime of citizenship and work;

what does matter is that it imposes a dictatorial and authoritarian model on the poor and presents people who have problems *as* problems.

In any case, Joe Clark is not the problem, nor does his perspective bear any relation to a solution. Once he has exhausted his usefulness to those in power he will be shoved aside, like so many before him. What will remain long after Joe Clark has been forgotten, however, are the problems of the inner-city schools, and the sadism in search of a story fueled by these kinds of images. As film viewers, we need to ask ourselves how our imaginations are being colonized and for what ends. Perhaps one cannot really blame filmmakers for opportunistically exploiting the racial hatreds and social vindictiveness of the motion picture audience. Hollywood filmmakers are in business to make money, and they have never hidden their willingness to exploit the darkest recesses of the human character to turn a profit for their investors. But at least they could have given this execrable film an appropriate title. In its internal message and social mission, it is not so much *Lean on Me* as *Step on Them.*

None of this is to deny the crippling effects of crime on our society, most of all on the inner city and its inhabitants. Nor is it to assert the irrelevance of discipline, order, self-control, and character for any individual or group. It is only to argue against simplistic and self-serving diagnoses of deep and complex social problems. Locating the origins of white anxieties in the alleged character deficiencies of people from aggrieved racial groups evades an honest engagement with the materialism, selfishness, and predatory competitiveness of *all* social groups in the wake of the changes that neoconservative economics and politics have brought. Nearly every reputable scholarly study shows that unemployment, inferior educational opportunities, and social inequalities are directly linked to increases in crime. People of color have simply been the ones hardest hit by these structural transformations. Declining numbers of blue-collar jobs, capital flight, discrimination by employers in the expanding retail sector of the economy, locating new businesses in suburban locations, residential segregation, and cutbacks in social programs and government employment have all contributed to increased rates of minority unemployment. For example, unemployment among African American youths quadrupled between 1961 and 1986, while white youth unemployment remained static.

It is understandable that fear of crime makes many people wish to respond with a strong show of force against lawbreakers. But force can create as well as restrain criminality. It can teach people that force is the accepted way of controlling others, especially if it is applied indiscriminately against whole populations. Studies show that exposure to boot-camp correctional facilities structured around humiliating disciplinary routines makes inmates more rather than less aggressive. Force is even more counterproductive when used against law-abiding citizens—the vast majority of people in poor and minority communities. Nearly 5 percent of African Americans report that they have been unjustly beaten by police officers, and African Americans are more than nine times as likely to die at the hands of police officers than are whites. Highly publicized cases like the Rodney King beating in Los Angeles and the killing of Jonny Gammage by police officers in Pittsburgh convince a large proportion of minority observers (and many who are not minorities as well) that a code of silence protects police officers from the consequences of their actions against members of aggrieved communities. Of the nearly 47,000 police brutality cases reported to the federal Department of Justice between 1986 and 1992 (not including complaints to municipal, county, and state agencies), only 15,000 were investigated, and only 128 led to prosecution of any kind. Most important, the most sophisticated social scientific studies show that while neither poverty nor racial discrimination alone *cause* crime, aggressive acts of violence are more likely to emanate from people under conditions of poverty, racial discrimination, and inequality. As Judith and Peter Blau observed nearly twenty years ago, "[A]ggressive acts of violence seem to result not so much from lack of advantages as from being taken advantage of."[4]

Fighting crime effectively entails addressing its constituent causes, not indulging in the counterproductive escapism, sermonizing, and muscle flexing advanced in films like *Lean on Me*. Yet while we are waiting for the broad structural solutions that we need, we still must address issues of individual morality, personal accountability, and disrespect for law and order. I propose that we start by strictly enforcing the laws that ban discrimination in housing and hiring, regulate environmental pollution and unsafe working conditions, and guarantee minimum wages, due process, and equal protection of the law to all citizens. In that vein, I suggest swift and certain punishment meted out against one individual who flaunted the law brazenly, who deliberately obstructed justice, and who denied citizens the protections guaranteed to them in the Constitution. In his book *The Color Line,* the great historian John Hope Franklin describes the actions of this individual clearly. Appointed to a post in the Department of Education by the president of the United States, this person refused to investigate complaints about racial and gender discrimination, forcing the plaintiffs to ask that he be placed in contempt of court for his refusal to do what the law required him to do. When asked at a hearing if he was violating the time frames established for civil rights enforcement in *Adams v. Bell,* if he was violating them "on all occasions" and violating them directly on complaints "most of the time" or at least "half of the time," this bureaucrat answered, "That's right." When asked if "meanwhile you are violating a court order rather grievously, aren't you?" he answered yes.

On the strength of this record, this individual was promoted to chair the Equal Employment Opportunity Commission. In the first year at that job, the time needed to process complaints went from five months to nine months. The backlog of unanswered complaints went from 31,000 at the time of his appointment to 61,686 complaints four years later. This performance earned him an appointment to a federal judgeship, where in one case, he refused to recuse himself from a dispute that involved the direct financial interests of his personal and professional patron, instead issuing a ruling that vacated a judgment of $10.4 million against his patron's family-owned business.[5] Perhaps readers can help me locate this malefactor and bring him to justice. His name is Clarence Thomas.

Clarence Thomas and Joe Clark prove that not all white supremacists are white, that white supremacist policies can be pursued by people from all backgrounds. This should come as no surprise; it is the way power works. No oppressed group in history has ever been immune to the opportunism of individuals who long to distance themselves from the stigma associated with their identity and who surmise they will be better off if they work on behalf of their oppressors. At the same time, if not all white supremacists are white, it follows that all whites do not have to be white supremacists.

Just as Joe Clark's blackness did not prevent him from acting on behalf of white supremacy, a white scholar named George Rawick made his life's work exposing and attacking the possessive investment in whiteness. The narrator of Chester Himes's 1940s novel, *If He Hollers Let Him Go,* reflects on the range of identities open to white people when he ruminates on "how you could take two guys from the same place" and "one would carry his whiteness like a loaded stick, ready to bop everybody else in the head with it; and the other guy would just simply be white as if he didn't have anything to do with it and let it go at that."[6] Much of my education about the role whites can play in antiracist activity came from Rawick, an irascible and exasperating individual with many shortcomings and an assortment of personal problems who got one thing absolutely right. He was a white man who knew where he stood in respect to racism. Through his activism and his scholarship he battled white supremacy, not solely out of sympathy for others but out of a sense of social justice and self-respect. The truths that appear in his scholarly writings will never make it onto the big screens of Hollywood, but they have something important to teach us about the role whites can play in fighting against white supremacy.

Born in Brooklyn in 1929, Rawick went to Erasmus High School, where one of his acquaintances was Al Davis, who later became famous for his temper tantrums, paranoia, and indifference to public opinion as the owner of the Oakland Raiders football team. Many of Rawick's friends observed that he often displayed social skills similar to those of his high school classmate. He fought with everyone he knew at one time or another, even his best friends. He could be obstinate, irritating, and rude. He could also be flexible, considerate, and caring. He once described himself as a descendant of radical rabbis and gun-running gangsters, and his professional demeanor displayed evidence of both sensibilities.

Educated in and out of school by trade-union militants, Rawick attended Oberlin College in Ohio after graduating from high school in the mid-1940s. He traveled by train to Ohio, carrying with him radical pamphlets and wearing a zoot suit, fashionable by Brooklyn standards, that provoked considerable consternation in Ohio. Rawick went on to do graduate work at the University of Wisconsin and the University of Chicago, but he remained committed to political work through his involvement with a variety of left-wing splinter groups. Rawick's doctoral research examined New Deal programs aimed at youth, but he became an expert on oral history when the civil rights movement erupted. He realized that his many years of study and critique of U.S. capitalism had left him completely unprepared for the mass mobilization by African Americans and their allies, and consequently he felt compelled to explore other kinds of information and evidence. Moreover, he realized that his formal education had taught him little about the history of racism.

In 1964, C.L.R. James asked Rawick if any materials existed portraying slavery in the United States from the slaves' point of view. Because of his research on the New Deal, Rawick knew about the Works Progress Administration (WPA) slave narratives—transcriptions of interviews with elderly blacks conducted during the 1930s, probing their memories of slavery. His search led him to microfilm records in the Library of Congress, which provided the raw material for a seventeen-volume series that Rawick got Greenwood Press to publish along with an introductory volume of his own, *From Sundown to Sunup,* which explained the significance of the collection. In the first six chapters of his book, Rawick presented an extraordinary history and interpretation of the activity of slaves, demonstrating the dialectical interplay between accommodation and resistance that characterized their existence. The final two chapters laid out an argument about the causes, functions, and contradictions of white racism based on the centrality of slavery to the history of all people in the United States.

Rawick described how "racism took its strongest hold among those people who most thoroughly participated in the new, revolutionary developments of the modern world." He explained how coalitions between white and black workers foundered, not just because of the material advantages that racial segregation brought to whites, but because racism provided an outlet for all the repressed anguish and frustration that workers felt with the transformation from preindustrial to industrial society. He explained that white workers created a debased image of African Americans that filled real needs for them; blacks became a locus of both contempt and envy onto which whites projected their own repressed desires for pleasure and unrestrained free expression. Rawick showed how working -class racism never existed alone, how it emerged out of the hardships and self-hatred imposed on white workers by the humiliating subordinations of class.[7]

I first encountered Rawick in the late 1970s when I was finishing my own dissertation at the University of Wisconsin and working under his supervision as a teaching assistant at the University of Missouri-St. Louis. He suffered from a variety of ailments at the time, including diabetes, and his health was further damaged by his refusal to take proper medication or to attend to other measures necessary to protect his well-being. He was prone to mood shifts and long periods of depression. I saw him give some of the best and some of the worst lectures I ever heard during those two years. Once he placed the War of 1812 in the wrong century (not an easy mistake to make) and depicted it as a conflict between competing approaches to exterminating Native Americans (not necessarily a bad idea, but a nuance that had escaped all previous investigators and that conflicted with nearly all the available evidence). When he completed that lecture he approached me in the back of the hall and asked, "How crazy was that?" I had to admit it was pretty crazy.

When Rawick felt healthy, he came through with well-crafted, entertaining, carefully researched lectures replete with brilliant insights and observations. I noticed that these occasions often depended upon the makeup of his audience. When his listeners included white working-class students or African Americans of any background he seemed to have a special understanding of their lives and to feel a special compulsion to reach them; he became a well-organized, scintillating lecturer capable of connecting the most complicated abstractions to vivid and unforgettable illustrative anecdotes. For me, his examples were always the best part, because they displayed a seemingly limitless understanding of and empathy with the joys and sorrows of working-class life.

George Rawick's lectures and the long conversations that always followed them provided me with an extraordinary education about social identities and social power. They made me aware of the power of conversation and the importance of the specific and the concrete, the legitimacy of personal stories as a way of understanding the world. From them I learned about a vast range of events and ideas, about the contours and contradictions of social movements ranging from the nineteenth-century Knights of Labor to the Missouri sharecroppers' strikes of the late 1930s, from the sectarian Left of the 1940s to the to the countercultures and antiwar mobilizations of the New Left of the 1960s. He told me about demonstrating against the Korean War in 1950 in New York with Bayard Rustin and David Dellinger, about picketing the U.S. embassy during an antiwar demonstration in London in 1967 with Allen Ginsberg and Mick Jagger. It got to the point where I half expected him to come up with a personal memory of everyone he analyzed, including Terence Powderly and Karl Marx. Yet he did have an enormous network of friends and associates with whom he kept in constant touch. They comprised a "who's who" of radical politics; so much so that once when he was running out of money, he decided not to pay his phone bill because he reasoned that the FBI would not tolerate losing the opportunity to eavesdrop on his conversations and consequently would prevent the phone company from discontinuing his service. We could never prove it, but his continued access to telephone service seemed to indicate that he was correct.

Rawick understood that social struggle begins with who people really are, not who we would like them to be; that political contestation takes multiple and varied forms, ranging from religious rituals to popular culture; and that struggle on the factory floor has always been connected to and dependent on struggles in other sites—on plantations and Native American reservations, on street corners and country roads, in high-tech laboratories and libraries. Most important, he understood the connections between the possessive investment in whiteness and the contradictions of the social movements of his time.

Growing up in an ethnic, immigrant working-class neighborhood during the 1930s gave George Rawick firsthand experience with social movements. During that decade the Great Depression overwhelmed the resources of traditional ethnic organizations such as fraternal orders, burial societies, and credit circles that linked ethnic identities to economic interests. The collapse of ethnic institutions came at a time when chain stores and mass marketing created new communities of consumers, when automated production methods broke down skill monopolies among ethnic groups and encouraged the concentration of diverse groups of unskilled and semiskilled workers in common workplaces, and when the emergence of mass organizing drives by the Congress of Industrial Organizations (CIO) drew young workers into what historian Lizabeth Cohen calls "a culture of unity."[8] Simultaneously, the popular front activities of the Communist Party, the cultural programs of the New Deal, and writings by ethnic activists and journalists including Louis Adamic, Langston Hughes, and Jack Conroy emphasized the multicultural origins of the United States. The culture of the 1930s glorified the "common man" and changed the reigning image of the immigrant from the unwanted alien banned by the 1924 Immigration Act into a redemptive outsider who had become American by choice and therefore personified the nation's true spirit. Fiorello La Guardia in New York and Anton Cermak in Chicago attained the office of mayor by pulling together interethnic electoral coalitions that celebrated their diversity. When Cermak's patrician opponent bragged about being part of a family that came over on the Mayflower and implied that his second-generation Czech immigrant opponent (nicknamed "Pushcart Tony") was unfit for high office, Cermak responded that his family might not have come over on the Mayflower, but they got here as fast as they could.[9]

The culture of unity of the 1930s broke down ethnic antagonisms among European Americans and forged a common identity that grew out of mass mobilizations on factory floors and city streets. Participants in the social movements of the 1930s sought and secured real institutional resources to replace the exhausted and inadequate ethnic self-help structures that had let them down when the Depression came. The "culture of unity" won bargaining recognition for industrial workers in mass-production industries, but also social security pensions and survivors' benefits, federally subsidized home loans, National Labor Relations Board protection for collective bargaining industries, federal responsibility for welfare, and other direct social benefits. These resources from the state made European Americans less dependent upon separate ethnic identities, and they helped create the standard of living, the suburban neighborhoods, the workplace opportunities, and the educational subsidies that enabled the children and grandchildren of immigrants to become middle class and to blend together into a "white" identity. Earlier in this book I have pointed out at great length the disastrous consequences that ensued from the ways in which these gains excluded communities of color and created a possessive investment in whiteness, but the gains themselves, the collective struggle for them, and the institutions and resources they provided help explain how unity might be constructed among members of diverse groups.

Although the victories secured by the culture of unity disproportionately benefited whites, the coalitions of the 1930s did cut across color lines. As James Baldwin recalled in 1976, "[I]n a way, we were all niggers in the thirties. I do not know if that really made us more friendly with each other—at bottom, I doubt that, for more would remain of that friendliness today—but it was harder then, and riskier to attempt a separate peace, and benign neglect was not among our possibilities."[10] The perception that a separate peace was dangerous made all the difference in key campaigns in crucial industries for the CIO, as a temporary alliance across racial lines won unprecedented victories. Unfortunately, not all parts of the coalition reaped the fruits of victory to an equal degree.

The CIO needed the cooperation and participation of African American, Mexican American, and Asian American workers to organize mass-production industries, in part because the same discriminatory practices that relegated those groups to dirty unpleasant jobs like foundry work also gave them key roles in production: if the foundry shuts down, the factory cannot run. Historians Robin D. G. Kelley and Vicki Ruiz (among others) present detailed descriptions of the importance of black workers to the organization of the CIO in Alabama and the centrality of Chicanas to organization in the canning industry on the West Coast.[11]

Yet postwar opportunities available to whites separated their interests from those of communities of color. In his provocative and enlightening book *Blackface/White Noise*, Michael Rogin presents an important anecdote that illuminates this general process. He describes a predominately Jewish group of war veterans who participated in a cooperative housing development in the Philadelphia suburb of Abington Township. That area had previously been restricted to white Christians by restrictive covenants, but under pressure from the veterans the new development broke the local barriers against Jewish residency. Yet while experiencing ethnic inclusion, these same veterans practiced racial exclusion, appeasing the anxiety of their new Christian neighbors by agreeing not to open their development to blacks. "We wanted to let Negroes in—they're veterans too," an organizer of the cooperative confessed, "but we've been advised that mortgage investors, unfortunately, will not take Negroes in a mixed project." When some veterans and Jewish activists objected to this bargain, the cooperative's representative stood firm, explaining that "only after every possibility was exhausted did we reluctantly arrive at the conclusion that we must have a 'white' community if we were to have any at all."[12]

Rogin's anecdote encapsulates the process of ethnic inclusion by racial exclusion that transformed the "culture of unity" of the 1930s into the social democratic version of the possessive investment in whiteness during the 1940s, 1950s, and 1960s. Many white immigrants and their descendants developed especially powerful attachments to whiteness because of the ways in which various Americanization programs forced them to assimilate by surrendering all aspects of ethnic organization and identification. As Patricia Williams explains, "Sometimes I wonder how many of our present cultural clashes are the left-over traces of the immigrant wars of the last century and the beginning of this one, how much of our reemerging jingoism is the scar that marks the place where Italian kids were mocked for being too dark-skinned, where Jewish kids were taunted for being Jewish, where poor Irish rushed to hang lace curtains at the window as the first act of climbing the ladder up from social scorn, where Chinese kids were tortured for not speaking good English."[13]

Yet shared experiences in social movements of the 1930s and a lingering concern for social justice helped connect some whites to the civil rights movement of the 1950s and 1960s in ways that called whiteness into question. George Rawick was one of those whites. He later told an interviewer that the politics of the Old Left were destroyed by the suddenness of the civil rights movement's successes. "No one anticipated it," he remembered. "I was fundamentally a racist because I had not thought about it and was challenged by it. Somehow I was convinced that the problem was me and I had to resolve the contradiction."[14]

Reasoning that the fact of exploitation was more important than the identity of the victim, Rawick threw himself into antiracist work in the 1950s and 1960s in both his activism and his academic work. Because he had been part of labor and civil rights groups with black leaders, it was easier for him to envision antiracist coalitions based on what he called the self-activity—the things people do by and for themselves in the face of repressive power—and social analysis of people of color themselves and to reject white paternalistic approaches, which all too often saw racism as a symptom of broader social problems rather than an issue in its own right. His experiences with the slave narratives and his careful reading of Du Bois gave him an advantage over other theorists of whiteness, because he drew upon the sophisticated version of "white studies" developed out of necessity by blacks.

Rawick wrote *From Sundown to Sunup* to reveal the connections between contemporary self-activity among African Americans and the rivers of resistance that could be traced back to the days of slavery. His book not only helped explain the self-activity of the civil rights movement but revealed the importance of work as a crucible for revolt, and illuminated the important lessons that could be learned by all workers from the forms of resistance undertaken by slaves to resist their subordination. He managed an incredibly difficult task— to write about oppression without obscuring resistance, and to write about resistance while acknowledging the terrible price that people pay for not having power. In his concluding chapters, he analyzed how and why racism functions in working-class life, how it enables individuals to externalize elements of self-hatred and self-loathing into contempt and fear of others.

Rawick thought his work was over when his introduction and the first seventeen volumes of the slave narratives came out, but during a speaking engagement at Tougaloo College outside Jackson, Mississippi, a friend suggested that they look in the Mississippi state archives to see if they contained any slave narratives not included in the Library of Congress collection. Five volumes emerged from the search in the Mississippi archives, and Rawick launched an inquiry into similar caches in other libraries and archives in Alabama, Missouri, Indiana, Oklahoma. He immersed himself in the stories told by ordinary people about the ways in which broad structural forces made their presence felt in everyday life. Today libraries all over the country contain dozens of volumes of WPA-collected narratives listed under the title, *The American Slave: A Composite Autobiography*.

Rawick never sought recognition from the main credentialing institutions of our society. No professional honor would ever have pleased him as much as a good conversation with a young worker. A story he often told about himself illustrates the depth of his feeling. Shortly after *From Sundown to Sunup* was published, Rawick boarded a bus in Detroit. To his amazement and delight he noticed a young black worker carrying a copy of his book. At the next stop, two more passengers got on the bus, each carrying a copy of the book. Figuring that this was a trend, he tried to calculate how many thousands of copies the book was selling in Detroit if every busload of passengers represented three copies. When the next stop produced a fourth passenger, with a fourth copy of the book, he began composing remarks for the mass conference of revolutionary workers that he was sure would follow from the success of the book. It was only when he could no longer contain his curiosity and he asked one man carrying the book that Rawick found out he had stumbled onto a black history study group carrying that week's assigned reading. Rawick told the story with self-deprecating humor, but I have always found it significant that the possibility of rank-and-file workers picking up his book meant more to George than all the laudatory reviews and extensive academic sales—indeed, it would have meant more to him than a Pulitzer Prize or a National Book Award.

Rawick also kept himself alert for the hidden possibilities of struggle in even the most conventional arenas. He once lived across the hall from St. Louis Cardinals football players MacArthur Lane and Ernie McMillan. They became symbols for him of the working class, while their boss, Cardinals owner Bill Bidwill, came to represent management. Rawick could describe all the dynamics of the class struggle through the relationship between Bidwill and his players; for him it was another episode in the history of industrial capitalism. When Bidwill turned his factory into a runaway shop and moved the team to Phoenix, following so many other St. Louis industries to the Sun Belt, Rawick was ready with the appropriate critique of management for its squandering of social possibilities. Because of his stories, the whole history of the working class and its connections across racial lines became accessible and tangible to me in new ways; I began to see patterns for the first time.

Of course, Rawick's best gift to all of us has been his writing; not just the slave narratives and *From Sundown to Sunup,* but decades of articles like the important one on self-activity in an early issue of *Radical America* and the ones written under pseudonyms for obscure leftist journals. They all evidence Rawick's abiding faith in the ingenuity and perseverance of the working class. They express his delight in the little symbolic victories with which people keep alive their hopes for a better future. Most of all, they show his capacity to listen to people, to take them seriously, and to fight alongside them rather than commanding or lecturing them into submission. Some people think that such writing is preaching to the already converted, but I think of it more as entertaining the troops, as showing us what we are capable of even under the most dire circumstances, and reminding us how many kindred spirits there have been and continue to be in this world. I know that the things that Rawick has taught me have informed everything I've written about the working class, and I'm sure that Robin D. G. Kelley, David Roediger, Peter Rachleff, Eileen Eagan, Margaret Creel Washington, Stan Weir, Katharine Corbett, Marty Glaberman, and many others would make similar testimonials. Of course that's just the tip of the iceberg; if every historian who lifted an idea from *Sundown to Sunup* had paid Rawick five cents, he would have had enough money to buy the Cardinal football team and move them back to St. Louis with MacArthur Lane as coach.

Hollywood will always prefer stories about the Joe Clarks of this world to stories about people like Fannie Lou Hamer. The true and useful history that George Rawick discovered in the WPA slave narratives will never eclipse the popular exposure given to the destructive lies told in *The Birth of a Nation, Gone with the Wind,* or *Lean on Me.* Neoconservative foundations and mainstream media outlets will always try to hide the possessive investment in whiteness, its causes, and its consequences. The makers of *Rocky* and *The Karate Kid* cannot be expected to understand the WPA slave narratives and the lessons they hold about power and struggle for people from all backgrounds. Gil Scott-Heron used to say that the revolution will not be televised, and we should not expect it to appear in the form of high-budget motion pictures from major studios either. Yet revolutionary potential remains among white people willing to resist racism and to struggle openly against it.

After a series of devastating and paralyzing strokes, George Rawick died in 1990. I miss him very much and wish more people knew how important he was. But I would be a poor student if I did not focus on the main lesson that he tried to bring to our attention. Rawick taught us that fighting racism was everyone's business; that the self-activity of oppressed people holds the key to the emancipation of everybody. For all his personal problems, he understood that white people have an important role to play in antiracist work. Whites cannot free themselves without acting against the poisonous pathologies of white supremacy—both referential and inferential. Anyone can make antiracist proclamations, but antiracist practices come only from coordinated collective action. The rewards offered to people from all races to defend the possessive investment in whiteness are enormous, while the dangers of challenging it are all too evident. But in every era, people emerge to fight for something better. Identifying racism and fighting against it may preclude us from joining the ranks of the makers and shakers and accomplices of this world, but at least it will enable us, in the words of Toni Cade Bambara, "to tell the truth and not get trapped."[15] As W.E.B. Du Bois observed many years ago about the possessive investment in whiteness in his own day, "Such discrimination is morally wrong, politically dangerous, industrially wasteful, and socially silly. It is the duty of whites to stop it, and to do so primarily for their own sakes."[16]

CHAPTER 8

"Swing Low, Sweet Cadillac": Antiblack Racism and White Identity

White children, in the main, and whether they are rich or poor, grow up with a grasp of reality so feeble that they can very accurately be described as deluded—about themselves and the world they live in. . . . The reason for this, at bottom, is that the doctrine of white supremacy, which still controls most white people, is itself a stupendous delusion: but to be born black in America is an immediate, a mortal challenge.—JAMES BALDWIN

People of color have never been merely passive victims of white supremacist power. The active agency of aggrieved communities has always served as an important counterweight to white power. In the process of defending themselves and advancing their own immediate interests, individuals and communities struggling against white supremacy have often created ways of knowing, forms of struggle, and visions of the future important to all people. Even seemingly insignificant cultural expressions often prove to be important reservoirs of collective memory and cultural critique about the possessive investment in whiteness. Scholarly studies of racism in the United States suffer when they fail to recognize the knowledge about social relations contained in music, literature, and folklore, but those scholars who develop respect and understanding for popular ways of knowing can create highly enlightening and important works.

To uninitiated listeners, Dizzy Gillespie's 1959 composition "Swing Low, Sweet Cadillac" might have sounded like a trivial, frivolous, and insignificant communication. In it, Gillespie combined fragments of the spiritual "Swing

Low, Sweet Chariot" with advertising jingles. He mixed jazz improvisation, Afro-Cuban drumming, Yoruba chants, rhythm-and-blues melodies, and quotes from General Douglas MacArthur's famous 1951 farewell speech. Gillespie's lyrics playfully imbued Cadillacs with the reverence that slaves a century earlier reserved for the chariots that they imagined would take them to heaven. He transposed General MacArthur's line "Old soldiers never die, they just fade away" to "Old Cadillacs never die, the finance company just fades them away." Yet for all its inventive contrasts, the humor and the seriousness encoded in "Swing Low, Sweet Cadillac" contained a communication of great significance.

Gillespie's mischievous conflation of divinity with consumer desire in the song brought to the surface the connections between the secular and the sacred in the history of slavery and segregation in the United States. The slaves who sang about chariots coming to carry them home actually had no homes in this world, though their uncompensated labor created comfortable homes for others. Slaves owned no commodities, but their labor made it possible for others to accumulate assets, to ride in fine carriages—while the legal and social systems transformed slaves from human persons to private property. In the ante-bellum period, abolitionists used spirituals like "Swing Low, Sweet Chariot" to remind the public of the slaves' humanity by focusing attention on their faith, on their own assumptions about themselves as people with souls entitled to the fellowship in Christ promised to all by Christianity. Yet after emancipation, as Jon Cruz's innovative research convincingly demonstrates, these same spirituals served fundamentally different purposes. As the slaves themselves turned away from spirituals and hastened to create music appropriate to their new circumstances as free people, folklorists revived the spirituals in a way that portrayed African Americans and their culture as fixed and finite, locating them more in nature than in history, and consequently legitimating as natural, necessary, and inevitable the low-wage labor and political disenfranchisement imposed on blacks by the regimes of white supremacy in the post-Reconstruction era.[1]

Dizzy Gillespie's references to "Swing Low, Sweet Chariot" in "Swing Low, Sweet Cadillac" evoked both of the spiritual's past meanings—as an icon of slaves' desire for escape, salvation, and freedom to be sure, but also as an instrument of racist sentimentality, condescension, and moral evasion. Gillespie's composition contained contradictions that confounded listeners and forced them to consider a number of possible meanings encoded in each part of the song. Most important, its meaning in 1959 depended on the ways it recaptured and reconfigured the past as part of the present. The ingenious and evocative historical references in "Swing Low, Sweet Cadillac" present history, but not the kind that conforms to the aims and standards of what we generally encounter as authoritative historical narratives. These aspire to comprehensive totality; they assert direct causal relations between events, and they encapsulate the diverse experiences of the past in coherent and unified narratives with beginnings, middles, and ends. In Gillespie's song, as in many of the significant communications emanating from aggrieved communities, the past becomes part of the present through genealogical practices that construct a chain of association between different historical moments to bring to the surface the sedimented hurts of history that hold enduring meaning for the present. Through this method, fragments from different historical moments direct our attention to the elements of the past that remain important in the present but that traditional historical narratives may not explain adequately.

For all its references to the past, "Swing Low, Sweet Cadillac" primarily addressed contemporary realities. The song served as a prop for Dizzy Gillespie's parodic campaign for president in the 1964 election. Throughout the early 1960s, Gillespie and his publicists used interviews, liner notes, and live appearances to link jazz music and politics. As he later explained in his memoir *To Be, or Not . . . to Bop*, "It wasn't just a publicity stunt. I made campaign speeches and mobilized people. I meant to see how many votes I could get, really and see how many people thought I'd make a good President. Anybody coulda made a better President than the ones we had in those times, dillydallying about protecting blacks in the exercise of their civil and human rights and carrying on secret wars against people around the world."[2]

In a campaign that predated the passage of the 1964 Civil Rights Act and the 1965 Voting Rights Act, Gillespie attacked the disenfranchisement of black voters and advocated mass boycotts of consumer products as a tactic to bring about radical change. He promised to end the war in Vietnam, extend diplomatic recognition to Communist China, and provide voters with universal free education and health care. Gillespie deployed humor as a weapon in his campaign, proposing to change the name of the White House to the Blues House, vowing to appoint bass player Charles Mingus as minister of peace ("because he'll take a piece of your head faster than anybody I know"), naming band leader and composer Duke Ellington secretary of state (because "he's a natural and can con anyone,"), and designating Malcolm X as his attorney general (because "he's one cat we want on our side").[3] Lampooning the extreme right-wing organization, the John Birch Society, Gillespie asked his followers to join a group bearing his first and middle names—the John Birks Society.

Gillespie advocated the abolition of the Federal Bureau of Investigation and suggested that the Senate Internal Security Committee "investigate everything under white sheets for un-American Activities." One plank of his platform called for the National Labor Relations Board to require everyone applying for jobs to wear sheets over their heads so that the "bosses won't know what they are until after they've been hired." He promised to appoint black prosecutors and judges in the South, proposed deporting Alabama's segregationist governor George Wallace to Vietnam while appointing Mississippi's Ross Barnett to direct the United States Information Agency offices in the Congo. He called for federal subsidies to the arts, including the establishment of civil service nightclubs to provide work for jazz musicians.

The humor of Gillespie's campaign depended, in part, on the conflation of two spheres usually thought of as mutually exclusive—show business and politics—although Ronald Reagan subsequently turned this into a different kind of joke when he proved that show business and politics were not so different after all. As a blend of elements from seemingly disparate spheres, "Swing Low, Sweet Cadillac" made an appropriate icon for the campaign. It displayed the trumpeter's ebullient humor and indisputable artistry magnificently, but it also combined elements of religion, politics, and commercial culture in such a way as to compel an unusual engagement with the politics of the present.

Gillespie's spoof of General MacArthur's farewell speech mocked a sacred icon of anti-Communist conservative politics with its equation of interests of the U.S. nation-state and the wishes of God. The mix of Cuban Santeria chants, Yoruba lyrics, and Latin rhythms referenced another kind of deity, at the same time juxtaposing MacArthur's imperial stance toward dark-skinned people in Asia, Africa, and Latin America and the affinities that might link aggrieved communities of color in the United States to anticolonialist struggles overseas. Gillespie started wearing African robes, hats, and shoes during the campaign "to emphasize that my candidacy meant a more progressive outlook toward Africa and the 'third world' "[4] The contrast in "Swing Low, Sweet Cadillac" between the embodied labor of slaves longing for divine chariots and the "body by Fisher" automobiles (often made by black labor and frequently coveted by black workers as emblems of economic affluence and cultural inclusion) framed the labor and consumer desire of blacks in the 1950s in a historical narrative about the fate of Africans in America over the centuries.

"Swing Low, Sweet Cadillac" transgressed the boundaries that divide the secular and the sacred, making a unified work out of a melange of Afro-American Christian spirituals, Afro-Cuban Santeria chants, jazz improvisation,

dance rhythms, advertising jingles, a political speech, and humor about economic insecurity. It established an irreverent and ironic stance toward sacred
icons of religion, politics, and advertising by locating life in the present within
an expansive historical grid that linked the conditions and concerns of the present to the injustices, oppressions, and artistic practices of the past.

Gillespie's composition and performance also transgressed the boundaries
of cultural categories that confine expressive forms into atomized and mutually
exclusive realms such as folk culture, high culture, and commercial culture.
"Swing Low, Sweet Cadillac" makes use of a religious spiritual that became a
folk song as well as a formal element of high culture (quoted by Dvorak among
others), that employs a modernist form of composition (bebop) to create a
commodity for sale within commercial culture. Consequently, "Swing Low,
Sweet Cadillac" is a commodity that critiques the commodity system while circulating within it.

Gillespie used the iconic status of Cadillacs for both racist and antiracist discourse to explore African American cultural politics and identity in this song.
His composition referenced the frequently voiced white supremacist slur portraying African Americans as impractical and incompetent consumers whose
poverty stems from undisciplined desire and foolish spending on flashy items
like Cadillacs rather than from racist discrimination in hiring, housing, and education. A decade later, Guy Drake scored a country and western hit with "Welfare Cadillac," a song about a welfare recipient with ten children who has never
worked much but always manages to own a brand new Cadillac.[5] Dizzy Gillespie's song, however, registers the ways in which people denied opportunities
to accumulate assets or move up in the world might well covet symbols of status and luxury like Cadillacs, even when their personal circumstances make
such desires impractical and force the "finance company" to haul their dreams
away.

The significance of Gillespie's communication in "Swing Low, Sweet Cadillac" becomes clearer when we see how it functions as an expression of collective memory and resistance within a chain of genealogical signifiers that together testify to the importance of collective memory and ideological critique
in African American culture. These expressions, though not related in a direct
causal way, are part of a shared social language with many points of origin and
many points of connection. Consider, for example, the utility of connecting the
Cadillac in Gillespie's song to another large automobile with significance in the
opening pages of African American author Chester Himes's 1971 autobiography. Himes recalls how his African American family offended their white neigh-

bors in rural Mississippi at the end of World War I by becoming the first owners of the first private automobile in their county. The sight of a black family
riding around in such a modern, expensive, and noisy vehicle (loud enough to
frighten their neighbors' mule teams) outraged white farmers to such a degree
that they got Himes's father fired from his job at Alcorn A&M University and
then forced the family to leave the state. Writing from a distance of more than
fifty years and in the aftermath of civil rights legislation ending de jure segregation, Himes insisted on the relevance of his childhood memory: "I must confess I find white people just the same today, everywhere I have been, if a black
man owns a big and expensive car they will hate him for it."[6]

The historical record reveals some instances that conform closely to Himes's
formulation. For example, in Amite County, Mississippi in 1944, local whites
coveted the 295-acre debt-free farm of black preacher Isaac Simmons. Rumor
had it that oil reserves lay beneath Simmons's land, and white speculators tried
to lay claim to the property. When Reverend Simmons hired an attorney to help
him protect his property, six white vigilantes attacked the sixty-six-year-old
preacher and his son, Eldridge. They forced the son to watch as they killed the
elder Simmons with three shots in the back; then they beat Eldridge, ordering
him to vacate the land in ten days. When Simmons's friends and family came to
claim the body, they found that all of the preacher's teeth had been knocked out
with a club, his arm broken, and his tongue cut out.[7] "They kept telling me that
my father and I were 'smart niggers' for going to see a lawyer," Eldridge Simmons later recalled.[8]

By translating an idiographic incident into a nomothetic generalization and
professing to find a broad principle at work whenever white people encounter
blacks with big cars, Himes mischievously appropriates the language of social
science to make a dramatic point about the enduring significance of white supremacy in U.S. society. Yet Himes's anecdote adds a new element to our understanding of "Swing Low, Sweet Cadillac." More than materialism and unmediated consumer desire motivates the pursuit of Cadillacs. For the Himes
family's white neighbors, automobile ownership symbolized a degree of status
and success inappropriate for blacks. Under such circumstances, the desire
among blacks to own a luxury automobile entails an implicit challenge to white
norms. At the same time, white opposition to the accumulation of assets by
African Americans has a long history, one manifest in a broad range of private
and public actions, including discrimination in home lending, employment,
and education as well as in racial zoning, restrictive covenants, blockbusting,
racially targeted urban renewal, and vigilante violence against people of color

who move into white neighborhoods. More than low wages or high interest rates make ownership of Cadillacs and other commodities symbolic terrain for African Americans; the obstacles to asset accumulation that they face are part of a structure of racialized power and unequal opportunity that pervades their personal experience but remains practically invisible in historical narratives about citizenship, economics, and power in the United States.

The story about his family's automobile serves as an appropriate introduction to Himes's autobiography, which at every turn emphasizes the unremitting pressures of white racism in the author's life, but his story is that of a person who not only suffers repression but relishes resistance. Immediately after detailing the incident about the family car, Himes concedes that part of the hostility manifested by whites came from his mother's "attitude": "She always carried a pistol on our car rides through the country, and whenever a cracker mule driver reached for his rabbit gun she beat him to the draw and made him drop it."[9] From this we learn that physical force and violence sustain white supremacy, and consequently that armed self-defense serves as an important symbol of resistance, self-activity, and subjectivity among African Americans. The gun that Chester Himes's mother used to defend her automobile and her family's right to own it can be connected to another gun in a narrative by one of Himes's contemporaries, Ralph Ellison.

In an early section of Ellison's *Invisible Man,* the narrator's grandfather calls his son to his side for a deathbed confession. "I never told you," the grandfather relates, "but our life is a war and I have been a traitor all my born days, a spy in the enemy's country ever since I give up my gun back in the Reconstruction. Live with your head in the lion's mouth. I want you to overcome 'em with yesses, undermine 'em with grins, agree 'em to death and destruction, let 'em swoller you till they vomit or bust wide open." With his last breath, the old man instructs his family to "learn it to the younguns."[10]

With his dying words, the narrator's grandfather establishes the disarming of African Americans during Reconstruction as a formative moment in U.S. race relations. Once blacks have given up their guns, they are powerless to resist white supremacy overtly and must resort to covert methods, as spies "in the enemy's country." Like Gillespie and Himes, Ellison identifies a foundational white supremacy in U.S. life and culture underlying surface appearances of progress and change. Yet the historical truth about the betrayal of Reconstruction and the ways it figuratively and literally disarmed African Americans is less important than its enduring legacy—the lies that lurk within the dominant discourses of history and race. In *Invisible Man* an old man who had been "the meekest of men" reveals on his deathbed that his "yesses" and "grins" have been forms of dissembling designed to "agree 'em to death and destruction."

At the same time, however, black people pay a terrible price for not being able to espouse their views directly. The tactics designed to fool the enemy may also fool one's allies and even oneself. For example, Dr. A. Hebert Bledsoe explains to Ellison's narrator why he collaborates with the power of whites in his job as president of a black college: "These white folks have newspapers, magazines, radios, spokesmen to get their ideas across. If they want to tell the world a lie, they can tell it so well that it becomes the truth; and if I tell them that you're lying, they'll tell the world even if you prove you're telling the truth. Because it's the kind of lie they want to hear."[11] Later we learn that Dr. Bledsoe means what he says. The narrator carries what he thinks is a confidential letter of recommendation from Bledsoe to help him secure temporary employment so that he can make enough money to return to school. He discovers that the letter actually says that he has been expelled secretly from the school, and it advises the prospective employer to deny him a job in order to teach him a lesson.

Taken by themselves, these passages from *Invisible Man* or Chester Himes's autobiography can be read as illustrative anecdotes about general problems—about intergenerational relations, family stories, and individual alienation. But when placed in historical context, they disclose a quite specific and quite racialized history with only incidental connection to the more general alienations expressed so often in modern literature. Impediments to asset accumulation are backed up by physical force in these accounts by Himes and Ellison, and the presence or absence of guns makes a difference. But both authors also call our attention to the ways in which dominant discourse prevents us from getting at the truths of historical experience. For Himes, the promises of universal inclusion through participation in market relations and consumption are belied by the practices of racialized exclusion that his family experienced in Mississippi. For Ellison's narrator, the reliance on indirect and covert forms of expression imposed on African Americans by the history of white supremacy makes it hard to discern the truth in any given situation. Moreover, the connection between the defensive lies and dissembling practices of his own community and the larger lies of history becomes evident in the link established by the narrator's grandfather in his deathbed confession with its emphasis on the legacy of Reconstruction.

Another fictional deathbed confession offers a genealogical link between Ellison's *Invisible Man* and the hurts of history that it seeks to address and to adjudicate. The same folklore community that in the postbellum period recontextualized songs like "Swing Low, Sweet Chariot" from emblems of the injustices of slavery into rationalizations for the political disenfranchisement and economic subordination of blacks discovered and disseminated a story popular among African Americans in Washington, D.C., in the 1880s. This story alleged that when George Washington lay on his deathbed, his last words to his friends and family were "Forever keep the niggers down." With only half-disguised amusement, scholars wrote that the story was "accepted as undoubtedly true by many, if not most, of the colored people over a wide area."[12]

The activity of collecting folklore in the nineteenth century often stemmed from paternalistic assumptions about the simplicity and naiveté of ordinary people. Like geographical expeditions, Wild West and minstrel shows, or jungle stories, it offered escapist fantasies about traditional peoples and their cultures as a way of easing the pains of modernity and the alienating self-regulating individualism it encouraged. Through that frame, the story about George Washington's dying wish plays a part in representing black people as nonempirical, superstitious, and gullible. Its possible function as a teaching device encapsulating important parts of the experiences of its authors did not strike the folklorists who collected it. Yet in the wake of the betrayal of Reconstruction, this story suggests a secret covenant at work in U.S. society that might explain the persistence of white supremacy among European Americans whose public affirmations often proclaimed the virtues of equal opportunity.

That wisdom rather than superstition undergirded the folktale about Washington's deathbed advice becomes clear if we make one final genealogical leap to a historical document. A letter written on March 23, 1802, by U.S. Postmaster General Gideon Granger to Georgia senator James Jackson helps us understand the historical roots of Dizzy Gillespie's "Swing Low, Sweet Cadillac," Chester Himes's autobiography, Ralph Ellison's *Invisible Man,* and the tale of Washington's deathbed words. Granger's letter explained his opposition to "employing negroes, or people of color, in transporting the public mails." Describing his comments as "too delicate to engraft into a report which may become public, yet too important to be omitted or passed over without full consideration," Granger drew a direct connection between post office hiring policies and the recent revolt in Haiti against slavery and colonialism. Arguing that "we cannot be too cautious in attempting to prevent similar evils in the four Southern States, where there are, particularly in the eastern and old settled parts of them, so great a proportion of blacks as to hazard the tranquillity and happiness of free citizens," the postmaster general noted that in Virginia and South Carolina "plans and conspiracies have already been concerted by them more than once, to rise in arms, and subjugate their masters."[13]

It is not surprising that the successful slave insurrection in Haiti frightened property owners and "free citizens" in the United States, or that it motivated federal officials to take defensive precautions. But the extent of Granger's actions, and his reasons for them, demonstrate important dynamics and dimensions of white supremacy and antiblack racism. With comprehensive and systematic logic, Granger argued in his confidential letter to Senator Jackson that banning blacks from positions as postal riders served the interests of slavery because "every thing which tends to increase their [black people's] knowledge of natural rights, of men and things, or that affords them an opportunity of associating, acquiring, and communicating sentiments, and of establishing a chain or line of intelligence, must increase your hazard, because it increases their means of effecting their object." He warned that "the most active and intelligent" blacks would gravitate to jobs as postal riders, that they would learn important information from their travels, and that they would "in time, become teachers to their brethren." To foreclose that end, Granger decided to deny them employment in those positions. "The hazard may be small and the prospect remote," he admitted, "but it does not follow that at some day the event would not be certain." Deploying the language of counterinsurgency that so often guides those with power to take repressive measures, Granger warned that "it is easier to prevent the evil than to cure it."[14]

Gideon Granger's letter to James Jackson is an important resource for analyzing and critiquing the production of racialized identities and hierarchies in U.S. literature and social life. No public pronouncement or statute announced any intention to discriminate against blacks, but through a policy of willful and systematic deception, an official at the highest level of government authored and authorized a policy of racial discrimination in order to protect the long-term interests of members of his own race. Slave owners may or may not have reaped direct benefits from Granger's actions, but other whites enriched themselves because of his decision. Whites hired as postal riders were not told that they received their positions because of racial privilege. The property and privileges they passed on to their descendants may have seemed like the fruits of competition in a free market, but they stemmed from systematic racial favoritism.

Black people denied employment as postal riders were led to believe that they failed to qualify for these jobs because of their deficiencies as individual applicants. Yet the opposite was true: their very potential for oppositional ideas and insurrectionary actions made them ineligible for these government jobs. We must certainly surmise that black people noticed the effects of Granger's decision and no doubt knew that a policy against their employment existed, but the privileges of power enabled Granger (and all whites) to escape responsibility for their actions.

The prose of Granger's letter hardly qualifies it for inclusion in the classical canon of U.S. literary history, although its frank disclosures of elite fears of popular protest make it of significant historical and sociological interest. When one considers that it came from a time in our nation's history when slavery was legal and when overt white supremacy perpetually imperiled the property and personhood even of free blacks, it is hardly the most racist document in our national papers of state. But Granger's letter represents an important dynamic, and it offers some important insights. For example, it enables us to cast the folktale about George Washington's dying wish in a new light. Secret communications among whites at the dawn of the Republic *did* consign black people to subordinate status. Even though they might not have had access to documents detailing exactly how their suppression was accomplished, the blacks in Washington, D.C., certainly saw the consequences of those actions in their own lives, as the story attests.

"Swing Low, Sweet Cadillac," Chester Himes's autobiography, Ralph Ellison's *Invisible Man,* and the folktale about George Washington are related to each other and to the larger body of texts (written and unwritten) that have authored and authorized the racialization of life chances in America; for example, the confidential City Survey appraisals for the Home Owners Loan Corporation (discovered by urban historian Kenneth Jackson) that covertly channeled federally guaranteed home loan funds toward whites and away from blacks between the 1930s and the 1970s; the prosecution and incarceration of a generation of community leaders through the Federal Bureau of Investigation's COINTELPRO activities in the 1960s and 1970s; and the sale of crack cocaine in the Los Angeles ghettos and barrios by individuals with ties to the CIA-supported contras in the 1980s.[15] But even more significant, Granger's letter, Gillespie's song, Himes's memories, Ellison's novel, and the story about George Washington's deathbed wish are texts from other times with special explanatory power for our own, because they present what Walter Benjamin called memories that flash up in a moment of danger.

During the days of slavery and segregation, we might have missed the true import of the genealogical connections linking Cadillacs, guns, and deathbed wishes encoded within these texts. In our own time, however, they speak powerfully to present circumstances by calling our attention to the ways in which public promises of inclusion can hide covert acts of exclusion, by demonstrating that direct, referential, and personal racism pales in comparison to the pernicious effects of indirect, inferential, and institutionalized racism. They show that racism can be systematic and effective even when unannounced in public; that rational considerations of self-interest and preservation of privilege can motivate racist behavior just as surely as private prejudice or irrational fear; that hypotheses about the nature and extent of white racism that might strike many whites as paranoid can sometimes be traced to accurate knowledge about history.

The presence or absence of social movements provides an important subtext for "Swing Low, Sweet Cadillac," Chester Himes's autobiography, *Invisible Man,* the story of George Washington's deathbed wish, and Gideon Granger's letter. Gillespie's campaign for president responded to the frustrations of civil rights activists of the 1950s and 1960s and served as a symbolic corollary to their struggle. Himes's autobiography, on the other hand, emerged after the assassinations of Malcolm X and Martin Luther King, in the midst of white America's war against the Black Panthers and its backlash against the egalitarian gains of the 1960s. Consequently, Himes's story about his father's dismissal from a black college established during Reconstruction emphasizes continuity rather than rupture, pointing out how little had changed over the years. His reference to his mother's armed self-defense, Ellison's narrator's reference to the disarming (and subsequent disenfranchising) of blacks during Reconstruction, and the folklore tale circulating just a few years after the Compromise of 1877 announced the end of Reconstruction are cultural expressions of a historical fact—the short-term victories and long-term defeats experienced by freed slaves. That long history of taking guns away from black people underscores an argument made brilliantly by historian Brenda Gayle Plummer about the Second Amendment as an essentially racialized right given to white people to insure their domination over Native Americans and blacks; it also testifies powerfully to the enduring power in the white mind of the Haitian Revolution at the end of the eighteenth and the start of the nineteenth century. Gideon Granger's secrecy, like most of the subsequent secret measures enacted to constrain opportunities among African Americans for accumulating assets or exercising political rights, emanated from efforts to suppress the egalitarian impulses and accomplishments of popular struggles like the Haitian Revolution and the U.S. Civil War.

The accurate knowledge and insight about U.S. history and culture that emerges from the genealogy of cars, guns, and deathbed wishes conflicts with some of the scholarship about the same subjects produced today by celebrated academics from elite institutions. For example, political scientists Paul Sniderman and Thomas Piazza provide an excellent example of the dangers of work on race that rests on surface appearances and remains rooted in dominant assumptions. In their 1993 book, *The Scar of Race,* they argue that racism today differs dramatically from the racism of the past, declaring that "race prejudice no longer organizes and dominates the reactions of whites; it no longer leads large numbers of them to oppose public policies to assist blacks across-the-board. It is ... simply wrong to suppose that the primary factor driving the contemporary arguments over the politics of race is white racism." Contending that few whites openly endorse discrimination or claim that blacks are innately inferior, Sniderman and Piazza rest their conclusions largely on data they assembled through survey-sample public opinion polls of whites in the San Francisco Bay area. They find in these surveys strong support for fair-housing laws and other pieces of legislation that outlaw discrimination. They learn from their interviews that educated people are less likely to approve of bigotry than people with limited schooling, and they discover that respondents who hold negative views of blacks in general are nonetheless willing to endorse government and private assistance for individual blacks who demonstrate good character. Perhaps most important, they use a sophisticated polling system to demonstrate that respondents who express bigoted opinions based on the belief that blacks disproportionately benefit from welfare can be persuaded to change their minds through aggressive counterarguments.[16]

Yet the picture presented by Sniderman and Piazza's interview data demonstrates the continuity of racism as well. Their findings disclose that 61 percent of whites believe that "most blacks on welfare could find work if they wanted to," that nearly 50 percent of whites agreed that "if blacks would only try harder, they would be just as well off as whites," and that an equal number of whites felt that "black neighborhoods tend to be run down because blacks simply don't take care of their own property." Indeed, the two political scientists concede that "what is striking is the sheer pervasiveness throughout contemporary American society of negative characteristics of blacks."[17]

How can Sniderman and Piazza declare that white racism has become less important when their own findings reveal such hostility to black people? Though not convincing, their answers are instructive. Although Sniderman and Piazza concede that simple prejudice does feed negative opinions about blacks among whites, they contend these opinions cannot be reduced to bigotry because they are essentially accurate. When their own evidence reveals that whites as a group hold pejorative opinions about an entire race of people, Sniderman and Piazza contend that these views are not racist because "these characterizations capture real features of everyday experience." (One wonders if they would have been as charitable about the views of German citizens in the 1930s toward Jews, which in their own way also probably reflected "real features of everyday experience.") To support this contention, and as examples of "real features of everyday experience," Sniderman and Piazza remind us that blacks "were responsible for one in every two murders" in 1990 and for "more than six in every ten robberies" in 1989, that in 1988 "63.7 percent of black births were out of wedlock," and that "the average Scholastic Aptitude Test score of blacks, in 1990, was 737, compared with an average white score of 993."[18]

Sniderman and Piazza present statistics like these ingenuously, as if they have never been challenged, even though they have been debunked many times by scholarly studies showing that such figures reveal less about innate racial characteristics than about the cultural biases and poor predictive capacities of standardized tests, the hostility of police officers and judges to black suspects, and the practical logic of extended households and female-headed families given current employment, wage, and welfare policies.

In addition, Sniderman and Piazza interrupt their scholarly project with speculations that their research does not support. Their original questions asked whether blacks on welfare could get jobs if they tried, if blacks could be as well off as whites if they would only try harder, if black neighborhoods tend to be run down because blacks don't take care of their property, if most blacks have a chip on their shoulder, and if blacks are more violent than whites. One might argue that the large numbers of blacks convicted of murder relates to the question about the supposed violent nature of black people, yet that particular question actually drew the lowest level of white agreement in their survey, with only 20 percent claiming that blacks are more violent than whites. But what is the relevance of SAT scores or births out of wedlock to views about keeping up neighborhoods or working hard? These spurious connections do not come out of the data, but are inserted by Sniderman and Piazza as motivating answers to questions about completely unrelated issues. Only if one assumes that any negative action by any black is evidence about all blacks (which is exactly what racism is), or that homeowners generally worry about their neighbors' SAT scores, could we possibly conclude that the "facts" cited by Sniderman and Piazza *explain* the opinions in their data.

Sniderman and Piazza also attempt to minimize the role of bigotry in shaping the negative comments their respondents make about black people by turning to data from the 1991 National Race Survey, which found that African Americans were even more likely than whites to agree that black people are aggressive and violent, boastful, complaining, lazy, and irresponsible. Because these results make it seem that black people have a low opinion of themselves, Sniderman and Piazza conclude that the negative comments made by whites in their own survey are justified and based on experience. Had this standard been in effect during the *Brown vs. Board of Education* case, Kenneth Clark's experiments showing that black children had negative self-images would have been used as justification for segregation rather than as a rationale for integration, as the Supreme Court decided. But more important, it should be noted that once again Sniderman and Piazza assume that any negative statement about blacks becomes equal to any other: if blacks think other blacks are boastful, imply Sniderman and Piazza, then whites are justified in thinking that the material advantages they enjoy in comparison to blacks should be attributed to black people's laziness rather than to unequal opportunity.

The authors of *The Scar of Race* take the answers given to them by white respondents at face value. Yet discerning scholars point out the dangers of such an unsophisticated approach. Leonard Steinhorn notes poll results indicating that 80 percent of whites claim that they have close personal friends who are black and observes that if this were the case, then "every American black, even those most isolated from whites, has five or six close white friends" —certainly an unlikely prospect. Christopher Doob addresses one poll in which only 6 percent of whites represent themselves as prejudiced against blacks, yet nearly half of the blacks note that they had encountered direct racial discrimination within the previous thirty days while shopping, dining out, working, riding public transportation, or dealing with police officers. Doob quips that if both results are taken as reliable then "that small percentage of whites must have remained very busy solidifying their racist reputations."[19]

Sniderman and Piazza do not ask blacks the same questions they ask whites, nor do they draw upon existing survey data collected by others about black opinions and attitudes. They ignore, for instance, the in-depth experiential survey by Joe R. Feagin and Melvin P. Sikes that forms the basis for *Living with Racism: The Black Middle Class Experience.* Feagin and Sikes's interviews with middle-class blacks reveal black attitudes toward whites, but they also disclose important evidence about how white people behave—an important counter to the self-serving representations of white open-mindedness so evident in *The Scar of Race.* The middle-class blacks surveyed by Feagin and Sikes detail the pervasiveness of racial insults and indignities in every sphere of American life, from navigating public places to pursuing an education, from building careers and businesses to securing shelter. The book's chapters about public space and educational institutions appeared in scholarly journals in 1991 and 1992, two years before the publication of Sniderman and Piazza's book.[20]

Yet the authors of *The Scar of Race* chose to use their own data and ideological justifications for what white people *say* rather than looking systematically at what white people *do* or how they appear to black people while they are doing it. Even here, Sniderman and Piazza are selective. They conclude that white people support fair-housing laws, for example, without noting that much depends on how one phrases questions on this issue. One 1980 survey, for example, found that nearly 90 percent of whites stated that black people have the right to live in any home they can afford; but in the same survey only 40 percent of whites said they would support a communitywide law requiring that "a homeowner cannot refuse to sell to someone because of their race and skin color." As Nancy Denton and Douglass Massey have shown, these data indicate that while expressing support for "fair housing" in the abstract, 60 percent of the white respondents said they would vote against practices mandated by the existing federal fair housing laws that had been on the books for twelve years at that time. Such laws had been so poorly enforced that most whites did not even know which practices were proscribed.[21] More than a decade later, the 1991 National Opinion Research Council (NORC) opinion survey found that nearly 40 percent of whites still *favored* legislation to give white home owners the legal right *not* to sell their house to a black person, a practice that would be in clear violation of federal law. This survey sample evidence hardly confirms the overwhelming support for fair housing among whites that Sniderman and Piazza allege. Of course, the thousands of cases of housing discrimination that take place every year raise more serious questions about how whites behave, no matter what answers they give to social science surveys.[22]

In their opening and concluding chapters especially, Sniderman and Piazza frame issues of rupture and continuity in U.S. race relations in a particularly deficient way—as a story of white innocence and generosity contrasted with self-serving and ungrateful behavior by blacks. Sniderman and Piazza construct a narrative that looks back to the civil rights era as a golden age when race "was a problem of the heart." In their account, defenses of de jure segregation before 1964 hinged solely on notions of black inferiority. They claim that the civil rights movement triumphed when a consensus formed around the idea that "it was wrong—unequivocally wrong, unambiguously wrong—to make it a crime for a black to drink from the same water fountain as a white, or to attend the same school."[23]

Sniderman and Piazza then claim that blacks shattered this integrationist consensus themselves when they (unaccountably) began to follow a "race conscious agenda" that violated the American creed. Race-conscious policies like affirmative action allegedly turned civil rights into pork barrel politics that Sniderman and Piazza claim alienated a number of whites so profoundly that "they have come to dislike blacks as a consequence." They charge that after the passage of the Civil Rights Acts of 1964 and 1965 "the voices of separatism began to drown out those of integration; and the headlines came to be dominated not by Martin Luther King, Jr., but by Stokely Carmichael and H. Rap Brown, then in the fullness of time, by Marion Barry, Tawana Brawley, and the Reverend Al Sharpton."[24]

Sniderman and Piazza offer no analysis of discourse, no sense that the voices dominating the headlines are filtered through gatekeepers with interests. To them, headlines are unmediated constructs, transparent windows into social reality, rather than historically created devices that represent the ways in which people with interests frame, shape, and inflect dissemination of the news. Moreover, the rhetorical flourishes in Sniderman and Piazza's conclusions make their book more revealing as a symptom of our current racial crisis than as a critique of it. In a book that points to a dramatic rupture in the history of U.S. race relations, trotting out Barry, Brawley, and Sharpton has a depressingly familiar ring to it—using instances of alleged black malfeasance to justify white racism is one of the oldest tropes of U.S. racism.

Careful readers might also note that Sniderman and Piazza's chronology fails to mention that Dr. King followed the Civil Rights Act with campaigns against housing discrimination in the North in 1966, that he championed opposition to America's "unjust and immoral war in Vietnam" as a civil rights issue in 1967, and that he died trying to build an interracial Poor People's Movement in 1968. If white people were as enthusiastic about his vision as Sniderman and Piazza imply, why did these campaigns attract so little support and fail so miserably to change public and private policies? In addition, by citing Marion Barry, Tawana Brawley, and Reverend Al Sharpton as evidence of how "the voices of separatism began to drown out the voices of integration," Sniderman and Piazza do not seem to be aware that Barry, Brawley, and Sharpton are not separatists; what unites them is that they are famous blacks who white people think are guilty of misbehavior. Further, this does not explain why their putative violations should consign black people to discriminatory treatment, when similar behavior by Mark Fuhrman, Richard Nixon, Charles Stuart, or Reverend Jimmy Swaggart does not seem to affect the life chances of European Americans.

As a *historical* narrative, Sniderman and Piazza's account is wrong in almost every respect. Concrete social struggle, not some amorphous consensus, secured passage of the civil rights laws. Direct-action protests by civil rights advocates provoked violent repression and sparked civil disorders that key opinion leaders sought to salve with meliorative reforms. The Civil Rights Acts of 1964 and 1965 were attempts to insulate the civil rights challenge to the narrowest possible terrains, not the fulfillment of the movement's goals. Contrary to Sniderman and Piazza's account, those who supported civil rights legislation had interests, not just "ideas" on their minds: Lyndon Johnson, for example, wanted to expand the potential pool of black voters in the South to counter growing Republican strength in white suburbs. Opponents of civil rights legislation did not rely solely on arguments about black inferiority, as the authors of *The Scar of Race* allege. Barry Goldwater, George Bush, and Ronald Reagan all opposed the 1964 law, not by citing the biological superiority of whites, but by claiming that the law violated states rights and that it threatened rather than enhanced racial harmony.[25] The white students at the University of Mississippi who wanted to deny Meredith access to married student housing after he became the first black student at that institution in 1962 did not claim that he was biologically inferior; they used the same arguments that white people use today to deny opportunities to people of color, claiming that Meredith was receiving "special privileges." A member of the university's student government received prolonged applause when he charged, "There are two sets of rules on this campus. There is one set for James Meredith and his friends and another for the 4,500 white students."[26]

Although offered as advice for liberals who want to build an electoral coalition that supports public policies aimed at helping blacks, *The Scar of Race* is curiously silent about the politics of whiteness in our society—about the open, public, and sustained discourse about race carried on by neoconservatives and their allies since the 1960s. From Spiro Agnew's public humiliation of black leaders in Baltimore for their "failure" to prevent riots when Dr. King was killed, to Richard Nixon's "southern strategy" promoting resistance to desegregation, from the legal and public relations campaigns waged by wealthy neoconservative foundations like the Heritage Foundation and John M. Olin Institute against affirmative action programs to the elevation of Clarence Thomas to the Supreme Court—race has been at the center of neoconservative efforts to build the countersubversive electoral coalition they needed to dismantle the welfare state and advance the agendas of big business. But Sniderman and Piazza evade any mention of these initiatives; they attribute the unraveling of the civil rights coalition primarily to the bad behavior of blacks. Whites have neither interest nor agency in their account, only attitudes.

While Sniderman and Piazza's account does not succeed as scholarship, it needs to be taken seriously as storytelling. *The Scar of Race* mobilizes and enacts our culture's double standards about race. Narratives of black misbehavior eroding the goodwill of whites have always fueled racist reaction: in our own day these are stories that writers love to write and publishers love to print, tales that reviewers routinely salute as "novel," even though they are as old as the nation itself. The success of these stories, however, gives us the opportunity to rethink the relationship between the transparently fictional stories about race that circulate in novels, short stories, motion pictures, and electronic journalism, and the much more powerful but purportedly true stories about race that circulate in politics and everyday discourse among whites.

All fiction written today by and about black people circulates in a network that includes fictions like the ones disguised as social science in Sniderman and Piazza's narrative. Their story is a social text as well as a book, a widely disseminated story that reinforces itself every time its basic contours are repeated in the speeches of politicians, in the content of television news and entertainment programs, in the comments of callers to talk-radio programs, and in the actions of social institutions like home lending agencies, realtors, zoning boards, personnel departments, and schools. The challenge to both scholars and citizens in this context is to avoid complicity in the erasures effected by stories that obscure actual social relations and hide their own conditions of production and distribution.

Sniderman and Piazza tell stories that assume what they should be proving, but an impressive body of new writings about race presents an effective and devastating alternative to their work through sophisticated, useful, and accurate accounts about the ways racial narratives get constructed and disseminated. Paul Gilroy, David Theo Goldberg, and Cornel West especially provide powerful tools for engaging and transcending racism in their books, *The Black Atlantic, Racist Culture,* and *Keeping Faith.* Each of these studies treats racism as a longstanding but decidedly dynamic and distinctly historical phenomenon. Each argues that race is a fiction, that no basis exists in biology or anthropology to categorize people along racial lines. Yet each also demonstrates that things that are made up are also real, that social constructs can have sinister social causes and consequences. Gilroy, Goldberg, and West reject definitions that relegate racism to the realm of purely personal prejudices and practices—what Goldberg calls the "law of universal reduction"—but they also challenge the idea of any innate, transhistorical, or universal racism.[27] Similarly, they reject methodologies that deny racism's independent existence and explain it only as a subordinate category within other forms of economic and political domination. Instead, they investigate, analyze, and interpret the emergence and endurance of Euro-American white supremacy as a historical phenomenon with enduring effects on our common intellectual, cultural, and social life.

Gilroy and Goldberg especially trace contemporary racism to the modern categories of the Enlightenment—nationality, ethnicity, authenticity, and cultural integrity.[28] John Locke's justification of the Royal Africa Company's slave expeditions as "just wars" and Immanuel Kant's belief in fundamental differences in the rational capacities of blacks and whites serve as revealing examples—not because they contradict the liberal ideals of the Enlightenment, but because they flow logically from its commitments to categorizing, classifying, and controlling. Gilroy notes that modern rationality originated, in part, in the slave-labor sugar plantations of the Caribbean, while Goldberg identifies racialized language and preconceptual elements of racism even in antiracist documents and arguments. These authors insist on viewing slavery and racism as "part of the ethical and intellectual heritage of the West" rather than as the special property or special problem of blacks.[29]

A central contribution of these books is their delineation of how racism and resistance against it get written into the commonplace practices of everyday life and culture. West offers powerful and persuasive critiques of the racialized assumptions ordering modern art and architecture, Goldberg produces a brilliant reading of urban spatial arrangements as the political unconscious of racism in cities all over the world, and Gilroy offers an original and inspired reading of the role of race in Richard Wright's modernism and internationalism.

Remembering the roles played by racism and slavery in the evolution of the Enlightenment is important for these authors, not to distance themselves from Western traditions of thought and reason but to claim a special place for antiracist thought within them. Because antiracist writers have had to confront directly the racist elements of Enlightenment thought that others have the luxury of ignoring, the antiracists—by necessity—must do the hard work of fulfilling the worthy goals of the Enlightenment without collaborating in its uninterrogated racist subtexts. As Gilroy explains, slavery and its aftermath forced diasporic Africans in the West "to query the foundational moves of modern philosophy and social thought, whether they came from the natural rights theorists who sought to distinguish between the spheres of morality and legality, the idealists who wanted to emancipate politics from morals so that it could become a sphere of strategic action, or the political economists of the bourgeoisie who first formulated the separation of economic activity from both ethics and politics."[30] Consequently, we need to read the work of antiracist writers because their critical marginality enables them to see aspects of reigning social relations that dominant texts obscure and avoid.

The critiques by Gilroy, Goldberg, and West enable us to shift the terms of racial debate away from those favored by traditional social science (why blacks aren't more like whites) toward an infinitely more constructive and instructive issue—what intellectuals and artists from aggrieved communities have been able to create as a result of the specific circumstances they confront. West describes a "New World African modernity" that emerges when "degraded and exploited Africans in American circumstances" use "European languages and instruments to make sense of tragic predicaments—predicaments disproportionately shaped by white supremacist bombardments on black beauty, intelligence, moral character, and creativity." He celebrates the skill of black artists and intellectuals in drawing on cultural traditions to critique white supremacy; he cites Horace Pippin's art, Bessie Smith's music, and Sterling Brown's poetry as creations that transcended the limited art of uplift and protest allowed blacks in the white world to articulate and affirm traditional African and African American paradigms of art as healing. West shows that New World Africans also gravitated toward newness and novelty, innovation and improvisation, as tools for changing their condition. Gilroy stresses this fundamental commitment to change as an important impetus toward modernism in black art and literature, showing how a "politics of fulfillment and transfiguration" appealed to aggrieved peoples who longed for change, not just out of an abstract artistic commitment to progress, but because of their fundamental struggles for justice. Perhaps most important, Gilroy shows how the lessons learned through struggle by diasporic Africans can serve all people because of their sophisticated critiques of exploitation and hierarchy.[31]

Cultural production provides important evidence for Gilroy, Goldberg, and West because they understand not only how social conditions influence cultural texts and the role of cultural texts in social life, but also the inevitable textualization of social life by dominant groups who circulate stories that represent their own power as necessary and inevitable. Following the intellectual traditions of antiracist resistance within aggrieved communities of ordinary people, they find epistemological and ontological principles vital to improving our understanding of social relations. Just as the burdens of slavery and racism are not the property of blacks alone, the insights and ideological critiques of aggrieved populations forced to open up the suppressed contradictions of the Enlightenment for themselves have generalizable validity for people from all backgrounds.

Self-reflexive about their roles as intellectuals, Gilroy, Goldberg, and West offer concrete programs for antiracist thought and action. Gilroy shows how a hermeneutics of suspicion and a hermeneutics of memory can guide intellectual critique and cultural practice grounded in "the mimetic functions of artistic performance in the processes of struggles towards emancipation, citizenship, and eventually autonomy." Goldberg offers a carefully conceived program of pragmatic antiracism based on the presumption that racialized definitions of self and social structure are so pervasive in our society that they cannot be altered by simple "color blind," "nonracial" thinking. West calls for intellectuals to become "critical organic catalysts" who blend the paradigms, viewpoints, and methods of traditional scholarship with the insights, ideas, and experiences of aggrieved communities. Crucial to this role is the development of "genealogical materialist analysis of racism" based on genealogical inquiry into the origins, evolution, and enabling conditions of racist practices, a microinstitutional and local analysis of the actual mechanisms that instantiate or resist racism in social life, and a macrostructural approach that connects class exploitation, police power, and bureaucratic domination to the maintenance and regeneration of racisms around the globe.[32]

By stressing the ways of knowing that emerge from antiracist intellectual and political struggle, Gilroy, Goldberg, and West demonstrate that multiculturalism is not just a matter of adding the experiences of "others" onto what we already presume to be true about culture and history. The significance of marginalized peoples to cultural studies does not lie in their marginality, but rather in the role that marginalization (not to mention oppression and suppression) plays in shaping intellectual and cultural categories that affect everyone. Like the feminist epistemologies of Sandra Harding, Donna Haraway, and Teresa de Lauretis, these books turn to the perspectives of aggrieved individuals and communities not because of who such individuals and groups are, but because of how they have been treated and what they have learned in the process.[33]

Both continuity and rupture pervade the analyses of racism offered by Gilroy, Goldberg, and West. Tracing present racist practices back to the core categories of modernity, they help us understand the endurance of racist hierarchies despite the long tradition of critique against them. Yet, they also contest the possibility of a universal or transhistorical racism impervious to social or intellectual challenges. "In contrast to the prevailing picture of a singular and passing racism," Goldberg writes, "I will be developing a conception of transforming racisms bound conceptually in terms of and sustained by an underlying culture."[34] This project holds particular importance precisely because it is historical, because it traces how racism changes over time, how there has always been racism in the United States at different times and different places—but never exactly the same racism.

In the spirit of that kind of attention to change over time, historians David Roediger and Robin D. G. Kelley offer even more finely delineated historical accounts of U.S. racial identities in Roediger's *Toward the Abolition of Whiteness* and Kelley's *Race Rebels*. Both authors are superb researchers who combine mastery of macrosocial economic and political history with an uncommon attention to the microsocial textures of everyday life as they are experienced by ordinary people. They offer insightful critiques of how dominant power relations become textualized in language and law, as well as of the ways in which the cultural creations of aggrieved communities author and authorize oppositional "texts" and practices.

Roediger reminds us that racial identities affect white people too, that whiteness is a category that requires historical explanation because it has been a social construction with calamitous consequences. Building on his previous study of the origins and evolution of white identity in the U.S. working class before the Civil War, Roediger traces the continuity and permutations in white identity as they have affected gender, work, social movements, ethnicity, language, and historical scholarship from the Civil War to the present. *Towards the Abolition of Whiteness* contains many brilliant moments, but among the best is Roediger's sensitive, knowing, and complex mapping of the role played by whiteness in both constructing and destabilizing European American ethnic identities. His account reveals much about the logic of new historicism because it underscores the impossibility of separating cultural texts from the textualization of cultural and social life. Roediger also offers a fascinating etymology of the word "gook," a racial epithet used by U.S. soldiers since the nineteenth century against indigenous populations in diverse locations, including Haiti, the Philippines, Nicaragua, the Arabic Middle East, Hawaii, Korea, and Vietnam.[35] This curiosity about the origins of white supremacist slang is indicative of Roediger's sophisticated grasp of social life as a totality made up of both macrosocial structural institutions and microsocial practices and experiences.

In a chapter that exemplifies the best possibilities of historically grounded cultural criticism, Roediger details the efforts of labor poet and humorist Covington Hall to popularize a new language of labor, race, and gender among southern timber workers in the early part of the twentieth century. In this discussion, Roediger shows how struggles over resources necessitate struggles over culture, and how enduring cultural conservatism can undermine political rad-

icalism.[36] Rejecting any temptation to draw simple and one-dimensional relationships between social structure and culture, Roediger accomplishes the far
more difficult feat of showing the mutually constitutive relationships that connect the culture of everyday life to the broad distribution of wealth, power, and
life chances in society.

Roediger's explorations of whiteness provide a perfect introduction to
Robin D. G. Kelley's *Race Rebels,* a stunningly original and illuminating history
of episodes in which poor and working-class people in America have mobilized
on behalf of their own interests in the face of systematic discrimination and exploitation. Ever since Herbert Gutman's generative 1973 essay, "Work, Culture,
and Society in Industrializing America," social historians have developed ever
more sophisticated ways of exploring popular resistance to concentrated wealth
and power, but Kelley raises this discussion to a new level.[37] Imagination and
ingenuity characterize his efforts, but Kelley's best skill is his mastery of empirical data—he has found more and better evidence than anyone in the field.

From Kelley's introductory reminiscences about working at a fast-food
restaurant when he was a teenager to his cogent observations about how wage
labor shaped the nature of the civil rights movement in Birmingham, *Race
Rebels* delineates the intersections of race and class in the United States in important and enlightening ways. It combines an attention to the quotidian that
often appears only in novels with a comprehensive and convincing analysis of
the broad social forces that shape individual and collective behavior. Most important, Kelley understands how prevailing power relations—and resistance to
them—often become written into everyday life as cultural performances.

Drawing on the cultural criticism of James Scott, Michel de Certeau, and
C.L.R. James, among others, Kelley explains how dressing up on Saturday
nights enabled southern blacks to answer back to the deprivations they suffered
as underpaid workers and to transform the indignities imposed on them by
their work uniforms that marked them as people with subordinate status. He
analyzes the role of dancing as a way of reclaiming the work body for pleasure,
and in his tour de force shows how Malcolm X's description of changing into
his zoot suit from his work uniforms as a Pullman porter and soda jerk proclaimed a self-affirmation that found full expression in the way the zoot uniform—with its wide shoulders and broad hats underscored by the zoot suiters'
characteristic walk—took up physical space on city streets.[38]

The forms of social critique practiced by Kelley and Roediger allow for no
easy answers about continuity and rupture in U.S. race relations. To be sure,
they remind us of the long duration of white supremacist practices and institu-

tions, but they also illuminate the innumerable instances of antiracist resistance growing out of the contradictions and inconsistencies necessitated by the insupportable fictions of race. Yet if racism has no absolutely determined innate trajectory in our nation's history, its presence poisons everything we are and everything we hope to become. It makes every moment a moment of danger, not just because of the potential for explosions of violence like the Los Angeles rebellion of 1992, but because of the ruined lives, wasted talents, and corrupt interpersonal and social relations that racism causes. But the very danger that racism represents can serve constructive ends if it motivates us to create new ways of knowing and acting.

The insights of contemporary antiracist intellectuals bring us full circle to "Swing Low, Sweet Cadillac" and its genealogical relationship to yet one more automobile, one described by Malcolm X, who worked for a short time as an automobile industry assembly-line worker in a truck factory in Detroit. Malcolm X used to tell his followers, "Racism is like a Cadillac, they bring out a new model every year." In his view, just as General Motors made adjustments in the surface features of its automobiles, racism changed its contours and dimensions. The racism of 1964 might not look like the racism of 1954, but it was still racism. Malcolm X warned against thinking that racism had ended because it had changed its appearance, at the same time cautioning his listeners that they could not defeat today's racism with yesterday's slogans and analyses.

If racism is like a Cadillac, and if old Cadillacs never die, we may never see a world without racial oppression. The long history of white supremacy in the United States may make many of us wish to second Cornel West's observation that "the extent to which race still so fundamentally matters in nearly every sphere of American life is—in the long run—depressing and debilitating."[39] Like the white neighbors that Chester Himes remembered from his childhood, many whites still seem disturbed and threatened by the prospect of black success—witness neoconservative ideologue Carol Iannone's ridicule of the literary awards bestowed on Toni Morrison and Alice Walker, characterizing them as consolation prizes awarded because of their race and gender rather than because of their superb skills as writers.[40] In Malcolm X's terms, they may turn out a new Cadillac every year, but it's still a Cadillac.

Racism may never disappear, but we know that it does change, that it contains explosive contradictions and is always susceptible to exposure and challenge. The white farmers who succeeded in driving the Himes family out of Mississippi did not convince Chester Himes that he did not deserve the good things in life; they only showed him that he would have to fight to get what he wanted. New racisms may always supplant old ones—just like this year's Cadillacs roll off the assembly lines to replace last year's. Old Cadillacs never die, but they sometimes become too expensive to maintain. White supremacy and antiblack racism may never die, but that shouldn't stop us from trying to see what we can do to help them fade away.

CHAPTER 9

"Frantic to Join . . . the Japanese Army": Beyond the Black–White Binary

I began to feel a terrified pity for the white children of these white people; who had been sent, by their parents, to Korea, though their parents did not know why. Neither did their parents know why these miserable, incontestably inferior, rice-eating gooks refused to come to heel, and would not be saved. But I knew why. I came from a long line of miserable, incontestably inferior, rice-eating, chicken-stealing, hog-swilling niggers—who had acquired these skills in their flight from bondage—who still refused to come to heel, and who would not be saved.

—JAMES BALDWIN

All communities of color suffer from the possessive investment in whiteness, but not in the same way. No magical essence unites aggrieved victims of white supremacy in common endeavors; all too often racial minorities seek to secure the benefits of whiteness for themselves by gaining advantages at each others' expense.[1] This polylateral process, however, always entails more than one minority group at a time interacting with a white center. It demands that communities of color be aware of one another and be prepared for unexpected alliances as well as unexpected antagonisms. African Americans and Asian Americans have often had antagonistic relationships with one another as competitors for scarce resources. Yet they have also often been allies, united by similar if not identical experiences as racialized subjects as well as by the racial undertones of U.S. foreign policy. In this chapter, I examine the importance of Asia for black nationalism and the ways in which U.S. foreign policy has had important ramifications for racial and ethnic identity at home.

In his celebrated autobiography, Malcolm X explains how he escaped the draft during World War II. At a time when "the only three things in the world that scared me" were "jail, a job, and the Army," the Harlem street hustler devised a plan to fool his foes. Aware that military intelligence units stationed "black spies in civilian clothes" in African American neighborhoods to watch for subversive activity, Malcolm (then named Malcolm Little) started "noising around" Harlem bars and street corners ten days before his scheduled preinduction physical exam. He told everyone withing earshot that he was "frantic to join . . . the Japanese Army." In case the military found his dramatic displays of disloyalty insufficient, Malcolm informed a psychiatrist at his physical exam that he was eager to enter the military. "I want to get sent down South," he asserted. "Organize them nigger soldiers, you dig? Steal us some guns, and kill crackers!" Not surprisingly, the Selective Service judged Malcolm Little mentally disqualified for military service, sending him home with a 4-F deferment on October 25, 1943.[2]

The distinguished historian John Hope Franklin secured a similar result for himself by very different means. Swept up in the patriotic fervor that followed the bombing of Pearl Harbor, Franklin *was* frantic to join . . . the U.S. Navy. He saw an advertisement indicating that the navy needed skilled office workers who could type, take shorthand, and run business machines. At that point in his life, Franklin had six years' experience at secretarial work, had won three gold medals in typing, had taken an accounting course in high school, knew shorthand, and had a Ph.D. in history from Harvard University. The navy recruiter told him that he was lacking one credential—color; they could not hire him because he was black.

Franklin next directed his efforts toward securing a position with the Department of War, then assembling a staff of historians. But here again, color mattered. The department hired several white historians without advanced degrees, but never responded to Franklin's application. When he went for his preinduction physical, a white doctor refused to let Franklin enter his office and made him wait for a blood test on a bench at the end of a hall near the fire escape until Franklin's protests got him admitted to the physician's office.

Years later, Franklin recalled that these experiences changed his attitude toward the war. They convinced him that "the United States, however much it was devoted to protecting the freedoms and rights of Europeans, had no respect for me, no interest in my well-being, and not even a desire to utilize my services." Franklin concluded that "the United States did not need me and did not deserve me. Consequently, I spent the remainder of the war years successfully and with malice aforethought outwitting my draft board and the entire Selective Service establishment." Instead of serving in the military, Franklin devoted his time to teaching, scholarship, and activism aimed at undermining the system of white supremacy.[3]

Although they started out with very different intentions, Malcolm X and John Hope Franklin both end up avoiding military service during World War II. Their actions were hardly typical; an overwhelming majority of Americans, and even an overwhelming majority of African Americans, who were eligible for the draft accepted induction and served effectively. Black draft resisters accounted for less than 5 percent of the 12,343 conscientious-objection cases processed by the Justice Department, and more than one million black men and women served in the armed forces during the war.[4] But the conflicts with the selective service system experienced by Malcolm X and John Hope Franklin bring into sharp relief the potentially explosive racial contradictions facing the United States during the war.

Franklin and Malcolm X expressed more than individual ingenuity and personal pique in their resistance to the draft. They articulated and acted upon a suspicion about the relationship between World War II and white supremacy widely held in their community: about the shortcomings of democracy in the United States, about the racialized nature of the war, about the potential power of nonwhite nations around the globe, and about the viability and desirability of covert and overt resistance to racism.

Although they expressed a decidedly minority view about the draft itself in their own communities during the war, they touched on shared social perceptions that gained majority approval afterward. The emergence of Malcolm X in the postwar period as a black nationalist leader who connected antiracist struggles in the United States with anti-imperialist efforts around the globe; Martin Luther King, Jr.'s role as the leading opponent of the U.S. war in Vietnam as well as the leader of civil rights and poor people's movements; and the actions of a generation of young people in the 1960s who used the research of scholars (including John Hope Franklin) to fashion their own understanding of their obligations to the nation at home and abroad, all testify to the generative nature of wartime tensions and conflict.

Most important, the strategic maneuverings of John Hope Franklin and Malcolm X in their struggles with the selective service system highlight the volatile instabilities sedimented within seemingly stable narratives of nation and race. Malcolm X initially presented himself as an admirer of America's enemies and as an active agent of subversion simply so he could stay on the streets and pursue his own pleasures as a petty criminal. Yet his eventual imprisonment for crimes committed on the streets led him to a religious conversion and political awakening that made him an actual opponent of U.S. foreign policy, turning his wartime charade into an important part of his life's work. John Hope Franklin initially approached the government as a superpatriot eager to enlist in the U.S. war effort, but the racism directed at him by the government led him to evade military service and embark on a lifetime of oppositional intellectual work and activism.

By feigning a desire to join the Japanese army and by announcing his interest in shooting southern segregationists, Malcolm X drew upon ideas and practices with deep roots in his own life and in the politics of his community. His threat to join the Japanese army in particular carried weight, because it played on the paranoia of white supremacy by posing the possibility of a transnational alliance among people of color. In the process, it brought to the surface the inescapably racist realities behind the seemingly color-blind national narrative of the United States and its aims in the war.[5]

Historically, the prospect of escape to Indian Territory, Canada, or Mexico and the assistance offered by European abolitionists made slaves and free blacks sensitive to international realities in the antebellum period. Robin D. G. Kelley's research on black Communists in Alabama in the 1930s indicates that charges of instigation by outside agitators influenced by Russia had little effect on the descendants of slaves who had been freed from bondage in part by an invading army from the North.[6] But the Japanese were not just any outsiders to African Americans in the 1940s; they were people of color with their own independent nation, a force capable of challenging Euro-American imperialism on its own terms, and possible allies against the oppressive power of white supremacy.

Paul Gilroy and others have written eloquently about a "black Atlantic"— about the importance of Africa and Europe as influences on the black freedom struggle in the United States, but there has been a "black Pacific" as well. Images of Asia and experiences with Asians and Asian Americans have played an important role in enabling black people to complicate the simple black-white binaries that do so much to shape the contours of economic, cultural, and social life in the United States.[7] In addition, it is not just elite intellectuals who have had an international imagination; working people whose labor in a global capitalist economy brought them into contact with other cultures have often inflected their own organizations and institutions with international imagery and identification.

The African American encounter with Japan has been especially fraught with contradictions. In their zeal to identify with a nonwhite nation whose successes might rebuke Eurocentric claims about white supremacy, blacks have often overlooked, condoned, and even embraced elements of Japanese fascism and imperialism. In the United States, Japanese agents sometimes succeeded in promoting the crudest kinds of racial essentialism and male chauvinism among black nationalist groups. But as Laura Mulvey observes, "It cannot be easy to move from oppression and its mythologies to resistance in history; a detour through a no-man's land or threshold area of counter-myth and symbolisation is necessary."[8] The African American engagement with Japan has provided a detour through a symbolic terrain sufficiently complex to allow an oppressed racial minority in North America to think of itself as part of a global majority of nonwhite peoples. In addition, as Malcolm X's performance at his physical demonstrated, imaginary alliances and identifications with Japan could create maneuvering room for dealing with immediate and pressing practical problems.

African American affinities with Asia have emanated from strategic needs and from the utility of enlisting allies, learning from families of resemblance, and escaping the categories of black and white as they have developed historically in the United States. These affinities do not evidence innate or essential characteristics attributable to race or skin color; on the contrary, they demonstrate the distinctly social and historical nature of racial formation. Neither rooted in biology nor inherited from history, racial identity is a culturally constructed entity always in flux. During World War II, the racialized nature of the Pacific war, the racist ideals of Nazi Germany, the legacy of white supremacy, segregation, colonialism, and conquest in the United States, and antiracist activism at home and abroad, all generated contradictions and conflicts that radically refigured race relations in the United States and around the world.

Global politics and domestic economic imperatives have shaped relations between Asian Americans and African Americans from the start. White planters and industrialists in the nineteenth-century United States favored the importation of Asian laborers to simultaneously drive down the wages of poor whites and gain even greater domination over slaves and free blacks. As immigrants ineligible for naturalized citizenship according to the terms of the 1790 Immigration and Naturalization Act, and as a racialized group relegated largely to low-wage labor, Asian Americans could offer little resistance to employer exploitation and political domination. White workers in California and elsewhere often took the lead in demanding that Asian immigrants be excluded from the U.S. labor market, but many manufacturers and entrepreneurs also came to view Asian immigrants as actual or potential competitors and to favor exclusion.[9] The U.S. Congress passed the first of several acts excluding Asians from immigrating to the United States in 1882, shortly after the Compromise of 1877 guaranteed the subjugation of southern blacks and therefore eliminated employers' needs for a group of racialized immigrants to compete with African American laborers. Significantly, one voice raised against the act in congressional debates was that of Senator Blanche K. Bruce of Mississippi, the only African American in the Senate.[10]

Contradictions between domestic racism and the imperial ambitions of the United States appeared as early as 1899, during the Filipino insurrection against occupying U.S. troops in the aftermath of what the United States calls the Spanish-American War. African American soldiers from the Twenty-fourth Infantry Regiment could not help but notice that white Americans used many of the same epithets to describe Filipinos as they used to describe them, including "niggers," "black devils," and "gugus." One black enlisted man in the regiment felt that the rebellion he was sent to suppress emanated from the fact that "[t]he Filipinos resent being treated as inferior," which he believed "set an example to the American Negro" that should be emulated. Similarly, the regiment's sergeant major, John Calloway, informed a Filipino friend that he was "constantly haunted by the feeling of how wrong morally . . . Americans are in the present affair with you."[11]

Filipinos fighting under the command of Emilio Aguinaldo made appeals to black troops on the basis of "racial" solidarity, offering posts as commissioned officers in the rebel army to those who switched sides. Most remained loyal to the U.S. cause, but Corporal David Fagen deserted the Twenty-fourth Regiment's I Company on November 17, 1899, to become an officer in the guerrilla army. He married a Filipina and served the insurrectionists with distinction, engaging U.S. units effectively and escaping time after time. Fearing that his example might encourage others to follow suit, U.S. officers offered extensive rewards and expended enormous energy to capture or kill Fagen. On December 5, 1901, U.S. officials announced that a native hunter had produced "a slightly decomposed head of a negro" and personal effects that indicated the skull belonged to Fagen. Although this may have been a ruse on Fagen's part to end the search for him, the gradually weakening position of the rebels made further resistance impossible, and, one way or the other, Fagen disappeared from the combat theater. But his example loomed large in the minds of military and diplomatic officials, especially when they contemplated military activity against nonwhite populations.[12] Nearly five hundred African American soldiers elected to remain in the Philippines at the conclusion of the conflict, and Filipino civilians later told stories to black U.S. soldiers stationed in their country during World War II about Fagen and about the black soldiers who refused to crush the Moro Rebellion in 1914.[13]

Just as some black soldiers from the Twenty-fourth Infantry Regiment viewed the Filipino independence struggle as a battle with special relevance to their own fight against white supremacy, individuals and groups in Japan took an interest in Marcus Garvey's Universal Negro Improvement Association around the time of World War I. Charles Zampty, a native of Trinidad and a leader of the Garvey movement in Detroit for more than fifty years, learned about the UNIA from Garvey's newspaper, *Negro World,* which he obtained from Japanese sailors in Panama while he worked at the Panama Canal.[14] As early as 1918, Garvey warned that "the next war will be between the Negroes and the whites unless our demands for justice are recognized," adding that, "with Japan to fight with us, we can win such a war."[15]

Other African American intellectuals also looked to Japan for inspiration. Shortly after the war between Russia and Japan, Booker T. Washington pointed to Japanese nationalism as a model for African American development.[16] W.E.B. Du Bois included the "yellow-brown East" in the "darker world" poised to resist "white Europe," in his novel *Dark Princess: A Romance,* in which he fantasized about an alliance linking an Asian Indian princess, a Japanese nobleman, and an African American intellectual.[17] In his 1935 classic study, *Black Reconstruction in America,* Du Bois counted U.S. support for colonialism and imperialism in Asia, Africa, and Latin America as one of the enduring consequences of the concessions to the South required to suppress African Americans in the years after the Civil War. "Imperialism, the exploitation of colored labor throughout the world, thrives upon the approval of the United States, and the United States gives that approval because of the South," he argued. Warning that war would result from the reactionary stance imposed upon the United States by its commitment to white supremacy, Du Bois reminded his readers, "The South is not interested in freedom for dark India. It has no sympathy with the oppressed of Africa or of Asia."[18]

At times black grass-roots organizations saw resemblances between their status and that of other racialized minorities. In San Francisco in the early years of the twentieth century, black community groups and newspapers opposed efforts to send Japanese American children to segregated schools because they recognized the demeaning nature of segregation from their own experiences. In addition, in their public mobilizations, they pointed repeatedly to the ways in which opposition to immigration from Japan manifested not just a generalized fear of foreigners, but the racist prejudices of white Americans.[19]

Malcolm X's Garveyite father and West Indian mother encouraged him to be internationalist in his thinking, to look to Africa, the Caribbean, and beyond, to render the hegemonic white supremacy of North America relative, contingent, and provisional. This tradition affected Malcolm X directly, but it also shaped the broader contours of relations between African Americans and people of Asian origin. In 1921, members of Garvey's UNIA and Japanese immigrants in Seattle joined forces to create a Colored People's Union open to all people "except the whites or Teutonic races."[20] In New York, a young Vietnamese merchant seaman regularly attended UNIA meetings and became friends with Garvey himself in the early 1920s. Years later he would apply the lessons he learned about nationalism from Garvey when he took on the identity Ho Chi Minh and led his country's resistance against Japanese, French, and U.S. control.[21]

Forty members of the Garvey movement in Detroit converted to Islam between 1920 and 1923, largely as a result of the efforts of an Ahmadiyah mission from India. Elijah Muhammad, then Elijah Poole, associated with Garveyites in Detroit during the 1930s before founding the Nation of Islam, which Malcolm Little would later join while in prison during the late 1940s. The Nation of Islam went beyond Garvey's pan-Africanism to include (at least symbolically) all "Asiatic" (nonwhite) people.[22]

During the 1930s, a Japanese national using the names Naka Nakane and Satokata Takahishi (sometimes spelled Satokata Takahashi) organized African Americans, Filipinos, West Indians, and East Indians into self-help groups, among them the society for the Development of Our Own, the Ethiopian Intelligence Sons and Daughters of Science, and the Onward Movement of America.[23] Born in Japan in 1875, Nakane married an English woman and migrated to Canada. He presented himself as a major in the Japanese army and a member of a secret fraternal order, the Black Dragon Society. Nakane promised financial aid and military assistance to African Americans in Detroit if they joined in "a war against the white race."[24]

Deported in 1934, Nakane moved to Canada and continued to run Development of Our Own through his African American wife, Pearl Sherrod. When he tried to reenter the United States in 1939, federal officials indicted him for illegal entry and attempting to bribe an immigration officer. The FBI charged in 1939 that Nakane had been an influential presence within the Nation of Islam (NOI), that he spoke as a guest at NOI temples in Chicago and Detroit, and that his thinking played a major role in shaping Elijah Muhammad's attitudes toward the Japanese government. As proof, the FBI offered a copy of a speech that the bureau claimed had been saved by an agent since 1933, in which Muhammad predicted "the Japanese will slaughter the white man."[25]

The Pacific Movement of the Eastern World (PMEW), founded in Chicago and St. Louis in 1932, advocated the unification of nonwhite people under the leadership of the empire of Japan. Led by Ashima Takis (whose pseudonyms included Policarpio Manansala, Mimo de Guzman, and Itake Koo), the group expressed its ideology of racial unity in the colors of its banners—black, yellow, and brown.[26] The PMEW implied that it had the backing of the Japanese government in offering free transportation, land, houses, farm animals, and crop seed to the first three million American blacks willing to repatriate to Africa.[27] Although Marcus Garvey expressly warned his followers against the PMEW, Takis frequently represented himself as an ally and even agent of the Garvey movement, and his group enjoyed considerable allegiance among Garveyites in the Midwest, especially in Gary, Indiana, and East St. Louis, Illinois.[28] Madame M.L.T. De Mena of the Universal Negro Improvement Association defied Garvey's prohibitions and arranged speaking engagements for Takis and his Chinese associate Moy Liang before black nationalist audiences.[29] "The Japanese are colored people, like you," Takis told African American audiences, adding pointedly that "the white governments do not give the negro any consideration." In 1940, Takis told one African American group that war would soon break out between the United States and Japan, and that they would receive rifles from Japan to help them mount an insurrection in the Midwest while Japanese troops attacked the West Coast.[30] In the 1930s, the leader of the Peace Movement of Ethiopia, Mittie Maud Lena Gordon, had asked newly elected President Franklin Roosevelt to help finance black repatriation to Africa. After the Japanese attack on Pearl Harbor, Gordon described December 7, 1941, as the day "one billion black people struck for freedom."[31]

Thus, Malcolm X's presentation of himself in 1943 as pro-Japanese and anti–white supremacist picked up on elements of his personal history as well as on significant currents of thought and action among black nationalists. He also exploited well-founded fears among government officials. Some recognized that the pathology of white supremacy posed special problems for the nation as it sought to fashion national unity in a war against German and Japanese fascism. White racism in the United States undermined arguments behind U.S. participation in the war and made it harder to distinguish the Allies from the Axis. Racial segregation in industry and in the army kept qualified fighters and factory workers from positions where they were sorely needed, while the racialized nature of the war in Asia threatened to open up old wounds on the home front. Most important, asking African American, Asian American, Mexican American, and Native American soldiers to fight for freedoms overseas that they did not themselves enjoy at home presented powerful political, ideological, and logistical problems. But other government officials worried more about conspiratorial collaboration between African Americans and agents of the Japanese government.

As far back as the 1920s, the Department of Justice and agents from military intelligence had expressed fears of a Japanese-black alliance. One report alleged: "The Japanese Associations subscribe to radical negro literature. In California a negro organization, formed in September, 1920, issued resolutions declaring that negros would not, in case of the exclusion of Japanese, take their place; a prominent negro was liberally paid to spread propaganda for the Japanese; and various negro religious and social bodies were approached in many ways." The report continued: "It is the determined purpose of Japan to amalgamate the entire colored races of the world against the Nordic or white race, with Japan at the head of the coalition, for the purpose of wrestling away the supremacy of the white race and placing such supremacy in the colored peoples under the dominion of Japan."[32]

Similar fears haunted policymakers during World War II. Secretary of War Henry L. Stimson attributed black demands for equality during the conflict to agitation by Japanese agents and Communists. Stimson recognized no legitimate grievances among African Americans but interpreted their demands for jobs in industry and positions in combat as evidence of Japanese-initiated efforts to interfere with mobilization for national defense. In the same vein, the Department of State warned against Japanese infiltration of black protest groups, like A. Philip Randolph's March on Washington Movement, as part of an effort "to direct the Negro Minority in a subversive effort against the United States."[33]

Southern journalist and racial self-proclaimed moderate Virginius Dabney feared African American identification with the Japanese war effort because, "like the natives of Malaya and Burma, the American Negroes are sometimes imbued with the notion that a victory for the yellow race over the white race might also be a victory for them."[34] These predictions could become self-fulfilling prophesies; by showing how frightened they were by the prospect of alliances between African Americans and people of color elsewhere in the world, anxious whites called attention to a resource in the bud for black freedom struggles that would eventually came to full flower in the 1960s in the form of opposition to the Vietnam War by the Student Nonviolent Coordinating Committee and the Southern Christian Leadership Conference and expressions of solidarity with anti-imperialist struggles in Asia, Africa, and Latin America by more radical groups.

Extensive surveillance and infiltration of Japanese American and African American organizations by intelligence agents conclusively found little reason to fear any significant systematic disloyalty or subversion. Yet once the war started, government officials moved swiftly and decisively against black nationalist draft resisters and organizations suspected of sympathy with Japanese war aims. F.H. Hammurabi, leader of World Wide Friends of Africa (also known as the House of Knowledge), was indicted in 1942 for delivering speeches praising Japan and for showing his audiences films of the Japanese attack on Pearl Harbor.[35]

Federal agents placed Ashima Takis under surveillance because of the PMEW's efforts to persuade black nationalists in New York to ready "the dark-skinned races for armed uprisings should Japanese forces invade United States soil."[36] He received a three-year prison sentence for having cashed a fraudulent money order some years earlier and served as a star witness in a federal prosecution of St. Louis–area members of the PMEW. Followers reported that Takis spoke German, French, and Spanish, that his English was perfect in private conversation but heavily accented in public speeches, and that he enjoyed success as a faith healer in black neighborhoods.[37] Robert A. Hill describes Takis as a Japanese who masqueraded as a Filipino under the pseudonym Policarpio Manansala, while Ernest V. Allen represents him as a Filipino who called himself Mimo de Guzman and Policarpio Manansala and. masqueraded as a Japanese national under the pseudonym Ashima Takis.

Prosecutors also brought charges of sedition and inciting draft resistance against leaders of the Peace Movement of Ethiopia and against the Nation of Islam. Federal agents arrested Elijah Muhammad in May 1942, and a federal judge sentenced him to a five-year prison term at the Federal Correction Institute in Milan, Michigan. FBI agents raided the Chicago Temple of the NOI in September 1942, tearing "the place apart trying to find weapons hidden there since they believed we were connected with the Japanese," one suspect later recalled. The agents found no weapons or documents linking the group to the

Japanese government, but those arrested all served three years in prison for draft evasion.[38]

Although Malcolm X later joined the Nation of Islam, where he fashioned an impassioned and precise critique of the connections linking U.S. imperialism overseas and antiblack racism at home, we have no reason to doubt his report in his autobiography that in 1943 his conscious motivations entailed little more than a desire to avoid "jail, a job, and the Army."[39] But he could not have failed to notice that the war against Japan gave him leverage that he would not have had otherwise. In that respect, his vision corresponded to that of millions of other African Americans.

Immediately after the Japanese attack on Pearl Harbor, Robert L. Vann, editor and publisher of one of the nation's most important black newspapers, the *Pittsburgh Courier,* called on the president and Congress "to declare war on Japan and against racial prejudice in our country." This campaign for "double victory" had actually started before the war, when A. Philip Randolph used the threat of a mass march on Washington in June 1941 to extract from President Roosevelt Executive Order 8802, which mandated fair hiring in defense industries. James Boggs, then a black auto worker in Detroit, recalled that "Negroes did not give credit for this order to Roosevelt and the American government. Far from it. Recognizing that America and its allies had their backs to the wall in their struggle with Hitler and Tojo, Negroes said that Hitler and Tojo, by creating the war which made the Americans give them jobs in the industry, had done more for them in four years than Uncle Sam had done in 300 years."[40]

Yet, even in the midst of a war against a common enemy, white Americans held onto their historic hatreds and prejudices. At the Packard main factory in Detroit, white war workers protesting desegregation of the assembly line announced that they would rather lose the war than have to "work beside a nigger on the assembly line." John L. De Witt of the Fourth Army Western Defense Command in San Francisco complained to the army's chief of classification when badly needed reinforcements that he had requested turned out to be African American soldiers. "You're filling too many colored troops up on the West Coast," De Witt warned. "There will be a great deal of public reaction out here due to the Jap situation. They feel they've got enough black skinned people around them as it is, Filipinos and Japanese. . . . I'd rather have a white regiment."[41]

Black workers had to wage unrelenting struggles to secure and keep high-paying posts in defense industries on the home front, while African American military personnel served under white officers in a largely segregated military.

The high command did its best to keep black troops out of combat so that they could not claim the fruits of victory over fascism.[42] On the other hand, in order to promote enthusiasm for the war among African Americans, the military also publicized the heroism of individual black combatants like Dorie Miller, a steward on the battleship *West Virginia,* which was among the vessels attacked at Pearl Harbor on December 7, 1941. According to the navy, Miller was stationed on the bridge near the ship's commanding officer when the enemy attacked. He reportedly dragged the ship's wounded captain from an exposed spot on the bridge and then manned a machine gun, shooting down two enemy planes, despite never having been trained on the weapon. Twelve weeks after the incident, the navy bowed to pressure from African American organizations and identified Miller, awarding him the Navy Cross.[43] Skeptics have subsequently raised doubts about whether Miller accomplished the feats for which he was decorated, but his fame made his fate an issue among African Americans regardless. They noted that, consistent with navy policy at the time, he received no transfer to a combat position but continued serving food and drink to white officers on the escort carrier *Liscombe Bay,* where he died when that ship sank on November 24, 1943.[44]

Black soldiers sought positions in combat but found themselves relegated to roles as garrison troops at Efate in the New Hebrides, at Guadalcanal in the southern Solomons, and at Banika in the Russels group. But black soldiers from the First Battalion of the Twenty-fourth Infantry Regiment (which had been David Fagen's unit in the Philippines) and members of the all-black Ninety-third Division eventually served with white soldiers in combat in March 1945 on Bougainville.[45] More than a million black men and women served in the armed forces during the war, more than half of them overseas in Europe or the Pacific.

Despite clear evidence of African American loyalty to the Allied effort, counterintelligence officers made black people special targets of surveillance, investigation, and harassment. Naval intelligence officials in Hawaii ranked "Negroes" second only to "Japanese" people as primary suspects of subversion.[46] The Federal Bureau of Investigation issued a wildly inflated estimate of more than 100,000 African American members of pro-Japanese organizations (perhaps counting those who escaped the draft in the way that Malcolm X did).[47] Yet, while mass subversion by blacks was largely a figment of J. Edgar Hoover's always active imagination, the racialized nature of U.S. policy and propaganda in relation to the Japanese did elicit strong responses from African Americans.

In *Lonely Crusade,* a postwar roman à clef based on his own wartime experiences as an African American assembly-line worker, Chester Himes writes of the complicated relationship between Japan and his lead character, Lee Gordon. When navy training exercises make him think for a moment that a Japanese invasion is in progress, Gordon exults, "They're here! Oh, God-dammit, they're coming! Come on, you little bad bastards! Come on and take this city." Himes writes: "In his excitement he expressed a secret admiration for Japan that had been slowly mounting in him over the months of his futile search for work. It was as if he reached the conviction that if Americans did not want him the Japanese did. He wanted them to come so he could join them and lead them on to victory; even though he himself knew that this was only the wishful yearning of the disinherited."[48]

The Office of War Information conducted a confidential survey of African Americans in 1942. Eighteen per cent of the respondents indicated that they expected their personal condition to improve if Japan invaded the United States; 31 percent thought that their circumstances would remain the same; 26 percent had no opinion or refused to answer.[49] The OWI concluded that only 25 percent of African Americans supported the war effort wholeheartedly and that 15 percent had "pro-Japanese" inclinations," yet a careful study of letters to the editor and editorials in the black press showed that most African Americans neither supported nor condemned Japan.[50]

Detroit journalist Gordon Hancock accused white government officials of "colorphobia" in their close surveillance of Japanese expansion in the Far East while virtually ignoring what Hancock saw as the manifestly greater dangers posed by German actions in Europe."[51] Chester Himes worked his reaction to the Japanese internment into another midforties novel, *If He Hollers Let Him Go,* by having his narrator, Bob Jones, identify the roots of rage against white supremacy: "[M]aybe it wasn't until I'd seen them send the Japanese away that I'd noticed it. Little Riki Oyana singing 'God Bless America' and going to Santa Anita [for internment] with his parents the next day. It was taking a man up by the roots and locking him up without a chance. Without a trial. Without a charge. Without even giving him a chance to say one word. It was thinking about if they ever did that to me, Robert Jones, Mrs. Jones's dark son, that started me to getting scared."

Gloster Current, the NAACP's director of branches, noted how these countersubversive measures against Japanese Americans raised special concern in the black community. When the government announced its plans to incarcerate more than 100,000 law-abiding Japanese Americans, Current observed,

"[M]any a Negro throughout the country felt a sense of apprehension always experienced in the face of oppression: Today *them*, tomorrow *us*. For once the precedent had been established of dealing with persons on the basis of race or creed, none of us could consider ourselves safe from future 'security' measures."[52] This interethnic solidarity among aggrieved racial groups was one of the main products of the World War II experience and one of its most important postwar legacies.

Before the war, African Americans and Japanese Americans lived in close proximity in many western U.S. cities. On Jackson Street in Seattle, Japanese restaurants and black barber shops catered to customers from both races as well as to customers of Filipino, Chinese, and Mexican ancestry. White-owned hotels, restaurants, and motion picture theaters denied service to black customers, but Japanese American entrepreneurs welcomed them.[53] In Los Angeles, African Americans and Japanese Americans shared several areas of the city, notably the neighborhood bounded by Silver Lake, Sunset, and Alvarado, the section near Vermont, Fountain, and Lucille, and the streets near Arlington, Jefferson, and Western. People in these neighborhoods shared experiences with discrimination as well; because of the "subversive" and "heterogeneous" nature of their communities, the Home Owners Loan Corporation Secret City Survey Files designated the property of home owners in these districts undesirable for federal loan support.[54]

Less than a week after the attack on Pearl Harbor, Seattle's black-owned and black-edited newspaper, *Northwest Enterprise*, opposed plans to evacuate Japanese Americans from the West Coast. "Don't lose your head and commit crimes in the name of patriotism," a front-page editorial cautioned. In terms its African American readers well understood, the newspaper reminded them that "the same mob spirit which would single them [Japanese Americans] out for slaughter has trailed you through the forest to string you up at some crossroad."[55]

Personal relationships between Japanese Americans and members of other racialized groups motivated individual responses to the internment. Chicano playwright Luiz Valdez remembers that the incarceration of Japanese Americans brought a temporary moment of prosperity to his family in Delano when the U.S. Army made his father manager of a farm previously run by Japanese Americans. Yet prosperity had its price. The Japanese farmer who lived on the land refused to go to the camps and hanged himself in the kitchen of the house that Valdez and his family inhabited for the duration of the war. The playwright remembers being afraid to enter the kitchen late at night and recalls that during one evening of telling ghost stories he and his cousins thought they could see the farmer's body hanging from a lamp. After the war, the Valdez family returned to the fields and life as impoverished farmworkers.[56]

At the Manzanar Relocation Center in 1944, authorities discovered that one of the Japanese Americans incarcerated in their camp was actually Mexican American. Ralph Lazo decided to present himself as a Japanese American at the time of the internment in order to stay with his high school friends. "My Japanese-American friends at Belmont High School were ordered to evacuate the West Coast, so I decided to go with them," Lazo explained. "Who can say I haven't got Japanese blood in me? Who knows what kind of blood runs in their veins?" When embarrassed relocation officials ordered his release from Manzanar, Lazo enlisted in the army. One African American in Seattle drove a Japanese family to the train scheduled to take them to a relocation center and stood by them until it was time to get on board. An interpreter overheard the black man tell a Japanese woman in the group, "You know that if there's ever anything I can do for you whether it be something big or something small, I'm here to do it."[57]

In the San Francisco Bay Area, the chair of the Alameda County Branch of the NAACP's legal committee wrote to the organization's national spokesperson, Walter White, in July 1942 to protest the "inhumane treatment of Japanese evacuees, and the simultaneously eased restrictions against white enemy aliens." Frank Crosswaith of the Negro Labor Committee criticized the Supreme Court's decision to uphold curfews on Japanese Americans on the West Coast as evidence of "the spread of Hitler's despicable doctrine of racism." When New York's usually liberal mayor Fiorello La Guardia objected to the placement of relocated Japanese Americans in that city in 1944, Roy Wilkins, editor of the NAACP's *The Crisis*, joined George Schuyler, then assistant editor of the *Pittsburgh Courier*, Fred Hoshiyama of the Japanese American Citizens League, and socialist Norman Thomas in addressing a mass protest rally. While Cheryl Greenberg is absolutely correct in arguing that the NAACP responded too timidly and too parochially to the internment—the organization attempted to take advantage of the internment by seeking to replace Japanese American farmhands in California's agricultural fields with blacks—she also demonstrates that the organization did more than most other civil rights or ethnic groups to defend Japanese Americans. Especially in California, the NAACP offered aid to returned evacuees and supplied them with extensive legal assistance.[58]

In 1945, Charles Jackson condemned attacks in California against Japanese Americans returning from the internment camps in an editorial in *The Militant*, the organ of the Socialist Workers Party. Jackson urged his fellow blacks to "go to bat for a Japanese-American just as quickly as we would for another Negro. These people are obviously being denied their full citizenship rights just as we are. They are pictured in the capitalist press as toothsome, 'brown-bellied bastards, and are described by the capitalist commentators as half-man and half beast.' This vicious type of prejudice indoctrination is familiar to every Negro."[59]

The interethnic identification between people with similar experiences with racism that characterizes Charles Jackson's response to the assaults on Japanese Americans proved important in reconfiguring racial politics during World War II. Members of racialized minority groups frequently found themselves compared to one another. For example, military officials and political leaders in California favored a plan to move urban Japanese Americans to farm work in rural areas, hoping that such a move would prevent the influx of "a lot of Negroes and Mexicans" into the farming regions. At the Poston internment camp, a staff person complained that many of the facility's officials knew little about Japanese Americans but "almost automatically transferred attitudes held about Negroes to the evacuees."[60]

When deployed in combat and support roles, African American service personnel were often confronted with the fear so characteristic of colonial officials everywhere that contact between native peoples and armed troops of their own race might "contaminate" the population. For example, when large numbers of black U.S. troops arrived in Trinidad, British colonial officials on that island protested that the "self-assurance" of the troops would spread to the islanders and make them uncontrollable. The U.S. Department of State agreed with the British officials and consequently ordered the troops replaced by Puerto Ricans who spoke mostly Spanish, and thus constituted less of a threat to the black Anglophone population.[61]

The Puerto Rican presence in Hawaii seemed to play a different role in race relations there. The thirty thousand African American sailors, soldiers, and war workers who came to Hawaii during the war discovered that the Hawaii census classified people of African origin as Puerto Rican—and therefore "Caucasian"—to distinguish them from native and Asian inhabitants of the islands. Thus, by moving to Hawaii, blacks could become white. Native Hawaiians often displayed sympathy for blacks in unexpected ways. One bus driver tried to help African Americans defeat their white tormentors when racial fights broke out on his vehicle. He kept the rear doors closed if blacks were winning, and then opened the doors to let them slip away when the fights ended. As a black war worker recalled, "There was what you would call an empathy from the local people as to what the black people had endured. They sort of, I guess, sympathized with us to a degree."[62]

Nonetheless, service in Hawaii hardly insulated blacks from racism. During the war, brothels in Honolulu's Hotel Street district refused to admit African Americans or Hawaiians of color because white servicemen and war workers from the mainland objected to their presence. Continually warned against associating with black men, local women sometimes viewed the African Americans with fear. One Chinese-Hawaiian wrote, "I am very scared of these Negro soldiers here in Honolulu. They make my skin shrivel and my self afraid to go near them."[63]

Communities of color found their fates intertwined during the war; they could not isolate themselves from one another. When large numbers of African American workers from the South moved to war production centers on the West Coast, city officials, realtors, and military authorities saw to it that they found housing in the sections of Seattle, San Francisco, and Los Angeles left vacant by the Japanese internment rather than in white neighborhoods.[64] At the same time, some Mexican Americans felt more vulnerable to racist attacks after the Japanese relocation. "In Los Angeles, where fantasy is a way of life," observed liberal journalist Carey McWilliams, "it was a foregone conclusion that the Mexicans would be substituted as the major scapegoat group once the Japanese were removed." After mobs of white sailors attacked Mexican American youths wearing zoot suits in June 1943, the *Los Angeles Times* printed a caricature of Japanese premier Tojo riding on horseback and wearing a zoot suit.[65]

A 1942 Gallup Poll discovered that "American" respondents held slightly more favorable opinions of Mexicans than of Japanese people, but Los Angeles County Sheriff's Department lieutenant Edward Duran Ayers proved an exception. He drew on many popular stereotypes and slurs in grand jury testimony where he paradoxically contrasted "violence-prone" Mexicans with "law abiding" Chinese and Japanese populations, of course not explaining why 100,000 law-abiding Japanese Americans had been shipped off to internment camps. Even more contradictorily, Ayers "explained" the propensity toward violence that he discerned among Mexicans as a result of the "oriental" background of their pre-Columbian ancestors, which left them with the "oriental" characteristic of "total disregard for human life."[66]

While racialized groups retained their separate (and sometimes antagonistic) interests and identities, panethnic antiracist coalitions emerged on occasion in support of Japanese Americans. Representatives of African American, Filipino, and Korean community groups met with delegates from sixteen federal, state, and local agencies at the Palace Hotel in San Francisco in January 1945 to establish the Pacific Coast Fair Play Committee. They agreed that "any attempt to make capital for their own racial groups at the expense of the Japanese would be sawing off the limbs on which they themselves sat." Sometimes, identification came from a perception of common problems. In the novel *Lonely Crusade,* Chester Himes has his black protagonist learn how black, Mexican, and Asian American residents share similar experiences with white racism when he reads a newspaper that reports on "a white woman in a shipyard" who "accused a Negro worker of raping her," on a group of white sailors who "had stripped a Mexican lad of his zoot suit on Main Street before a host of male and female onlookers," and about a "Chinese girl" who had been "mistaken for Japanese" and "slapped on a crowded streetcar by a white mother whose son had been killed in the Pacific."[67]

By the end of the war, race had become a visible and clearly contested element in all areas of U.S. life. The humiliation and indignity imposed on the Japanese during their incarceration left lasting scars, demonstrating once again how state policy marked Asian Americans as permanently foreign in a manner quite dissimilar to every other immigrant group. During the war, Japanese Americans not only lost years of their lives and millions of dollars in property that went mostly to whites, but they suffered a systematic assault on their culture by incarceration and surveillance policies aimed at wiping out the key conduits of Japanese culture in America.[68] In addition, a wave of violent attacks against Japanese American persons and property swept the West Coast toward the end of the war, and the leniency shown the perpetrators by law enforcement officials and juries portended permanent second-class status for Americans of Japanese ancestry.[69]

Yet Japanese Americans secured some victories in the postwar period. In 1948, California voters rejected efforts to institutionalize and extend the state's anti-Japanese Alien Land Law by a vote of 59 percent against and only 41 percent in favor. The 1952 McCarren-Walter Immigration Act reversed the ban on nonwhites becoming naturalized citizens, on the books since 1790, even though the national origins quotas in the act still displayed strong prejudice against immigrants from Asia. Large-scale migration by African Americans and Mexican Americans seeking work in war industries changed the composition of the region's nonwhite population during the war: California's black population increased from 124,000 to 462,000, and the population of Seattle quadrupled between 1941 and 1945 as African Americans replaced Japanese Americans as the city's largest minority group.[70] In some ways, whites' hatred for blacks and

Mexicans eased some of the pressures on Japanese Americans. For example, as Roger Daniels points out, the same voters who rejected the 1948 Alien Land Law Referendum in California also voted overwhelmingly against a Fair Employment Practices measure aimed mainly at prohibiting job discrimination against African American and Mexican American workers.[71]

For African Americans, the Pacific war contributed to a new militancy. Struggles to secure high-paying jobs in defense industries and positions on the front lines in combat led logically to postwar activism, which ranged from massive campaigns for voting rights in the South to access to jobs and housing in the North. A. Philip Randolph organized resistance to the draft among African Americans in the postwar period until President Truman capitulated and ordered the desegregation of the military in 1948. But the war did more than incubate a certain amount of militancy; it taught lasting lessons about the inescapably racialized nature of power and politics in the United States.

African Americans responded with mixed emotions to what they had learned about white racism in their wartime experiences. In a postwar rumination, James Baldwin recalled, "The treatment accorded the Negro during the Second World War marks, for me, a turning point in the Negro's relation to America. To put it briefly, and somewhat too simply, a certain hope died, a certain respect for white Americans faded." John Hope Franklin had some of the same feelings. "Obviously I was pleased with the outcome of the war," he recalled, "but I was not pleased with certain policies pursued by our government. I wish that the government could have been less hypocritical, and more honest about its war aims. I wish that it could have won—and I believe it could have—without the blatant racism that poisoned the entire effort; without its concentration camps for our Japanese citizens, which smacked too much of Hitlerism; and without the use of the atomic bomb."[72]

A black soldier stationed in the Philippines, Nelson Peery, drew a parallel between the postwar fate of African Americans and the destiny of the Filipino people he had come to know during his time in the service: "I knew. No one had to tell me. I knew that America was going to beat us back into line when we got home. The Negro troops got a taste of racial equality in foreign lands. As they came home, that had to be beaten and lynched and terrorized out of them before they would go back to building levees and picking cotton. I could see no reason to expect that the Filipinos, also referred to as 'niggers,' were going to get any better treatment. It was the reason I felt such a deep sense of unity with, and loyalty to, the islands and their people." In a book published immediately after the surrender of Japan, Walter White observed that "World War II has given to the Negro a sense of kinship with other colored—and also oppressed—peoples of the world. Where he has not thought or informed himself on the racial angles of colonial policy and master-race theories, he senses that the struggle of the Negro in the United States is part and parcel of the struggle against imperialism and exploitation in India, China, Burma, South Africa, the Philippines, Malaya, the West Indies, and South America."[73]

The postwar period also served as a crucible for antiracist thought and action among members of other aggrieved racial groups. Chicano scholar and author Americo Paredes (see chapter 3) served as a Pacific staff correspondent and editor for the U.S. military's newspaper *Stars and Stripes* during the war. He entered Japan with the U.S. occupation forces and, after meeting and marrying a Japanese national, he remained in that country after the war to report on the trials of Japanese leaders charged with atrocities. The racial insults directed against the accused by the military reminded Paredes of things he had heard said about Chicanos back home in south Texas, and in that context he felt an affinity for the accused. Paredes went on to work as a journalist in Korea and China during the postwar years, and his student and biographer, Jose Limon, notes that Paredes "developed an attachment to these Asian peoples and a conviction that racism had played a key role in the extension of American military power in that part of the world. This conviction was reinforced when he and his wife decided to return to the United States and encountered racist immigration quotas for Japanese designed to discourage marriages such as his."[74]

Malcolm X certainly embraced a similar anti-imperialism and internationalism after he converted to Islam in a Massachusetts prison in the late 1940s. When the Korean War broke out, he wrote a letter from prison (which he knew would be read by that institution's censors as well as by outside intelligence agents) explaining, "I have always been a Communist. I have tried to enlist in the Japanese Army last war, now they will never draft or accept me in the U.S. Army." Paroled in 1953, he secured employment moving truck frames and cleaning up after welders at the Gar Wood factory. FBI agents visited him at work demanding to know why he had not registered for the draft. He pretended that he did not know that ex-convicts had to register, and the FBI apparently believed him. His draft board in Plymouth, Michigan, denied his request for status as a conscientious objector but judged him "disqualified for military service" because of an alleged "asocial personality with paranoid trends."[75]

Black encounters with Asia became increasingly important between 1940 and 1975, as the United States went to war in Japan, the Philippines, Korea, China, Vietnam, Laos, and Cambodia. These U.S. wars in Asia have played an important role in reconfiguring race relations in North America. They have augmented racist tendencies to conflate Asian Americans with the nation's external enemies, as evidenced most clearly by hate crimes against people of Asian origin in the wake of the war in Vietnam and the emergence of economic competition between Asian and North American industries.[76] But U.S. wars in Asia have also repeatedly raised the kinds of contradictions faced by communities of color during World War II. For example, Gerald Horne and Mary L. Dudziak have shown how the Supreme Court's 1954 decision in Brown v. Board of Education responded in part to the imperatives of the Cold War: segregation made it difficult for the United States to present itself as the defender of freedom to emerging nations in Asia, Africa, and Latin America.[77]

In addition, U.S. wars in Asia and their costs to communities of color generated new critiques of the nation's domestic and foreign policies. Amiri Baraka (formerly LeRoi Jones) argues that the Korean conflict created many of the preconditions for the modern-day civil rights movement, and indeed many Korean War veterans, including James Foreman and Bobby Seale, played prominent roles in African American protest groups during the 1950s and 1960s.[78] Ivory Perry, a prominent community activist in St. Louis, always credited his service at Camp Gifu, Japan, and in combat in Korea as the crucible for his own subsequent activism. Meeting Japanese and Korean citizens who seemed refreshingly nonracist compared to the white Americans Perry had known helped him see that white supremacy was a primarily a phenomenon of U.S. national history, not of human nature. In addition, the contrast between the freedoms he was sent overseas to defend and the freedoms he could not realize at home made him more determined than ever to bring about changes in his own country. As he remembers thinking on his return to the United States from the war, "I shouldn't have been in Korea in the first place because those Korean people they haven't ever did anything to Ivory Perry. I'm over there trying to kill them for something that I don't know what I'm shooting for. I said my fight is here in America."[79]

When Muhammad Ali (whose conversion to Islam involved the direct intervention and assistance of Malcolm X) refused to fight in the Vietnam War because "I ain't got no quarrel with them Viet Cong," his celebrated case not only established that anti-imperialist and internationalist thinking had a broad base of support among African Americans, it also helped publicize, legitimate, and proselytize for an antiwar movement that was interracial in many significant ways.[80] As Edward Escobar, Carlos Munoz, and George Mariscal have shown, the Chicano Moratorium in Los Angeles in 1970 demonstrated mass opposition to the war among Mexican Americans, but it also played a crucial role in building the Chicano movement itself.[81] Antiwar protest among Chicanos held particular significance because it required them to oppose the official positions of important institutions in the community, including the Catholic church, trade unions, and veterans groups.[82]

Just as U.S. wars in Asia brought to the surface the racial contradictions facing African Americans and Mexican Americans, antiracist movements among blacks and Chicanos helped Asian Americans address their unresolved grievances in respect to white supremacy in the United States. During the Vietnam War, militant Asian American political and cultural groups emerged as important participants in interethnic Third World coalitions. African American examples often guided these groups. Rie Aoyama, a Japanese American activist from Seattle explains, "We had no role models for finding identity. We followed what blacks did. Within the whole Asian American identity, part of the black identity came with it. Usually when you say Asian American, you are going to have some aspect of black experience too." Nancy Matsuda similarly attributes her politicization to her recognition while in high school of the parallels between Asian Americans and blacks: "I realized how blacks were an oppressed people, and I saw how Asians were oppressed too. So for me, it was a complete turn around from wanting to be associated with the whites to wanting to be associated with the blacks, or just a minority."[83] In 1968, Toru Sakahara, a Japanese American attorney and community leader in Seattle, organized a discussion group that brought representatives of the Black Panther Party in dialogue with members of the Japanese American Citizens League and Jackson Street business owners whose property had been damaged during a civil insurrection in that city.[84]

Thus, we can see that the racialized nature of the Pacific war has had enduring consequences for race relations in the United States. It exacerbated the antagonisms and alienations of race, while at the same time instigating unexpected alliances and affinities across communities of color. Yet it is important to understand that fights between men of different races often involved competition for power over women or over access to them. The prophetic currents of African American and interethnic antiracist activity during World War II addressed important issues about race, nation, and class, but they did precious little to promote an understanding, analysis, or strategy about the ways in which hierarchies of gender initiated, legitimated, and sustained social inequalities and injustices.

The black nationalist organizations that identified with Japan and other "nonwhite" nations during the 1920s and 1930s also advocated a rather consistent subordination of women to men. In some of these groups women did attain visibility as organizers and activists: government agents shadowed Mittie Maud Lena Gordon because of her work as head of the Peace Movement of Ethiopia, and they put Madame M.L.T. De Mena under surveillance because of her public association with Ashima Takis. Pearl Sherrod took over Satakota Takahishi's newspaper column in local papers after he was deported, and she served as well as nominal leader of the society for the Development of Our Own. Takahishi himself spoke out forthrightly for women's rights, condemning the "peculiar ideas prevailing among a certain group of men, that the women should not hold any office in an organization, nor even have a voice at the meetings." Counseling respect between men and women, Takahishi reminded his followers that a woman held the post of international supervisor in his organization. That woman, however, did most of her speaking to white audiences that Takahishi refused to address. In addition, he demonstrated his respect for women by having an affair with a young female follower while Pearl Sherrod Takahishi ran his organization for him. This development led Sherrod to report her husband to the Immigration and Naturalization Service herself when he tried to return to the United States in 1939.[85]

The white servicemen who attacked Mexican American youths in Los Angeles in the 1943 Zoot Suit Riots justified their actions as a defense of white women from the predatory attentions of nonwhite "hoodlums." At the same time, many Mexican American youths saw the zoot suiters as heroic defenders of Mexican women from advances by white men. In an article about the riots for the NAACP journal, *The Crisis,* Chester Himes compared the sailors to storm troopers, dismissing them as uniformed Klansmen. But he portrayed the riots as primarily a fight about access to women. Condemning the "inexplicable" and "incomprehensible" ego that allows "southern white men" to believe that they are entitled to sex "with any dark skinned woman on earth," Himes explained that Mexican American and black youths objected to white men dating women of their races because "they, the Mexican and negro boys, cannot go out in Hollywood and pick up white girls."[86]

Himes analyzed the ways in which the war in the Pacific emboldened white men about approaching women of color. He recounted an incident that he witnessed on a streetcar when three white sailors on leave from the "Pacific skirmishes" began talking loudly about "how they had whipped the Japs." Himes noted sarcastically, "It seems always to give a white man a wonderful feeling when he whips a Jap." One sailor boasted about his prowess in combat, and then bragged, "Boy, did those native gals go fuh us." Looking around the street-car, one of them announced that a white man could get any woman he wanted, in a clear attempt to intimidate two "Mexican" youths in the company of an attractive girl. Himes complained that African American and Mexican American men could not protest remarks like these made to their wives and sweethearts by white men and, even worse, that unescorted black women would "get a purely commercial proposition from every third unescorted white man or group of white men."[87] Although he fashioned a sensitive and perceptive critique of how official sanction for the attacks on zoot suiters replicated the rule by riot that dominated the lives of blacks in the South, Himes never identified the role played by gender in constructing racial identities, or the ways in which desires for equality based on equal male privileges over women undermined the egalitarian principles and hopes that he saluted elsewhere.

Part of the prejudice toward black soldiers originated from white servicemen who warned the women they met about the dangers of being molested and raped by black men. A Japanese American woman in Hawaii noticed how her views had been channeled in that direction one day after she shared an uneventful bus ride with four African American servicemen. Surprised that they had not accosted her, she wrote to a friend, "Gee, I was very frightened. . . . Funny isn't it how I am about them. One would be that way after hearing lots of nasty things about them.[88] On the home front and overseas, battles between black and white war workers, service personnel, and civilians stemmed from struggles over sex—over rumors of rape, competition for dates, and symbolic and real violations of the privileges of white masculinity."[89]

In his important analysis of government distribution of pin-up photos among U.S. servicemen during World War II, Robert Westbrook shows how the maintenance of white male prerogatives and privileges involved much more than the regressive thinking or selfish behavior of individuals (see chapter 4). Westbrook makes a persuasive case that the entire war effort had to be presented as a defense of middle-class male norms in order to solve some difficult ideological problems raised by the government's need for popular sacrifice. Westbrook explains that liberal capitalist states have difficulty providing compelling reasons for their citizens to go to war. Given its promises of insulating private property and personal happiness from demands by the state, how can the liberal capitalist state ask its subjects to surrender property, happiness, liberty, and life in pursuit of collective goals?

In the United States during World War II, the answer came from couching public obligations as private interests, by stressing military service as the defense of families, children, lovers, friends, and an amorphously defined but clearly commodity-driven "American Way of Life." Just as wartime advertisers' promises about the postwar period featured full refrigerators rather than the four freedoms, just as Hollywood films presented soldiers sacrificing themselves for apple pie, the Brooklyn Dodgers, and the girl they left behind rather than for the fight against fascism, the U.S. government chose to supply its fighting men with pictures of Betty Grable in a swimsuit as an icon of the private world of personal pleasure that would be restored to them when the war was won. Grable's identity as a blonde, white, wholesome, middle-class, and married beauty made her an appropriate symbol, fitting the war effort firmly into the conventions, history, aspirations, and imagery of middle-class European American life and culture.[90] Consequently, when white men engaged in racist violence against soldiers and civilians of color, they acted upon an understanding of their privileges and prerogatives that the government and other important institutions in their society had encouraged.

After World War II, U.S. economic expansion and military engagement in Asia led to a new stage of racial formation. The same propagandists who deployed alarmist images of violated white women as the reason to resist "yellow feet" on U.S. soil during the war now fashioned fables of romantic love between white U.S. servicemen and Asian women as allegories of empire. In his perceptive analysis of race as the "political unconscious" of American cinema, Nick Browne shows how World War II occasioned a displacement of some of the U.S. film industry's traditional images of African Americans onto Asia. In films including *The Teahouse of the August Moon* (1956) and *Sayonara* (1957), the U.S. presence in Asia becomes naturalized by a grid of sexual relations in which white males have general access to all women, white women are prohibited from sex with nonwhite men, nonwhite men have access to nonwhite women only, and nonwhite women submit to both nonwhite and white men. Consequently, in Browne's formulation, the social world created by the complicated intersections of race, gender, nation, and class attendant to the U.S. presence in Asia relies upon a unified "gender-racial-economic system built as much on what it prohibits as what it permits."[91] This use of gendered imagery to make unequal social relations seem natural and therefore necessary endures today as a particularly poisonous legacy of the Asia Pacific war, especially at a time when so much of the project of transnational capital depends upon the low-wage labor of exploited Asian women workers.

During World War II, African Americans found in Asia a source of inspiration and emulation whose racial signifiers complicated the binary black-white divisions of the United States. They exposed the internationalist past and present of U.S. race relations, and they forged intercultural communications and contacts to allow for the emergence of antiracist coalitions and consciousness. Liberal narratives about multiculturalism and cultural pluralism to the contrary, race relations in the United States have always involved more than one outcast group at a time acting in an atomized fashion against a homogenous "white" center. Interethnic identifications and alliances have been powerful weapons against white supremacy. All racial identities are relational; communities of color are mutually constitutive of one another, not just competitive or cooperative.

The history of interethnic antiracist coalitions among even ostensibly essentialist and separatist black nationalist groups points toward potentially effective strategies for the present. Yet to abstract race from the other social relations in which it is embedded would be to seriously misread the nature of racial formation and the social construction of identities. As Susan Jeffords points out, "[T]he complex intersections between all of the manifestations of dominance in patriarchal structures will vary according to historical moments and location, and must be specified in each situation in order to be adequately understood and challenged."[92]

In our own time, when the rapid mobility across the globe of capital, commodities, images, ideas, products, and people creates fundamentally new anxieties about identities connected to nation, race, class, and gender, the relevance of transnational interracial identifications and alliances prefigured during World War II should be manifestly evident. Race is as important as ever; people are dying every day all around the world because of national narratives with racist preconditions. But at a time when women make up so much of the emerging low-wage world work force, when patriarchal narratives continue to command the allegiance of killers for so many causes, it is also evident that the same imagination and ingenuity that allowed for unlikely coalitions across continents in the past on issues of race must now include a fully theorized understanding of gender as it intersects with identities based on narratives of nation, race, and class.

California: The Mississippi of the 1990s

It is not true that people become liars without knowing it. A liar always knows that he is lying, and that is why all liars travel in packs: in order to be reassured that the judgment day will never come for them. They need each other for the well-being, the health, the perpetuation of their lie. They have a tacit agreement to guard each other's secrets, for they have the same secret.—JAMES BALDWIN

During the 1960s, comedian Jackie "Moms" Mabley frequently told a story about voting rights in Mississippi. According to her tale, an African American attorney attempts to register to vote at the local registrar's office. Pulling out the literacy tests that have been used historically to disenfranchise black voters in that state, the registrar asks the applicant to recite the names of all the books of the Bible in order—backwards and forwards. The question is a difficult one, but being a black Baptist from Mississippi, the lawyer answers it easily. The next question asks him to interpret an arcane clause in the Mississippi state constitution. Most voters would be stumped here, but being a law school graduate and a practicing attorney, the applicant answered that one correctly as well. Finally, in frustration, the registrar pulls out a Chinese language newspaper, throws it at the attorney, and orders sharply, "Tell me what that says!" Nonplused, the attorney picks up the paper calmly, peruses it carefully, and says slowly, "Oh, that's easy. This says that no matter *what* I do, you're not going to let me vote here in Mississippi."[1]

A friend of mine often invokes Moms Mabley's story as a way of describing the frustrations he faces in trying to get private businesses and government agencies to obey civil rights laws and to implement the nondiscriminatory policies they claim to support. Like the attorney in her story, he finds that previously unannounced rules, regulations, and principles mysteriously emerge whenever the possessive investment in whiteness is threatened. "How did it go today?" someone will ask him in respect to a meeting about discrimination in housing or unfair employment and promotion practices. "They handed me the Chinese newspaper." he'll reply. It sometimes seems as if he gets a Chinese newspaper every day, almost as if he had a subscription.

My friend is not deterred by his recognition of the innate unfairness of established bureaucratic procedures, of their stubborn resistance to substantive change and their disingenuous disavowal of racial intent. The humor in Moms Mabley's story comes from recognition, not resignation—from unmasking procedures that purport to be fair as actually unfair. Today the story invokes memories of a difficult but ultimately successful struggle in the past. We know in the 1990s that, despite its limits, the civil rights movement of the 1960s won some lasting and irreversible victories. Moms Mabley's joke raised the consciousness and the morale of participants in that movement, and today the attorney in her story would be able to vote. In fact, given the rapid emergence of alliances among aggrieved communities of color, that attorney today might even know how to read Chinese.

Yet Mabley's metaphor also reveals the complexity and contradictions of whiteness. Being asked to read a Chinese newspaper is only absurd if China is figured as the master trope of foreignness, as the opposite of "American" identity. It reminds us that literacy tests were not only devices used against blacks, but also key mechanisms for denying entry and citizenship to immigrants.[2] Encoded in Mabley's joke is the assertion that no matter how despised they may be, blacks are American and therefore entitled to the privileges denied them by white supremacy. Yet the operative assumption behind this assertion is that it is unreasonable to expect someone who is "American" to be able to read a Chinese newspaper. This is in no way to belittle the black claim for inclusion contained in Mabley's story, only to warn that in the current multiracial and international context in which racial identities are made and unmade, a simple black-white binary, or indeed any binary opposition, will not help us address or redress the possessive investment in whiteness.

Precisely because of the possessive investment in whiteness, the destinies and self-definitions of Asian Americans and African Americans have long been linked Shortly after the Civil War, southern planters proposed importing large numbers of Chinese laborers to replace freed slaves as agricultural workers. They followed a well-established path with this proposal; throughout the Americas labor migrations from Asia and especially China followed soon after the abolition of slavery—in the West Indies and South America as well as in the United States.[3] Although only a small number of Chinese workers came to the southern United States however, many of them settled in Mississippi, where their presence complicated the local racial economy. Some married African Americans and many others conducted business in African American neighborhoods. Some cities required Chinese residents to attend separate segregated schools and be buried in their own cemeteries. Some of the Mississippi Chinese filed suit asking to have themselves declared "white."[4]

Informed audiences in the 1960s knew that Moms Mabley's story contained fact as well as fiction, at least in respect to literacy tests. The "understanding clause" of the Mississippi constitution of 1890 required prospective voters to demonstrate that they could read any section of the state constitution—or at least understand it when it was read to them by giving "a reasonable interpretation of it."[5] Although it did not specifically mention race, the clear intention of this clause since its inception in 1890 was to give registrars discretionary power to prevent blacks from voting. Like the poll tax, the grandfather clause, the white primary, and other features of civic life in the South outlawed by the 1965 Voting Rights Act, this clause in the state constitution was but one of many institutional practices designed to produce racially differentiated results while disavowing any racial intent.

Racially exclusive policies in Mississippi before the 1960s relied as much on covert as overt racism. No law said that African Americans could not vote in Mississippi, because no such law was needed. White people knew that voting registrars would protect the possessive investment in whiteness by finding all (or nearly all) of the black applicants "unqualified" because they could not pass the literacy test. No state law barred people of color from attending the state's all-white universities because no such law was needed. When Clennon King, a thirty-seven-year-old black teacher attempted to enroll in summer courses at the University of Mississippi at Oxford in 1958, highway patrol officers arrested him and had him committed to a state mental hospital, because "any nigger who tried to enter Ole Miss must be crazy." Authorities kept King in custody for two weeks, refusing to declare him competent to leave the institution until he promised to move to Georgia upon his release.

Similarly, in 1959, Clyde Kennard applied for admission to Mississippi Southern University in Hattiesburg. An African American army veteran who had successfully completed two years of study at the University of Chicago, Kennard sought to complete his education when he returned home to Mississippi to run the family farm after illness incapacitated his stepfather. School and state officials urged Kennard to withdraw his application, but he refused. Police officers, aware of a law that barred convicted felons from attending state colleges, then arrested Kennard and charged him with stealing twenty-five dollars' worth of chicken feed from a warehouse. Despite what historian David M. Oshinsky describes as "clear evidence of a frame-up," a jury composed entirely of whites took only ten minutes to find the defendant guilty, and a state judge sentenced Kennard to seven years at Parchman Prison Farm. In jail, the authorities denied him medical treatment and check-ups even though he had cancer of the colon, and Kennard died of cancer in 1963, shortly after an international protest campaign secured his release from jail through a pardon from Governor Ross Barnett.[6]

State officials in Mississippi never admitted at the time that their refusal to admit Kennard and King to the state's white universities had anything to do with color. To do so would be to admit that the state was violating the Fourteenth Amendment to the Constitution and the subsequent civil rights laws emanating from it. Instead, they argued that the problem with the two applicants was not the color of their skin, but the content of their character. They claimed that King was crazy and that Kennard was a criminal. Of course, they knew these characterizations were lies, and their supporters knew they were lies. Certainly King, Kennard, and their allies knew they were lies. No one was fooled, but no one had to be. State officials were handing King and Kennard the Chinese newspaper.

The politicians who pursued these policies did not always enjoy undiluted popularity. Some white Mississippians felt guilt about their complicity with this system and many more experienced an uneasiness that made them avert their eyes and avoid knowing too much about the policies carried out in their names. Their leaders made them ashamed of themselves. But segregationist politicians knew they could always count on the possessive investment in whiteness; they could always secure support from a significant segment of the electorate by offering them the pleasures of participating in a game that was fixed, by salving their wounds in a competitive society by ensuring that members of another race would always be beneath them. The sadistic pleasures offered to this constituency depended in no small measure on a cynical combination—disingenuous disavowal of racist intent coupled with conscious deployment of policies having clear racist consequences.

Most of the time, the majority of white Mississippians did not think of themselves as racists, yet they supported and sustained a white supremacist system. Most viewed themselves as moderates unfairly burdened by the legacy of past practices that they imagined they would have opposed had then been alive in those days. They believed themselves to be enlightened opponents of primitive racialist thinking, but also practical realists who feared that rapid changes in race relations would give blacks freedoms for which they were not prepared, and consequently undermine economic efficiency, burden taxpayers, and increase social disorder.

The combination of racism and disavowal that characterized Mississippi politics during the 1960s had distinct local inflections, but it evidenced a national problem of long standing. Disavowals of racist intent do not mean that racism is not in effect; on the contrary, that is the way racism usually works. A paradoxical and nettling combination of racism and disavowal has always permeated the possessive investment in whiteness. In his excellent study of soldiers and civilians during World War II, historian Takashi Fujitani identifies "the systematic disavowal of racism coupled with its ongoing reproduction" as the driving force behind the treatment of Japanese Americans in that era." He notes the curious rhetoric of Franklin Delano Roosevelt on February 1, 1943, in announcing the establishment of the 442nd Combat Team, a military unit composed exclusively of Japanese American soldiers. "No loyal citizen of the United States should be denied the democratic right to exercise the responsibilities of citizenship, regardless of his ancestry," the president proclaimed. He added, "The principle on which this country was founded and by which it has always been governed is that Americanism is a matter of the mind and the heart; Americanism is not, and never was, a matter of race of ancestry. A good American is one who is loyal to this country and to our creed of liberty and democracy."[7]

Roosevelt's claims about Americanism as a matter of the mind and heart rather than of race and ancestry contradicted his racial practices. The president's speech came almost exactly one year after he issued Executive Order 9066 mandating the forced incarceration of more than 100,000 loyal Japanese American civilians and the confiscation or compulsory sale of their property. The 442nd Combat Team would be part of a military ruled by whites that had already relegated African Americans to underequipped and poorly supported segregated units of their own. Roosevelt's proclamation about race's irrelevance to the American creed did not motivate him to close the internment camps, offer reparations to the people incarcerated in them, or reverse U.S. laws restricting naturalized citizenship to "white" immigrants and banning immigration from Asian nations. The president took no action to oppose state laws that denied Japanese Americans the right to own property or to marry partners of their choice if they happened to be of another race. Instead, in a move characteristic of the possessive investment in whiteness, he extended to the members of the 442nd Combat Team the responsibilities of citizenship without its rewards—the opportunity to fight and possibly die for a country that relegated them to second-class status precisely because of their ancestry and race. Roosevelt invoked antiracist principles, but only to perpetuate racist practices.

President Roosevelt's rhetoric about race no doubt reflected the pressures of practical politics as well as his own personal predispositions. He served as the leader of a political coalition that contained both open white supremacists and spokespersons for communities of color. Establishing the 442nd Combat Team enabled him to make a concession to Japanese Americans without offending the settled expectations or direct interests of whites. Roosevelt's allusions to the enduring traditions of inclusion in the United States may have been a tactical move to legitimate a progressive yet controversial policy, to incorporate within the contours of tradition changes emerging from the radical transformations in social relations engendered by the war.

Beyond Roosevelt's personal motivations, however, the practice of pursuing policies designed to have detrimental effects on nonwhites while at the same time disingenuously disavowing any racial intent is characteristic of traditional "Americanism." The framers of the U.S. Constitution coyly avoided referring to race directly in their document, but its passages about ending the slave trade and its formula for counting persons held in servitude to determine representation in Congress acknowledge racist realities too divisive and discomforting to allow direct mention. The key legislative achievements of Roosevelt's own New Deal—the Federal Housing Act, the Wagner Act, and the Social Security Act—contained no overt racial provisions, but the racialized categories in FHA appraisers' manuals and the denial of Wagner Act and Social Security coverage to farmworkers, domestics, teachers, librarians, and social workers made these measures systematic subsidies to white males at the expense of people of color and women.

Roosevelt's simultaneous disavowal and embrace of racism illustrates a broader pattern. Racism in the United States sometimes proceeds through direct, referential, and overt practices of exclusion. But it manifests itself more often through indirect, inferential, and covert policies that use the denial of overt racist intent to escape responsibility for racialized consequences. By avoiding direct endorsement of white supremacy, by denying the salience of race in determining life chances and opportunities in the present and the past, by relegating racism to some previous era now passed, civil rights rhetoric like Roosevelt's sanctions the promotion and extension of racist practices. Thus Roosevelt's language in establishing the 442nd Combat Team ultimately tells us less about the personal hypocrisy of the president or the contradictions of the New Deal than about civil rights rhetoric that waves the banner of inclusion while practicing exclusion, maintaining and extending the privileges attendant to the possessive investment in whiteness.

In the process of connecting whiteness with the maintenance of economic security, stability, and predictability, Mississippians of the 1960s resembled their parents and their grandparents more than they recognized. Their confidence in the progress that had already been made in race relations and their certainty that rapid change would bring chaos followed a well-worn path. Disapproval of yesterday's racism as ideological justification of today's was not new in the 1960s; it had characterized the entire history of the state's racial economy. James Baldwin identified the core contradictions of this mind-set in his analysis of the racial philosophy of the great Mississippi writer William Faulkner. In Baldwin's view, Faulkner was "seeking to exorcise a history which is also a curse. He wants the old order, which came into existence through unchecked greed and wanton murder, to redeem itself without further bloodshed—without, that is, any further menacing of itself—without coercion. This, old orders never do, less because they would not than because they cannot. They cannot because they have always existed in relation to a force which they have had to subdue. Their subjugation is the key to their identity and the triumph and justification of their history, and it is also on this continued subjugation that their material well-being depends."[8]

Baldwin's diagnosis of Faulkner connects racial attitudes to economic interests. For more than a century the plantation system sustained Mississippi's economy and shaped the contours of its race relations. Whatever else white racism was in Mississippi, it was also a system for insuring a predictable supply of docile low-wage workers for a labor-intensive economy. As the economy changed, earlier forms of racial subordination became obsolete and new forms emerged. Conflicts over racial identities in Mississippi during the 1960s touched on matters of conscience, but they also emanated from contradictions caused by the transformation from one economic order to another. The traditional low taxes, low wages, and management control over the point of production that Mississippians inherited from the preindustrial era sometimes helped their state attract northern capital as it began to industrialize during the 1960s, but racial antagonisms, the power of local land owners, and the weaknesses of the state's social and industrial infrastructure inhibited growth and development.

Northern corporations wanted to take advantage of the state's low wages, but Mississippi's social structure caused them problems. Their vulnerability to customer boycotts and stockholder protests made the presence of de jure segregation in southern states an economic liability for national and multinational firms like Woolworth's drug stores and Crown-Zellerbach paper company.[9] The turmoil in Mississippi in the 1960s represented a settling of accounts from more than a century of racial subordination, but it also reflected a struggle for authority and power in the context of dramatic economic and social change. The question was how traditional racial categories would influence and shape that change. White racism in Mississippi during the 1960s reassured whites that they would retain the privileges to which they had become accustomed despite the upheavals caused by economic transformation and change.

National economic growth after World War II extended the reach of the industrial system to the remotest corners of Mississippi, a state still dominated in many ways by preindustrial institutions, and created a time of transition during the 1950s and 1960s from which new social relations emerged. Mississippi's political leaders during the 1960s did not prevent the dawn of a new day in their state, but in their ferocious resistance to change they defeated the radical and democratic changes proposed by Fannie Lou Hamer and the grass-roots activists in the Mississippi freedom movement. To whites in the rest of the nation, they demonstrated the utility of breaking the law and resisting federal court orders. Their resistance laid the groundwork for Richard Nixon's southern strategy, for the assault on civil rights and affirmative action that defined the Reagan coalition, and for the timid leadership on issues of racial justice displayed by the Clinton administration. It is no accident that Mississippians Trent Lott and Haley Barbour emerged as leaders of the Republican Party by the 1990s. The diehard white supremacists in Mississippi certainly felt they lost the war in their state in the 1960s, but by preserving the value and strategic importance of whiteness, they actually triumphed. The rest of us have paid a terrible price for their victory.

In our own time, equally dramatic transformations are taking place, caused by key characteristics of the postindustrial era—globalization, economic restructuring, computer-generated automation, and the planned shrinkage of social services provided by the state. Today too, demagogic politicians try to reassure white people that whatever else they lose, they will retain the possessive investment in whiteness. Symbols and signs of racial change in Mississippi thirty years ago take on special significance in contemporary political debates.

In 1997, Minnesota senator Paul Wellstone journeyed to Mississippi to retrace Robert Kennedy's much publicized tour of the state three decades earlier. Kennedy's visit in 1967 drew national attention to the nature and extent of poverty in the Mississippi Delta, and Wellstone hoped to use his visit to "put the issues of race, gender, poverty, and children back on the public agenda." Although he pledged to travel the length and breadth of the country from Los Angeles to New York in future visits, Wellstone used the symbolic importance of Mississippi in the national imagination to dramatize his opposition to the draconian, mean-spirited, and inhumane welfare reform bill passed by Congress and signed by President Clinton in 1996, with its "disgraceful lack of concern for the downtrodden."[10]

As one might expect, the senator's allies applauded his gesture while his opponents attacked it. Bennie G. Thompson, Mississippi's sole black representative to the U.S. Congress at the time, accompanied Wellstone on his tour of Tunica County and declared, "We have several thousand families that still don't have running water. This is one of the wealthiest countries in the world and if there are individuals who want to highlight the plight of these families, I can't say that person is doing anything but trying to help." Mississippi governor Kirk Fordice, on the other hand, in an unfortunate choice of words, complained that Wellstone was "using Mississippi as a whipping boy," adding, "I'm sick of it."[11] Fordice, however, did not indicate that he was sick of Mississippi having one of the worst records in the nation in respect to poverty, infant mortality, and illiteracy. In 1990, black per capita income in Mississippi remained less than half of white per capita income, and for all citizens the state ranked near the bottom in per capita income. Almost half of the state's 400,000 black children lived in families whose income put them below the poverty line.[12]

Wellstone's allies and his opponents alike correctly understood the ways in which Mississippi's history made the state a highly charged setting for discussions about race and poverty. Yet it is hard to imagine that many useful lessons about the present can be drawn by the public through references to Mississippi, precisely because the state's image is so connected to the past. Governor Fordice was not wrong to say that Mississippi has become an easy target, a state's whose past has been so bad that it can be summoned up as the negative example against which any injustice of today can easily be rationalized and accepted. The picture of Mississippi during the 1960s that has come down to us through political discourse, popular journalism, fiction, and the motion pictures *Mississippi Burning* and *Ghosts of Mississippi* (which probably frame memory of that period for the greatest number of people) strips the struggle in that state of all context and complexity. It presents a simple story about the victory of good whites over bad ones, while submissive and cowed blacks look on with fear and apprehension. Vigilante violence by poor whites emerges as the main problem in this fictive 1960s Mississippi, while the disciplined and determined struggle by blacks for jobs, education, housing, and political power disappears from view. Elite white protection of black interests serves as a legitimating excuse to promote the most vicious and condescending stereotypes about working-class whites. This portrait distorts the past, to be sure, but it also distorts the present by confining all the worst evils of racism to the past—to one group of people in one state during one time period. It gives us a history that hides the present rather than illuminating it, that serves to protect present social relations from examination, analysis, and critique.

Hollywood actor James Woods, star of *Ghosts of Mississippi*, offers proof of the intellectual paralysis that the iconic status of Mississippi in the 1960s engenders. Woods played Byron de la Beckwith, the fertilizer salesman who assassinated Medgar Evers but escaped punishment for more than thirty years until grass-roots pressure finally forced a new trial, which brought a conviction. Discussing his preparation for the role, the MIT-educated Woods told a reporter that he once encountered de la Beckwith but refused to meet with him "on moral grounds. I just don't like him, and I thought it would make him feel special, that I would further inflame his narcissism." Woods's contempt for de la Beckwith as an individual is understandable, but the actor's understanding of racism leaves a lot to be desired. When asked if the South had changed since Evers's assassination, Woods replied, "Well, they convicted him. And California didn't convict O.J. Simpson did they?"[13]

Woods's answer ignores some important differences between the two cases. Police investigators discovered de la Beckwith's fingerprint on a rifle found in a vacant lot near the killing. They established that de la Beckwith owned a rifle and a scope like the one used in the murder. They produced two cab drivers who testified that de la Beckwith had inquired about Evers's address prior to the killing. During his first trial, the accused waved to friends in the courtroom, drank soda pop, sat with his legs on another chair, offered cigars to the prosecutor, and had to be escorted by a bailiff back to his chair when he strolled to the jury box to exchange pleasantries with the jurors. Members of the Mississippi Sovereignty Commission helped the defense with jury selection. It took thirty-one years to get de la Beckwith convicted of a crime that he frequently bragged about committing.[14] Residents of de la Beckwith's hometown held a parade in his honor when the first jury announced it could not agree on a verdict. A second trial also resulted in a hung jury. After those two trials, local of-

ficials appointed Evers's murderer as an auxiliary police officer with full powers of law enforcement.[15]

In addition, James Woods surely knows that, however worthy they may have
been as human beings, Simpson's alleged victims, Nicole Brown Simpson and
Ron Goldman, were not murdered to silence a political movement and disenfranchise a whole race of people. Simpson's wealth rather than his color secured
him the best defense money could buy. De la Beckwith, on the other hand, had
only his whiteness to protect him from prison, but for thirty-one years that was
enough. Yet Woods did not confine himself to comparing the Simpson and de
la Beckwith cases; he went on to raise the issue of affirmative action. Responding to a question about whether the South had really changed since 1963, Woods
opined, "I really think we've accomplished much more than we realize, but
things like affirmative action are actually holding back progress, reducing dignity. I have a ton of black friends and they hate the idea that people might think
they gained their position based on some kind of quota, rather than on the basis of their talent. It's insulting. It's like people keep adding on to and building
their house, and they sometimes have to be told that it's done, it's time to live in
the house. This country needs to shut up already and get going. Stop whining
and start living. There's too much yakking and not enough thinking."[16]

His answer indicates that Woods could stand to do a little less yakking and
a little more thinking (and reading) himself. One should not necessarily expect
an actor to have a sophisticated grasp of politics (witness Ronald Reagan), but
Woods's analogy comparing affirmative action to needless tinkering with an already built house is seriously flawed. James Woods probably lives in a dwelling
that needs no more fixing, but the nation at large still needs to get its house in
order. Racial discrimination lowers the gross national product by nearly 2 percent every year—a total of more than $100 billion. It squanders the skills and
talents of women and minority workers while providing an unearned bonus to
white men by protecting them from the fullest possible field of competitors. For
whom is the house finished, when blacks hold less than 4 percent of the 260,000
jobs in magazine and newspaper journalism, when only thirty-seven of the
twenty thousand partners in major accounting firms are black, when black attorneys make up less than 2 percent of the lawyers employed by the two hundred fifty largest law firms and less than 1 percent of the partners in these businesses? Black professionals and managers are almost twice as likely to be
unemployed as whites in similar job categories, and a black person who earns
more than $50,000 a year is just as likely to live in a segregated neighborhood
as someone who earns $2,500.[17]

In his reply to the reporter's question, Woods makes a rhetorical move common to many defenders of white privilege. He relegates black grievances against whites to the past while situating white complaints about blacks in the present. The actor deflects attention away from the racism practiced against blacks in the South by raising corollary (and presumably equal) objections to what he presumes to be the special privileges enjoyed by O.J. Simpson and black beneficiaries of affirmative action. Woods doesn't seem concerned that affirmative action remedies came into existence because of white resistance to desegregation, that the quotas he describes are illegal and nonexistent, and that weaknesses in the structure and enforcement of civil rights laws make affirmative action programs both necessary and desirable.

If Woods's black friends really do "hate the idea that people might think they gained their position based on some kind of quota, rather than on the basis of talent," one wonders how insulted Woods's white friends must feel, those who inherited money from their parents, got their jobs through family connections or prep school contacts, who enjoyed the benefits of a healthy environment or a decent education because of their favored position in a discriminatory housing market. The stigma that is supposed to haunt those helped by affirmative action evidently does not apply to white people, for example, to the 20 percent of Harvard undergraduates who received preferential treatment because their parents were alumni, consequently increasing by three times their likelihood of admission compared to applicants not connected to the college through family ties. At Harvard, alumni children are twice as likely to be admitted as a Latino or black student. The class of 1992 at that institution included two hundred marginally qualified applicants who gained admission because their parents attended Harvard, a number greater than the combined total of black, Chicano, Native American, and Puerto Rican members of the class.[18] Apparently advantages only carry a stigma when people of color receive them.

Minority students with slightly lower test scores or grade point averages are often *better* students than those who score above them because they achieve results under more difficult conditions. Minority students are concentrated in the schools with the least funding, the fewest experienced teachers, and the sparsest resources. They are less likely than their white counterparts to have the money to enable them to take standardized tests over and over again so that their scores improve, to purchase the expensive courses that private entrepreneurs offer to boost scores on standardized tests, and to be in schools that offer advanced placement and other enrichment courses that colleges value in making decisions about admissions. James Woods expresses no anguish about these inadequate schools, inexperienced teachers, or financial pressures, but he raises his voice against affirmative action programs that help members of minority groups succeed in spite of all the obstacles placed in their path.

The familiar arguments against affirmative action that James Woods articulates are the product of a pervasive propaganda campaign, the fruits of the public relations reach of a handful of wealthy corporations and the neoconservative think tanks they finance. For example, in the late winter of 1995, newspapers around California reported the start of a bold new initiative against affirmative action. A story on the front page of the March 30, 1995, *San Francisco Chronicle* attributed the genesis of this campaign to the private frustrations of one aggrieved individual, Tom Wood. "After losing a coveted teaching job to a minority woman," the story began, "Tom Wood has turned his private frustration into a public crusade that threatens to end America's 30-year experiment with affirmative action." Wood explained that he had been a candidate for a position in the philosophy department at a California university, that he was clearly "the most qualified applicant" for the job, but that the hiring committee passed over him because he was not "the right race or the right sex."[19] Yet Wood refused to identify the position for which he applied, raising doubts about whether the incident had happened at all.

Wood presented himself as an apolitical individual, a liberal who believed in the teachings of Martin Luther King, Jr., and now an innocent white male victim of the excesses of affirmative action. He did not tell the press that he was affiliated with the conservative National Association of Scholars, a group created and funded lavishly by right-wing extremist foundations. (In 1992, the National Association of Scholars received $375,000 from the Scaife Foundation, $125,000 from the John M. Olin Foundation, and $72,500 from the Bradley Foundation.)[20] When Wood described himself to the press as the most qualified candidate for the job he did not receive, he did not disclose that he had not published any scholarly work in any venue in the first fifteen years after he received his Ph.D. degree—a record of productivity that would disqualify him for employment at any serious research university. Portraying himself as "an academic," Wood did not reveal that he had never been employed in a permanent college teaching position, that except for two one-year positions as a visitor at different universities, he worked as a computer programmer in a San Francisco bank and as a part-time instructor at a psychology institute where he earned $1200 a course. When the television newsmagazine *Dateline* looked into his case, they discovered that five jobs were listed for which Wood might have applied, and that four of these went to white male candidates. The fifth went to a woman who was far superior to Wood in academic achievement—as indeed nearly every candidate for all five of these positions must have been.[21]

Tom Wood's picture of himself as an innocent victim of affirmative action turned out to be false; the truth was that he was a white male who chose to blame women and minorities for his own shortcomings as a job candidate. Yet the special privileges he enjoyed as a white male and the massive amounts of money poured into his cause by right-wing foundations and the Republican Party led reporters to write stories about his campaign that uncritically repeated his charges and read largely like press releases from the National Association of Scholars.[22] As planned, Wood soon picked up a powerful ally in Governor Pete Wilson, who saw an attack on affirmative action as a means of giving a distinctive slant to his campaign for the Republican nomination for the presidency. Acting in concert with his longtime African American ally, Ward Connerly of the University of California Board of Regents, Wilson broke a long tradition of leaving the university system free of political meddling and mobilized the regents he had appointed to pass two measures banning affirmative action programs in student admissions, faculty hiring, and contracting.

Wilson and Connerly used the same combination of racism, disavowal, and dissembling that characterized Tom Wood's public posture in their campaign against the only proven effective tools for promoting diversity in the University of California system. Connerly contended that affirmative action was a form of "slavery," because "if we carefully examine the definition of slavery, we find its most important characteristics—'dependency' and 'under the domination of another'—present in affirmative action."[23] Purists might want to point out that Connerly's understanding of slavery ignores its history as a system of permanent, hereditary, racialized servitude reducing human persons to the status of property, legally defenseless against beatings, whippings, and rapes—surely a far cry from receiving fifty extra points out of three thousand when applying for admission to college. But definitions aside, if Connerly was so concerned about dependency, one wonders why his whole career has depended upon the largesse and insider connections provided by his patron Pete Wilson, or why Connerly followed Wilson's wishes in transforming the state university into a vehicle for the advancement of the governor's electoral ambitions.

Connerly has himself been a beneficiary of affirmative action. Although he first denied to reporters that he had ever benefited from "minority preferences," Connerly soon conceded that he certified a firm he co-owns in equal partnership with his white wife as a 51 percent minority-owned company in order to win Energy Commission contracts worth more than one million dollars. Connerly's long association with Wilson probably also did not hurt his chances of winning contracts with fifteen California communities to administer Community Development Block grants. This is an odd history for someone who favors ending others' access to affirmative action programs, who champions private enterprise as superior to working for the state, and who complains that affirmative action encourages dependency and makes blacks "perpetuate the self-defeating and corrosive myth that we cannot do it without help from someone else—and we all too often don't even try."[24]

Wilson, Connerly, and their allies on the Board of Regents argued that affirmative action in student admissions gave special preferences to applicants from underrepresented groups, that these preferences were undeserved, and that they undermined the quality of the student body. Regent Leo Kolligan, an attorney from Fresno, announced that he voted for the resolutions introduced by Wilson and Connerly "because I believe in equal rights. To me, when you give preferential treatments you're not exercising equal rights. That's not what I understand the Constitution to be."[25] Yet Kolligan and the other regents took a different view when it came to the children of their friends and business associates. A few months before his vote against affirmative action in the UC system, Kolligan privately contacted admissions officers at UCLA and pressured them to admit the daughter of a white Fresno builder who had taken no high school honors classes and who scored an anemic total of 790 on standardized tests, despite her slightly above-average high school grade point average. Because of the regent's intervention on her behalf, the applicant secured admission, leap-frogging over more than five hundred prospective students with credentials stronger than her own. Almost all of the regents who supported ending affirmative action, including Ward Connerly, had engaged in similar successful lobbying for personal friends and business associates. In one case, a student backed by one of the regents secured admission even though six thousand candidates for admission had better test scores and grade point averages than he did. When student, faculty, and community groups protested against the gap between the regents' philosophy about what others should do and their own behavior, the regents complained that they felt persecuted by such criticism. Regent Stephen Nakashima worried that the protests would be unfair to wealthy children and the regents' own children because they made it sound as if having connections would now count against applicants. "It seems it would be ridiculous for a child of mine to apply to UC-Berkeley," he moaned.[26]

In the summer of 1995 when they pushed their plan through the University of California regents, Wilson and Connerly denied that their motives were political. Yet Wilson made his victory over affirmative action in the university system a prominent part of his campaign for the presidency. In December, Connerly announced that he would head the campaign effort to pass Proposition 209, the statewide ballot initiative launched by the National Association of Scholars and Tom Wood. While campaigning to "free" blacks, minorities, and women from the "dependency" of affirmative action, Connerly did not disclose that he serves as a trustee of the National Association of Scholars and that the campaign on behalf of Proposition 209 depended upon infusions of cash from wealthy individuals and right-wing foundations who have never shown much interest in freeing the same groups from dependency on low wages, unsafe working conditions, or discrimination in education, employment, and housing.[27] Nor did Connerly deal with the fact that the supporters of Proposition 209 needed him to head the campaign precisely because his identity as an African American helped shield them from taking responsibility for the racist sentiments mobilized by their campaign. "It was like using affirmative action to defeat affirmative action," admitted Joe C. Gelman, who had been the campaign manager for Proposition 209 when Connerly was recruited to take his place. "We were being pretty cynical, I have to admit."[28]

As the November election approached, Wilson frantically lobbied business leaders in September to secure donations to the media campaign against affirmative action. In a confidential telephone conference call to prospective donors to the Republican Party, Wilson made no mention of slavery, fairness, equal opportunity, or even affirmative action, but described the campaign as a "wedge issue" designed to divide the Democrats and to bring more Republican voters to the polls. Speaker of the House Newt Gingrich joined in on the call and described the ballot initiative as crucial to the hopes of the national Republican Party: "We have to be competitive in California to keep control of the House." As *Los Angeles Times* columnist Peter King observed, "[T]he only thing shocking about all this is its utter nakedness, the absence of any semantical coyness."[29]

Yet even if Wood, Wilson, and Connerly treat it like a game, the fight against affirmative action has all too real social consequences. The cynical demagogues who secure short-term gain from fueling white resentment will not be the ones who have to face the consequences of their actions. Ending affirmative action cuts off avenues of upward mobility that have proven of great importance to aggrieved communities. Minority contractors cut off from entry into the construction business by overt discrimination, unfair lending practices, and covert exclusion from insider networks gain one of the few possible sources of asset accumulation by minorities through affirmative action programs. The loyalty of minority medical school graduates to the communities from which they come provides one of the only hopes their communities have of receiving decent medical care. Affirmative action opens up opportunities for decent paying jobs to groups traditionally excluded from them at every income level, and it provides one of the few effective mechanisms for offsetting the effects of continuing discriminatory practices in the public and private sectors alike. College students, professionals, and skilled workers are important role models in inner-city communities, expanding the range of possibilities for those around them. Schools, businesses, and governments also benefit from the presence of the broadest possible range of students, workers, and leaders, because diversity is rewarding in itself but also because the greatest amount of talent always comes from the broadest possible pool.

The new admissions policies mandated by the University of California regents received their first test during the 1996–1997 academic year. Only fourteen African American applicants secured admission in a class of 792 students at the law school at the University of California at Berkeley. To make matters worse, all fourteen chose to go to other institutions in protest against the adoption of an admissions policy that elevated performance on often criticized standardized tests over demonstrated success in law school and professional life by African Americans (who often scored lower on standardized tests than their white counterparts). With one stroke of the pen, the regents turned the state's best law school into a provincial place unable to offer its students a cosmopolitan and diverse atmosphere. "That's the bad news, yes," conceded Ward Connerly, who then protested that "[n]o one talks about the good news, that fourteen black students were admissible and, if they had chosen to attend, no one would have questioned their right to be there."[30] He expressed no concern over the loss to all of the students incurred by learning the law in a segregated environment, no concern over an admissions policy that demands that minority taxpayers subsidize the educations of those who successfully discriminate against them, and no concern that the $3.6 million that Connerly and his allies spent on Proposition 209 to protect the possessive investment in whiteness might have been better spent on improving the educational opportunities and resources available to minorities if better education had actually been their goal.

Connerly further embarrassed himself by citing the research of Professor Claude M. Steele as justification for Proposition 209. Steele's research has shown that black students experience great anxiety in testing situations because they know that whites have negative opinions about blacks and consequently

fear that any mistakes they make will be interpreted as evidence of their inferiority. Connerly argued that Proposition 209 would lessen that anxiety by taking away "preferences" that he claimed reinforce the idea that black students are
inferior. Yet Claude Steel rejected Connerly's interpretation of his research, argued that eliminating affirmative action would "almost certainly not" rid campuses of stereotypes, and called instead for mentoring programs and accelerated classes to demonstrate the state's trust in the potential of underachieving
black students.[31]

With the implementation of the regents' ban on affirmative action and the
success of Proposition 209, young people of color interested in higher education in California face a stark new reality. Already victimized by diminished
state spending on recreation centers, libraries, counseling services, health, and
schools, they now face a program targeted expressly against those among them
who have the most ambition, who have studied the hardest, and who have
stayed away from drugs and gangs. The success of students from these backgrounds in higher education and in the professions in the past now means nothing. Now students will have to outperform their suburban rivals on standardized tests, completely unreliable indicators of how well these students will do
once they arrive at college. If inner-city minority students drop out of school,
take drugs, join gangs, and commit crimes, the state is willing to spend huge
amounts of money on prisons for them. But if they work hard, succeed in
school, and have ambition, the state is willing to hand them the equivalent of
Moms Mabley's Chinese newspaper.

California's leaders advance these regressive policies while patting themselves on the back about how much progress has been made and how much better things are today in the fight against racial discrimination. Ward Connerly
claims that the battle against discrimination was won in the early 1980s, that in
California "we're at a 9 or a 10 with 10 being the best." Connerly contrasted California's record on discrimination with that of other states and concluded, "In
other states, things are probably at a 7 or 8. I'm not sure a Mississippi is at the
same point as a California."[32] Connerly agrees with James Woods about affirmative action, but argues that California is ahead of Mississippi; he disagrees
with Paul Wellstone about affirmative action and welfare reform, but agrees
that Mississippi provides the power of a negative example.

Yet the arguments advanced by Connerly and his patrons have far more in
common with the defense of white supremacy in Mississippi in the past and
present than they recognize. In their anti–affirmative action and anti-immigrant
rhetoric, California's leaders in the 1990s deploy the same combination of

racism and disavowal that proved so poisonous in Mississippi during the 1960s. Because their speeches rarely contain direct racist epithets, they may seem more benign than the Ross Barnetts and James Eastlands of yesterday. But as we enter a new economic era where educational and technical training become more important than ever before in determining opportunities and life chances, Governor Wilson and his allies are harming more people in more permanent ways than Ross Barnett and his cohorts ever did in the 1960s. The amount of suffering and strife engendered by California's leaders today is greater in both quantity and quality than anything Mississippi's white supremacists did to their citizens thirty years ago. The violent upheaval in Los Angeles in 1992 reflected only a small portion of the rage, despair, and cynicism permeating California as a result of the racialized effects of the transformation from a national industrial economy to a global postindustrial economy. The possessive investment in whiteness plays an insidious role in these realities: it occludes the crisis that we all face as a result of declining wages, environmental hazards, and social disintegration, while it generates racial antagonism as the only available frame for comprehending how individuals imagine themselves as a part of society.

Yet it is precisely the urgency of the present crisis and the need for presence of mind about it that makes it dangerous to compare the largely binary struggle between blacks and Whites in Mississippi in the 1960s with the intercultural conflict and cooperation that characterize California today. What happened in Mississippi in the 1960s was that in a moment of crisis, elements of the state's past reappeared with a vengeance and undermined opportunities for peaceful, democratic, and egalitarian social change. That same dynamic is now at work in California, but with a different history and facing a different kind of crisis, that state has deployed the possessive investment in whiteness in different ways. California is both the Mississippi of the 1960s and an evil of its own. It is as bad as Mississippi was in the 1960s in many respects, but it is different as well.

California's harsh racial history rivals that of any state in the union, including Mississippi The Native American population fell from more than 300,000 when white settlers first entered the state to less than 150,000 at the time of statehood in 1850. White aggression cut the number to less than 30,000 in the first decades of statehood through impressment of Native Americans for labor gangs and outright physical assaults on them, in the belief that such attacks protected white property. White settlers murdered at least 4,500 Native Americans in the state between 1848 and 1880. Shortly after statehood the California legislature passed a law forbidding testimony by Native Americans in le-

gal proceedings that involved whites, while another statute made it illegal to supply them with firearms or ammunition. The legislature initially denied Native
Americans admission to public schools; when forced to change the policy, the
legislature relegated Native American students to segregated schools and classrooms.[33] When slavery was outlawed by the state constitution of 1850, the legislature passed a law that allowed any white to arrest any Native Americans not
presently working for whites and force them to "work off" the costs of bail
through involuntary servitude. Many of the white miners who struck it rich did
so with the aid of unpaid Native American labor.[34]

As white Californians used legal and illegal means to compel Native Americans to labor on their behalf, they used similar force against Chinese immigrants to prevent them from working. In the 1860s and 1870s "Anti-Coolie
Clubs" lobbied for legislation to end Asian immigration to the United States,
organized boycotts of goods made by Chinese workers in America, committed
arson against factories suspected of hiring Chinese workers, and physically as-
saulted individual Chinese workers in the streets. Legislative acts prevented the
Chinese from voting in California elections and barred their participation in
public works projects financed by state funds.[35] A state court ruling in 1854 held
that, like Native Americans, blacks, and mulattos, Chinese residents of California could not testify in court in cases that involved whites.[36]

Through laws that did not expressly mention race but had clear racial consequences, municipal and state authorities alike conspired to prevent the Chinese from accumulating assets. For example, San Francisco and other cities outlawed the operation of laundries in wood buildings inside the city limits but
enforced the act only against Chinese-owned businesses. In 1870, San Francisco
enacted a "cubic air" ordinance requiring inexpensive lodging houses to
provide at least five hundred cubic feet of clean air for each adult resident, then
enforced the act only in Chinatown. The 1890 San Francisco Segregation Ordinance designated all Chinese residents for removal from a residential neighborhood when speculators cast a covetous eye on the neighborhood near downtown (see chapter 2). Even though many of these laws ultimately proved
unconstitutional, they effectively hindered Chinese immigrants from accumulating assets, thereby granting a de facto subsidy to white business owners and
workers who were not encumbered by either restrictive ordinances or the need
to wage a long and costly legal struggle against them.

Despite the guarantees of the Treaty of Guadalupe Hidalgo, Mexicans in
California also suffered from racial oppression. An early antivagrancy act defined vagrants as "all persons who [were] commonly known as 'Greasers' or the

issue of Spaniards or Indian blood . . . and who [went] armed and [were] not peaceable and quiet persons," a definition that made resistance against Anglo incursions on land titles supposedly protected by the treaty all but impossible. A "Foreign Miner's Tax" that demanded twenty dollars monthly from "foreign" but not "American" miners led to taxing U.S. citizens of Mexican ancestry as well Mexican immigrants, but not Anglos. When taxation proved too clumsy a means, Anglo miners used physical force and direct attacks to drive Mexican miners from the gold-producing regions of the state.[37] Although legal categories officially designated people of Mexican origin as "white" and extended the possible benefits of citizenship to them, concerted action among Anglos disarmed and disenfranchised many Mexicans, denied them opportunities for asset accumulation and for education, and used legal and illegal means to relegate most people of Mexican origin to a segment of the work force where they would be unable to compete with whites.

From the start, African Americans also faced institutionalized racism in California. The state constitution prevented African Americans from voting, holding public office, testifying in court in cases involving whites, serving on juries, attending public schools, or homesteading land.[38] As with other groups, denial of African American's citizenship rights affected their opportunities to accumulate assets. For example, in the early 1860s Rodney Schell, a white man, robbed a millinery shop owned by a black proprietor. The store owner was powerless to complain to the police because state law prevented him from testifying in court in a case involving a white man. When African American civil rights activist George Gordon complained to the police about the case, Schell shot and killed Gordon. This incident and the political mobilization it spawned led to a change in the law and the granting of the right to testify in court in California to African Americans. Yet blacks won this right at the expense of the state's Chinese population by arguing that respectable Christian and American blacks should be allowed to testify in court and not be constrained by a law originally aimed at the Chinese, whom black spokespersons derided for their "filthy habits," idolatrous religion, and loose sexual morality. Just as Chinese residents in Mississippi won some gains for themselves at the expense of blacks by suing for "white" status, California blacks won the right to testify in court by promoting themselves as allies in the defense of whiteness against the foreign Chinese.[39]

The long history of racial oppression and interracial conflict in California shows that Mississippi is not the only state with ghosts from its past and skeletons in its closet. California has long been a racialized state, systematically channeling opportunities for asset accumulation and the exercise of citizenship rights toward whites and away from communities of color. Dramatic events like the Japanese internment, the Zoot Suit Riots, the repeal of fair-housing legislation in 1964, the Watts Riots, Proposition 187, and Proposition 209 flow logically from a history of state protection for the possessive investment in whiteness. Yet just as the Mississippi that produced James Eastland, and Ross Barnett, and Byron de la Beckwith also produced Fannie Lou Hamer, and Medgar Evers, and Bill Moore, Californians are divided on issues of race, property, and politics.

If the Mississippi Freedom Democratic Party had triumphed in the 1960s and 1970s, the state of Mississippi and the entire country would be in better shape today. Similarly, if antiracist individuals and groups in California succeed in creating interethnic antiracist coalitions that grasp the international, intercultural, and intersectional quality of contemporary race relations, they may save themselves, their state, and their nation from the dreadful polarization already well underway. The struggle in California today has some direct links to the struggles in Mississippi during the 1960s, but it is not the same struggle. The opposition between black and white that shapes so much of our racial imagination no longer suffices when both whiteness and blackness emerge in relation to other expressly racialized categories and other intersectionally racialized identities, such as the immigrant noncitizen, non-American labor, the female low-wage worker, the sexual subject who does not conform to the heterosexual ideal, the homeless, the unemployed youth, and a declining middle class stripped of its security and marketable skills by computer-generated automation, outsourcing, capital flight, and the looting of productive corporate assets by speculators. Investment in individual group identities can challenge the possessive investment in whiteness, but such efforts always run the risk of reifying the very categories they seek to destroy. Aggrieved groups will not magically unite simply because they are separately oppressed, but coalitions within and across identity categories can be built by open and honest discussion of the ways in which all of us have been differently racialized, gendered, and infused with complex and composite identities and interests. In the long run, a politics based on ideology, interests, and ideas is required if we are ever to move beyond the possessive investment in whiteness and the identity politics it encourages and sustains.[40]

Yet even while much distinguishes the California of the 1990s from the Mississippi of the 1960s, one constant remains—the cowardice and craven opportunism of elected officials eager to gain and regain power at any cost. Our leaders are long on noble pronouncements but short on noble deeds. They preach the politics of inclusion, but they pursue the practices of exclusion. They proclaim their faith in the work ethic, but their politics declare war on working people and their institutions. They profess a desire to get government out of our lives, but they perpetuate invasions of privacy through restrictions on reproductive rights, bans on gay and lesbian marriages, and proposals to mandate compulsory prayer in the schools. They promise to curtail government spending, but they deploy state power ruthlessly to promote capital accumulation and protect the property of the rich. They propose new initiatives about education, but they spend their money on incarceration. They preach the love of God, but they practice the love of gain.

We need to ask ourselves why whiteness works this way and what we are going to do about it. What enables the recipients of unearned privileges to present themselves as put-upon victims? If we were to apply the methodology that Charles Murray and Richard Herrnstein deploy in *The Bell Curve* to explain the behavior of black people, we might be tempted to ask questions about which genes account for white America's predilection for plunder and seeming incapacity for complex thought. But we know better. The problem with white people is not our whiteness, but our possessive investment in it. Created by politics, culture, and consciousness, our possessive investment in whiteness can be altered by those same processes, but only if we face the hard facts openly and honestly and admit that whiteness is a matter of interests as well as attitudes, that it has more to do with property than with pigment. Not all believers in white supremacy are white. All whites do not have to be white supremacists. But the possessive investment in whiteness is a matter of behavior as well as belief.

Recently I delivered a lecture about the possessive investment in whiteness at an eastern college. After my talk I was approached by a young student who was greatly disturbed by the things I had said. "I think you're too hard on white people," she offered. I told her that no one would be more delighted than I to be proven wrong, to find out that the possessive investment in whiteness is not as strong as I believe it to be. But I told her that this was not a matter for idle speculation. In the years ahead we will have ample opportunities to see what white people are made of, to see whether we can transcend our attachments to the mechanisms that give whiteness its force and power. We need to learn why our history has been built so consistently on racial exclusion and why we continue to generate new mechanisms to increase the value of past and present discrimination. How can we account for the ways in which white people refuse to acknowledge their possessive investment in whiteness even as they work to increase its value every day? We can't blame the color of our skin. It must be the content of our character.

N O T E S

Introduction. Bill Moore's Body

The epigraph is from James Baldwin, *The Devil Finds Work* (New York: Dell, 1976), # 7.

1. See, for example, Thomas Edsall and Mary Byrne Edsall, *Chain Reaction* (New York: Norton, 1991).
2. Harvard Sitkoff, *The Struggle for Black Equality, 1954–1980* (New York: Hill and Wang, 1981), 124.
3. Congress of Racial Equality [CORE] Papers, State Historical Society, University of Wisconsin, MSS14, box 5, folder 40, p. 3.
4. "White Foe of Segregation Slain on a Protest Trek in Alabama," *New York Times*, April 25, 1963.
5. Sitkoff, *The Struggle for Black Equality*, 135; CORE Papers, MSS14, box 5, folder 40, page unnumbered, "White Foe of Segregation."
6. Foster Hailey, "Alabama Holds Two in Hiker's Slaying," *New York Times*, May 2, 1963.
7. "White Foe of Segregation."
8. Claude Sitton, "Dozen to Resume Slain Postman's Walk Tomorrow," *New York Times*, April 30, 1963.
9. "Alabama Jury Refuses to Indict in Murder of Hiking Postman" and "One Negro on Jury," *New York Times*, September 14, 1963.
10. Taylor Branch, *Parting the Waters: America in the King Years, 1954–63* (New York: Touchstone, 1988), 750.
11. Foster Hailey, "8 Negroes Seized in Alabama Walk," *New York Times*, May 2, 1963.
12. Claude Sitton, "Dozen to Resume Slain Postman's Walk Tomorrow," *New York Times*, April 30, 1963.
13. Stephan Lesher, *George Wallace: American Populist* (Reading, Mass.: Addison Wesley, 1990), 180.
14. Sitkoff, *The Struggle for Black Equality*, 135–36; John Hope Franklin, *From Slavery to Freedom: A History of Negro Americans*, 4th ed. (New York: Knopf, 1974), 483.

15. Claude Sitton, "11 Seized Trying Postman's Walk," *New York Times*, May 20, 1963.

16. Foster Hailey, "Alabama Holds 2 in Hiker's Slaying," *New York Times*, April 26, 1963.

17. Claude Sitton, "March to Continue," *New York Times*, April 28, 1963.

18. Sitkoff, *The Struggle for Black Equality*, 151; Franklin, *From Slavery to Freedom*, 483. This is, of course, the incident dramatized in the 1996 film *Ghosts of Mississippi*.

19. Franklin, *From Slavery to Freedom*, 483.

20. Sitkoff, *The Struggle for Black Equality*, 176.

21. John Dittmer, *Local People: The Struggle for Civil Rights in Mississippi* (Urbana: University of Illinois Press, 1995), 109.

22. CORE Papers, MSS 14, letter from Gordon Carey to Bill Moore, March 20, 1963; "White Foe of Segregation."

23. Kay Mills, *This Little Light of Mine: The Life of Fannie Lou Hamer* (New York: Penguin, 1993), 87; Erich Harrison, "Secret Files to Shed Light on State-Sanctioned Racism," *Los Angeles Times*, August 18, 1997, sec. A.

24. James W. Silver, *Mississippi: The Closed Society* (New York: Harcourt, Brace and World, 1966); Chad Mitchell Trio, "We're Going to Miss Ole Miss"; Phil Ochs, "Here's to the State of Mississippi," Nina Simone, "Mississippi Goddamn."

25. Charles Payne, *I've Got the Light of Freedom: The Organizing Tradition and the Mississippi Freedom Struggle* (Berkeley and Los Angeles: University of California Press, 1996), 340.

26. Mills, *This Little Light of Mine*, 51.

27. Sitkoff, *The Struggle for Black Equality*, 181.

28. Mills, *This Little Light of Mine*, 125.

29. Payne, *I've Got the Light of Freedom*.

30. Dittmer, *Local People*, 23.

Chapter 1. The Possessive Investment in Whiteness

The epigraph is from Baldwin, *The Devil Finds Work*, 1.

1. Raphael Tardon, "Richard Wright Tells Us: The White Problem in the United States," *Action*, October 24, 1946. Reprinted in Kenneth Kinnamon and Michel Fabre, *Conversations with Richard Wright* (Jackson: University Press of Mississippi, 1993), 99. Malcolm X and others used this same formulation in the 1960s, but I believe that it originated with Wright, or at least that is the earliest citation I have found.

2. Toni Morrison points out the ways in which African Americans play an essential role in the white imagination, how their representations both hide and reveal the terms of white supremacy upon which the nation was founded and has been sustained ever since. See *Playing in the Dark: Whiteness in the Literary Imagination* (Cambridge: Harvard University Press, 1992).

3. Richard Dyer, "White," *Screen* 29, 4 (fall 1998): 44.

4. I thank Michael Schudson for pointing out to me that since the passage of civil rights legislation in the 1960s whiteness dares not speak its name, cannot speak in its own behalf, but rather advances through a color-blind language radically at odds with the distinctly racialized distribution of resources and life chances in U.S. society.

5. Walter Benjamin, "Madame Ariane: Second Courtyard on the Left," in *One-Way Street* (London: New Left Books, 1969), 98–99.

6. See Lisa Lowe, *Immigrant Acts: On Asian American Cultural Politics* (Durham, N.C.: Duke University Press, 1996), 11–16; Gary B. Nash, *Red, White, and Black: The Peoples of Early*

America (Englewood Cliffs, N.J.: Prentice-Hall, 1974); Ronald Takaki, *A Different Mirror: A History of Multicultural America* (Boston: Little, Brown, 1993), 177–83.

7. Nash, *Red, White, and Black,* 292–93.
8. Howard R. Lamar, *Texas Crossings: The Lone Star State and the American Far West, 1836–1986* (Austin: University of Texas Press, 1991), xiii.
9. Cedric J. Robinson, *Black Movements in America* (New York and London: Routledge, 1997), 44. See also chapter 9, "Frantic to Join."
10. Nash, *Red, White, and Black,* 294.
11. Robinson, *Black Movements in America,* 43–44.
12. Takaki, *A Different Mirror,* 187–88; Peter Narvaez, "The Influences of Hispanic Music Cultures on Afro-American Blues Music," *Black Music Research Journal* 14, 2 (fall 1994): 206; Ernest V. Allen, "'When Japan Was Champion of the Darker Races'": Satokata Takahishi and the Flowering of Black Messianic Nationalism," *Black Scholar* 24, 1: 27–31.
13. See Kenneth Jackson, *Crabgrass Frontier: The Suburbanization of the United States* (New York: Oxford University Press, 1985), and Douglas S. Massey and Nancy A. Denton, *American Apartheid: Segregation and the Making of the Underclass* (Cambridge: Harvard University Press, 1993).
14. I thank Phil Ethington for pointing out to me that these aspects of New Deal policies emerged out of political negotiations between the segregationist Dixiecrats and liberals from the North and West. My perspective is that white supremacy was not a gnawing aberration within the New Deal coalition but rather an essential point of unity between southern whites and northern white ethnics.
15. Records of the Federal Home Loan Bank Board of the Home Owners Loan Corporation, City Survey File, Los Angeles, 1939, Neighborhood D-53, National Archives, Box 74, RG 195.
16. Massey and Denton, *American Apartheid,* 54.
17. John R. Logan and Harvey Molotch, *Urban Fortunes: The Political Economy of Place* (Berkeley and Los Angeles: University of California Press, 1987), 182.
18. Ibid., 114.
19. Arlene Zarembka, *The Urban Housing Crisis: Social, Economic, and Legal Issues and Proposals* (Westport, Conn.: Greenwood, 1990), 104.
20. Jill Quadagno, *The Color of Welfare: How Racism Undermined the War on Poverty* (New York: Oxford University Press, 1994), 92, 91.
21. Logan and Molotch, *Urban Fortunes,* 130.
22. See Gary Gerstle, "Working-Class Racism: Broaden the Focus," *International Labor and Working Class History* 44 (fall 1993): 36.
23. Logan and Molotch, *Urban Fortunes,* 168–69.
24. Troy Duster, "Crime, Youth Unemployment, and the Underclass," *Crime and Delinquency* 33, 2 (April 1987): 308, 309.
25. Massey and Denton, *American Apartheid,* 55.
26. Quadagno, *The Color of Welfare,* 105, 113; Massey and Denton, *American Apartheid,* 204–5.
27. Logan and Molotch, *Urban Fortunes,* 113.
28. Robert D. Bullard, "Environmental Justice for All," in *Unequal Protection: Environmental Justice and Communities of Color,* ed. Robert Bullard (San Francisco: Sierra Club, 1994), 9–10.
29. Robert D. Bullard, "Anatomy of Environmental Racism and the Environmental Justice Movement," in *Confronting Environmental Racism: Voices from the Grass Roots,* ed. Robert D. Bullard (Boston: South End, 1993), 21.
30. Bullard, "Environmental Justice for All," 13.

31. Charles Lee, "Beyond Toxic Wastes and Race," in *Confronting Environmental Racism: Voices from the Grass Roots,* ed. Robert D. Bullard (Boston: South End, 1993), 49. Two corporate-sponsored research institutes challenged claims of racial bias in the location and operation of toxic and hazardous waste systems. Andy B. Anderson, Douglas L. Anderton, and John Michael Oakes made the corporate case in "Environmental Equity: Evaluating TSDF Siting over the Past Two Decades," *Waste Age,* July 1994. These results were trumpeted in a report by the Washington University Center for the Study of American Business, funded by the John M. Olin Foundation. But the study by Anderson, Anderton, and Oakes was sponsored by the Institute of Chemical Waste Management, an industry trade group. The researchers claimed that their results were not influenced by corporate sponsorship, but they limited their inquiry to urban areas with toxic storage, disposal, and treatment facilities, conveniently excluding seventy facilities, 15 percent of TSDFs, and 20 percent of the population. The world's largest waste company, WMX Company, contributed $250,000 to the study, and the study's research plan excluded from scrutiny two landfills owned by WMX: the nation's largest commercial landfill, located in the predominately African American city of Emelle, Alabama, and the nation's fifth largest landfill, in Kettelman City Hills, California, a predominately Latino community.
32. Bunyan Bryant and Paul Mohai, *Race and the Incidence of Environmental Hazards* (Boulder, Colo.: Westview, 1992).
33. Lee, "Beyond Toxic Wastes and Race," 48.
34. Robert D. Bullard, "Decision Making," in Laura Westra and Peter S. Wenz, eds., *Faces of Environmental Racism: Confronting Issues of Global Justice* (Lanham, MD: Rowman and Littlefield, 1995), 4.
35. Bullard, "Anatomy of Environmental Racism," 21.
36. David L.L. Shields, 'What Color is Hunger?" in David L.L. Shields, ed., *The Color of Hunger: Race and Hunger in National and International Perspective* (Lanham, MD: Rowman and Littlefield, 1996), 4.
37. Centers for Disease Control, "Nutritional Status of Minority Children: United States, 1986," *Morbidity and Mortality Weekly Reports (MMWR)* 36, 23 (June, 19, 1987): 366–69.
38. Peter S. Wenz, "Just Garbage," in Laura Westra and Peter S. Wenz, eds., *Faces of Environmental Racism: Confronting Issues of Global Justice* (Lanham, MD: Rowman and Littlefield, 1996), 66; Robert D. Bullard, "Decision Making," in Laura Westra and Peter S., Wenz, eds., *Faces of Environmental Racism,* 8.
39. Laura Pulido, "Multiracial Organizing Among Environmental Justice Activists in Los Angeles," in Michael J. Dear, H. Eric Shockman, and Greg Hise, eds., *Rethinking Los Angeles* (Thousand Oaks, CA, London, New Delhi: Sage, 1996): 175.
40. Charles Trueheart, 'The Bias Most Deadly," *Washington Post,* October 30, 1990, sec. 7, cited in Shields, *The Color of Hunger,* 3.
41. George Anders, "Disparities in Medicare Access Found Among Poor, Black or Disabled Patients,: *Wall Street Journal,* November 2, 1994; Lina R. Godfrey, "Institutional Discrimination and Satisfaction with Specific Government Services by heads of Households in Ten Southern States," paper presented at the Rural Sociological Society annual meeting, 1984, cited in Shields, *The Color of Hunger,* 6,13.
42. Jeffrey Shotland, *Full Fields, Empty Cupboards: The Nutritional Status of Migrant Farmworkers in America,* (Washington: Public Voice for Food and Health: 1989) cited in Shields, *The Color of Hunger,* 3.
43. Linda A. Wray, "Health Policy and Ethnic Diversity in Older Americans: Dissonance or Harmony," *Western Journal of Medicine* 157, 3 (September 1992): 357–61.
44. Eva Bertram, Morris Blachman, Kenneth Sharpe, and Peter Andreas, *Drug War Politics:*

The Price of Denial (Berkeley and Los Angeles: University of California Press, 1996), 38–42; Alexander C. Lichtenstein and Michael A. Kroll, "The Fortress Economy: The Economic Role of the U.S. Prison System," in Elihu Rosenblatt, ed., *Criminal Injustice: Confronting The Prison Crisis* (Boston: South End, 1996), 21, 25–26.

45. Ibid., 41.
46. Massey and Denton, *American Apartheid,* 61.
47. Gertrude Ezorsky, *Racism and Justice: The Case for Affirmative Action* (Ithaca, N.Y.: Cornell University Press, 1991), 25.
48. Logan and Molotch, *Urban Fortunes,* 116.
49. Jim Campen, "Lending Insights: Hard Proof that Banks Discriminate," *Dollars and Sense,* January–February 1991, 17.
50. Mitchell Zuckoff, "Study Shows Racial Bias in Lending," *Boston Globe,* October 9, 1992.
51. Paul Ong and J. Eugene Grigsby III, "Race and Life-Cycle Effects on Home Ownership in Los Angeles, 1970 to 1980," *Urban Affairs Quarterly* 23, 4 (June 1988): 605.
52. Massey and Denton, *American Apartheid,* 108.
53. Gary Orfield and Carol Ashkinaze, *The Closing Door: Conservative Policy and Black Opportunity* (Chicago: University of Chicago Press, 1991), 58, 78.
54. Logan and Molotch, *Urban Fortunes,* 129.
55. Campen, "Lending Insights," 18.
56. Alicia H. Munnell, Lyn E. Browne, James McEneany, and Geoffrey M. B. Tootel, "Mortgage Lending in Boston: Interpreting HMDA Data" (Boston: Federal Reserve Bank of Boston, 1993); Kimberly Blanton, "Fed Blocks Shawmut's Bid to Gain N.H. Bank," *Boston Globe,* November 16, 1993.
57. Ellis Cose, *Rage of a Privileged Class* (New York: HarperCollins, 1993), 191.
58. Gregory Squires, "'Runaway Plants,' Capital Mobility, and Black Economic Rights," in *Community and Capital in Conflict: Plant Closings and Job Loss,* ed. John C. Raines, Lenora E. Berson, and David McI. Gracie (Philadelphia: Temple University Press, 1983), 70.
59. Ezorsky, *Racism and Justice,* 15.
60. Orfield and Ashkinaze, *The Closing Door,* 225–26.
61. Peter Downs, "Tax Abatements Don't Work," *St. Louis Journalism Review,* February 1997, 16.
62. "State Taxes Gouge the Poor, Study Says," *Long Beach Press-Telegram,* April 23, 1991, sec. A.
63. "Proposition 13," *UC Focus,* June/July 1993, 2.
64. William Chafe, *The Unfinished Journey* (New York: Oxford University Press, 1986), 442; Noel J. Kent, "A Stacked Deck: Racial Minorities and the New American Political Economy," *Explorations in Ethnic Studies* 14, 1 (January 1991): 11.
65. Carey Goldberg, "Hispanic Households Struggle as Poorest of the Poor in the U.S.," *New York Times,* January 30, 1997, sec. A.
66. Kent, "A Stacked Deck," 13.
67. Melvin Oliver and James Johnson, "Economic Restructuring and Black Male Joblessness in United States Metropolitan Areas," *Urban Geography* 12, 6 (November–December 1991); Gerald David Jaynes and Robin M. Williams, Jr., eds., *A Common Destiny: Blacks and American Society* (Washington, D.C.: National Academy Press, 1989); Reynolds Farley and Walter R. Allen, *The Color Line and the Quality of Life in America* (New York: Russell Sage Foundation, 1987); Melvin Oliver and Tom Shapiro, "Wealth of a Nation: A Reassessment of Asset Inequality in America Shows At Least One-Third of Households Are Asset Poor," *Journal of Economics and Sociology* 49, 2 (April 1990); Jonathan Kozol, *Savage Inequalities: Children in America's Schools* (New York: Crown, 1991); Cornell West, *Race Matters* (Boston: Beacon, 1993).

68. Orfield and Ashkinaze, *The Closing Door,* 46, 206.
69. Bart Landry, "The Enduring Dilemma of Race in America," in *America at Century's End,* ed. Alan H. Wolfe (Berkeley and Los Angeles: University of California Press, 1991), 206; John Hope Franklin, *The Color Line: Legacy for the Twenty-First Century* (Columbia: University of Missouri Press, 1993), 36–37.
70. Kathleen Hall Jamieson, *Dirty Politics: Deception, Distraction, and Democracy* (New York: Oxford University Press, 1992), 100.
71. Edsall and Edsall, *Chain Reaction.*
72. Nathan Glazer makes this argument in *Affirmative Discrimination* (New York: Basic Books, 1975).
73. I borrow the term "overdetermination" from Louis Althusser, who uses it to show how dominant ideologies become credible to people in part because various institutions and agencies independently replicate them and reinforce their social power.
74. Rogena Schuyler, "Youth: We Didn't Sell Them into Slavery," *Los Angeles Times,* June 21, 1993, sec. B.
75. Jim Newton, "Skinhead Leader Pleads Guilty to Violence, Plot," *Los Angeles Times,* October 20, 1993, sec. A.
76. Antonin Scalia, "The Disease as Cure," *Washington University Law Quarterly,* no. 147 (1979): 153–54, quoted in Cheryl I. Harris, "Whiteness as Property," *Harvard Law Review* 106, 8 (June 1993): 1767.
77. Harris, ibid., 1993.
78. The rise of a black middle class and the setbacks suffered by white workers during deindustrialization may seem to subvert the analysis presented here. Yet the black middle class remains fragile, far less able than other middle-class groups to translate advances in income into advances in wealth and power. Similarly, the success of neoconservatism since the 1970s has rested on securing support from white workers for economic policies that do them objective harm by mobilizing countersubversive electoral coalitions against busing and affirmative action, while carrying out attacks on public institutions and resources by representing "public" space as black space. See Oliver and Shapiro, "Wealth of a Nation." See also Logan and Molotch, *Urban Fortunes.*
79. Johnny Otis, *Upside Your Head! Rhythm and Blues on Central Avenue* (Hanover, N.H.: Wesleyan/University Press of New England, 1993). Mobilizations against plant shutdowns, for environmental protection, against cutbacks in education spending, and for reproductive rights all contain the potential for panethnic antiracist organizing, but too often neglect of race as a central modality for how issues of employment, pollution, education, or reproductive rights are experienced isolates these social movements from their broadest possible base.
80. Benjamin, "Madame Ariane," 98, 99.

Chapter 2. Law and Order

The epigraph is from Baldwin, *The Devil Finds Work,* 69.
1. Charles McClain, *In Search of Equality: The Chinese Struggle against Discrimination* (Berkeley and Los Angeles: University of California Press, 1994), 223–33.
2. The realtors' national code and local rules are described in Dennis R. Judd and Todd Swanstrom, *City Politics: Private Power and Public Policy* (New York: HarperCollins, 1994), 198.

3. Thomas Sugrue, "Crabgrass-Roots Politics: Race, Rights, and the Reaction against Liberalism in the Urban North: 1940–1964," *Journal of American History,* 82, 2 (September 1995): 551–78; Arnold Hirsch, "Massive Resistance in the Urban North," *Journal of American History,* 82, 2 (September 1995): 522–50.

4. David Theo Goldberg, *Racist Culture: Philosophy and the Politics of Meaning* (London: Blackwell, 1993), 195.

5. Massey and Denton, *American Apartheid,* 188.

6. Zarembka, *The Urban Housing Crisis,* 101–3.

7. Quadagno, *The Color of Welfare,* 98–99.

8. Massey and Denton, *American Apartheid,* 189–90,191–92.

9. Quadagno, *The Color of Welfare,* 99.

10. Ibid.

11. Massey and Denton, *American Apartheid,* 196–200.

12. Ibid., 196.

13. Ibid., 190.

14. Quadagno, *The Color of Welfare,* 109–10.

15. Zarembka, *The Urban Housing Crisis,* 16–17.

16. Massey and Denton, *American Apartheid,* 105.

17. Zarembka, *The Urban Housing Crisis,* 103.

18. Ibid., 129.

19. Massey and Denton, *American Apartheid,* 206.

20. Franklin, *The Color Line,* 20.

21. Massey and Denton, *American Apartheid,* 207–8.

22. Zarembka, *The Urban Housing Crisis,* 106; Quadagno, *The Color of Welfare,* 114.

23. Zarembka, *The Urban Housing Crisis,* 8.

24. Melvin L. Oliver and Tom Shapiro, *Black Wealth/White Wealth* (New York: Routledge, 1995), 142.

25. Harris, "Whiteness as Property," 1754.

26. Ibid., 1755.

27. Nathaniel R. Jones, "Civil Rights after *Brown:* 'Stormy the Road We Trod,'" in *Race in America: The Struggle for Equality,* ed. Herbert Hill and James E. Jones, Jr. (Madison: University of Wisconsin Press, 1993), 100.

28. Wiley A. Branton, "Race, the Courts, and Constitutional Change in Twentieth-Century School Desegregation Cases after *Brown,*" in *African Americans and the Living Constitution,* ed. John Hope Franklin and Genna Rae McNeil (Washington, D.C.: Smithsonian Institution Press, 1995), 86; Harris, "Whiteness as Property," 1756.

29. Jones, "Civil Rights after *Brown,*" 103.

30. Ibid.; Harris, "Whiteness as Property," 1756.

31. Quadagno, *The Color of Welfare,* 30.

32. Ibid., 127.

33. Gary Orfield, "School Desegregation after Two Generations: Race, Schools, and Opportunity in Urban Society," in *Race in America: The Struggle for Equality,* ed. Herbert Hill and James E. Jones, Jr. (Madison: University of Wisconsin Press, 1993), 240.

34. Ibid., 245, 240, 237.

35. Charles Lawrence III and Mari J. Matsuda, *We Won't Go Back: Making the Case for Affirmative Action* (New York: Houghton Mifflin, 1997), 45.

36. Carter A. Wilson, "Exploding the Myths of a Slandered Policy," *Black Scholar,* May/June 1986, 20; Harris, "Whiteness as Property," 1770.

37. Harris, "Whiteness as Property," 1773.
38. David W. Bishop, "The Affirmative Action Cases: Bakke, Weber, and Fullilove," *Journal of Negro History* 67, 3 (fall 1982): 231.
39. John Larew, "Why Are Droves of Unqualified, Unprepared Kids Getting into Our Top Colleges?" *Washington Monthly*, June 1991, 10.
40. Kozol, *Savage Inequalities,* especially 72–73, 236–37.
41. Lawrence and Matsuda, *We Won't Go Back,* 73.
42. Harris, "Whiteness as Property," 1731.
43. Quadagno, *The Color of Welfare,* 23.
44. George Lipsitz, *Rainbow at Midnight: Labor and Culture in the 1940s* (Urbana: University of Illinois Press), 1994.
45. Herbert Hill, "Black Workers, Organized Labor, and Title VII of the 1964 Civil Rights Act: Legislative History and Litigation Record," in *Race in America: The Struggle for Equality,* ed. Herbert Hill and James E. Jones, Jr. (Madison: University of Wisconsin Press, 1993), 263.
46. William H. Harris, *the Harder We Run: Black Workers since the Civil War* (New York: Oxford University Press, 1983), 123–37.
47. Quadagno, *The Color of Welfare,* 64.
48. George Lipsitz, *A Life in the Struggle: Ivory Perry and the Culture of Opposition* (Philadelphia: Temple University Press, 1995), 84–85.
49. Franklin, *From Slavery to Freedom,* 483.
50. Peter B. Levy, "The Civil Rights Movement in Cambridge, Maryland, during the 1960s," *Vietnam Generation* 6, 3–4 (1995): 101.
51. Quadagno, *The Color of Welfare,* 63, 67.
52. Hill, "Black Workers, Organized Labor," 267.
53. Helene Slessarev, *The Betrayal of the Poor* (Philadelphia: Temple University Press, 1997), 39–41.
54. Hill, "Black Workers, Organized Labor," 269–70, 170.
55. Quadagno, *The Color of Welfare,* 64–65.
56. Slessarev, *The Betrayal of the Poor,* 70, 74.
57. Quadagno, *The Color of Welfare,* 73–75.
58. Alphonso Lumpkins to James F, Conway, September 5, 1980, James F. Conway Papers, records group 7, series 2, box 11, Civil Rights Enforcement Agency File, Washington University Libraries, St. Louis, Mo.
59. Edward H. Kohn, "Judges Called Adverse to Anti-Bias Suits," *St. Louis Post-Dispatch,* February 11, 1980.
60. Ezorsky, *Racism and Justice,* 25.
61. Richard Child Hill and Cynthia Negry, "Deindustrialization and Racial Minorities in the Great Lakes Region, USA," in *The Reshaping of America: Social Consequences of the Changing Economy,* ed. D. Stanley Eitzen and Maxine Baca Zinn (Englewood Cliffs, N.J.: Prentice-Hall, 1989), 168–78.
62. Harris, "Whiteness as Property," 1783.
63. Ibid., 1778; Derrick Bell, "Remembrances of Racism Past: Getting beyond the Civil Rights Decline," in *Race in America: The Struggle for Equality,* ed. Herbert Hill and James E. Jones, Jr. (Madison: University of Wisconsin Press, 1993), 80.
64. Robert L. Carter, "Thirty-five Years Later: New Perspectives on *Brown,*" in *Race in America: The Struggle for Equality,* ed. Herbert Hill and James E. Jones, Jr. (Madison: University of Wisconsin Press, 1993), 86, 88.
65. Ibid., 86.

66. Bell, "Remembrances of Racism Past," 76.

67. Ibid., 80.

68. *The Life and Death of Malcolm X*, Sitmar Entertainment VHS 2768, videocassette.

Chapter 3. Immigrant Labor and Identity Politics

The epigraph is from Baldwin, *The Devil Finds Work*, 134.

1. Quoted in Lawrence Levine, *The Opening of the American Mind: Canons, Culture, and History* (Boston: Beacon Press, 1996), 123.

2. Kitty Calavita, "The New Politics of Immigration: 'Balanced Budget Conservatism' and the Symbolism of Proposition 187," *Social Problems* 43, 3 (August 1996): 284–306.

3 Mark Potter, "San Diego: City of Shame," *San Diego Reader* 25, 32 (August 8, 1996): 1, 8–10.

4. Holly Sklar, *Chaos or Community* (Boston: South End, 1995), 96.

5. Patrick J. McDonnell, "Immigrants a Net Economic Plus, Study Says," *Los Angeles Times*, May 18, 1997, sec. A.

6. David Bacon, "Labor Slaps the Smug New Face of Union-Busting," *Covert Action Quarterly* no. 60 (spring 1997), 38–39.

7. Lisa Lowe repeats the basic contours of this argument in *Immigrant Acts*, 20, 174–75.

8. Potter, "San Diego," 8–10.

9. Rafael Perez-Torres, *Chicano Poetry* (New York: Cambridge University Press, 1995), 101.

10. Janice Shields, "Social Dumping in Mexico under NAFTA," *Multinational Monitor*, April 1995, 24.

11. Ibid., 22.

12. Ibid.

13. Yen Le Espiritu, *Asian American Women and Men: Labor* (Thousand Oaks, Calif.: Sage, 1997).

14. Lowe, *Immigrant Acts*, 60–83.

15. Juan Flores, "'Que Assimilated, Brother, Yo Soy Assimilao': The Structuring of Puerto Rican Identity in the U.S.," *Journal of Ethnic Studies* 13, 3: 1–16; Jack D. Forbes, *Black Africans and Native Americans: Color, Race, and Caste in the Evolution of Red-Black Peoples* (Oxford: Basil Blackwell, 1988); Gary Y. Okihiro, *Margins and Mainstreams: Asians in American History and Culture* (Seattle: University of Washington Press, 1994), 31–63; Peter Narvaez, "The Influences of Hispanic Music Ccultures on African-American Blues Musicians," *Black Music Research Journal* 14, 2 (fall 1994): 206; Kevin Gaines, *Uplifting the Race: Black Leadership, Politics, and Culture in the Twentieth Century* (Chapel Hill: University of North Carolina Press, 1996), 56; James Howard, *Shawnee! The Ceremonialism of a Native Indian Tribe and Its Cultural Background* (Athens: University of Ohio Press, 1981), 21–23. I thank Rachel Buff for calling Howard's work to my attention and for her own superb scholarship, which has influenced my understanding of panethnic antiracism in significant ways.

16. Teresa de Lauretis, "Eccentric Subjects," *Feminist Studies* 16, 1 (summer 1990):115–51.

17. Ramón Gutiérrez, *When Jesus Came, the Corn Mothers Went Away* (Stanford, Calif.: Stanford University Press, 1990).

18. George Sanchez, *Becoming Mexican American* (New York: Oxford, 1993).

19. Vicki Ruíz, *Cannery Women/Cannery Lives: Mexican Women, Unionization, and the California Food Processing Industry, 1930–1950* (Albuquerque: University of New Mexico Press, 1987); David Montejano, *Anglos and Mexicans in the Making of Texas, 1836–1986* (Austin: University of Texas Press, 1987); Neil Foley, *The White Scourge* (Berkeley and Los Angeles: University of California Press, 1997); Rosaura Sánchez, *Telling Identities: The Californio Testimonios* (Minneapolis: University of Minnesota Pess, 1995).

20. David Gutiérrez, *Walls and Mirrors: Mexican Americans, Mexican Immigrants, and the Politics of Ethnicity* (Berkeley and Los Angeles: University of California Press, 1995).
21. José David Saldívar, *Border Matters* (Berkeley and Los Angeles: University of California Press, 1997); Carl Gutiérrez-Jones, *Rethinking the Borderlands: Between Chicano Culture and Legal Discourse* (Berkeley and Los Angeles: University of California Press, 1995); Ramón Saldívar, *Chicano Narrative: The Dialectics of Difference* (Austin: University of Texas Press, 1990), 7.
22. Rosa Linda Fregoso, *The Bronze Screen* (Minneapolis: University of Minnesota Press, 1994); Gloria Anzaldúa, *Borderlands: La Frontera: The New Mestiza* (San Francisco: Spinsters/aunt lutte, 1987), 30; José Limón, *Dancing with the Devil: Society and Cultural Poetics in Mexican-American South Texas* (Madison: University of Wisconsin Press, 1994).
23. Yvonne Yarbro-Bejarano, "The Female Subject in Chicano Theatre: Sexuality, 'Race,' and Class," *Theatre Journal* 38, 4 (December 1986): 389–407; Normal Alarcón, "Chicana's Feminist Literature: A Revision through Malintzin/ or Malintzin: Putting Flesh Back on the Object," in *This Bridge Called My Back: Writings by Radical Women of Color,* ed. Cherríe Moraga and Gloria Anzaldúa (Watertown, Mass.: Persephone, 1981), 182–90; Steven Loza, *Barrio Rhythm: Mexican American Music in Los Angeles* (Urbana: University of Illinois Press, 1993); James Diego Vigil, *Barrio Gangs: Street Life and Identity in Southern California* (Austin: University of Texas Press, 1988), 117, 121; Brenda Bright, "Remappings: Los Angeles Low Riders," in *Looking High and Low,* ed Brenda Bright and Liza Bakewell (Tucson: University of Arizona Press, 1995).
24. I must add here out of deference to Bob Marley that, while he shot the sheriff, he did not shoot the deputy.
25. .Américo Paredes, *With His Pistol in His Hand* (Austin: University of Texas Press, 1958), 171–72.
26. Robert Farris Thompson, *The Flash of the Spirit* (New York: Oxford University Press, 1984).
27. Renato Rosaldo, *Culture and Truth: The Remaking of Social Analysis* (Boston: Beacon, 1989), 150–55 (quote on p. 151). See also Limón, *Dancing with the Devil,* 76–94.
28. Lowe, *Immigrant Acts.*
29. *CAAAV Voice* 9, 1 (winter 1997): 3; *CAAAV Voice* 9, 2 (summer 1997): 11.
30. Lowe, *Immigrant Acts,* 165–66.
31. Mike Davis, "Kajima's Throne of Blood," *The Nation,* February 12, 1996, 18–21.
32. Eric Mann and Chris Mathis, "Civil Rights Consent Decree? Legal Tactics for Left Strategy," *Ahora Now,* no. 4 (1997): 1–11.
33. James Baldwin, *No Name in the Street* (New York: Dial, 1972), 129.

Chapter 4. Whiteness and War

The epigraph is from Baldwin, *The Devil Finds Work,* 93.
1. Yen Le Espiritu, *Asian American Panethnicity: Building Institutions and Identities* (Philadelphia: Temple University Press, 1992), 141–43; see also the film by Renee Tajima and Christine Choy, *Who Killed Vincent Chin?.* 1988.
2. Helen Zia, "Violence in our Communities: 'Where Are the Asian Women?'" in *Making More Wives: New Writing by Asian American Women,* ed. Elaine H. Kim, Lilia v. Villaneuva, and Asian Women United of California (Boston: Beacon, 1997), 208.
3. Darrell Y. Hamamoto, *Monitored Peril: Asian Americans and the Politics of TV Representation* (Minneapolis: University of Minnesota Press, 1994), 165; Yen, *Asian American Panethnicity,* 155–56.
4. Hamamoto, *Monitored Peril,* 166–67; Mike Clary, "Rising Toll of Hate Crimes Cited in Slaying," *Los Angeles Times,* October 10, 1992, sec. A.

5. Lowe, *Immigrant Acts*, 6–22; Yen, *Asian American Women and Men*, 9–13; Okihiro, *Margins and Mainstreams*.

6. Espiritu, ibid. 90.

7. Reginald Horsman, *Race and Manifest Destiny: The Origins of American Anglo-Saxonism* (Cambridge: Harvard University Press, 1981); David Roediger, *Toward the Abolition of Whiteness: Essays on Race, Politics, and Working-Class History* (New York: Verso, 1994).

8. Michael Rogin, *Ronald Reagan, the Movie: And Other Stories in Political Demonology* (Berkeley and Los Angeles: University of California Press, 1987).

9. Kathleen Hall Jamieson, *Eloquence in an Electronic Age* (New York: Oxford University Press, 1988), 162, 163.

10. Lefty Frizzell, "Mom and Dad's Waltz," Columbia Records 20837, appears in *Billboard* on August 18, 1951, and stays on the charts for twenty-nine weeks; Joel Whitburn, *Top Country Hits, 1944–1988* (Menomonee, Wis.: Record Research, 1989), 107; Robert Westbrook, "'I Want a Girl Just Like the Girl that Married Harry James': American Women and the Problem of Political Obligation in World War II," *American Quarterly* 42, 4 (December 1990): 587–615; Amy Kaplan, "Romancing the Empire: The Embodiment of American Masculinity in the Popular Historical novel of the 1890s," *American Literary History* 2, 4 (winter 1990): 659–90.

11. Robert Westbrook, "Private Interests and Public Obligations in World War II," in *The Power of Culture: Critical Essays in American History*, ed. Richard Wightman Fox and T. J. Jackson Lears (Chicago: University of Chicago Press, 1993), 195–222.

12. Benedict Anderson, *Imagined Communities* (New York: Verso, 1983).

13. Hobson quoted in Kaplan, "Romancing the Empire," 677.

14. Francis X. Clines, "Military of U.S. 'Standing Tall,' Reagan Asserts," *New York Times*, December 13, 1983.

15. Kevin Bowen, "'Strange Hells': Hollywood in Search of America's Lost War," in *From Hanoi to Hollywood: The Vietnam War in American Film*, ed. Linda Dittmar and Gene Michaud (New Brunswick, N.J.: Rutgers University Press, 1991), 229.

16. James William Gibson, "The Return of Rambo: War and Culture in the Post-Vietnam Era," in *America at Century's End*, ed. Alan Wolfe (Berkeley and Los Angeles: University of California Press, 1991), 389, 390.

17. William Adams, "Screen Wars: The Battle for Vietnam," *Dissent*, Winter 1990, 65.

18. See Lynne Cheney, "Report," in *On Campus* 7, 3 (November 1987): 2, as well as Lynne Cheney, "Report to the President, the Congress, and the American People," *Chronicle of Higher Education* 35, 4 (September 21, 1988): A18–19.

19. It was reported that the *Mayaguez* carried only paper supplies for U.S. troops, but as a container ship its cargo could have included much more sensitive material for surveillance or combat, which may account for the vigorous government reaction to its capture. See Marilyn Young, *The Vietnam Wars, 1945–1990* (New York: HarperCollins, 1991), 301; see also Thomas J. McCormick, *America's Half Century: United States Foreign Policy in the Cold War* (Baltimore: Johns Hopkins University Press, 1989), 178–79.

20. "A Force Reborn," *U.S. News and World Report*, March 18, 1991, 30; Harry G. Summers, Jr., "Putting Vietnam Syndrome to Rest," *Los Angeles Times*, March 2, 1991, sec. A; E. J. Dionne, Jr., "Kicking the 'Vietnam Syndrome,'" *Washington Post*, March 4, 1991, sec. A; Kevin P. Phillips, "The Vietnam Syndrome: Why Is Bush Hurting If There Is No War?" *Los Angeles Times*, November 25, 1990.

21. Robert McKelvey, "Watching Victory Parades, I Confess Some Envy: Vietnam Vets Weren't Feted by Parades," *Los Angeles Times*, June 16, 1991, sec. M; James S. Barron, "A Korean War Parade, Decades Late," *New York Times*, June 26, 1991, sec. B.

22. Young, *The Vietnam Wars*, 314.

23. George C. Herring, *America's Longest War* (New York: Wiley, 1968), George McT. Kahin,

Intervention (New York: Knopf, 1986), and Stanley Karnow, *Vietnam: A History* (New York: Viking, 1984) present different perspectives on the war, but their cumulative evidence reveals the untenable nature of any hypothesis blaming internal division in the United States for the war's outcome.

24. Thomas Ferguson and Joel Rogers, *Right Turn: The Decline of the Democrats and the Future of American Politics* (New York: Hill and Wang, 1986), 79, 80.

25. Katherine S. Newman, "Uncertain Seas: Cultural Turmoil and the Domestic Economy," in *America at Century's End,* ed. Alan Wolfe (Berkeley and Los Angeles: University of California Press,1991), 116.

26. Ibid., 116, 117, 121; Chafe, *The Unfinished Journey,* 449.

27. See Michael I. Luger, "Federal Tax Incentives as Industrial and Urban Policy," in *Sunbelt/Snowbelt: Urban Development and Regional Restructuring,* ed. Larry Sawers and William K. Tabb (New York: Oxford University Press, 1984), 201–34.

28. Christian G. Appy, *Working Class War: American Combat Soldiers and Vietnam* (Chapel Hill: University of North Carolina Press, 1993), 6, 11.

29. There were, of course, important exceptions to this pattern. Antiwar activists supported coffeehouses, draft counseling centers, and antiwar newspapers at dozens of military bases. Many local peace coalitions united trade unionists, intellectuals, suburban liberals, students, and poor people, and—especially after 1970—the antiwar counterculture had a substantial working-class presence. But almost nowhere did any of this produce a class-based critique of why the war was fought and who had to fight it. Of course, the antiwar movement emerged as an ad hoc coalition based on college campuses with few other institutional resources. McCarthyism's destruction of the Old Left and the timidity of social democrats left the work of radicalism to politically inexperienced children of the middle class.

30. Billy Joel, "Allentown," Columbia Records 03413, entered *Billboard* charts on November 27, 1982, rose as high as number seventeen, and remained on the charts twenty-two weeks; Bruce Springsteen, "Born in the USA," Columbia Records 04680, entered *Billboard* charts November 10, 1984, rose to number nine, and remained on the charts seventeen weeks; see Joel Whitburn, *Top Pop Singles* (Menomonee Falls, Wis.: Record Research, 1987), 266, 475. Bobbie Ann Mason, *In Country* (New York: Perennial Library, 1985).

31. Adams, "Screen Wars," 71–72.

32. Frank Burke, "Reading Michael Cimino's *The Deer Hunter:* Interpretation as Melting Pot," *Film and Literature Quarterly* 20, 3 (1992): 252–53.

33. Adams, "Screen Wars," 72; Gaylin Studlar and David Dresser, "Never Having to Say You're Sorry: Rambo's Rewriting of the Vietnam War," in *From Hanoi to Hollywood: The Vietnam War in American Film,* ed. Linda Dittmar and Gene Michaud (New Brunswick, N.J.: Rutgers University Press, 1991), 111, 108; Stephen Prince, *Vision of Empire: Political Imagery in Contemporary American Film* (New York: Praeger, 1992), 66, 69.

34. Susan Jeffords, *The Remasculinization of America: Gender and the Vietnam War* (Bloomington and Indianapolis: Indiana University Press, 1989).

35. Lynda Boose, "Techno-Muscularity and the 'Boy Eternal': From the Quagmire to the Gulf," in *The Cultures of United States Imperialism,* ed. Donald Pease and Amy Kaplan (Durham: Duke University Press, 1994), 588–99, 600, 602.

36. Jeffords, *The Remasculinization of America,* 180; Philip Slater, *A Dream Deferred: America's Discontent and the Search for a New Democratic Ideal* (Boston: Beacon, 1991).

37. Cole and LaHaye are quoted in Michael Lienesch, *Redeeming America: Piety and Politics in the New Christian Right* (Chapel Hill: University of North Carolina Press, 1993), 60, 54, 58.

38. "Talk Radio Lowlights," *Extra! Update* (newsletter), December 1996, 2.
39. Chaim F. Shatan, "'Happiness Is a Warm Gun'—Militarized Mourning and Ceremonial Vengeance: Toward a Psychological Theory of Combat and Manhood in America, Part III," *Vietnam Generation* 3, 4 (1989): 147.
40. Jamieson, *Eloquence in an Electronic Age,* 161.
41. Hobson quoted in Kaplan, "Romancing the Empire," 679.
42. Shatan, "'Happiness Is a Warm Gun,'" 140–41.
43. O'Brien is quoted in Young, *The Vietnam Wars,* 329.
44. George Marsical, "'Our Kids Don't Have blue Eyes, but They Go Overseas to Die': Chicanos in Vietnam," paper read at the conference "America and Vietnam: From War to Peace," University of Notre Dame, South Bend, Ind., December 4, 1993.
45. Kitty Calavita, "The New Politics of Immigration: 'Balanced Budget Conservatism' and the Symbolism of Proposition 187," *Social Problems* 43, 3 (August 1996), 284–306.
46. See for example Rita Chaudry Sethi, "Smells Like Racism: A Plan for Mobilizing against Anti-Asian Bias," in *the State of Asian America: Activism and Resistance in the 1990s,* ed. Karen Aguilar-San Juan (Boston: South End, 1994), 235–50.
47. Timothy J. Dunn, *The Militarization of the U.S.-Mexico Border, 1978–1992* (Austin, Tex.: Center for Mexican American Studies, 1996), 87–89.
48. Mark Dow, "Behind the Razor Wire: Inside INS Detention Centers," *Covert Action Quarterly,* no. 57 (summer 1996): 35.
49. Jesse Katz, "Marine is Cleared in Texas Border Death," *Los Angeles Times* August 15, 1997, sec. A; Sam Howe Verhovek, "Pentagon Halts Drug Patrols After Border Killing," *New York Times,* July 31, 1997, sec. A.
50. W.E.B. Du Bois, *Black Reconstruction in America, 1860–1880* (New York: Touchstone, 1992), 696.

Chapter 5. White Fear: O.J. Simpson and the Greatest Story Ever Sold.

The epigraph is from Baldwin, *The Devil Finds Work,* 71–72.
1. Alexander Saxton, *The Rise and Fall of the White Republic* (New York: Verson, 1992); David Roediger, *The Wages of Whiteness* (New York: Verso, 1991); Rogin, *Ronald Reagan, the Movie;* and Michael Rogin, *Blackface/White Noise* (Berkeley and Los Angeles: University of California Press).
2. Ward Churchill and Jim Vander Wall, *Agents of Repression: The FBI's Secret Wars against the Black Panther Party and the American Indian Movement* (Boston: South End, 1988), 79, 85, 87–88, 409.
3. Ibid., 90, 91, 406.
4. M. Wesley Swearingen, *FBI Secrets: An Agent's Exposé* (Boston: South End, 1995), 84–86.
5. Edward J. Boyer, "Pratt Retrial Bid May Ride on Definition of 'Informant,'" *Los Angeles Times,* December 30, 1996, Metro section.
6. Mumia Abu-Jamal, "Parole Denied for Geronimo Pratt—Again," *New Pittsburgh Courier,* April 17, 1996, sec. A; Boyer, "Pratt Retrial Bid."
7. Edward Boyer, "Judge Reverses Conviction of Geronimo Pratt," *Los Angeles Times,* May 30, 1997, sec. A.
8. "Taxing: The O.J. Simpson Trial," *The Economist,* June 17, 1995, 31.
9. Joe Mandrese and Jeff Jensen, "'Trial of a Century,' Break of a Lifetime," *Advertising Age,* October 9, 1995, 1.
10. Rich Brown, "The Juice Powers Some Players," *Broadcasting and Cable,* October 9, 1995, 10.
11. Mandrese and Jensen, "'Trial of a Century,'" 41.

12. Ibid., 1; Michael Wilke, "O.J. Verdict: 'Hero' Days Are Over," *Advertising Age,* October 2, 1995, 8.

13. Cynthia Littleton, "Verdict Propels Tabloid Ratings," *Broadcasting and Cable,* October 9, 1995, 7.

14. Brent Staples, "Millions for Defense," *New York Times Book Review,* April 28, 1996, 15; Adam Hochschild, "Closing Argument," *New York Times Book Review,* April 28, 1996, 15.

15. Hochschild, "Closing Argument," 15.

16. Steve McClellan, "All Eyes on O.J.," *Broadcasting and Cable,* October 9, 1996, 6; Mandrese and Jensen, "'Trial of a Century,'" 1.

17. Joe Mandrese and Thomas Tyler, "Simpson Shakes New TV Season," *Advertising Age,* October 16, 1995, 48.

18. Ibid.; Jim McConville, "Down Is Up for Cable Networks," *Broadcasting and Cable,* October 30, 1995, 51.

19. Littleton, "Verdict Propels Tabloid Ratings," 7.

20. Julie Johnson, "O.J. Scores Again on '95 Covers," *Advertising Age,* January 1, 1996, 4.

21. Mark Berniker, "CNN Web Site Flooded with O.J. Interest," *Broadcasting and Cable,* October 9, 1995, 71.

22. J.M., "O.J. Simpson Interview Scores Big for BET," *Broadcasting and Cable,* January 29, 1996, 7.

23. Richard Barnet and John Cavenagh, *Global Dreams: Imperial Corporations and the New World Order* (New York: Simon and Schuster, 1994), 325–29.

24. Hochschild, "Closing Argument," 14.

25. John Fiske, *Media Matters: Everyday Culture and Political Change* (Minneapolis: University of Minnesota, 1994), xix.

26. Nancy Armstrong, *Desire in Domestic Fiction* (New York: Oxford University Press, 1985); Roddy Reid, *Families in Jeopardy* (Stanford: Standford University Press, 1994).

27. Fiske, *Media Matters,* xix.

28. Joel Kovel, "Rationalization and the Family," *Telos,* no. 37 (1978): 13–14.

29. William Howze, "John Ford's Celluloid Canvas," *Southwest Media Review,* vol. 3 (1985): 20–25.

30. C.L.R. James, *American Civilization* (New York: Blackwell, 1994), 127.

31. Ibid., 158, 148.

32. Christopher Stern, "Cameras in Courts Take a Hit," *Broadcasting and Cable,* October 9, 1995, 10.

33. Jack White, "A Double Strand of Paranoia," *Time,* October 9, 1995, 39.

34. Jimmie Reeves and Rich Campbell, *Cracked Coverage* (New York: NYU Press, 1994); Herman Gray, *Watching Race: Television and the Struggle for "Blackness"* (Minneapolis: University of Minnesota Press, 1995), esp. pp. 14–34.

35. Gray, *Watching Race,* 23.

36. Ralph Ellison, "Change the Joke and Slip the Yoke," reprinted in *Shadow and Act* (New York: Vintage, 1972), quoted in Sandra Gunning, *Race, Rape, and Lynching: The Red Record of American Literature, 1890–1912* (New York: Oxford University Press, 1996), 3.

37. Nathan Irvin Huggins, *Harlem Renaissance* (New York: Oxford University Press, 1978), especially chapter six.

38. Baldwin, *No Name in the Street,* 88 (see chap. 3, n. 33).

39. Fiske, *Media Matters,* xvi.

40. Lewis R. Gordon, "A Lynching Well Lost," *Black Scholar* 25, 4 (1995): 37.

41. Peniel E. Joseph, "'Black' Reconstructed: White Supremacy in Post–Civil Rights America," *Black Scholar* 25, 4 (1995): 53.

42. Ibid., 52.

Chapter 6. White Desire: Remembering Robert Johnson

The epigraph is from Baldwin, *The Devil Finds Work,* 147.

1. "Every Crossroads Has a Story," *Living Blues,* November/December 1996, back cover.
2. Michael Schumacher, *Crossroads: The Life and Music of Eric Clapton* (New York: Hyperion, 1995), 19, 63, 99–100; Harry Shapiro, *Eric Clapton: Lost in the Blues* (New York: Da Capo, 1992), 11, 14.
3. Peter Guralnick, *Searching for Robert Johnson* (New York: Dutton, 1982); Francis Davis, *The History of the Blues: The Roots, the Music, the People, from Charley Patton to Robert Cray* (New York: Hyperion, 1995), 126; Marla C. Berns, ed., *"Dear Robert, I'll See You at the Crossroads": A Project by Renee Stout* (Santa Barbara: University Art Museum, 1995); Walter Mosley, *RJ's Dream* (New York: Simon and Schuster, 1994); Walter Hill (director), *Crossroads,* Columbia Pictures, 1986; Ben Cromer, "Robert Johnson Tapes Found: Set Remastered," *Billboard,* December 7, 1996, 39.
4. Thompson, *Flash of the Spirit,* 19, 93.
5. Ibid., 19; See also Samuel A. Floyd, *The Power of Black Music: Interpreting Its History from Africa to the United States* (New York: Oxford University Press, 1995), 74, and Robert Palmer, *Deep Blues* (New York: Penguin, 1981), 59.
6. Hill, *Crossroads.*
7. Mosley, *RJ's Dream,* 143.
8. Nancy Rosenblum, "Romanticism," in *A Companion to American Thought,* ed. Richard Wightman Fox and James T. Kloppenberg (Oxford: Basil Blackwell, 1995), 601.
9. Shapiro, *Eric Clapton,* 14, 13.
10. Schumacher, *Crossroads,* 18, 19.
11. Ibid., 205, 206; Shapiro, *Eric Clapton,* 145.
12. Guralnick, *Searching for Robert Johnson,* 15.
13. Ibid., 17.
14. Palmer, *Deep Blues,* 113.
15. Guralnick, *Searching for Robert Johnson,* 12.
16. Palmer, *Deep Blues,* 57, 101.
17. Guralnick, *Searching for Robert Johnson,* 10–11.
18. Palmer, *Deep Blues,* 112.
19. Guralnick, *Searching for Robert Johnson,* 11, 20.
20. Palmer, *Deep Blues,* 59.
21. Ibid., 62, 122.
22. Davis, *The History of the Blues,* 128; Palmer, *Deep Blues,* 80.
23. Palmer, *Deep Blues,* 119.
24. Lawrence Levine, *Black Culture and Black Consciousness: Afro-American Folk Thought from Slavery to Freedom* (New York: Oxford University Press, 1977), 10–11.
25. Edward Krehbiel, *Afro-American Folk Songs: A Study in Racial and National Music* (New York: Schirmer, 1914). I thank Jon Cruz for calling this quote to my attention.
26. Guralnick, *Searching for Robert Johnson,* 31.
27. Palmer, *Deep Blues,* 120–21, 113, 175.
28. Chris Waterman, "'Corrine Corrina' and the Excluded Middle of the American Racial Imagination," in *Music and the Racial Imagination,* ed. P. Bohlman and R. Radano (Chicago: University of Chicago Press, 1998); B. B. King with David Ritz, *Blues All Around Me* (New York: Avon, 1996), 23.
29. Marla Berns, "On Love and Longing: Renee Stout Does the Blues," in Berns, *"Dear Robert, I'll See You at the Crossroads,"* 42.
30. Holland Cotter, "Art That's Valued for What It Can Do," *New York Times,* July 18, 1993, sec. H.

31. Michael D. Harris, "Resonance, Transformation, and Rhyme: The Art of Renee Stout," in *Astonishment and Power,* ed. Wyatt MacGaffey and Michael D. Harris (Washington, D.C.: National Museum of African Art/Smithsonian Institution, 1993), 109.
32. Paul Gilroy, *Ain't No Black in the Union Jack* (Chicago: University of Chicago Press, 1987), 156, 158, 159.
33. George Rawick, *From Sundown to Sunup* (Westport, Conn.: Greenwood, 1972); Sterling Stuckey, *Slave Culture: Nationalist Theory and the Foundations of Black America* (New York: Oxford University Press, 1987).
34. Herman Gray, *Watching Race: Television and the Struggle for "Blackness"* Minneapolis: University of Minnesota Press, 1995), quoted in Leland Ferguson, *Uncommon Ground: Archaeology and Early African America, 1650–1800* (Washington, D.C.: Smithsonian Institution Press, 1992), xiv.
35. Robert Farris Thompson, "he Song that Named the Land: The Visionary Presence of African-American Art,"in *Black Art Ancestral Legacy: The African Impulse in African-American Art,* ed. Alvia Wardlaw (Dallas: Dallas Museum of Art, 1989), 97, 102, 127, 132.
36. Charles Joyner, *Down by the Riverside* (Urbana: University of Illinois Press, 1984), xxi.
37. Stuckey, *Slave Culture;* Sterling Stuckey, *Going through the Storm: The Influence of African American Art in History* (New York: Oxford University Press, 1994); Joseph E. Holloway and Winifred K. Vass, *The African Heritage of American English* (Bloomington and Indianapolis: Indiana University Press, 1993); Melville Herskovitz, *The Myth of the Negro Past* (Boston: Beacon, 1958); LeRoi Jones, *Blues People* (New York: Morrow, 1963); Ben Sidran, *Black Talk* (New York: Holt, Rinehart, and Winston, 1971); John F. Szwed and Morton Marks, "The Afro-American Transformation of European Set Dances and Dance Suites," *Dance Research Journal* 20, 1 (summer 1998): 29–36.
38. Arthur Schlesinger, Jr., *The Disuniting of America: Reflections on a Multicultural Society* (New York: Norton, 1991), 15, 82, 83, 85.
39. Of course, some Afrocentrists do work that conforms to Schlesinger's caricatures. But his citations of them are largely from journalistic sources; he offers little evidence that he has actually read their work. Moreover, his ignorance about the African presence in American leaves him poorly equipped to answer even these arguments, a circumstance he could have avoided simply by consulting the outstanding research of such writers as Sterling Stuckey, Lawrence Levine, Peter Wood, Robert Farris Thompson, Margaret Washington Creel, and George Rawick.
40. Carter G. Woodson, *The Negro in Our History* (Washington, D.C.: Associated Publishers, 1922), 628, quoted in Stuckey, *Going through the Storm,* 127.
41. Herskovitz, *Myth of the Negro Past;* Rawick, *Sundown to Sunup;* Jones, *Blues People;* Sidran, *Black Talk.*
42. Lawrence Levine, "Clio, Canons, and Culture," *Journal of American History* 80, 3 (December 1993): 849–67. See also the exchange of letters between Levine and Schlesinger in *Journal of American History,* 81, 1 (June 1994): 367–68.
43. Arthur M. Schlesinger, Jr., "The Cult of Ethnicity, Good and Bad: A Historian Argues that Multiculturalism Threatens the Ideal that Binds America," *Time,* July 8, 1991, 21.
44. Renee Stout quoted in Julia Barnes Mandle, "Artists in the Exhibition/Interviews," in *Sites of Recollection: Four Altars and a Rap Opera,* ed. Williams College Museum of Art (Williamstown, Mass.: Williams College, 1992), 85.
45. Harris, "Resonance, Transformation, and Rhyme," 11, 114, 149.
46. Robert Farris Thompson, "Illuminating Spirits: 'Astonishment and Power' at the National Museum of African Art," *African Arts* 26 (October 1993): 66.

47. Harris, "Resonance, Transformation, and Rhyme," 114.
48. Ibid., 111, 114, 149.
49. Florence Rubenfeld, "Renee Stout," *Arts Magazine,* May 1991, 79.
50. Thompson, "Song that Named the Land," 132, 131.
51. Thompson, "Illuminating Spirits," 68.
52. Harris, "Resonance, Transformation, and Rhyme," 111.
53. Thompson, "Song that Named the Land," 103.
54. Gylbert Coker, "African Art and the Black Folk Artist," in *African American Art,* ed. San Antonio Museum of Art (San Antonio: San Antonio Museum of Art, 1994), 41.
55. Alvia J. Wardlaw, "Private Visions," in *Black Art Ancestral Legacy: The African Impulse in African-American Art,* ed. Alvia Wardlaw (Dallas: Dallas Museum of Art, 1989), 188.
56. Jontyle Theresa Robinson, "Recent Exhibitions: Black Art Ancestral Legacy," *African Arts* 24, 1 (January 1991): 29; Alvia J. Wardlaw, "Reclamations," in *Black Art Ancestral Legacy: The African Impulse in African-American Art,* ed. Alvia Wardlaw (Dallas: Dallas Museum of Art, 1989), 231.
57. Curtia James, "Astonishment and Power: Kongo Minkisi and the Art of Renee Stout," *Art News* 92, 8 (October 1993): 171.
58. Harris, "Resonance, Transformation, and Rhyme," 151–52, 142, 153.
59. Stuckey, *Slave Culture,* 11.
60. Mandle, "Renee Stout," 85; Harris, "Resonance, Transformation, and Rhyme," 120; Thompson, "Song that Named the Land," 292.
61. Mandle, "Renee Stout," 91.
62. Ibid., 85.
63. Thompson, "Song that Named the Land," 100.
64. Gylbert Coker, "Nineteenth-Century African Art," in *African American Art,* ed. San Antonio Museum of Art (San Antonio: San Antonio Museum of Art, 1994), 8.
65. Alvia J. Wardlaw, "A Spiritual Libation: Promoting an African Heritage in the Black College," in *Black Art Ancestral Legacy: The African Impulse in African-American Art,* ed. Alvia Wardlaw (Dallas: Dallas Museum of Art, 1989), 54.

Chapter 7. *Lean on Me:* Beyond Identity Politics

The epigraph is from Baldwin, *The Devil Finds Work,* 134–35.
1. Jeffrey Page, "Joe Clark Faults Black Leaders," *Bergen Record,* November 15, 1989, sec. A.
2. Mike Kelly, "Time for the Boot," *Bergen Record,* November 14, 1989, sec. B.
3. Jeffrey Page, "Clark Asks Workers' Compensation," *Bergen Record,* September 6, 1990, sec. B.
4. Bernard D. Headley, "Black on Black Crime: The Myth or the Reality?" *Crime and Social Justice* 20 (n.d.), 53; Jesse Jackson, "A Bold Call to Action," in *Inside the L.A. Riots,* ed. Don Hazen (New York: Institute for Alternative Journalism, 1992), 149.
5. Franklin, *The Color Line,* 15, 16 (see chap. 1, n. 69); Jane Mayer and Jill Abramson, *Strange Justice: The Selling of Clarence Thomas* (New York: Plume, 1995), 163.
6. Chester Himes, *If He Hollers Let Him Go* (New York: Thunder's Mouth Press, 1986), 41.
7. In this summary of Rawick's work I draw upon David Roediger's characteristically insightful essay "Notes on Working Class Racism" in his indispensable collection *Towards the Abolition of Whiteness,* 61–68. I have also learned much from Paul Buhle's "Preface: Visions of Emancipation—Daniel De Leon, C.L.R. James, and George Rawick," in *Within the Shell of the Old: Essays on Workers' Self-Organization,* ed. Don Fitz and David Roediger (Chicago: Kerr, 1990), 1–4.

8. Lizabeth Cohen, *Making a New Deal* (Cambridge: Cambridge University Press, 1990), 323–61.

9. Roger Daniels, *Coming to America: A History of Immigration and Ethnicity in American Life* (New York: Harper, 1990), 282.

10. Baldwin, *The Devil Finds Work,* 29–30.

11. Ruiz, *Cannery Women, Cannery Lives* (see chap. 3, n. 19); Robin D. G. Kelley, *Hammer and Hoe: Alabama Communists during the Great Depression* (Chapel Hill: University of North Carolina Press, 1990), 138–51.

12. Rogin, *Blackface/White Noise,* 253 (see chap. 5, n. 1).

13. Patricia J. Williams, *The Rooster's Egg: On the Persistence of Prejudice* (Cambridge: Harvard University Press, 1996), 65.

14. David Roediger, "Black Freedom and the WPA Slave Narratives: Dave Roediger Interviews George Rawick," in *Within the Shell of the Old: Essays on Workers' Self-Organization,* ed. Don Fitz and David Roediger (Chicago: Kerr, 1990), 10.

15. Toni Cade Bambara quoted in Darlene Clark Hine, Elsa Barkley Brown, and Rosalyn Terborg-Penn, eds., *Black Women in America: An Historical Encyclopedia* (Bloomington and Indianapolis: Indiana University Press, 1993), 80.

16. W.E.B. Du Bois quoted in Gaines, *Uplifting the Race,* 175 (see chap. 3, n. 15).

Chapter 8. "Swing Low, Sweet Cadillac": Antiblack Racism and White Identity

The epigraph is from Baldwin, *No Name in the Street,* 128–29.

1. Jon Cruz, *Culture on the Margins* (Princeton, N.J.: Princeton University Press, forthcoming). See also Christopher Small, *Music of the Common Tongue* (New York: Riverrun, 1994), 94.

2. Dizzy Gillespie (with Al Fraser), *To Be, or Not . . . to Bop* (Garden City, N.Y.: Doubleday, 1979), 453.

3. Ibid., 452–61. I thank Kevin Gaines for calling my attention to Gillespie's campaign in his fine paper for the 1997 American Studies Association conference.

4. Ibid., 454.

5. See "Welfare Cadillac: Disgusting Racism," *Rolling Stone,* March 19, 1970, 12. I thank Dave McBride for bringing this article to my attention.

6. Chester Himes, *The Quality of Hurt: The Early Years,* vol. 1 of *The Autobiography of Chester Himes* (New York: Paragon House, 1990), 8.

7. Charles Payne, *I've Got the Light of Freedom: The Organizing Tradition and the Mississippi Freedom Struggle* (Berkeley and Los Angeles: University of California Press, 1996), 14–15.

8. Dittmer, *Local People,* 15 (see introduction, n. 21.).

9. Himes, *The Quality of Hurt,* 8.

10. Ralph Ellison, *Invisible Man* (New York: Vintage, 1972), 16.

11. Ibid., 140–41.

12. Levine, *Black Culture and Black Consciousness,* 88 (see chap. 6, n. 24).

13. Gideon Granger to James Jackson, March 23, 1802, *American State Papers,* quoted in Stan Weir, "Early U.S. Labor Policy Revealed by Archiives Find," *Random Lengths* 7, 12 (November 1986): 16. I thank Stan Weir for calling my attention to this document and its significance, and acknowledge as well the work of Laurence Reinhold and Ernest Rice McKinney in discovering this document in the first place.

14. Ibid.

15. Jackson, *Crabgrass Frontier* (see chap. 1, n. 13).

16. Paul M. Sniderman and Thomas Piazza, *The Scar of Race* (Cambridge: Harvard University Press, 1993), 5, 40, 98, 124, 47, 76, 11, 137.

17. Ibid., 40–42, 50.

18. Ibid., 43–44.

19. Leonard Steinhorn, "On Race, Americans Only Talk a Good Game," letter to the editor, *New York Times,* November 19, 1997, sec A.; Chistopher B. Doob, "For Whites, Confusion," letter to the editor, *New York Times,* November 19, 1997, sec. A.

20. Joe R. Feagin, "The Continuing Significance of Race: Antiblack Discrimination in Public Places," *American Sociological Review* 56, 1 (February 1991): 101–16; Joe R. Feagin, "The Continuing Significance of Racism," *Journal of Black Studies* 22, 4 (June 1992): 546–78.

21. Massey and Denton, *American Apartheid,* 91 (see chap 1, n. 13).

22. Joe R. Feagin and Milvin P. Sikes, *Living with Racism: The Black Middle Class Experience* (Boston: Beacon, 1994), 227.

23. Sniderman and Piazza, *The Scar of Race,* 1.

24. Ibid., 177, 129, 8, 177.

25. Lipsitz, *A Life in the Struggle* (see chap. 2, n. 48); Cornell West, *Keeping Faith: Philosophy and Race in America* (New York: Routledge, 1993), 271–91; Sitkoff, *The Struggle for Black Equality* (see introduction, n. 2).

26. "Students Score University," *New York Times,* April 24, 1963.

27. Goldberg, *Racist Culture,* 104 (see chap. 2, n. 4).

28. Paul Gilroy, *The Black Atlantic: Modernity and Double Consciousness* (Cambridge: Harvard University Press, 1993), 2.

29. Ibid., 47, 49; Goldberg, *Racist Culture,* 47.

30. Gilroy, *The Black Atlantic,* 39.

31. West, *Keeping Faith,* xii; Gilroy, *The Black Atlantic,* 37.

32. Gilroy, *The Black Atlantic,* 71, 57; Goldberg, *Racist Culture,* 213; West, *Keeping Faith,* 27, 268.

33. Donna J. Haraway, *Simians, Cyborgs, and Women: The Reinvention of Nature* (New York: Routledge, 1991), 183–201; de Lauretis, "Eccentric Subjects" (see chap. 3, n. 16); Sandra Harding, *The Science Question in Feminism* (Ithaca, N.Y.: Cornell University Press, 1986).

34. Goldberg, *Racist Culture,* 8.

35. Roediger, *Toward the Abolition of Whtieness,* 181–98, 117–20 (see chap. 4, n. 7).

36. Ibid., 127–80.

37. Herbert Gutman, "Work, Culture, and Society in Industrializing America," *American Historical Review* 78, 3 (June 1973): 531–88.

38. Robin D. G. Kelley, *Race Rebels* (New York: Free Press, 1994), 147–68.

39. West, *Keeping Faith,* 15.

40. Carol Iannone, "Literature by Quota," *Commentary* 91, 2 (March 1991): 12–13.

Chapter 9. "Frantic to Join . . . the Japanese Army": Beyond the Black-White Binary

The epigraph is from Baldwin, *The Devil Finds Work ,* 100–101.

1. Arnold Shankman, *Ambivalent Friends: Afro-Americans View the Immigrant* (Westport, Conn.: Greenwood, 1982); Rosaura Sanchez, *Telling Identities: The Californio Testimonios* (Minneapolis: University of Minnesota Press, 1995), 50–95; Phil Ethington, *The Public City: The Political Construction of Urban Life in San Francisco, 1850–1900* (New York: Cambridge University Press, 1994), 170–206.

2. Malcolm X and Alex Haley, *The Autobiography of Malcolm X* (New York: Grove, 1965),

104–5, 106. Robin D. G. Kelley's adroit analysis of this incident in his splendid and indispensable book *Race Rebels* (p. 171) directed my attention to the significance of Malcolm's story. FBI Surveillance File on Malcolm X, November 30, 1954, quoted in Ferruccio Gambino, "Malcolm X, Laborer: From the Wilderness of the American Empire to Cultural Self-Identification, Colloque 1984 de L'Association Française d'Études Americaines Dourdan, 25–27 Mai, 1984," unpublished manuscript in the author's possession, 17.

3. John Hope Franklin, "Their War and Mine," *Journal of American History* 77, 2 (September 1990): 576–77, 578.

4. Brenda Gayle Plummer, *Rising Wind: Black Americans and U.S. Foreign Affairs, 1935–1960* (Chapel Hill: University of North Carolina Press, 1996), 74–75. Plummer's comprehensive, persuasive, and fascinating book makes a major contribution to rethinking the roles of race and nation in the U.S. past and present.

5. On the African American trickster tradition, see Rawick, *From Sundown to Sunup,* 98 (see chap. 6, n. 33). For the definitive analysis of the racialized nature of the Pacific war see John Dower, *War without Mercy: Race and Power in the Pacific War* (New York: Pantheon, 1986).

6. Kelley, *Hammer and Hoe.*

7. Gilroy, *The Black Atlantic;* Joseph E. Holloway, ed., *Africanism in American Culture* (Bloomington and Indianapolis: Indiana University Press, 1991); George Lipsitz, *Dangerous Crossroads* (London: Verso, 1994).

8. Laura Mulvey, "Myth, Narrative, and Historical Experience," *History Workshop,* vol. 23 (spring 1984): 3–19..

9. Okihiro, *Margins and Mainstreams,* 44, 45 (see chap. 3, n. 15); Daniel Rosenberg, "The IWW and Organization of Asian Workers in Early Twentieth-Century America," *Labor History* 36, 1 (winter 1995): 77–87; Richard White, *It's Your Misfortune and None of My Own* (Tulsa: University of Oklahoma Press, 1991).

10. On exclusion acts, see Lowe, *Immigrant Acts,* 180–81 (see chap. 1, n. 6). On the importation of Asian immigrant labor, Reconstruction, and exclusion, see Okihiro, *Margins and Mainstreams,* 46–48.

11. Michael C. Robinson and Frank N. Schubert, "David Fagen: An Afro-American Rebel in the Philippines, 1899–1901," *Pacific Historical Review* 64, 1 (February 1975): 71, 72.

12. Ibid., 75, 81–82.

13. Nelson Peery, *Black Fire: The Making of an American Revolutionary* (New York: New Press, 1994), 277–78.

14. Tony Martin, *The Pan-African Connection: From Slavery to Garvey and Beyond* (Dover, Mass.: Majority, 1983), 64.

15. Garvey quoted in Ernest V. Allen, "When Japan Was 'Champion of the Darker Races': Satokata Takahishi and the Flowering of Black Messianic Nationalism," *Black Scholar* 24, 1: 29.

16. Ibid.

17. Michiko Hase, "Race, Status, and Culture in Trans-Pacific Perspective: African American Professionals in Japan," paper presented at the American Studies Association meetings, Nashville, Tenn., October 28, 1994, 9–10 (manuscript in the author's possession); W.E.B. Du Bois, *Dark Princess* (Jackson: University Press of Mississippi, Banner Books, 1995). See also Gilroy, *Black Atlantic.*

18. Du Bois, *Black Reconstruction in America* (see chap. 4, n. 49), 706, 704.

19. David J. Hellwig, "Afro-American Reactions to the Japanese and the Anti-Japanese Movement, 1906–1924," *Phylon* 37, 1 (1977): 94–96.

20. Quintard Taylor, "Blacks and Asians in a White City: Japanese Americans and African Americans in Seattle, 1890–1940," *Western Historical Quarterly* 23, 4 (November 1991): 426.

21. Karl Evanzz, *The Judas Factor: The Plot to Kill Malcolm X* (New York: Thunder's Mouth, 1992), 22.

22. E. U. Essien-Udom, *Black Nationalism: A Search for Identity in America* (Chicago: University of Chicago Press, 1962), 44–45, 74–75; Rony Martin, *Race First: The Ideological and Organizational Struggles of Marcus Garvey and the Universal Negro Improvement Association* (Westport, Conn.: Greenwood, 1976), 74–77; Humphrey J. Fischer, *Ahmadiyah* (Oxford: Oxford University Press, 1963); Gambino, "Malcolm X, Laborer," 25–26.

23. Dominic J. Capeci, Jr., *Race Relations in Wartime Detroit: The Sojourner Truth Housing Controversy of 1942* (Philadelphia: Temple University Press, 1984), 53; Evanzz, *The Judas Factor*, 24, 138; Dower, *War without Mercy*, 174.

24. Capeci, *Race Relations in Wartime Detroit*, 53.

25. The record of the Federal Bureau of Investigation in counterintelligence is such that any document the organization releases should be met with suspicion. Yet even if fabricated, this document at the very least shows the anxiety felt at high levels of government about the possiblity of African Americans feeling allegiance to Japan because it was a nonwhite country. Evanzz, *The Judas Factor*, 138.

26. Ernest Allen, Jr., "Waiting for Tojo: The Pro-Japan Vigil of Black Missourians," *Gateway Heritage* 15, 2 (fall 1994): 19, 26.

27. Robert A. Hill, ed., *The Marcus Garvey and UNIA Papers* (Berkeley and Los Angeles: University of California Press, 1983), 596; Bob Kumamoto, "The Search for Spies: American Counterintelligence and the Japanese American Community, 1931–1942," *Amerasia Journal* 6, 2 (1979): 50.

28. Hill, *Marcus Garvey and UNIA Papers*, 506–7.

29. Allen, "When Japan Was 'Champion,' " 37.

30. Hill, *Marcus Garvey and UNIA Papers*, 506, 507.

31. Allen, "When Japan Was 'Champion,' " 25.

32. Gary Y. Okihiro, *Cane Fires: The Anti-Japanese Movement in Hawaii, 1865–1945* (Philadelphia: Temple University Press, 1991), 116–17.

33. Kumamoto, "The Search for Spies," 54.

34. Dabney quoted in Dower, *War without Mercy*, 173–74.

35. Allen, "When Japan Was 'Champion,' " 37.

36. Capeci, *Race Relations in Wartime Detroit*, 54.

37. Allen, "Waiting for Tojo," 27, 28, 19.

38. Essien-Udom, *Black Nationalism*, 48–49, 67.

39. Malcolm X and Haley, *The Autobiography of Malcolm X*, 107.

40. Beth Bailey and David Farber, *The First Strange Place: Race and Sex in World War II Hawaii* (Baltimore: Johns Hopkins University Press, 1992), 133; James Boggs, *The American Revolution: Pages from a Negro Worker's Notebook* (New York: Monthly Review, 1963), 79. I thank Suzanne Smith for calling my attention to this quote.

41. Walter White and Thurgood Marshall, *What Caused the Detroit Riot? An Analysis by Walter White and Thurgood Marshall* (New York: National Association for the Advancement of Colored People, 1943), 15; Roger Daniels, *Concentration Camps USA:Japanese Americans and World War II* (New York: Holt, Rinehart, and Winston, 1971), 36.

42. Lipsitz, *Rainbow at Midnight*, 73–83 (see chap. 2, n. 44); Bernard C. Nalty, *Strength for the Fight: A History of Black Americans in the Military* (New York: Free Press, 1986), 143–203.

43. Dennis Denmark Nelson, "The Integration of the Negro into the United States Navy, 1776–1947," master's thesis, Howard University, 1948, 28–29; Otto Lindenmeyer, *Black and Brave: The Black Soldier in America* (New York: McGraw-Hill), 88; Robert Ewell Greene, *Black Defenders of America, 1775–1973* (Chicago: Johnson, 1974), 202.

44. Nalty, *Strength for the Fight,* 186.
45. Ibid., 166, 169.
46. Bailey and Farber, *The First Strange Place,* 159.
47. Cheryl Greenberg, "Black and Jewish Responses to Japanese Internment," *Journal of American Ethnic History* 14, 2 (winter 1995): 22.
48. Chester Himes, *Lonely Crusade* (New York: Thunder's Mouth Press, 1986), 46.
49. Allen, "When Japan Was 'Champion,'" 37.
50. Dower, *War without Mercy,* 174.
51. Capeci, *Race Relations in Wartime Detroit,* 53; Himes, *If He Hollers Let Him Go,* 3 (see chap. 7, n. 6).
52. Greenberg, "Black and Jewish Responses," 19–20.
53. Taylor, "Blacks and Asians," 408, 413.
54. Records of the Federal Home Loan Bank Board of the Home Owners Loan Corporation, City Survey File, Los Angeles, 1939, Neighborhood D-50, D-33, D-30, National Archives, Box 74, RG 195.
55. Taylor, "Blacks and Asians," 425.
56. Luis Valdez, *Envisioning California,* Keynote Address Publications Series, publication no. 3 (Sacramento: Center for California Studies, 1995), 7.
57 Beatrice Griffith, *American Me* (Cambridge: Houghton Mifflin, 1948), 321; Taylor, "Blacks and Asians," 424.
58. Greenberg, "Black and Jewish Responses," 15, 18, 16, 18, 19.
59. Charles Jackson, "Plight of Japanese Americans," *Militant,* March 10, 1945, reprinted in C.L.R. James, George Breitman, and Edgar Keemer, *Fighting Racism in World War II* (New York: Monad, 1980), 342.
60. Daniels, *Concentration Camps USA,* 59, 105.
61. Nalty, *Strength for the Fight,* 167.
62. Bailey and Farber, *The First Strange Place,* 139, 161.
63. Ibid., 103, 162.
64. Daniels, *Concentration Camps USA,* 163.
65. Quoted in Mauricio Mazon, *The Zoot-Suit Riots: The Psychology of Symbolic Annihilation* (Austin: University of Texas Press, 1984), 19, 52. On the "zoot suit" riots, see Lipsitz, *Rainbow at Midnight,* 83–86 (see chap. 2, n. 44).
66. Mazon, *The Zoot-Suit Riots,* 23.
67. Daniels, *Concentration Camps USA,* 158; Himes, *Lonely Crusade,* 207. I thank Lisa Lowe for reminding me of the ways in which anti-Asian racism entails this rendering of Asian Americans as "permanently foreign."
68. Kumamoto, "The Search for Spies," 66–68.
69. Daniels, *Concentration Camps USA,* 159, 168.
70. Ibid., 162; Taylor, "Blacks and Asians," 428.
71. Daniels, *Concentration Camps USA,* 170. See also Kevin Allen Leonard, "'Is That What We Fought For?' Japanese Americans and Racism in California: The Impact of World War II," *Western Historical Quarterly* 21, 4 (November 1990): 480.
72. Baldwin, *The Fire Next Time* (New York: Dial), 63; Franklin, "Their War and Mine," 579.
73. Peery, *Black Fire,* 200; Walter White quoted in Dower, *War without Mercy,* 177–78.
74. Limón, *Dancing with the Devil,* 78 (see chap. 3, n. 22).
75. Gambino, "Malcolm X, Laborer," 18, 19.
76. Espiritu, *Asian American Panethnicity,* 134–60 (see chap. 4, n. 1).
77. Mary L. Dudziak, "Desegregation as Cold War Imperative," in *Critical Race Theory,* ed. Richard Delgado (Philadelphia: Temple University Press, 1995), 110–21.
78. LeRoi Jones, *Blues People* (see chap. 6, n. 37).

79. Lipsitz, *A Life in the Struggle,* 63 (see chap. 2, n. 48).
80. Thomas R. Hietala, "Muhammad Ali and the Age of Bare Knuckle Politics," in *Muhammad Ali: The People's Champ,* ed. Elliott J. Gorn (Urbana:Universitiy of Illinois Press, 1995), 138; Franklin, *From Slavery to Freedom,* 474 (see introduction, n. 14).
81. Edward Escobar, "The Dialectics of Repression: The Los Angeles Police Department and the Chicano Movement, 1968–1971," *Journal of American History* 74, 4 (March 1993), 1483–1504; Carlos Munoz, *Youth, Identity, Power: The Chicano Movement* (London: Verso, 1989).
82. George Mariscal, "'Chale Con La Draft': Chicano Antiwar Writings," *Vietnam Generation* 6, 3–4:130.
83. Yasuko Il Takezawa, *Breaking the Silence: Redress and Japanese American Ethnicity* (Ithaca, N.Y.: Cornell University Press, 1995), 147, 148–49. See also Gutierrez, *Walls and Mirrors* (see chap. 3, n. 20), for a discussion of how the Chicano movement grew from a similar desire to identify with blacks rather than with whites.
84. Quintard Taylor, *The Forging of a Black Community: Seattle's Central District from 1870 through the Civil Rights Era* (Seattle: University of Washington Press, 1994), 225–26.
85. Allen, "When Japan Was 'Champion,'" 33–37, 25.
86. Chester B. Himes, "Zoot Riots Are Race Riots," *The Crisis,* July 1948, 200.
87. Ibid., 200, 201.
88. Bailey and Farber, *The First Strange Place,* 162.
89. Lipsitz, *Rainbow at Midnight,* 81–86 (see chap. 2, n. 44).
90. Westbrook, "'I Want a Girl'" (see chap. 4, n. 10).
91. See Nick Browne's significant "Race: The Political Unconscious of American Film," *East-West Journal* 6, 1 (1992): 9.
92. Jeffords, *The Remasculinization of America,* 180 (see chap. 4, n. 34).

Chapter 10. California: The Mississippi of the 1990s

The epigraph is from Baldwin, *No Name in the Street,* 186 (see chap. 3, n. 33).
1. I thank Melvin Oliver for calling this story—and its significance—to my attention. John H. Burma presents a story similar to Mabley's an an example of folk humor deployed as a technique in race conflict by African Americans, and it seems likely that she derived her joke from this story. See John H. Burma, "Humor as a Technique in Race Conflict," in Alan Dundes, ed., *Mother Wit from the Laughing Barrel: Readings in the Interpretation of Afro American Folklore* (New York and London: Garland, 1981), 624.
2. Hyung-chan Kim, *A Legal History of Asian Americans, 1790–1990* (Westport, Conn.: Greenwood, 1994), 104, 111.
3. Mary E. Young, *Mules and Dragons: Popular Culture Images in the Selected Writings of African-American and Chinese Women Writers* (Westport, Conn.: Greenwood, 1996), 2.
4. James W. Loewen, *The Mississippi Chinese: Between Black and White,* 2d ed. (Prospect Heights, Ill.: Waveland, 1988).
5. Dittmer, *Local People,* 6 (see introduction, n. 21).
6. David M. Oshinsky, *"Worse than Slavery": Parchman Farm and the Ordeal of Jim Crow Justice* (New York: Free Press, 1996), 231–32.
7. Takashi Fujitani, "Nisei Soldiers as Citizens: Japanese Americans in U.S. National Military and Racial Discourses," paper presented at the Conference on the Politics of Remembering the Asia/Pacific War, East-West Center, Honolulu, Hawaii, September 8, 1995, 5.
8. Baldwin, *No Name in the Street,* 46 (see chap. 3, n. 33).
9. I make this argument at greater length in *A Life in the Struggle* (see chap. 2, n. 48).

10. Edwin Chen, "Senator Becomes Road Warrior in Battle against Poverty," *Los Angeles Times,* May 30, 1997, sec. A.

11. Tom Hamburger, "Some Mississippians Not Thrilled about Wellstone's 'Poverty' Tour," *Minneapolis Star-Tribune,* May 21, 1997, sec. A; Chen, "Senator Becomes Road Warrior."

12. Dittmer, *Local People,* 427 (see introduction, n. 21).

13. Henry Cabot Beck, "Woods Noted for MIT Intellect," *Newark Star-Ledger,* January 3, 1997, Ticket section, 5.

14. Payne, *I've Got the Light of Freedom,* 288–89 (see introduction, n. 25).

15. Ibid., 323.

16. Beck, "Woods Noted for MIT Intellect."

17. Walter J. Updegrave, "Race and Money," *Money,* December 1989, 152–62.

18. Larew, "Why Are Droves," 10–11 (see chap. 2, n. 39).

19. *San Francisco Chronicle* quote from Peter H. King, "Story of a Story," *Los Angeles Times,* April 5, 1995, sec. A.

20. Jean Stefancic and Richard Delgado, *No Mercy* (Philadelphia: Temple University Press, 1996), 126.

21. "Affirmative Reaction," correspondent Josh Mankiewicz, prod. Cathy Singer, *Dateline,* NBC News, original broadcast January 24, 1996, program #2828–01, transcript.

22. See, for example, Steve Schmidt, "Scholars in Liberal Bastion Plot to End Legacy of 1960s," *San Diego Union-Tribune,* March 19, 1995, sec. A.

23. Ward Connerly, "Affirmative Action Has Outlived Its Usefulness," *Black Enterprise,* November 1995, 157.

24. Ibid.

25. Ralph Frammolino, Mark Gladstone, and Amy Wallace, "Some Regents Seek UCLA Admissions Priority for Friends," *Los Angeles Times,* March 16, 1996, sec. A.

26. Amy Wallace, "VIPS Do Influence Some Admissions, UC Provost Says," *Los Angeles Times,* May 17, 1996, sec. A.

27. Stefancic and Delgado, *No Mercy,* 128.

28. Barry Bearak, "Questions of Race Run Deep for Foe of Preferences," *New York Times,* July 27, 1997, 11.

29. "Private Call by Wilson Beckons Prop. 209 Votes," *San Francisco Examiner,* September 8, 1996, sec. B; Peter King, "The Curtain Pulled Back, for a Moment," *Los Angeles Times,* September 11, 1996, sec. A.

30. Bearak, "Questions of Race Run Deep," 10.

31. Claude M. Steele, "Student Self-Doubts Are No Reason to End Minority Preferences," *New York Times,* August 3, 1997, sec. E; Bearak, "Questions of Race Run Deep," 10.

32. Bearak, "Questions of Race Run Deep," 10.

33. Tomas Almaguer, *Racial Fault Lines: The Historical Origins of White Supremacy in California* (Berkeley and Los Angeles: University of California Press, 1994), 133.

34. White, *It's Your Misfortune,* 338–39 (see chap. 9, n. 10).

35. Ibid., 341.

36. Almaguer, *Racial Fault Lines,* 162.

37. Takaki, *A Different Mirror,* 178, 179 (see chap. 1, n. 6).

38. Almaguer, *Racial Fault Lines,* 38.

39. Ethington, *The Public City,* 185–88 (see chap. 9, n. 1).

40. Lisa Lowe offers a most impressive argument along these lines in *Immigrant Acts* (see chap.1, n. 6) and elsewhere. I am indebted to her for these insights and for her constructive and principled challenges to my own positions.

ACKNOWLEDGMENTS

My debts to others are endless, and the space available for acknowledgments is limited. I wish I were eloquent enough to express fully the deep gratitude I feel toward everyone who has helped to educate me, but I know that no matter what I say I will never be able to say enough or say it well enough to do justice to the care, concern, and kindness that others have shown me.

My colleagues in the Department of Ethnic Studies at the University of California, San Diego are an inspiration. Their superb scholarship, devoted teaching, and passionate sense of social justice exemplify the best possibilities of our present moment. The research vision and academic leadership of Ramón Gutiérrez have created an unusual and precious space for serious, socially grounded scholarship, and we all owe a great debt to him for his efforts. It is a rare privilege in life to encounter an individual like Yen Le Espiritu—an exemplary colleague and an exemplary person whose presence makes everyone around her better. Working with Ramón and Yen to build a department has been an amazing and wonderful experience. Every day of my life is enriched by my interaction with them and with our brilliant colleagues Charles Briggs, Jane Rhodes, Jonathan Holloway, Leland Saito, Ross Frank, and Paule Cruz Takash. In addition, being at UCSD brings us in contact with an extraordinary group of colleagues from other departments including David Gutiérrez, Takashi Fujitani, Michael Bernstein, Ivan Evans, Ricardo Stanton-Salazar, Cecil Lytle, George Lewis, Anthony Davis, Jann Pasler, George Mariscal, Quincy Troupe, Lisa Yoneyama, Rosaura Sánchez, Rosemary George, Judith Halberstam, Michael Murashige, Marta Sánchez, Olga Vasquez, Vince Rafael, Susan Davis, Dan Schiller, and Ellen Seiter. The Campus Black Forum offers regeneration every week: thanks to Dr. Philip Raphael, Linda Young, Manuelita Brown, and Willie Brown especially.

Like everyone who works on whiteness in our society, I owe a tremendous debt to David Roediger, whose pioneering research established the categories with which we work. David is also a valued friend, ally, and confidant, someone who offers a moral and political compass for the rest of us. It has also been a privilege to read research and secure greatly needed assistance and insight from Michael Rogin, Sterling Stuckey, David Theo Goldberg, Joe Feagin, and Sherry Ortner. None of my research on whiteness would have existed had it not been for the inspiration, advice, and example of Melvin Oliver, whose fine book, *Black Wealth/White Wealth*, co-authored with Tom

Shapiro, sets the standard of excellence in the field. In addition, everything that I write about race profits from the things that I learned from Ivory Perry and George Rawick.

The American Studies Association has emerged as the most important academic site for the study of social identities, culture, and power. I am grateful for the leadership shown on these issues by my good friend Jan Radway, president of the ASA, and by ASA members including Lucy Maddox, Barry Shank, Susan Douglas, Earl Lewis, George Sánchez, Paul Lauter, David W. Noble, José Saldívar, Sharon O'Brien, Wahneema Lubiano, Amy Kaplan, Mary Helen Washington, Robyn Wiegman, Jack Tchen, Ned Blackhawk, Chandra Mohanty, Stelamaris Coser, Jay Mechling, Herman Gray, and Rosa Linda Fregoso. I have also learned a great deal from exchanges with Don Brenneis, Daniel Segal, David Thelen, Kimberle Crenshaw, and Patricia Williams.

Old and trusted friends deserve acknowledgment too: Elizabeth Long, Ed Hugetz, Ed Robbins, Michael M.J. Fischer, Paul Buhle, Mari Jo Buhle, Maria Damon, Richard Leppert, and Nick Browne. Dan Czitrom has no popular-front illusions. Johnny Otis, Preston Love, Marisela Norte, and Stan Weir do what they do in ways that are unique and awesome. This particular book has been especially enriched from interventions by Brenda Bright, Tom Dumm, Gayle Plummer, James Horton, Austin Sarat, John Bodnar, Wendy Kozol, Marla Berns, Bennetta Jules-Rosette, Denis Constant-Martin, and Gordon Hutner. Barbara Tomlinson's attention to evidence and passion for social justice always enrich my work, and I thank her for all the ways in which she has helped this project.

Toni Morrison, Stuart Hall, and Catherine Hall inspire me in ways beyond my capacity for expression. Susan McClary and Rob Walser provide sweet harmony and rhythms that Freddie Greene would envy. Tricia Rose knows what needs to be said, why, and when; her friendship and support are greatly appreciated. Ann duCille blends intellectual brilliance, moral passion, and life-affirming wit; I count myself very lucky to know her. Lisa Lowe is to ethnic studies what Aretha Franklin is to music—i.e., indispensable. Her extraordinary scholarship, dedicated teaching, and principled political engagement have been a crucial part of my education, and her collegiality, critical acumen, and friendship all enrich my life immeasurably. Robin D.G. Kelley deserves the last word. He is the O.G., the original Gramscian, whose writing breaks everything down for us, from Malcolm to Monk, from EPMD to E.P. Thompson. But his best work doesn't even appear in his own books; it makes itself manifest mainly through the ways he empowers and inspires others. On behalf of many of us, I want to say thanks.

Some parts of individual chapters have been published previously, in different versions, in the following articles and chapters. I thank those publishers for permission to reprint.

"The Possessive Investment in Whiteness: Racialized Social Democracy and the 'White Problem' in American Studies," *American Quarterly* 47, 3 (September 1995).

"Dilemmas of Beset Nationhood: Patriotism, the Family, and Economic Change in the 1970s and 1980s," in John Bodnar, ed., *Bonds of Affection: Americans Define Their Patriotism* (Princeton: Princeton University Press, 1996).

"The Greatest Story Ever Sold: The Marketing of the O.J. Simpson Trial," in Toni Morrison and Claudia Brodsky Lacour, eds., *Birth of a Nation'hood: Gaze, Script, and Spectacle in the O.J. Simpson Case* (New York: Pantheon, 1997).

"Diasporic Intimacy in the Art of Renee Stout," in Marla C. Berns, ed., *Dear Robert: I'll See You at the Crossroads* (Santa Barbara, CA: University Art Museum, 1995).

" 'Swing Low, Sweet Cadillac': White Supremacy, Antiblack Racism, and the New Historicism," *American Literary History* 7, 4 (winter 1995).

" 'Frantic to Join . . . the Japanese Army': The Asia Pacific War in the Lives of African American Soldiers and Civilians," in Lisa Lowe and David Lloyd, eds., *The Politics of Culture in the Shadow of Capital* (Durham, NC: Duke University Press, 1997).

INDEX